'Luthuli has long needed a serious biographer, consigned as he was to a homogenised nationalist pantheon. Couper has unearthed contemporary records to strip out the tendentious mythology and reconstruct Luthuli as a distinctive and assertive personality, a moral heavyweight, at odds with his movement and his times.'

— Tom Lodge, Professor of Peace and Conflict Studies, University of Limerick, Ireland

'Three widely held beliefs about Albert Luthuli are accepted as beyond question: that after Sharpeville, Mandela succeeded in convincing him to abandon his commitment to non-violence; that Luthuli's death on the railway tracks at Groutville was a political assassination by the apartheid regime; that his life and work can only properly be understood from a political perspective. In this work of fine scholarship and meticulous research, Couper casts considerable doubt on all three beliefs – and skilfully marshalls evidence to support his controversial view. This is a must-read for all interested in recent South African history.'

— Paddy Kearney, award-winning author of *Guardian of the Light: Denis Hurley: Renewing the Church, Opposing Apartheid*

'Basing his narrative and assessment on a considerable body of primary material, Scott Couper argues that Luthuli refused to give his support to violence and as a result was eventually sidelined within the liberation movement. This is a very important study for all who seek to understand the contemporary political situation in South Africa, the issues that have historically divided the ruling party, and the ambiguous role of the church and Christian faith within this context.'

— John W. de Gruchy, Emeritus Professor of Christian Studies, University of Cape Town, South Africa

Albert Luthuli

Bound by Faith

SCOTT COUPER

UNIVERSITY OF KwaZulu-Natal Press

Published in 2010 by University of KwaZulu-Natal Press
Private Bag X01
Scottsville, 3209
South Africa
Email: books@ukzn.ac.za
Website: www.ukznpress.co.za

ISBN: 978-1-86914-192-9

Managing editor: Sally Hines
Editor: Jane Argall
Typesetter: Patricia Comrie
Indexer: Christopher Merrett
Cover design: lucky fish
Cover photograph by The Reverend Nadia Sutch (1922–2010), American Board
    missioner

Printed and bound by Interpak Books, Pietermaritzburg

Contents

Acknowledgements

SO THAT I never sacrificed my vocational responsibilities in researching and writing, my family (Susan, Micah and Madeline) forfeited my free time with them for the better part of four years. All three bring tremendous joy to my life. I dedicate this book to them.

To turn a very verbose and soporific Ph.D. dissertation into an enjoyable and readable text for the lay and professional person interested in South Africa's history is a daunting task. Jane Argall beautifully synthesised many chapters, appropriately wove several theses throughout and subtly dissolved academic theory and vocabulary into an accessible narrative.

The editor's difficult task was that of 'conversion', therefore any errors herein are entirely my own responsibility. Because this is the first biography to be written on Albert Luthuli, errors are inevitable. The success of any seminal text is dependent upon its ability to inspire others to critique, amend and improve.

Thank you to Jeff Guy, my initial supervisor before his retirement. Thank you to my co-supervisors, Vukile Khumalo and Keith Breckenridge. Vukile always answered my excited phone calls, alerting him to the newest information learned, and never expressed any frustration with my constant interruptions. Keith's mind I covet. His prowess as a historian never ceases to amaze me. *Viva* UKZN's Historical Studies Seminar!

Thank you to 'Gatling Gun' (Catherine) Burns, whose exhausting three-hour Theory and Method lectures provided my foundation in the discipline of interpreting and writing history.

Thank you to the University of KwaZulu-Natal Press who agreed to publish this study despite the fact that, in my ignorance as a first-time author, I committed every 'don't do' when proposing a manuscript for publication. Thank you to Sally Hines, Debra Primo and Adele Branch for their professionalism.

To the United Church of Christ, the Christian Church (Disciples of Christ) and the United Congregational Church of Southern Africa, for the opportunity to serve, *Siyabonga*!

I owe much appreciation to the members of the Groutville Congregational Church, who welcomed me into their community and first told me of the heroic man of faith who was laid to rest behind the sanctuary.

Thank you to Ms Rooksana Omar, former director of the Luthuli Museum in Groutville, for her stellar work at the museum and the support she provided during my research. I am grateful that I was called upon by the thoughtful staff (particularly Paul, Thulani and Barbara) to attend and assist however possible whenever events were held, important visitors were expected and interviews were to be conducted at the museum and church. I have donated all of my research documents to the museum and therefore they can be found in its collection.

Thank you to Nellie Somers and Mwelela Cele at the Killie Campbell Collections for assisting my research and for permission to reproduce photographs in this book. Thank you also to the KwaZulu-Natal Local History Museums, Inanda Seminary and Harvard University for the use of their facilities and/or permission to publish photographs in their collections.

Thank you to the Luthuli family, who have always given their father to the nation and to the world. I appreciate very much the trust they placed in me as their pastor and family friend.

To Baba Luthuli: Had I been with you before you died, I would have assured you that you were faithful, that nothing you fought for was in vain. I would have prayed Simeon's prayer for you: 'Sovereign Lord, as you have promised, dismiss now your servant in peace' (Luke 2:29).

Abbreviations

AAC	All-African Convention
ABCFM	American Board of Commissioners for Foreign Missions
ABM	American Board Mission
ACA	American Committee on Africa Collection
ACAA	American Congregational Association Archives
ACOA	American Committee on Africa
ANC	African National Congress
ANCYL	African National Congress Youth League
APC&SA	Alan Paton Centre and Struggle Archives (University of KwaZulu-Natal, Pietermaritzburg)
ARC	Amistad Research Centre (Tulane University, New Orleans)
ARM	African Resistance Movement
AWGC	Allison Wessels George Champion (University of South Africa, Pretoria)
BAPA	Bailey's African Photo Archives (Johannesburg)
BCC	Bantu Congregational Church
CCSA	Christian Council of South Africa
CJE	Congresses' Joint Executive
COPCP	Charlotte Owen and Peter Corbett Papers (Luthuli Museum, Groutville)
CUSA	Congregational Union of South Africa
DCAS	Documentation Centre for African Studies (University of South Africa, Pretoria)
FLN	National Liberation Front (of Algeria)
FSAW	Federation of South African Women
HPAL	Howard Pim Africana Library (University of Fort Hare, Alice)
ICU	Industrial [and Commercial] Workers' Union
IDAMF	Interdenominational African Ministers' Federation
IFP	Inkatha Freedom Party

IUSY	International Union of Socialist Youth
KCAL	Killie Campbell Africana Library (University of KwaZulu-Natal, Durban)
KZN	KwaZulu-Natal
KZNA	KwaZulu-Natal Archives Depository (Pietermaritzburg)
LM	Luthuli Museum
LMS	London Missionary Society
MAD	Manuscripts and Archives Department (University of Cape Town)
MK	Umkhonto we Sizwe (Spear of the Nation)
MYP	Masabalala Yengwa Papers (Luthuli Museum, Groutville)
NAR	National Archives Repository (Pretoria)
NEC	National Executive Committee (of the ANC)
NGO	non-governmental organisation
NIC	Natal Indian Congress
NIV	New Internationalist Version (Bible)
NNC	Natal Native Congress
NRC	Native Representative Council
NRSV	New Revised Standard Version (Bible)
NUSAS	National Union of South African Students
NWC	National Working Committee (of the ANC)
OAU	Organisation of African Unity
PAC	Pan-Africanist Congress
PAFMECSA	Pan-African Freedom Movement of East, Central and Southern Africa
PAR	Pietermaritzburg Archives Repository
RIMA	Robben Island Mayibuye Archives (University of the Western Cape, Cape Town)
SABC	South African Broadcasting Corporation
SACC	South African Council of Churches
SACPO	South African Coloured People's Organisation
SACTU	South African Congress of Trade Unions
SADET	South African Democracy Education Trust
SAIC	South African Indian Congress
SAIO	South African Indian Organisation
SAIRR	South African Institute of Race Relations
SWANU	South West African National Union
SWAPO	South West Africa People's Organisation

TANU	Tanganyika African National Union
TUC	Trade Union Congress
UCBWM	United Church Board for World Ministries
UCCSA	United Congregational Church of Southern Africa
UCT	University of Cape Town
UF	(South Africa) United Front
UFH	University of Fort Hare
UKZN	University of KwaZulu-Natal
UNISA	University of South Africa
UP	United Party
UW	University of the Witwatersrand (Johannesburg)
UWC	University of the Western Cape
WCC	World Council of Churches
WCL	William Cullen Library (University of the Witwatersrand)
ZAPU	Zimbabwe African People's Union
ZIPRA	Zimbabwe People's Revolutionary Army

Introduction

IN 2004 AND 2005, the former president of South Africa, Thabo Mbeki, and the former president of Zambia, Kenneth Kaunda, respectively, gave the Albert Luthuli Memorial Lecture at the University of KwaZulu-Natal (UKZN).[1] Mbeki waxed eloquent about Chief Albert Luthuli's life and place in South African history. The lecture was cerebral, disembodied and littered with academic references. Kaunda's lecture proved very different. His offering was simple, embodied and, one might say, parochial. In his untitled address, he quoted no poets, philosophers or historians. The only quotation he used derived from Martin Luther King Junior (1929–1968).[2]

Mbeki's lecture, entitled 'The Tempo Quickens', made only one mention of Luthuli's Christian 'prescriptions'. Kaunda, for half his lecture, belaboured the influence of faith that was inarguably the foundation of Albert Luthuli's life and politics. Such a Christian emphasis revealed Kaunda's own bias. The son of an ordained minister in the Church of Scotland, Kaunda was schooled in and shaped by a Christian theological and educational environment, much the same as Albert Luthuli had been. To contextualise Luthuli, Kaunda's lecture explicitly referred to God and/or Christianity eight times and non-violence five times. Violent oppression and violent resistance were only twice given brief and vague mention. In contrast, Mbeki cited political (as opposed to theological) motivations, and violent (as opposed to militant non-violent) resistance to oppression. He made eight references to violent oppression and four references to violent resistance to oppression. He downplayed Luthuli's Christian orientation and elaborated instead on more philosophical and utilitarian principles to justify the African National Congress's (ANC) move to an armed struggle.

Perhaps there was something in Kaunda's lecture that sought to offer an alternative view and challenge the contemporary nationalist understanding that Luthuli supported the ANC's 16 December 1961

1

initiation of violence in the hopes of achieving South Africa's liberation. He said:

> Given his deep belief in non-violence, it can rightly be assumed that [Luthuli] clearly understood that in their journey to attain justice, freedom and nationhood, different tactical options may be preferred by various wings of the same struggle. It is important however, to stress the fact that, in spite of this pronouncement, he continued with his method of non-violence campaign [sic] to his death.[3]

This view was shared also by Joaquim Chissano, former president of Mozambique, who addressed the same forum in October 2007 saying that Luthuli had had his detractors, presumably within the ANC, who 'condemned his policy of non-violent struggle' and who, in December 1961, deviated from the policy for which he earned the Nobel Peace Prize.[4]

Luthuli's ecclesiastic roots ran much deeper than his political roots. It was Anglican Bishop Alpheus Zulu who said in 1977 that Luthuli became so 'famous for his political exploits' that his many other qualities paled away. But, those who knew the man intimately, the bishop said, knew well that Luthuli 'would have desired to be remembered first as a Christian'.[5] For many others, the designation 'Christian' is easily ignored or dismissed as trivial. In this book, I suggest that any historical inquiry that ignores the role of Luthuli's Christian faith, and more specifically, his faith tradition, fails to analyse him adequately.

Raised by his uncle, Martin Luthuli (1847–1921), and his mother in the Congregational church tradition, Albert Luthuli acclaimed the primacy of democracy, education, multiracialism and egalitarianism, and it was these values that propelled him to the heights of political leadership prior to 1961. Following 1961, these same seminal emphases rendered him obsolete as a political leader within an increasingly radicalised and desperate political environment that saw the ANC's initiation of violence in the struggle for liberation in South Africa. Luthuli's capacity to lead the movement became drastically curtailed by the government's harassment and repeated imposition of banning orders. Yet, I also suggest that he was additionally marginalised by his colleagues in the underground structures of congresses united in the liberation movement, rendering him only the titular leader of the ANC until his tragic death.

In the same month that Luthuli died, June 1967, the military wing of the ANC formed the Luthuli Detachment, naming it after the late president general. In what became named the Wankie Campaign, led by Mongameli Tshali, known in Umkhonto we Sizwe (Spear of the Nation, MK) circles as Lennox Lagu, and Chris Hani (1942–1993), the detachment crossed the Zambezi River into Rhodesia at the end of July 1967, en route to South Africa. Some members of the detachment joined forces with the Zimbabwe African People's Union's (ZAPU) Zimbabwe People's Revolutionary Army (ZIPRA) to establish a base in north-east Rhodesia. The combined forces endured fierce fighting in several skirmishes with members of the Rhodesian security forces. Of the eighty members of the Luthuli Detachment, twenty-five were killed. Five ZAPU fighters and eight members of the Rhodesian security forces were also killed. In 2007, the president of South Africa conferred the Order of Mendi for Bravery (in gold: for 'conspicuous bravery') on the detachment, describing it as 'a metaphor for freedom earned through the sweat of the oppressed's brow, and [representing] the possibility of victory against the system until then thought to be impregnable'.[6] At best, dedicating an armed guerrilla unit in Albert Luthuli's name suggests that the ANC has, since the launch of MK, never fully appreciated the man and his political convictions. At worst, the commemorative gesture can be seen to be a disingenuous means by which to justify the armed struggle in the name of a man whose political, social and physical death rendered him unable to continue to speak to the values for which he received the Nobel Peace Prize.

Much public historical mythology asserts that Chief Albert Luthuli, the one-time leader of Africa's oldest liberation movement, launched an armed struggle on the very evening he returned to South Africa after receiving the Nobel Peace Prize in 1961. This profound irony engenders what is arguably one of the most relevant and controversial historical debates in South Africa, with recent scholarship suggesting that Luthuli did *not* countenance the armed movement. Today, Luthuli remains a figure of great debate not least because of his domestic and international prominence and his impeccable moral character. Icons of the liberation struggle, political parties and active politicians frequently interpret the history of the struggle for freedom in South Africa within his given historical memory. And often that memory is *not* compatible with the archival record.

With the dawning of a non-racial democracy in South Africa in 1994, several leading figures in the liberation struggle set about compiling their memoirs, capturing for posterity their experiences of a life in the struggle.

Principal among these is Nelson Mandela's *Long Walk to Freedom* (1995). Likewise, several biographies have emerged that recount the roles played by other leading figures. Curiously, few historians have interpreted the life of Chief Albert Luthuli, and no formal biographies have emerged in spite of Mandela's call for a definitive account of the life of Africa's first Nobel Peace Prize winner, one that would 'be a useful addition to the sparse material' that existed then and is still insufficient today.[7] Gerald Pillay provided a brief biography of Luthuli in *Voices of Liberation*, Volume 1 (1993), contextualising Luthuli's speeches and statements and generally affirming his non-violent stand. Paul Rich's contribution on Albert Luthuli in Henry Bredenkamp and Robert Ross's *Missions and Christianity* (1995) is missiological in its approach and comes the closest to highlighting Luthuli's life of faith in the Congregational church tradition. Edward Callan's *Albert John Luthuli and the South African Race Conflict* (1962) and Mary Benson's *Chief Albert Lutuli of South Africa* (1963) pre-date Luthuli's death and provide little retrospective contextual analysis.[8] Neither posited substantive arguments regarding Luthuli's stand on violence, though both concluded he opposed its use. In *Religion and Resistance Politics in South Africa* (1995), Lyn Graybill generically agreed that Luthuli was non-violent in approach, but she did not delineate the nuances of his position, in particular, that although he supported non-violent methods, he was not a pacifist. Indeed, Luthuli appears to have acceded to the use of arms in the struggle for liberation elsewhere in Africa.

In contrast, several film documentaries, notably the National Film and Video Foundation's production of *The Legacy of a Legend* (2005) and the KwaZulu-Natal (KZN) Office of the Premier's production of *Servant of the People* (2007), provide ample testimony from contemporary figures such as Sibusiso Ndebele, Jacob Zuma, Nelson Mandela, Thabo Mbeki, Billy Nair and Kader Asmal – to all intents, the primary public interpreters of Luthuli's life in the context of the liberation struggle – who liberally express the opinion, suggest or infer, that Luthuli supported the ANC's turn to violence. At times, their assertions can be confusing. For example, in July 2007 KZN premier, Sibusiso Ndebele, told the provincial legislature that Luthuli 'believed in the four pillars of struggle . . . *peaceful resistance*, international mobilisation, the political underground and the *armed struggle*'.[9]

Nationalist history is a popular genre of literature in today's South Africa. The public finds it accessible in terms of purchase and comprehensibility. Often, these nationalist histories are biographic in nature or are history texts sponsored by a government instrumentality. Often, too, they assert that Albert Luthuli, president general of the ANC, supported the decision to form MK, thus initiating the armed struggle as the primary method by which to achieve liberation. This genre of literature contrasts with many more scholarly contributions, including those from Thomas Karis and Gwendolen Carter (1997), Elaine Reinertsen (1985), Gerald Pillay (1993), Lyn Graybill (1995), Jabulani Sithole and Sibongiseni Mkhize (2000) and, most recently, the South African Democracy Education Trust (SADET, Vol. 1, 2004). All generally conclude that Luthuli never came to support the turn to violence.

This account of Albert Luthuli's life broaches the manifestations of his faith tradition and links them directly to his specific political vantage point. Contrary to a nationalist-inspired historical perspective, it concludes that Luthuli did *not* support the initiation of violence in December 1961. Evidence suggests that Luthuli only reluctantly yielded to others' decision to not discipline those who undertook to form (not launch) an armed movement that would be separate from the ANC. This he did in July 1961, three months *before* the announcement in October 1961 that he would be awarded the (1960) Nobel Peace Prize in December 1961. *After* the announcement, Luthuli vociferously argued against the use of violence until April 1962. From April 1962 to his death in 1967, Luthuli only advocated non-violent methods and did not express support or condemnation of the ANC's use of violence.

Linked to the understanding that Luthuli supported armed resistance is an unsubstantiated suggestion that the apartheid regime assassinated him. The rationale behind this conviction is that if Luthuli fully supported the armed resistance and, in his role as president general of the ANC, if he acted as *a*, if not *the*, commander-in-chief, then the apartheid regime was sufficiently motivated to orchestrate his death. Given the degree of distrust accorded to the state, it is almost inconceivable that any 'accident' would not arouse accusations of foul play. The characterisation of Luthuli's death as 'mysterious' persists today in spite of the absence of criminal or documentary evidence implicating the apartheid government. As I have suggested above, Albert Luthuli was rendered politically impotent by, on the one hand, the apartheid government's successful attempts to silence and isolate him, and on the other, by his growing marginalisation in the ANC. These latter conditions suggest that the South African government did not view him enough of a threat to orchestrate his death. Also, Luthuli's health conditions and the immediate events of the time therefore suggest this conclusion to be accurate.

The premier's office in the KZN government declared 2007 as 'The Year of Luthuli'. It intended that events throughout the year would highlight various characteristics of Luthuli's leadership. In spite of introducing in his office's documentary a contradiction into the historical memory of Albert Luthuli, Sibusiso Ndebele humbly and earnestly appealed to the people of South Africa and KZN to do justice to the memory of Luthuli. He said:

> We ask our writers to write, we ask our researchers to research, we ask our singers to sing, we ask our poets to write poems, and this is how [Luthuli] will live on and on. Let us use this forty years anniversary of Nkosi Albert Luthuli to record his wonderful history, this wonderful life that lived amongst us that we are privileged to have him as part of this province and in remembering we will try to emulate his lessons.[10]

This book aims to remember Albert Luthuli more accurately so that the witness he provided is better emulated by all who honour him.

1

The Home of my Fathers

Pre-1897–1927

The revolution which Christianity brought into the lives of converts was profound, as can perhaps be imagined. Conversion meant an entirely new way of life, a new outlook, a new set of beliefs – the creation, almost, of a new kind of people. They were still Zulus to the backbone – that remained unchanged except for a few irrelevant externals. But they were Christian Zulus, not heathen Zulus, and conversion affected their lives to the core.

— Albert Luthuli, *Let My People Go*

THE LUTHULI FAMILY Bible is today a treasured item in the custodianship of the Luthuli Museum, which is located at the historic home of Albert Luthuli in Groutville, on the KwaZulu-Natal north coast. The Bible is a modest volume, hard-covered, though worn and frayed with use. Its first few pages barely hang on to the binding. Only a few stubborn strands of binder's twine hold them together. On these loosened pages, in somewhat haphazard fashion, are inscribed by hand the names of members of the Luthuli family, complete with the recording of birth and death dates, the last being that of Nokukhanya Luthuli (MaBhengu) who died on 14 December 1996. The fifth page contains a record of the original progenitor of the clan, Madunjini Luthuli, a polygamist who 'gave rise' to many sons, the eldest of whom was named Ntaba. In his autobiography, *Let My People Go* (1962), Albert Luthuli does not mention his great-grandfather, Madunjini. Instead, he traces his genealogy back to Ntaba Luthuli, who, born in the early part of the nineteenth century, became the first convert of Aldin Grout, a missioner of the American Board of Commissioners for Foreign Missions (ABCFM or American Board), who was based near the Umvoti River, north of Durban.[1] His grandmother, Titisi Mthethwa, also converted to Christianity, and not long after, on 1 May 1847, the local American Board Mission (ABM) constituted the 'church' in the area. Only after the turn of the twentieth century did local residents name the area Groutville and the church, the Groutville Congregational Church.

Luthuli deeply honoured his Christian forebears for their zeal and described them as 'the founders of the Luthuli Christian line'. Like many who have commented upon his life, he did not highlight the unique *Congregational* nature of the ancestral line.[2] And while his own parents, John and Mtonya Luthuli, settled in the Bulawayo area of Rhodesia (Zimbabwe) where Luthuli was born in 1897, he soon returned to the Umvoti Christian community where his uncle, Martin Luthuli, took responsibility for his upbringing.[3]

Perhaps Luthuli, like other commentators, did not see his *particular* faith tradition as formative. However, he came to stand as the quintessential product of a mission education provided by the American Board. It even showed in his speech. According to Nobel laureate, Nadine Gordimer, his American Board background seeped into the manner in which Luthuli spoke English: 'with a distinct American intonation, acquired along with his education at schools run by American missionaries'.[4]

Most ANC leaders during the 1960s received their education at Christian mission schools. Duma Nokwe (1927–1978), for example, was educated at the Anglican church's St Peter's, Rosettenville, in Johannesburg; Oliver Tambo (1917–1993) at Holy Cross, a Roman Catholic missionary school at Flagstaff in the Eastern Cape, and later at St Peter's; Wilson Conco (1919–1996) was educated at the Catholic Mariannhill College; Ashby Mda (1916–1993) at the Catholic mission schools of St Francis in Aliwal North and Mariazell in East Griqualand; both Robert Sobukwe (1924–1978) and Nelson Mandela were educated at the Methodist school in Healdtown, near Fort Beaufort in the Eastern Cape; and Walter Sisulu (1912–2003) was educated at All Saints Catholic mission school at Qutubeni in the Transkei. While these schools provided the intellectual tools with which their students would in time prosecute the liberation struggle, they did not usually succeed in instilling a theological ethos that would form the basis of their identities. Rarely did their specific faith traditions determine the seminal basis of who they were and how they thought. Perhaps only Zachariah Keodirelang (Z.K.) Matthews's (1901–1968) Methodism approaches the degree to which a specific faith tradition influenced an ANC leader to the extent that Congregationalism influenced Luthuli. Roy Briggs and Joseph Wing described the extent to which Luthuli's faith tradition was etched in his very being:

> The true worth of this great and good man was often misrepresented in the land of his birth, but as a Congregationalist he stood for those values which are an integral part of the Congregational witness for which our fathers suffered – the liberty and the unity of all men within the family of God. Luthuli believed that the unity between races which had been achieved in Congregationalism, where our oneness in Christ transcends our racial differences, was a practical policy for South Africa. Never once did Luthuli advocate a narrow, black nationalism – he stood for a form of political partnership in which each group would make its own contribution to the 'growing fullness' and enrichment of all.[5]

Luthuli's roots in Congregationalism were deep and extensive, stretching back three generations. It defined his home, school, vocation and spiritual life, and his political life never superseded these aspects of his being. Though those political colleagues who knew and worked with Luthuli became very affectionate of him and deeply respected his integrity, a distance between them grew, caused by the profound gravity with which the Christian and Congregational faith bound him.

No less than the American burr in his speech, Luthuli's politics were profoundly influenced by the ideals of Congregational ecclesiology which had been transplanted from the United States. The American Board that reared, educated, mentored, employed and preached to Luthuli throughout his formative years instilled in him a reverence for the values espoused, though not always implemented, by the western world.

Congregationalism

An understanding of Congregationalism's emphasis on religious, political and individual liberty reveals a source of Luthuli's lifelong motivation to free South Africa's black majority from the yoke of white supremacy. Democracy is the cornerstone of Congregational polity. However, in the early European and American history of the Congregational church, the democratic ideal was at times more than imperfectly realised. The Puritans in England, a Protestant grouping which grew out of the Reformation and coalesced after Henry VIII's 1534 secession from the Roman Catholic

Church, went on to establish theocracies in both the Old and the New World, contrary to their ethos. So named because they desired purity in worship, church governance and personal life, the Puritans represented an early expression of Congregationalism. In 1649, under Oliver Cromwell (1599–1658), these Congregationalists became in effect the establishment church in England with ministers accepting government grants, salaried subsidies and privileged appointments from the state. After the restoration of Charles II in England, Congregationalism was forced underground and again became more non-conformist and independent in nature.

A group of Puritans, later led by John Winthrop (1588–1649), crossed the Atlantic in 1630 to establish an independent society in New England on the east coast of America. Winthrop became governor of Massachusetts, serving twelve terms of office between 1639 and 1648. While he was admired as a political leader, writer and religious thinker and famous for his 'City upon a Hill' sermon delivered aboard the *Arabella* sailing for the New World, Winthrop expressed a scepticism towards democracy claiming it lacked scriptural basis.

Down the ages democratic practice was secured in degrees as the Congregational church fought to free itself from authoritative and hierarchical systems of ecclesiastical polity. In its modern expression, therefore, Congregationalism espouses a strong commitment to resist state interference in the life of the church. It emphasises and holds as supreme the 'gathered congregation' in matters related to church governance, with property ownership and decision-making concentrated at local church level. The brand of Congregationalism to which Luthuli was exposed emphasised individual (private) land ownership and thus fostered a strong work ethic and a desire for upward socio-economic mobility. For Luthuli, 'civilisation' was represented by progress in these terms and was the desired composite product of scientific, political, cultural and moral (religious) progress.[6]

Congregationalism upholds a commitment to unity and ecumenism, and at the same time values the dignity of all, with a biblical concern for justice and freedom as key elements in the Christian life. Above all, it upholds the right to dissent and to fight for justice and liberation. The early American Congregational church arguably led the anti-slavery movement in the United States as early as 1790 with the founding of the Connecticut Anti-Slavery Society, the American Anti-Slavery Society and the American Missionary Association.

Congregationalism also holds as a fundamental or classical tenet the objection to the use of creeds in worship or as tests of membership. This tenet affirms that contexts change as do theological perspectives. Creeds are not final – but they bear witness to specific historical contexts. To the same extent that creeds elucidate and explain concepts, creeds can limit and stifle understanding. Creeds also exclude.

Albert Luthuli, despite his strong convictions, refused to hold on to dogmatic views in either the religious or the secular spheres. He refused to ostracise those with differing ideologies so long as they had as their primary goal the overthrow of white supremacy. His ecumenical leanings maintained a 'broad church', uniting in solidarity Indians, whites, Africans, communists, liberals, Christians, Muslims, modernists and traditionalists within the ANC, thus enabling the survival and future growth of the anti-apartheid struggle and the creation of the present-day democratic South Africa.

Pre-eminently, Congregationalism places a strong emphasis on education. In 1636, the Congregational church's Puritan forebears founded Harvard University in Boston, Massachusetts; later they founded Yale University in New Haven, Connecticut. Both sites were used to train ministers. In the mission field, and in South Africa in particular, the Congregational church also founded several premier educational institutions such as Inanda Seminary, Tiger Kloof and Adams College.

Albert Luthuli declared that his uncle, Martin Luthuli, and John L. Dube (1871–1946), his one-time principal, both propelled him in his endeavour to be educated. Fundamental to the education imperative was the need to enlighten the conscience. From a book prized on his bookshelf, Luthuli once read the following bold historical declaration:

One must not read back into Seventeenth Century New England the perfected philosophy of a democratic society, but leaders of the little [New England] commonwealth knew by sound instinct that 'if people were to follow the dictates of conscience, that conscience must be enlightened. If people were to govern themselves in church and state, opportunity for education must be provided'. They laid the foundation of a public school system which was to continue in later years across the continent and become, perhaps, the finest single aspect of American life . . . What New England did for education was, therefore, done by Congregationalism.[7]

Luthuli passed this emphasis on education to his children. A daughter, Albertinah (also known as Ntombazana), once remarked:

> For his part, he was indulgent and concerned about progress in school. He would test us in our schoolwork and urge us on to do better. When we left home and lived in boarding schools and later became college students, our letters were always returned to us with grammar and spelling corrected in red ink.[8]

Tracing the history of Congregationalism in South Africa, Roy Briggs and Joseph Wing quote from Vernon Miller, secretary of the Congregational Union of South Africa (CUSA) between 1937 and 1967, who, in 1960, described its impact thus:

> In the early days it produced men of ability and courage who fearlessly championed the cause of non-Europeans in the highest courts of the land – men who altered the course of South African history just as much as did some of the great political leaders of the day. It has brought non-whites and whites together in a fellowship of Christian witness and service and into a unity which is becoming increasingly precious. It has maintained a platform from which liberal principles may be proclaimed and expounded. It has created a fellowship of Christian men and women who are sympathetic toward all forms of enterprise in matters of race relationships. It has striven at all times to give practical expression to the fundamental teaching of our Lord concerning the Fatherhood of God and the brotherhood of man.[9]

London Missionary Society antecedents

Congregational history in southern Africa began in 1799 when the American Board's equivalent in Europe, the London Missionary Society (LMS), dispatched four missioners to the Cape. The LMS had been established just four years earlier. Initially multi-denominational in character, it became predominantly Congregational following the withdrawal of the Presbyterian and Anglican churches to found their own mission instrumentalities.

Two of the four missioners set out to live among the Khoisan (indigenous southern Africans) in Namaqualand, and two set out to serve the Africans in the Eastern Cape. The early years of mission activity were not easy. While lack of communication and weak leadership created much instability, over time, the LMS established missions in what are known now as the Northern Cape province, Botswana, Zimbabwe and Gauteng. A brief outline of the lives and work of these four men help establish a historical context for the fixing of the Congregational ethos which so shaped and inspired Albert Luthuli.

In 1803 Johannes van der Kemp (1747–1811) founded a mission station at Bethelsdorp, near present-day Uitenhage. The mission benefited the Khoisan and focused as much on development as evangelism. Van der Kemp laid a priority on education, agriculture, entrepreneurism and self-sufficiency, as did Luthuli in later times when he served as chief of Groutville. A school, a church and gardens were established as well as an export business in indigenous plants. A forge was created to repair the wheels of wagons and carts. Leatherworking helped repair the bridles and harnesses of horses.

Van der Kemp surrounded himself with controversy. He offended missiological and racial sensibilities by taking as a wife a young slave girl, conducting interracial worship services and promoting literacy among his parishioners. Adopting a traditional Khoisan lifestyle, he constantly argued with local authorities over his mission, making him a most vilified nuisance. Van der Kemp offered a safe haven for the Khoisan who suffered much oppression, exploitation and racism by the colonists. As such he served his indigenous constituency as a renegade human rights activist. After his death in 1811, the first circuit court (nicknamed the 'Black Circuit') was established. It was flooded by cases, mostly of murder, brought by the Khoisan against the Boer settlers.

John Philip (1775–1851), a prominent Congregationalist, arrived in southern Africa in 1819 to investigate charges that many LMS missioners inappropriately carried out their vocations. After settling in Cape Town, he accepted an invitation to pastoral ministry, provided that the church meeting was to be the governing authority of the church. Thus, he established in 1820 the first Congregational church in South Africa.[10]

Luthuli identified Philip in his Nobel Peace Prize speech as an 'illustrious [man] of God' because his faith led him to advocate for human rights in southern Africa, noting also that Philip's name was 'still anathema to some South Africans'.[11] In the early 1800s, Philip's championing of the oppressed quickly made him a very controversial figure and many described him as a cantankerous fool. The historian, Frank Welsh, called

him 'the chief Boer bugbear'.[12] However, through his numerous tours in
the region and the regular reports he received from outlying missioners,
he knew more about what was going on in the Cape than the local
governing authorities did. He first ran afoul with white settlers through
his prolific advocacy for the Khoisan. Later, as an arbiter for the Treaty
System introduced in 1836, he lobbied for more favourable colonial policies
toward the Xhosa and Sotho-Tswana. Much to the chagrin of white
supremacists, he consistently argued that the races were equal in cerebral
capacity. He wrote that it was the lack of education that created a difference
in intellectual achievement. Accused of meddling in race matters, he wrote
that he could only plead guilty to the charge.

Luthuli also admired David Livingstone (1813–1873), a Congregationalist and missioner of considerable fame. Like Van der Kemp,
Livingstone proved particularly adept at immersing himself in the
indigenous context, often being accused of 'going native'. Wherever he
went, he worked assiduously to learn the local language, always eating
with and residing amongst the native population. Livingstone spoke out
scathingly against slavery and used his reputation as an explorer to lobby
vociferously for its abolition. For him, slavery resulted in the destruction
of a people and his ire was so raised by it that he would often express
public rage on his speaking circuit.

Livingstone's contribution to human rights in Africa is not well known.
His support of the Hottentot Rebellion of 1851 and his justification of
the rights of Africans to use violent resistance against Boers and English
settlers alike are not mentioned in most of the biographies that have
emerged on his life. Andrew Ross, who wrote a biography on John Philip,
suggests that Livingstone's stances were not compatible with nineteenth
and twentieth century ecclesiastical historiography that shied away from
casting a shadow on British imperialism.[13] Even within ecclesiastic history
texts, his human rights work is not given much merit, perhaps on account
of his resignation from the LMS in 1856 and the church's tendency to
marginalise those clergy who took up secular vocations. It was a growing
phenomenon in southern African Congregationalism. Though inspired
by their Congregational brand of Christianity, many leaders, including
Luthuli, found the church to be too conservative and lethargic an
instrument by which to achieve ambitious socio-political goals.

Another illustrious figure, John Mackenzie (1835–1899), came to
Congregationalism from the Presbyterian Church of Scotland, apparently

finding that it suited him far better than the more authoritarian and hierarchical ecclesiology that too resembled the Anglican episcopacy. He soon became convinced that 'Congregational Independency [was] the form of government laid down in the New Testament for the Churches of Christ'.[14] In 1873, the LMS appointed Mackenzie to oversee the Moffat Mission at Kuruman. Like so many Congregational missioners, and similar to Luthuli, the confines of the church proved too restrictive and the call of the Gospel led beyond parish leadership to political leadership. While at Kuruman, Mackenzie became a strident advocate of land rights for indigenous Africans. In the 1880s he campaigned vigorously to prevent the Boer republics of Stellaland and Goshen from expropriating land from the Batswana. His efforts to enlist the British government's intervention eventually led him to England where the London Convention of 1883–1884 effectively guaranteed protection for the Batswana within British Bechuanaland. In doing so, Mackenzie earned from the infuriated Boers the distinction of being labelled a 'meddling missionary'.

American Board of Commissioners for Foreign Missions

The mission arm of the United States based Congregationalist church, the ABCFM or American Board, was founded in 1810 at Andover Seminary in Massachusetts. In its earliest days, like the LMS, it was an ecumenical or interdenominational entity, comprising Presbyterian, Congregational and Dutch Reformed missioners. Both organisations later became, for all intents and purposes, Congregational.

In 1812 the American Board initiated early mission activities in India. Some scholars argue that mission work started a few years earlier in 1806 when, at the Haystack prayer meeting held in Williamstown, Massachusetts, five seminarians, inspired by a terrifying thunderstorm, pledged themselves to propagate mission work. Nevertheless, for the next twenty years from 1812, the American Board expanded its reach to Ceylon, Turkey, Greece, Hawaii and to western and central Africa. The first mission to Africa failed owing to the infiltration of traders and colonial powers prejudicing the indigenous populations against the missioners. It was a failure that likely haunted the American Board. Later, when conditions in the southern African mission became similarly unviable, it became skittish about continuing the mission there and was poised to abort the work, even against the wishes of the missioners on site.

The American Board's presence in southern Africa was catalysed by
John Philip who was appointed by the LMS as superintendent of the
mission in southern Africa. In 1835, upon Philip's referral, six American
Board missioners and their wives were sent to establish missions in
southern Africa – an inland mission under Daniel Lindley (1801–1880),
Alexander Wilson (1803–1841) and Henry Venable (1811–1878), and a
maritime mission under Aldin Grout (1803–1894), George Champion
(1810–1841) and Newton Adams (1804–1851). The inland mission failed
when Dutch settlers destroyed the site's structures in an attack on the
Matabele, leading the missioners to consolidate their efforts in the
maritime mission in Natal. By May 1836, Adams had settled on the Umlazi
River (Natal), Champion and Grout on the Umsunduzi River (Zululand),
Lindley at Illovo River (Natal) and Venable and Wilson on the Umhlatuzi
River (Zululand).

Some individuals, such as the missioner Captain Allen Francis
Gardiner (1794–1851) in 1834, preceded the American Board's arrival in
Natal. The Reverend Francis Owen (1802–1854) arrived in Natal in 1837.
While the American Board was the first mission entity to arrive in Natal
to establish mission stations, it was certainly not the last. Historian Vukile
Khumalo claimed that from 1850 to 1900 Natal was one of the 'most
heavily evangelised regions of the globe'.[15] His claim was not exaggerated.
Fellow historian, Norman Etherington, asserted the following:

> No other quarter of nineteenth century Africa was so thickly invested
> with Christian evangelists. The Secretary of the American Board of
> Commissioners for Foreign Missions estimated in 1880 that the number
> of missionaries in Natal was proportionally greater to any other
> community on the globe two or three times over. By the turn of the
> century in Natal alone there were 40 000 communicants and 10 000
> adherents to Christianity. Most of the converts lived in mission reserves
> and they occupied about 175 000 acres of land.[16]

Just as conflict between Dutch settlers and the Matabele under Mzilikazi
(c. 1790–1868) caused the abandonment and destruction of the inland
mission, so the maritime mission in Natal was destroyed and abandoned
due to conflict between English settlers and Zulus under Zulu king,
Dingane kaSenzangakhona Zulu (1795–1840). Lindley began
independently serving the Dutch in Pietermaritzburg. He justified this

decision to serve the white population with a surprising degree of prescience given the evils of the apartheid regime that began some one hundred years later. In an 1839 letter to Boston, he said:

> I do sincerely believe that the cheapest, speediest, easiest way to convert the heathen here is to convert the white ones first. More, the whites must be provided for, or we labour in vain to make Christians out of the blacks. These two classes will come so fully and constantly in contact with each other, that the influence of the whites, if evil, will be tremendous – will be irresistible, without a miracle to prevent. To their own vices the aborigines will add those of the white men, and thus make themselves two-fold more the children of hell than they were before.[17]

By August 1843, when the American Board decided to abort the mission in southern Africa altogether, Philip pleaded with them to allow the work to continue. The American Board, though embarrassed by Newton Adams's support of his work with the proceeds from his medical practice, Daniel Lindley serving the Dutch Voortrekkers as their *predikant* and Aldin Grout accepting a government commission to continue his ministry, relented and decided to continue the mission. From this point on the mission work flourished, comparatively speaking, with Grout founding a church near the Umvoti River where he served for twenty-five years until his retirement in 1870, and Adams confirming the first Zulu convert, Mbulasi Makhanya, to the Christian faith.

Lindley, Adams and Grout were the flag-bearers for the work of the American Board in southern Africa. Their influence was felt not only in their own contributions, but also in contributions of the indigenous descendants nurtured within the Christian environments that they engendered. Like the American Congregationalists before them who established Harvard and Yale, American missioners in South Africa founded educational institutions that produced some of South Africa's most distinguished leaders, among them Pixley Isaka ka Seme, the founder of the ANC, and John Dube, first ANC president and founder of the industrial Ohlange Institute. Yet, leadership grooming was not the primary aim of mission education. The propagation of the faith had pre-eminence. For women in the nineteenth and twentieth centuries, the American Board saw education as a means of forming 'suitable companions for native pastors and teachers'. A board report of 1866 adds that 'in every native community there may be at least one household illustrative of the fruits of Christian culture'. Such households would 'act as leaven to promote the social and moral regeneration of the people, and will especially tend to the elevation of the female sex'.[18]

Daniel and Lucy Lindley initiated the Inanda Seminary for girls in 1869 and since then it has produced many of South Africa's African female doctors, teachers and lawyers, and in recent times, cabinet and deputy ministerial positions in government. The first principal sent by the American Board, Mary Kelly Edwards (1829–1927), arrived in November 1868 after a three-month journey and served at the school for almost sixty years. The seminary continues to thrive today as the only school under the auspices of the Congregational church, having survived the ravages of the apartheid regime's Bantu Education policy that led to the closing of other mission schools across the country, among them, Adams College in Amanzimtoti and Tiger Kloof at Vryburg.

Inspired by Newton Adams who was a missioner and medical doctor, James McCord (1870–1950) and thereafter Alan Taylor (1893–1969) established a hospital in Durban, the first facility to cater for the medical needs of Africans. McCord Zulu Hospital also went on to become the first to train indigenous nurses (including one of Luthuli's daughters), many of whom graduated from Inanda Seminary.

Aldin Grout and Groutville
Born on 9 September 1803 in Pelham, Massachusetts, Aldin Grout founded the Umvoti (Groutville) mission station from which Albert Luthuli hailed. Grout had graduated from Andover Seminary in Boston, a distinctly Congregationalist or Independent seminary that inspired him to pursue ministries overseas.[19]

Following the death of his first wife and his return to Africa with his second, Charlotte Bailey, Grout found the mission environment significantly weakened by the political environment. The overthrow of Dingane kaSenzangakhona Zulu in June 1839 and his death at the hands of the amaSwazi in March 1840 led to the installation of Zulu king, Mpande kaSenzangakhona Zulu (1789–1872), who was, for all intents and purposes, a vassal of the Voortrekkers. A pattern of ambiguous dependency was first established with the American missioners when on 6 August 1840 Grout took an oath of loyalty to the *volksraad*, the Boer administration in Zululand.[20]

With Boer approval, Mpande granted Grout permission to establish a mission station at Empangeni. The Inkanyezi mission prospered under Grout and his wife, largely with the support of Mfungumfu Dube, his protector and interpreter. Hundreds of students attended the mission school where Charlotte taught, and Grout proved to be quite an agriculturalist, planting rye, wheat, barley, corn, pumpkins, melons, beans, sugar and sorghum. He became well known in the area as a rainmaker, a chief and even a rival power against Mpande.

Commentators have noted Grout's dismissive attitude to Mpande's power and implied that it was Grout's arrogance that caused Mpande's suspicion of him. Grout overestimated Mpande's trust of him and the extent to which the king would allow his Zulu subjects to be influenced by a missioner. In reality, Mpande's interest and benevolence extended to Grout only in so far as it was the royal kingdom that prospered. But, Grout fostered another kingdom, Christendom, and this kingdom was at theological and cultural odds with the Zulu king. Tragically for Grout, as well as for any Christian mission in Zululand for some time, Mpande's subjects paid for their dual allegiances with their lives. Grout's followers believed his tutelage of them to be sanctioned by Mpande. However, as the two rivals became ever more suspicious and doubtful of each other's intentions, the Zulus in Grout's mission became trapped – hesitant to demonstrate obeisance, and afraid to show disrespect for Mpande. On 25 July 1842, Mpande launched a surprise attack on the mission, 'eating up' (killing) those close to Grout.[21] Dube warned Grout to abandon the mission station and flee. The Grouts barely escaped with their lives.

Dube led them south across the Tugela River where, in the same year, they settled a station on the north side of the Umvoti River at Nkukhwini. A small church with a thatched roof was built with bricks that Grout taught his members to make. Here Dube proved to be a very able preacher. Grout respected his abilities to such an extent that he left him in charge of the mission station and crossed the Umvoti River to establish another church on the south side. There were two reasons for this move: Nkukhwini's abundant river sand was not suited to Grout's green thumb, and, further, the south side of the, then very large, Umvoti River, allowed more time for a getaway in the event of attack by royal impis from the north. By 1847 the church was constituted and by 1849 Grout had built a church nine metres wide and sixteen metres long, with a corner for a study.

After Natal became a British colony in 1843, large tracts of land were granted to Boers for farming. Perhaps there was a feeling of obligation by the Crown to dispense land to the American Board also as Grout and other missioners had settled in Natal and Zululand a year prior to the Boers. Land was duly promised and, in 1856, twelve self-contained mission stations of five hundred acres each were allocated at Umvoti (Groutville), Mapumulo, Inanda, Umsunduze, Itafamasi, Esidumbini, Table Mountain, Amanzimtoti (Adams), Imfume, Amahlongwa, Ifafa and Mtwalume. When considering Sabbath attendance, pupils and membership, Umvoti was the largest mission station in 1860.[22] These mission stations still exist today, though smaller in size, under the auspices of the United Congregational Church of Southern Africa (UCCSA), a union of Congregational churches formed in 1967. At the stations, the Congregational missiological emphasis on land tenure promoted the establishment of individual tenure for indigenous adherents. A village plan aimed to create small land-lease settlements on mission reserves where the amakholwa (Christian converts) could farm and graze cattle.

It was this emphasis on land tenure that nurtured Albert Luthuli's preoccupation and concern with the inadequacy of land in South Africa. The enactment of the 1913 Land Act legally confined Africans to high-density reserves and deprived them of the right to purchase land outside those reserves. Luthuli's role as chief in the latter half of the 1930s and throughout the 1940s enlightened him on the systemic injustice of land rights, and his autobiography and speeches are peppered with censorious references to the Act.

The Congregational emphasis on land tenure created in time a class of educated commercial agriculturalists and entrepreneurs who quickly outgrew the small landholdings they were allotted. As chief, Albert Luthuli often acted as an arbiter between the state and the amakholwa, and between the amakholwa themselves when the restrictive land laws caused conflict within the mission reserve. Nadine Gordimer summarised simply the problems Luthuli confronted on the mission reserve:

[T]he Chief found that most of the things that made the people in his reserve unhappy were things that could not be put right by careful advice or a chief's wisdom. There was not enough land for the five thousand people in the reserve to grow their crops of sugar cane and vegetables and graze their cattle. As the sons of the families grew up, they could not buy or rent more land, because Africans were not allowed to own or farm outside the reserves in South Africa.[23]

Ntaba Luthuli

After their conversion and baptism by Aldin Grout, Ntaba and Titisi Luthuli renounced polygamy and became *amakholwa*. Both Ntaba and Titisi were zealous in their faith and began a line of Luthuli *amakholwa* that remains strong to this day. Ntaba became the second chief (*inkosi*) to be appointed to serve the Umvoti Mission Reserve's *abasemakholweni*, or community of converts, and the first of four Luthulis who served as chief. He was also the first teacher to serve in one of several schools organised in the area. He abolished the drinking of alcohol throughout the village. His example was a strong influence on Albert Luthuli who remained a teetotaller throughout his life.

In his autobiography, Albert Luthuli recalls a story about Ntaba that provides a glimpse into the political tensions that permeated the lives of American Board products, creating conditions that Shula Marks referred to as 'ambiguous dependency'. Asked on one occasion to pray for the Queen's forces to prevail over the Zulus, the prayer stuck in his throat. 'O God,' he prayed eventually, 'protect the victims of whoever is the aggressor in this war!'[24]

Titisi gave birth to four sons, Martin, John, Daniel and Henry. Ntaba's cousin, Ngubane, became the Christian chief after Ntaba. Martin, Ntaba's son (and Luthuli's uncle), became chief after Ngubane. Ntaba's second-born, John, married a recent Christian convert, Nozililo Mtonya Gumede, whom Albert Luthuli described as a 'fluent, devoted and assiduous reader of the Bible in the vernacular'.[25] A well-trained teacher at the Groutville Congregational mission, John sought to augment his income by purchasing oxen and a wagon and entering the transport business. Many from Groutville embarked upon commercial ventures of one kind or another as the only professions available for literate *amakholwa* were in the lower paying teaching profession and the civil service. Historian Robert Houle described Groutville as the 'most fully realised pastoral village' saying:

> By 1867, its 433 residents owned nearly 50 wagons, many more ploughs and carts, and hundreds of trained oxen to pull them. Transport-riding was a particularly popular and lucrative career for Groutville's *kholwa* community, allowing them to tend their farms while using their unique

position as Zulu Christians to do business in both the traditional and
Western worlds of Natal, buying grain from Zulu neighbours and
reselling it to the white community. The residents of Groutville poured
these profits back into the markers of their Christian identity – their
64 Western-style homes (including those made of brick), Victorian
wardrobe, farming implements and small libraries.[26]

John Luthuli departed north with the British South Africa Army forces
where he likely served logistically as well as linguistically. At some time,
his wife, Mtonya, ventured north to join him. On a chance encounter in
Bulawayo, John met some Seventh-Day Adventist missioners who expressed
the desire to establish a school for orphaned children. Sufficiently
impressed with John's teaching abilities, the missioners invited him to
take charge of the school at the Solusi mission. But first, John had to
mend his ways. Virgil Robinson, who recorded the history of Solusi,
reported that John was a heavy drinker: 'He passed the idle hours away by
drinking more and more heavily, nearly drinking himself to death.'[27]
Finally, a doctor was sent for. Warned of the dangers he faced, one
presumes that John recovered enough to take on the position. He remained
in Bulawayo working as an evangelist, interpreter and teacher for the
Seventh-Day Adventists and proved to be competent despite the meagre
resources at his disposal – no equipment, no books, no blackboard.
Robinson reports that John told his students: 'Your textbook is going to
be your Bible. Your songbook is going to teach you English.'[28]

John Luthuli's leadership of the school was short-lived, however. The
mission grieved when he died unexpectedly in mid-1898. What is known
of the cause of his sudden death is puzzling. Robinson reports that after
a grave illness involving a fever and a brief recuperation, the missioner
Anderson reported that John received a gift of corn from a friend.
'Thinking they would taste good, [John] Ntaba asked his wife to cook a
half dozen ears, which he ate, with fatal results.'[29] John more than likely
died of malaria which had assumed epidemic proportions following heavy
rains that year that devastated Bulawayo and the Solusi mission.

John Luthuli left his wife widowed with the eldest son, Alfred Nsusana,
and their six-month-old son, Albert John Mvumbi Luthuli. Some
commentaries indicate that Albert Luthuli preferred the name 'Mvumbi'
('Continuous Rain') to his English names. However, no evidence suggests
this claim is correct though he is occasionally referred to as 'Madlanduna',

the Luthuli clan name. Albert was the third of three sons born of John and Mtonya. Alfred, the first-born son, died in 1941. Though only partially educated, he did his best to succeed his father on behalf of the Seventh-Day Adventists. The second son was Mpangwa, who died at birth.

Martin Luthuli

From Rhodesia, Albert Luthuli returned with his family to Natal, spending some time en route in Vryheid. Back in Groutville, he was brought up in two Congregational households, first that of his uncle, Martin Luthuli, and later in his mother's household. It was an upbringing saturated with Christian piety. Luthuli recalls in his autobiography that in Martin's home he was particularly influenced by his aunt who was highly regarded in the local church. 'All the time,' he remembered, 'unconsciously, I was busy absorbing the Christian ethos of home, and church congregation, and the social ethos of the community.'[30] It was an ethos that created lasting personal habits. Morning, evening and mealtime prayers were regular rituals for the family that, for Luthuli, the passage of time failed to dissipate. In a 2007 tribute to Luthuli, Nomzamo Winnie Madikizela-Mandela reminisced that when she entertained Luthuli as ANC president general, he would say a prayer before dinner, paying little attention to those who, for their own reasons, felt uncomfortable with the practice.[31]

Martin Luthuli was raised and educated at the American Board mission in the Groutville area. As a farmer and wagon maker, he suffered financially during an economic downturn in the 1880s and resorted to offering his services as translator and interpreter to the desperate *usuthu* (Zulu royalists) as they struggled to communicate appeals to the colonial government and the metropole. Serving as a secretary and attaché of sorts for the *usuthu* brought Martin in frequent contact with Bishopstowe, the mission station of the Anglican Bishop John William Colenso (1814–1883). It also brought him into the powerful circles of Theophilus Shepstone (1817–1893) and the colonial government. In the eyes of the Colenso family, this made Martin somewhat suspect.[32]

During the 1880s, Martin Luthuli also acted as secretary to Zulu king, Dinizulu kaCetshwayo Zulu (1868–1913). He was the first of several Groutville *kholwa* notables who later served in this capacity. He became chairperson of the Pastors' Conference of the Congregational church, a second, and lower, leadership instrumentality within the Congregational church. At the turn of the century, Martin, with Saul Msane (c. 1856–

1932), John Dube, Josiah Tshangana Gumede (1870-1947) and others, founded the Natal Native Congress (NNC) and, with H.C. Matiwane as secretary, became its chairperson for three years.[33] Following Luthuli's term, Skweleti Nyongwana succeeded him as chair.[34] The congress advocated for increased representation for Africans and for several other social changes such as the introduction of private land ownership.

In 1908, he was the first chief to be elected democratically by the *abasemakholweni* at Umvoti (the previous two having been appointed). Martin was certainly the community's popular choice and he cut a dashing figure in this role. From the American Board secretary, Cornelius H. Patton (1860-1939), after his visit to the Groutville, we hear that the congregation was 'not only civilised, but educated and prosperous', and the chief [Martin Luthuli] 'was garbed like a city gentleman, long black coat, starched shirt and all the paraphernalia of civilisation with not a detail omitted, even to the necktie pin. He was a Christian and a highly prosperous man, being the owner of a sugar plantation.'[35]

Historian Vukile Khumalo rightly points out in an unpublished paper that the NNC membership was based at the mission stations.[36] The government was uncomfortable with the NNC because it advocated for increased representation in Parliament during a time when segregationist policies were being formulated and implemented. In 1904, Martin Luthuli argued before the Native Affairs Commission of 1903-1905: '. . . sometimes we discuss about how we should approach the government to let the Natives have the franchise, so that Natives can have a voice in the Parliament; because here in Natal we have no voice in Parliament whatever.'[37]

In the early 1910s, together with other mission chiefs, Martin Luthuli argued, as the lesser of two evils, for the complete territorial and racial separation subject to a more equitable distribution of land. Like so many *amakholwa* leaders at the turn of the century, his life was one caught in the crosshairs of tradition and modernity. Two worlds pulling in opposite directions, one customary and indigenous and the other Christian and modern, vied for his allegiance.

Many aspects of Martin Luthuli's life were echoed later in the life of his nephew, Albert Luthuli. So, too, Albert Luthuli's life appeared to follow the vocational path of a more distant uncle, Ngazana Luthuli, who was born in Groutville in 1874 and was sub-editor of the Zulu-language weekly *Ilanga lase Natal*.[38] Ngazana attended the local Groutville primary school, was educated at Adams College and graduated in 1897. Like Albert Luthuli, Ngazana was a school master by profession (1888–1890) and taught at Adams College (1899–1915), departing only five years prior to Albert's arrival as a student. Ngazana also had a connection with Dube's Ohlange Institute, serving as its secretary. *The African Yearly Register* listed music as Ngazana's hobby and, like Albert Luthuli, he was a choirmaster.[39]

The links that Albert Luthuli's forebears had with the American Board, which was responsible for educating and training an emerging black elite in the mission field, are extensive enough to assert that they constructed the core of his being. Other early 1960 ANC leaders, although trained in mission schools, did not possess the broad and multi-generational *amakholwa* associations to the same extent and depth as Albert Luthuli did. And it is these similarities between Albert Luthuli and his American Board forebears that help explain how faith bound him throughout his life.

John Langalibalele Dube

Only one other Congregationalist rivals Albert Luthuli's political prominence: John Langalibalele Dube (1871–1946), founder and principal of the Ohlange Institute in Inanda. Luthuli attended the institute for two terms upon his completion of Standard Four, having attended the local Congregational mission school, Aldinville Primary in Groutville, from 1910 to 1914. Luthuli's short time at Ohlange made little impression on him; however, he emerged from it deeply influenced by Dube.

James Dube (d. 1882), a convert of Daniel Lindley's and John Dube's father, had been one of three indigenous Congregational lay leaders ordained by the American Board in 1870, a move which ended the dominance of white missioners in the ordained ministry. Like Martin Luthuli, James was the son of a prominent chief. Therefore, Albert Luthuli and John Dube were both chiefs' grandsons. The parallels between Albert and John do not end there.

John Dube attended Adams College where he came into the good graces of his mentor and sponsor, the Reverend William Wilcox (1850–1928), a missioner of the American Board. He subsequently raised the finance to accompany Wilcox on a journey to the United States in 1887. Soon after their arrival, Dube enrolled in the Oberlin Preparatory Academy before becoming a student at Oberlin College. This first visit to the United States lasted until 1892 when poor health forced him to return to Natal, not having formally obtained his degree at Oberlin. Upon his return, John Dube, like Luthuli, taught at Adams College. He then travelled to the United States a second time, presumably to raise money for an indigenous trade school he wished to found. In 1897, he took up residence in Brooklyn Heights, New York, and was ordained into the Congregational ministry at the Lewis Avenue Church located in the Bedford-Stuyvesant area. Dube then returned to South Africa and, in August 1901, during the Anglo-Boer War, founded the Zulu Christian Industrial School (in 1917 renamed Ohlange Institute).

John Dube could be an outspoken man. During the war he locked horns with the Natal colonial government when he expressed the opinion that Africans should have political control of the country. For this he was detained. In 1908 he resigned his pastorate at the Inanda mission, where his father James served before him, after seven years service as minister. His resignation followed closely on the heels of the Bhambatha Uprising of 1906 and upon his being hauled before the governor and told to moderate his opinions. The resignation may have been the result of differences due to the American Board's sensitivities to being labelled an 'Ethiopian' church, advocating indigenous rights, as it permitted African ministers to lead congregations unsupervised by a white person.

Never departing from his educational vocation, between 1904 and 1927, Dube made three more trips to the United States to raise funds for Ohlange. In 1912 the ANC elected him *in absentia* as its first president and elected another ordained Congregationalist, Walter B. Rubusana (1858–1936), as one of its first vice presidents.

John Dube's life seemed a precursor for Luthuli's. The common American Board heritage, faith, polity, education and travel to the United States ensured that their life paths would be similar. In *A History of Christianity in South Africa* (1994), Hofmeyr and Pillay identified three of Dube's defining characteristics:

Firstly, he was an educator and much energy went into making the Ohlange Institute viable. Secondly, he was a political leader and was among those who protested against the 1913 Native's Land Act. He accompanied the delegation to London in 1914 to protest to the British government. Thirdly, he sought peaceful coexistence between black and white South Africans, taking part in the Smuts Native Conferences (only for a few years before he left because it had no real power), the

Joint Council Movement in the 1920s and church conferences. In 1926 he was part of the South African delegation to the international missionary conference at Le Zoute in Belgium.[40]

All of the above three characteristics apply to Luthuli. One need simply substitute names and dates. Luthuli was an educator, a political leader and a Christian ambassador seeking racial reconciliation through peaceful means. Even their disappointments with the conservative nature of the church and the impotence of political forums run parallel.

The same unique ecclesiastical polity that reared both ANC presidents fundamentally influenced their political views. For Dube and Luthuli, education and hard work were the tools by which to achieve liberation. Violence and revolution were not a part of the recipe. While in Brooklyn, Dube attended Booker T. Washington's lectures on the dignity of labour and on methods for what William Marable, in his 1976 dissertation on John Dube, called teaching 'Negroes to become moral, self-supporting and useful citizens'.[41] In this respect, Luthuli strove to emulate Dube.

Both served together on the Adams College and Inanda Seminary advisory boards that provided Africans with a forum to shape mission education during the mid-1930s. In 1940, both served on the independent governing council of Adams College Incorporated. Both Luthuli and Dube used Christian biblical teachings and a progressive concept of civilisation as the basis for their arguments. Both articulated the central theme that the distinctly Congregational ethic, fusing ecclesiastical and political polity, was a means to forward the progressive nature of history. According to Dube, the Bible stated that a just government ruled from the consent of the governed. For him, the time had come for Africans to have some way of influencing the legislative processes that affected them. The Gospel demanded it.

Dube was not re-elected as president of the ANC in 1917, not, according to Hofmeyr and Pillay, for his rejection of violence, but because many progressive and impatient forces within the congress viewed his leadership as too conservative. Undoubtedly, Dube was troubled by recurrent tensions within the congress between those who maintained conservative and gradualist ethics (commonly referred to as *hamba kahle* politics or 'go easy' politics) engendered by American Board mission institutions, and those who were attracted to more assertive methods to establish equal rights in the land of their birth. This motif later troubled his younger cousin, Pixley Isaka

ka Seme, and other congress presidents such as Dr Alfred Bitini Xuma
(1893–1962), Dr James S. Moroka (1891–1985) and Luthuli. For the
remainder of his political career, Dube led only the Natal branch of the
ANC. He served on the Native Representative Council (NRC) from 1936.
In 1945 he suffered a stroke; he died the following year. After an election,
Luthuli replaced him as a member of the NRC.

Pixley Isaka ka Seme

Another figure that helps to shed light on Luthuli's intellectual history is
Pixley Isaka ka Seme (1881–1951). The Mount Hermon School file gives
us a solid basis for establishing Seme as an ecclesiastical ancestor to Luthuli.
Like his older cousin, John Dube, Seme was born at the Inanda mission
station. He studied for three years at Amanzimtoti Institute (later the
Adams Training School for Boys) learning, among other things, photo-
graphy. Seme studied the equivalent of Matric at the Mount Hermon
School in Massachusetts and continued at Columbia University after being
denied an opportunity to study at Yale, his first choice. His American
missioner mentor, the Reverend Stephen Pixley, whose name Isaka adopted
as a tribute during his studies, sponsored him and saw to his upkeep.
John Dube and other benefactors also assisted a great deal along the way.
At Columbia University, Seme delivered an award-winning speech entitled
'The Regeneration of Africa' in which he enunciated the central themes
in his spiritual and political worldview: an optimistic understanding of
history, an infusion of biblically based theology and a strategy of gradualism.
He said:

> Man knows his home now in a sense never known before. Many great
> and holy men have evinced a passion for the day you are now witnessing
> – their prophetic vision shot through many unborn centuries to this
> very hour. 'Men shall run to and fro', said Daniel, 'and knowledge
> shall increase upon the earth'. Oh, how true! See the triumph of genius
> today! Science has searched out the deep things of nature, surprised
> the secrets of the most distant stars . . . and has brought foreign nations
> to one civilised family. This all-powerful contact says even to the most
> backward race, you cannot remain where you are, you cannot fall back,
> you must advance! A great century has come upon us! No race possessing
> the inherent capacity to survive can resist and remain unaffected by
> this influence of contact and intercourse, the backward with the

advanced. This influence constitutes the very essence of efficient progress and of civilisation.[42]

Some years later, in 1912, subsequent to his return to South Africa, Seme organised a meeting in Bloemfontein, drawing together personalities from African communities all over South Africa, to establish the South African Native National Congress, the forerunner of the ANC. In his keynote address he proclaimed that the congress's purpose was to form a union to defend the rights and privileges of Africans. Ultimately, his leadership proved inadequate for the congress. He did not move with the times. In 'Discovering Seme' (2006), historian Tim Couzens described his leadership of the ANC from 1930 to 1937 as 'conservative, lacklustre and autocratic', thus leading to a state of 'culpable inertia' in the congress.[43] Like Dube before him, Seme was retired for not keeping up with radicalised developments in the organisation. Several other ANC leaders, including Luthuli, were to suffer the same fate in later years.

Early education

In 1915, Albert Luthuli attended Edendale College, near Pietermaritz-burg. It was here that he participated in his first act of civil disobedience. Together with other students, he joined a student strike and stay-away to protest against the use of manual labour as a form of discipline. The mass action failed and for it, Luthuli received a public thrashing from his uncle, Martin.

Luthuli remembered that it was at Edendale where he was first exposed to white (or European) teachers, and that this perhaps led to his developing, although subconsciously, his understanding of a synthesis of African and European cultures that could contribute to 'world civilisation'. In his autobiography, while recounting his times at Edendale, he disputed the charge that mission schools were producing 'black Englishmen'. At Edendale, rather, 'two cultures met, and both Africans and Europeans were affected by the meeting. Both profited, and both survived enriched.'[44]

Upon completing his two-year lower teacher's course at Edendale, Luthuli accepted the position of principal at a rural school at Blaauwbosch in the Natal midlands. While serving at Blaauwbosch, Luthuli resided with a Methodist evangelist's family (Xaba) and, with no local Congregational church at his disposal, he became the protégé of the ageing local Methodist minister, the Reverend Mtembu. Luthuli was confirmed in the Methodist church and shortly thereafter became a lay preacher under the mentorship of this old and benevolent minister. The fact that Luthuli worshipped and became a lay leader in this local Methodist mission school has led many sources to document incorrectly that Luthuli was a Methodist. Becoming a Methodist lay leader was a matter of very short-term local logistics only.

At Blaauwbosch, Luthuli first encountered Charles Templeman Loram (1879–1940), Natal's Chief Inspector for Native Education. Loram had mentored Z.K. Matthews, assisting him to secure scholarship support for further studies. He did the same for Luthuli, recommending him for a bursary to study in 1920 for the Higher Teacher's Diploma at Adams College.

Teacher training

After two years of study at Adams College, Luthuli remained a worthy investment to his benefactors, excelling academically. For him, however, Adams College was not just about academics. It was here that he learnt something about faith too.

> Adams taught me what Edendale did not, that I had to *do* something about being a Christian, and that this something must identify me with my neighbour, not dissociate me from him. Adams taught me more. It inculcated, by example rather than precept, a specifically Christian mode of going about work in a society, and I had frequent reason to be grateful for this later in life (original emphasis).[45]

When Charles Loram again offered Luthuli a scholarship, this time to attend Fort Hare University in the Eastern Cape, he declined. He opted instead to earn a salary to provide for his ageing mother. For a talented, conscientious and educated African person at the time, Luthuli could pursue few vocations other than teaching, for which he was in high demand following his graduation. Father Bernard Huss, principal at St Francis College, a Roman Catholic institution at Mariannhill in Natal, offered Luthuli a post even though Luthuli was a Protestant. A.E. Le Roy, the ordained principal of Adams who served from 1901 to 1926, also offered Luthuli a post at the 'Normal College'. This Luthuli accepted and his first responsibilities were to teach music as the college choirmaster (his favourite role), and the Zulu language, the latter without textbooks. As

Luthuli gained in experience and competence, 'School Organisation' was added to his portfolio and eventually he was made the first black South African supervisor of teachers-in-training in all satellite schools.

Adams College

A great number of prominent members of the twentieth-century southern Africa intelligentsia were educated and groomed to be leaders at the Adams institution. Many proceeded to study further at the University of Fort Hare at Alice in the Eastern Cape. Much has been written about Adams College as it was a point of contestation for and reconciliation of African and western theological, social and scientific values. Much of the evaluative literature on Adams is romantic and idealistic or, conversely, cynical and pejorative. In his autobiography, Luthuli himself acknowledges the contradictions between the values (idealistic and benevolent) articulated by American Board institutions, epitomised by Adams College, and the always imperfect, and on occasion contradictory, manner in which those ideals were implemented in practice.

The Amanzimtoti Institute, which later became Adams College, was the flagship school by which the American Board sought to train Congregational pastors and teachers. The American Board established the school in 1853 and closed it in 1956.[46] Adams's educational high standards attracted African students from all over southern Africa. In its heyday, the college consisted of a high school, a theological school, a 'practising' school (for teacher training), an industrial school, an agricultural school and a music school. According to the inaugural issue of its student publication, Iso Lomuzi (1931), the school stood for 'Sound Knowledge and Trained Ability, Modern Methods and Upright Character, a Clean Body and Spiritual Development'.[47]

In his autobiography, Luthuli names Z.K. Matthews, Karl Roger Brueckner (1882–1965), F.J. de Villiers (1898–1980), Edgar Brookes (1897–1979) and W.C. Atkins as the most influential personalities at Adams. Collectively and individually, they had a profound influence on his spirituality and helped germinate his faith-based political philosophy.

It was Brueckner, head of the industrial school, who advised Albert Luthuli to 'give a charitable interpretation to every man's actions until you can prove that such an interpretation is unsound'.[48] Luthuli was not an aggressive character. The absence of animus was the quality Nokukhanya most admired in her husband. In one biographical profile of Nokukhanya, she said Luthuli was incapable of hate. 'He never so much as criticised anyone. He felt he had no right to point a finger.'[49] Luthuli constantly looked for mitigating circumstances in the ill behaviour of others and tried to explain their conduct. No more was this evident than in his struggle to deal with his son's dysfunction, when Luthuli commented in a 1956 letter to his close friend, Mary-Louise Hooper: 'I must confess, I am beginning to lose hope: not that I would scold him if I saw him – No.'[50]

Such was the influence of Brueckner's counsel. Luthuli resolutely refused to be hostile even to those who physically assaulted him. Later, he could not show hostility to liberals on behalf of Africanists who wanted nothing to do with them and spurned their aid; he could not reject communists who were reviled by liberals. Most significantly, to his last days he continued to support non-violence as a means by which to attain freedom for South Africa's majority population.

It was F.J. de Villiers, a teacher at Adams, who sensitised Luthuli to the manner in which apartheid South Africa socialised whites to hate people of colour. Denied ordination in the Dutch Reformed Church because of his apparently liberal views on race, De Villiers, according to Luthuli, 'seemed closer to the Africans on the staff than did most white teachers . . . [and] associated with us more freely and more often than did his white fellows'.[51] He explained to Luthuli that Afrikaners were 'victims of their own past', whose hatred for people of colour was acculturated into their society rather than inherent. This interpretation of white supremacy offered Luthuli a 'real protection against hatred and bitterness' and was perhaps the source of his belief that, after a good deal of soul-searching and repentance, white supremacy would dissolve. Much to Luthuli's dismay, De Villiers later became the director of Bantu Education in Pretoria and complicit with Hendrik Verwoerd (1901–1966) in the destruction of African education, Adams College and other quality mission schools.

Adams principal, Edgar Brookes, too, made a deep impression on Luthuli for being utterly sincere in his religious practice and 'one of South Africa's greatest champions of public and private sanity and morality'.[52] Luthuli held this view of Brookes in 1961, despite the fact that in 1935, while Luthuli still taught at Adams College, Brookes passionately defended the continued control of educational institutions by white missioners against Charles Loram who suggested a rapid devolution of authority to

Africans. Rightly or wrongly, Luthuli likely observed benevolent motivations in both.

W.C. Atkins, head of the Teachers' Training College and principal, typified for Luthuli the ethos of Adams that he held to be most valuable and enduring. As principal, Atkins was devoted to the call of the Gospel to serve society. '[H]e had no hesitation,' said Luthuli, 'in involving us deeply in the affairs of the African communities which lay within reach of Adams. Possibly this was really the combined achievement of Adams, but Atkins remains in my memory as a symbol of it.'[53]

These Christian laymen convinced Luthuli that the Christian life was 'not a private affair without relevance to society'.

> It was, rather, a belief which equipped us in a unique way to meet the challenges of our society . . . which had to be applied to the conditions of our lives; and our many works – they ranged from Sunday School teaching to road-building – became meaningful as the outflow of Christian belief.[54]

Most of these personalities (with the exceptions of the Reverend Mtembu at Blaauwbosch and Z.K. Matthews) were white liberal male lay Christian educators. Under their influence, Luthuli was unable later to advance into the realm of armed struggle that he feared would quickly descend into a race war. When the question of violence arose within the congress movement, Luthuli's cloud of saintly witnesses would undoubtedly have disapproved. These mentors, these unseen and seen witnesses, strategically bound Luthuli when others, less influenced by white liberal Christians, perceived the resort to violence to be the only viable option enabling them to exit the perceived strategic cul-de-sac. Brookes, Atkins, De Villiers and Brueckner, despite the contradictions inherent in their liberal politics, influenced Luthuli to be 'bound by faith'. For them, this Christian mode could not countenance the use of violence in the South African context. While enhancing his relevancy to the ANC in 1952, it was these mentors that contributed to his irrelevancy in 1961.

John Reuling

Though not mentioned in Luthuli's autobiography, the Congregationalist John Reuling (1906–1990) mentored and supported Luthuli longer than any other. Luthuli intentionally did not mention many notable people in his autobiography. For this he apologised, saying the account was written for an international audience and names of domestic importance required sacrificing. In the preface, he wrote, 'It may be noticed that names, which might have been expected in a book of this type, do not appear. The reason for this is not churlishness on my part, or a lack of honour where it is due.'[55] However, it is also possible that Luthuli did not mention Reuling by name so as not to jeopardise Reuling's ability to obtain travel visas needed for his regular visits to South Africa's American Board missions.

John Reuling served the American Board as the Africa regional secretary from 1946 to 1962. Documenting the history of Congregationalism in South Africa, Roy Briggs and Joseph Wing judged Reuling to be the chief mover in 1960 for the dissolution of the American Board mission in Natal, and the establishment instead of an indigenous church that would enable South African Congregationalists in KwaZulu and Natal to be fully autonomous and thus self-governing.[56] With the surge in anti-colonial nationalism after the Second World War, Reuling and others resolved to streamline and thus make more efficient the American Board's global endeavours. To achieve this missiological downsizing, the American Board encouraged and equipped overseas missions to become sovereign. If mission churches were to be truly Congregational, autonomy was a prerequisite. In a 1962 letter to Luthuli, Reuling said that the relinquishing of foreign control meant that missioners would be 'working on the fringes as it were, serving by teaching or, as in the case of church advisors, giving help when requested'.[57] In 1962, Reuling became the executive general secretary for the American Board's institutional successor, the United Church Board for World Ministries (UCBWM) formed in 1961. He held this position until his retirement in 1971.

Reuling's history with southern African mission history is long, beginning in 1927 when he taught at Adams College with his wife, Eleanor. He served Adams in various capacities: as dean of men, head teacher (director) of the Teachers' Training College and as the vice principal. For nine years (1927–1935), Luthuli and Reuling were colleagues at Adams and their relationship continued long after their mutual time together there. They corresponded regularly until at least 2 September 1964.[58]

Reuling always remained very interested in Luthuli and news from Inanda Seminary's principal, Lavinia Scott (1907–1997), to Reuling frequently included a news bulletin about Luthuli, complete with information about his banning status and efforts to secure bursaries for Luthuli's daughters, Hilda and Albertinah. The UCBWM did not wish the state to perceive that the church involved itself politically, so there was a need to avoid direct or frequent communication that could be intercepted between Luthuli and Reuling. Missioners such as Scott acted as intermediaries between Reuling and Luthuli. Howard Trumbull, an American Board financial administrator for the Bantu Congregational Church (BCC), also acted as a conduit by sending and receiving telegrams between Reuling and Luthuli.

In the early 1960s, Reuling and Luthuli enjoyed many substantive discussions. They both felt a special camaraderie and Luthuli remained interested and involved in church dynamics from behind the scenes. Commonalities brought them together in the classroom, the sanctuary, the mission field and even in matters related to the use of land. When Reuling served at one time as the Adams farm manager, providing more scientific, modern and commercial methods of horticulture, Luthuli assisted by supplying agricultural knowledge derived from his childhood, shepherding mules in Vryheid and performing chores in Groutville. Luthuli transferred information about indigenous methods and plants while Reuling transferred commercial skills.

When Luthuli later returned to the land as chief, he founded and chaired the Zululand Bantu Cane Growers' Association. Bans had forced him to retire from the campaign trail and to subsist on farming. To his dying day, Luthuli remained a farmer. In fact, the inquest form prepared by the Stanger police identified Luthuli as a 'farmer'.

Marriage

After the customary negotiations, on 19 January 1927 Albert Luthuli married Nokukhanya Bhengu, a colleague on the staff at Adams College in the 'Practising School' and the boarding establishment. Like her husband, Nokukhanya was raised in the Congregationalist tradition. Her father, Maphitha, the eldest son of Chief Ndlokolo, and her mother were probably of the early converts at the American Board mission station at Umgeni near Durban.[59] Nokukhanya went to school at the Inanda Seminary from 1917 to 1919. Although in his autobiography, Luthuli does not say how, he surmises that the two must have been together at Ohlange High School which he briefly attended in 1914. She proceeded to Adams College to train as a teacher where she attended his Zulu language and School Organisation classes. After marrying, Albert and Nokukhanya Luthuli established a permanent home in Groutville with his mother Mtonya (also known as 'MaHangu'), where, in 1929, the first of their seven children, Hugh Bunyan Sulenkosi, was born. Those that followed were: Albertinah Nomathuli, Hilda Thandeka, Eleanor S'mangele (1936– 2002), Jane Elizabeth Thembekile, Christian 'Boyi' Madunjini (1942– 2009) and Edgar Cyril Sibusiso (1943–1993).

We can obtain a picture of the Luthuli's home during the time he taught at Adams from a relative, raised as a daughter but often referred to as a sister, Charlotte Goba (1918–1999), who later taught at Inanda Seminary.

> Dinner was a family affair. It began with prayer. Albert would ask one of his children to bring the Bible and hymn books. After dinner, we often sang hymns. He would then pat the young ones gently and playfully send them off to bed with a, 'Go, go and put on your nightie and get into bed.' The older children remained to discuss current affairs. He would make a statement to provoke discussion. He might suddenly break into what one of us had been saying with a sharp, 'Angivumi' (I don't agree with you) and that would begin a protest, 'But Baba,' and Baba would put us through a whole process of logic and get us to look at the provocative statement from different points of view. He thus shaped our minds.[60]

2

The Christian Mode
1928–1959

I am in Congress precisely because I am a Christian.
— Albert Luthuli, *Let My People Go*

BETWEEN 1928 AND 1959, many people, organisations and campaigns shaped Albert Luthuli's political views and instilled within him an appreciation for western democracy, multiracial co-operation and non-violence, and it was these values that later catapulted him to the presidency of the ANC. As a young teacher and chief, Luthuli's involvement with indigenous co-operatives, be they vocational, agricultural or political, brought with it many leadership challenges, especially as it dawned on him that the government would manipulate ethnic nostalgia to thwart a progressive developmental path. The earliest of these engagements was with the Natal Native Teachers' Association and the Zulu Language and Cultural Society. Luthuli quickly outgrew these humble institutions. His strong moral character and leadership abilities catalysed his meteoric rise to the heights of political power.

Natal Native Teachers' Association
In 1928, Albert Luthuli, then on the staff at Adams College, was elected as secretary of the Natal Native Teachers' Association, serving under the presidency of his friend and colleague, Z.K. Matthews. In 1933, he became the association's president.

The association had a threefold agenda. In the first place, it focused on improving the material conditions under which African teachers were employed. Secondly, it aimed to motivate its members to broaden their skills and keep abreast of the times through continuing education. Thirdly, it encouraged its members to participate in sports, music, debates, games and social meetings under what Luthuli described as 'the spell of a cup of tea or the cloud of the smoke of a pipe'.[1]

Despite four years of preoccupation with 'material matters', the association had made little, if any, progress in that regard. One of the few things it is remembered for is its vigorous opposition to Charles Loram's proposal in 1921 that Africans be educated in practical and utilitarian functions. For Luthuli, Loram's idea that people should 'develop along their own lines' later served as an ideological platform for the National Party's Bantu Education that enforced inferior education on all people of colour. Nonetheless, he believed Loram's motives to be altruistic, writing, 'He had, I do not doubt, the best of intentions'.[2] Loram's efforts to inspire the American Board to devolve authority in education to its African converts as a means of maintaining its influence and to continue its work in improving race relations may have inspired Luthuli's sympathetic appraisal of him. Perhaps, remembering that Loram arranged his bursary to Adams, Luthuli's characterisation of him was strikingly free of bitterness.

The earliest archived samples of Luthuli's writing date back to this period, in correspondence that conveys his belief in divine providence tempering and consoling his discontent with the South African government. When Allison Wessels George Champion (1893–1975), general secretary of the Industrial [and Commercial] Workers' Union (ICU),[3] was banned from the city of Durban for three years, Luthuli wrote to the ICU thus:

> My President has desired me, on behalf of the Natal Native Teachers' [Association] to write and express sympathy with you gentlemen on the unfortunate step taken by the so[-]called [M]inister of Justice in banishing Mr Champion, your General Secretary. Words really fail one to express adequately the feelings of regret and sorry [sic] that we have on this matter, and I am sure that in this, I am not only expressing the feelings of the president and myself, but of all the teachers who know Mr Champion and the organisation that owes so much to his indefatigable efforts on its behalf. We trust that the God, the Father Almighty, will keep him safe in his banishment and allow him to return to his work to carry it out to an even more successful issue than before, may be much to the disgust [sic] and disappointment of the so[-]called Minister of Justice and we hope that with God's guidance you shall be able to get a worthy acting General Secretary who shall keep up the work, in the

meantime, so ably carried on by Mr Champion . . . We trust that God shall take care and provide in His own way for his family.[4]

The Zulu Language and Cultural Society

Disillusioned by a lack of progress in improving teachers' material lot, Luthuli refocused his efforts by co-founding in 1935 an auxiliary of the Teachers' Association, the Zulu Language and Cultural Society. The Zulu king, Dinizulu kaCetshwayo Zulu, served as one of the society's patrons, and John Dube served as its first president. Charles Mpanza (1895–1960), a fellow Congregationalist, as well as chairperson of the American Board's *umkandlu* (council) and member of the Adams College advisory board, served as the society's secretary.

Before the society's inception, Luthuli wrote that he hoped it 'would undertake to secure the standardisation of necessary "Zuluised" words' and 'form new modes of expressing foreign [e.g. scientific] ideas'.[5] He also proposed that the society initiate mass adult education. Rather than preserve Zulu culture in some early nineteenth-century time capsule, Luthuli described the objective of the society as to 'preserve what is valuable in our heritage while discarding the inappropriate or outmoded'.[6]

Luthuli's time with the society was short-lived on account of his call to serve as chief in Groutville. His withdrawal prevented him from having any significant direct involvement with the society's development, and as it matured, it deviated from his original intentions. Of its own accord, it failed, much as the Teachers' Association had failed, to realise its own objectives. Shula Marks argued that the society primarily sought to attain 'state recognition of the scion of the Zulu royal house as Paramount, and added to it a concern for the preservation of Zulu tradition and custom'.[7] The society, rather than agitate the government for quality mass education, benignly collected Zulu folklore and traditions for publication. Such beneficent activities, according to Marks, attracted the support of the government, in particular the Chief Native Commissioner of Natal, Harry C. Lugg (1882–1978). According to Dr Mordeciah Gumede (1917–1993), speaking at a 1982 memorial service to pay tribute to Albert Luthuli, the government's largesse compromised the society, detracting from its autonomy and causing many teachers to withdraw their membership from the early 1940s until the society eventually collapsed in 1946.[8]

Luthuli expressed in his autobiography his perception that, in addition to the grant in aid and office space accepted from the Native Affairs

Department in Pietermaritzburg, the society's involvement in the politics of the Zulu royal house fostered its demise. The society's co-opted relationship with the government led it to preserve a caricature of Zulu culture and stunted, if not prevented, an otherwise dynamic and progressive contribution to the great stream of civilisation. Luthuli deduced this civilisation to be a synthesis of many cultures, including African.[9] The society's ethos proved too conservative, even retrograde. Thus, according to the historian Shula Marks, the Zulu Christian intelligentsia viewed it as a benign pawn of a malevolent government.[10]

The inability of the Teachers' Association and Zulu Society to initiate any meaningful change spurred Luthuli to reject the government as a co-operative partner. In more assertive tactics Luthuli participated in the 1946 boycott of the Native Representative Council (NRC), and, as leader of the Natal ANC, in the 1952 Defiance Campaign. Their failures also led to his vociferous objection in 1959, and beyond, to Africans' participation in the Bantustan framework.

Political and ecclesiastic chieftaincy

For two years from 1933, Albert Luthuli resisted appeals from the Groutville community elders to contest the chieftainship held since the 1920s by Josiah Mqwebu (d. 1952), an unpopular figure at the time. Luthuli's candidacy was supported also by the resident missioner. By December 1935, he relented, making himself available as a candidate. More likely than not, the process of vetting his candidacy by both the American Board and the government was a prerequisite for his election.

The Code of Native Law required for juridical purposes that there be a chief of the reserve. Any candidate who passed through the judicial gauntlet could then be presented to the community for ratification by democratic vote. The chieftainship of a mission community consisted of three roles: a traditional leader (*inkosi*) accountable to the local community, a civil servant (judge) accountable to the government and an unordained ecclesiarch (deacon) accountable to the wider and local church. Any candidate for the chieftaincy therefore needed the approval of the wider church and then the state, before being elected by the local community. In all events, the state exercised the power of veto as was demonstrated in the election which initially brought Josiah Mqwebu to the chieftaincy in 1920.

In 1935 Luthuli and Mqwebu squared off in an election conducted by the Native Commissioner. Luthuli won by sixty-eight votes to forty-three.[11] Though the church likely participated with the state in engineering Luthuli's position as chief, it cannot be considered to have been in league with the government, but rather submissive and subservient to it. Following the election, Luthuli left Adams College. By approving his candidacy, the American Board would bring him further into the Congregationalist fold and thus render him accountable to it.

In January 1936, Luthuli began his duties as chief, although he had to wait until the end of February to have criminal jurisdiction especially conferred upon him. His constituency was small and generally comprised educated members. Conflicts were few and he encouraged community members to resolve them amicably rather than through litigation. He soon realised that his appointment severely limited his earning potential and he lamented his low salary as he struggled to properly educate many children. In a June 1940 letter written to the Native Commissioner, Luthuli itemised his income for the year and complained that his income of £150 per year as a teacher had plummeted to £45–50 per year as the chief.[12] In his autobiography, he indicated that the government therefore gave him an extra responsibility and, therefore, remuneration as a liaison officer.[13]

Though experience with the Teachers' Association and the Zulu Society no doubt provided Luthuli with some administrative and financial experience, it was not until he became chief that he acquired the role of a public leader. He admitted that the position of chief was not particularly glamorous, nor did it predispose one to be a popular leader of a community or a country. In his autobiography, one senses the disdain he initially held for his very reluctantly accepted position. There were aspects of his uncle's tenure as leader of the *amakholwa* that repelled him. Now, in his uncle's shoes, he experienced the chieftaincy as 'taxing' and 'petty', and likened the position to an 'appointed boss-boy'.[14]

Whereas Adams engendered theoretical (theological, philosophical and pedagogical) epiphanies for Luthuli, the chieftaincy engendered practical ones. Away from the hermetically sealed comfort of what was very much an artificial community, motivated by an ethereal benevolence and protected from physical hardships, the chieftaincy allowed Luthuli to see 'almost for the first time, the naked poverty of my people, the daily hurt to human beings'.[15] Rather than being proud of and confident in his role as a traditional leader, he became disillusioned as he observed 'evidences of an inadequate tribal structure breaking up under the pressures of modern conditions . . .'[16] He soon perceived Groutville to be a microcosm of the greater context affecting all South Africans of colour. Macro-conditions were limiting micro-possibilities. A lack of access to arable land, migrant labour, poor availability of credit and a deficiency of mechanical agro-chemical technology negatively affected Groutville. Pretoria's policies created a shortage of land, money, employment, educational and health services and thus stunted the people's achievements. Structural injustices that stymied communities had to be confronted as no measure of self-contained efforts would ameliorate the dire circumstances. In a particularly memorable passage from his autobiography, Luthuli explained how, if the chieftaincy was to be constructive in serving the people, it had to move from addressing the petty to the substantive.

> [W]hen I became Chief I was confronted as never before by the destitution of the housewife, the smashing of families because of economic pressures and the inability of the old way of life to meet the contemporary onslaught. The destruction of our families is not the least of the crimes which white avarice has perpetrated against us. It continues, it increases, in spite of pleading voices raised against it.[17]

Agricultural, civil society and ecumenical advocacy organisations

The 1936 Sugar Act limited the production of sugar in order to artificially raise its price. Quotas were imposed on the amount of sugar cane that could be processed and sold and these quotas were especially limiting for the independent, rural, African cane grower. In response to this legislation, Luthuli, Gideon Mzoneli and two hundred others revived the Groutville Cane Growers' Association so as to make collective bargaining and advocacy more efficacious. The work was arduous, with the founders waking up at three in the morning to cut the cane themselves during the harvest. Two humble victories, the restoration of advances for production costs and the institution of 'globular' (comprehensive) quota amounting to the sum of individual quotas, led Luthuli to 'unionise' other growers on a regional scale.

The Zululand Bantu Cane Growers' Association, founded and chaired by Luthuli, aimed to make united representations to those who regulated the market at the expense of African farmers. It enjoyed a few small victories, among them, securing indirect representation to the central board via a 'non-European' advisory board in regard to sugar production, processing and marketing. The indirect representation provided by the Native Affairs Department had proved futile.

Luthuli organised cane growers until 1949. As with his involvement with the Teachers' Association, he seemed to grow disillusioned with the Growers' Association's lack of achievement. In whatever minor political dabbling he became involved, the participation, obstinacy and outright hostility of the government undermined substantive progress. Ultimately, the structural nature of the white supremacist society prevailed over its interests and advocacy efforts, and the association ultimately proved to be little match for the equivalent white commercial growers' associations.

Not all blame rested with the government or competition. In *Let My People Go* Luthuli lamented that Africans proved 'apathetic and un-cooperative' and thus difficult to unite.[18] He claimed that the government's all too successful divide-and-rule tactics had the effect of balkanising the oppressed. This dynamic persisted throughout Luthuli's leadership of the ANC, particularly with the Africanists, and perhaps led him to seek close ties with confident, assertive, established and co-operative white liberals. Nonetheless, as late as 1951, Luthuli continued to organise and support black cane growers, for example, using his links with the American Board to procure for the co-operative a donated tractor and ploughs. He continued to be the sole black representative on the central board until 1953.

Luthuli's participation in local politics extended past his agricultural advocacy efforts. At around this time he also served on the Durban Joint Council of Europeans and Africans, a precursor to the South African Institute of Race Relations (SAIRR), organisations in which few if any of his more militant colleagues held leadership positions. The SAIRR provided a forum for various churches and institutions to discuss matters concerning race, presenting findings to the government that were, more often than not, ignored. Co-operating with benevolent, white and primarily Christian members of various civil society organisations ingrained in him a conviction that racial integration was possible and universal suffrage inevitable.

As a member of the Joint Council, Luthuli corresponded with Zululand's Senator Edgar Brookes and other representatives of the 'natives' to advocate relief from onerous legislation. In an April 1941 letter (writer unknown) to Luthuli regarding opposition to the Burnside Amendment of the Motor Carrier Transportation Amendment Bill, the writer broke the news that 'we had quite a long struggle over that and other parts of the Bill, but we were unsuccessful'.[19] The Act discriminated against non-Europeans involved in the transport industry by revoking their certificates, imposing ten-fold increases in deposits for certificates and restricting taxis to certain areas and times. The same letter to Luthuli stated, 'Senator Brookes and I did all we could to protect non-European bus and taxi owners and had a strenuous struggle'.

During the early 1940s, Luthuli's service to the church was not limited to the Congregational community. In response to the Durban City Corporation's efforts to convert a rural and agricultural Anglican glebe in Umlazi into a residential dumping ground for African workers employed in Durban, Luthuli and others resurrected the Mission Reserve Association.[20] The original objective of the association was to lobby for individual, rather than communal, ownership of land. The revived Reserve Association dealt specifically with protecting the rights of the faith community within the Umlazi mission station. Representations were given a half-hearted reception. Ultimately, however, the National Party's 1948 electoral victory rendered the corporation's scheme obsolete. Again, Luthuli's advocacy efforts produced glimmers of optimism with exhausting, slow and disappointing results.

International Missionary Conference trip, India

As a delegate of the Christian Council of South Africa, Albert Luthuli attended the December 1938 International Missionary Conference at Tambaram, near Madras (Chennai), in India. In his autobiography, he speaks of the experience as having provided him with 'wider sympathies and wider horizons'.[21] The conference was called to discuss the missiological role of indigenous churches. John Mott, chairman of the conference, indicated that the central theme of the meeting 'would be the uplifting of the younger churches as part of the historic universal Christian community'.[22] Allan Boesak noted that participants of the gathering discussed questions related to racism and colonialism.[23] Whatever the agenda, the conference was a revelation for Luthuli. In an ecumenical setting, the conference dealt with comparative interracial relations, mission education and poverty alleviation, opening Luthuli's eyes to the shortcomings of Christianity as it was practised in South Africa. He departed from India an 'incisive critic' of the church at home.[24] In India he had experienced dynamic debate and been impressed with the vigour of delegates as they discussed and implemented Christianity. These qualities he contrasted to the apathy, diffidence to society and complicity of the Christian church in South Africa. They were features evident even in members of his own delegation. Luthuli expressed a very dry sense of humour when he remarked that 'the boat did not sink' when his own delegation's restriction on inter-racial worship was relaxed on board.

Returning to South Africa, Luthuli resumed responsibilities as chief in Groutville. Though sobered by the Madras conference, he remained very active in the church. In an article published in *South African Outlook* in October 1940, Luthuli warned that if the church neglected to capture the passion and potential of the youth, 'other agencies inimical to the realisation of the Kingdom will harness them'. He specifically mentioned communism and nationalism as competing forces. His evangelistic zeal for youth and the tone and intensity of his Christocentric beliefs are evident:

> Evangelism means the unreserved surrender of the individual to God through faith in Jesus Christ; and the deepening of the individual's faith and the regeneration of Society through saved souls. Our aim in evangelism should definitely be to confront the individual with Christ and to challenge him or her to decide for Christ. And we should not be satisfied until the individual unreservedly surrenders himself. Our efforts in evangelism mean little if we do not secure through Christ changed lives; consecrated lives; new men and women living a new way of life, as shown by our Lord and Master Jesus Christ when he said, 'I am the Way, the Truth, the Life, no man cometh unto the Father but by Me'.[25]

Evident, too, is the corporate importance of spirituality. Despite the highly individualistic nature of spirituality, Luthuli alluded to 'the regeneration of society', and, in other parts of the article, to the need for 'social study groups', 'the service of others', and interracial exchanges 'for the sake of winning the whole of Africa for Christ'.[26]

Natal Missionary Conference
Prior to his involvement with the ANC, Luthuli sharpened his political and administrative acumen by holding office in many ecclesiastic entities, one of them, the Natal Missionary Conference. The conference, comprising mostly white missioners, sponsored annual ecumenical gatherings where,

among other things, it formed education policy. Missions controlled ninety-five per cent of the schools for Africans and thus acted as grantees for the schools. The missioners' function necessitated regular meetings with the conference's advisory board and the Department of Education in Pietermaritzburg.

At its 1941 gathering in Durban, the conference elected Luthuli as chairperson. To elect an African, local layperson to preside over a predominantly white, expatriate and clerical association was bold to say the least and it excited much criticism. And the election reinforced Luthuli's perennial optimism in the ultimate viability of multiracial co-operation. His appointment confirmed for him the church's overall beneficence and strengthened the bond between him and like-minded white, liberal Christians. As his most recent trip to India had shown, and his future trip to the United States would later confirm, holding leadership positions in multiracial organisations conscientised him on the importance of solidarity movements and the key role Christian activists could play in mobilising international public opinion in support of resistance to white supremacy.

Native Representative Council
In 1937 the NRC was formed as a means by which to compensate and thus mollify the African population from the legislated loss of their limited franchise in the Cape Province arising from the passage of the Hertzog Bills in 1935. The government authorised Luthuli's first candidature for election as a member of the NRC in 1942. Before his second candidacy for the NRC in 1944, Luthuli became a member of the ANC.[27]

Luthuli's involvement with the NRC only arose through his success in a by-election held following John Dube's death in 1946, when he defeated ANC veteran Selby Msimang by a considerable margin. Aware that people were deeply disillusioned with the council by this time, his election nevertheless provided the first substantive window through which he entered national politics.

At this time, the mood of the liberation struggle was becoming increasingly militant, particularly amongst the youth. Founded in December 1943, with the intention of increasing the pace of reform, the ANC Youth League (ANCYL) placed much pressure on the NRC to adjourn permanently given that the Smuts and the National Party governments paid it no heed. Luthuli recognised these sentiments.

'What is the use', they asked me, 'of your going to the NRC in Pretoria? They do nothing but talk. Where has this council got us?' It was only too true. For years now they had talked. Nobody listened. I was disillusioned myself, and could only reply. 'There are people beyond South Africa who sometimes hear what we say. All we can do is try to shout to the world. All I can do is to help us shout louder'.[28]

Luthuli served on the NRC for a very short time, realising, as many others had before him, that its efforts proved futile. At a meeting of the body following the government's brutal suppression of a 1946 miners' strike, Luthuli stated his concurrence with his colleagues' decision to adjourn indefinitely. It was his very first meeting with the government where he served as NRC delegate. Chairman Major F. Rodseth expressed the government's disappointment in Luthuli, the young novice representative, who had been a trusted chief. The NRC was brought together again later, and again, adjourned indefinitely. Its own members rendered it defunct, effectively, refusing to co-operate with the government or its representative frameworks. The new National Party government eventually scrapped the body in 1951.

In a latter-day counter-defence from those who perceived his leadership of KwaZulu as collaborationist, Mangosuthu Buthelezi argued:

> In my opinion, to say that we have 'accepted' apartheid, by serving our people within the framework of the South African government policy would be as nonsensical as to say that when great African leaders like the late Chief Albert Luthuli, Dr Z.K. Matthews and others, served their people within the framework of the United Party government policy of segregation as members of the Native Representatives Council, that they did so because they 'accepted' the segregationists policies of the United Party government. Nothing could be further from the truth.[29]

Buthelezi's justification misled his audience. Luthuli resigned and refused to participate in the body from the first NRC meeting he attended. Buthelezi's often manipulated reference to the NRC, as a defence of his own participation in apartheid structures, is ironic given that the failure of the NRC to achieve any of its goals was perhaps the seminal event by which Luthuli learned that collaborative structures would prove 'pointless, wasteful and futile'.[30]

American Board and North American Missionary Conference trip, United States

Within the American Board, John Reuling sensed that Africans were overlooked in being given opportunities to travel to the United States to provide to the American churches first-hand indigenous perspectives on the various mission fields. In 1948, a joint venture between the American Board and the North American Missionary Conference sponsored a speaking tour to the United States. Luthuli was sent after several influential people, including Edgar Brookes, recommended that he would be the most outstanding candidate to present a report on the Natal mission.

Newspaper articles provided varied reports concerning the purpose of Luthuli's speaking tour in the United States. Some suggested the tour's purpose was to explain African economic, mission and rural development issues. Others thought it would focus on segregation, race problems and race reconciliation, the latter a preoccupation of the North American Missionary Society. Luthuli's own stated purpose – to deliver lectures on African rural and mission development and on evangelisation, particularly for the youth – would have been more palatable to the South African government to which he was beholden for a passport. Whatever stated purpose, the tour had a profound impact on him, enabling him to 'see South African issues more sharply, and in a different and larger perspective'.[31]

Shortly after his arrival in June 1948, Luthuli spoke to the American Board Prudential Committee at their annual meeting. In an address entitled 'Africa Looks to American Christian Friends', he concentrated on racial issues, also an important topic in Congregational circles at the time. During the last week of June, he delivered lectures as a faculty member at the Wilbraham Pilgrim Summer Fellowship Conference in Massachusetts. The December 1948 issue of *Missionary Herald* reprinted Luthuli's correspondence to the Reverend Frank Loper, Dean of the Conference, in which he reflected on the communion of races:

> The fellowship at the conference brought to me most forcefully and vividly, but most happily, the realism of our oneness in Christ, irrespective of our race or colour. Here I was, not only a stranger, but a man of another colour and nation, and yet I felt myself one with the fellowship. I have never sung with greater joy and understanding the song: 'In Christ there is no East or West, In Him no South or North,

[But] one great fellowship of love throughout the whole wide earth.'
The climax of this feeling of oneness was reached when the whole
fellowship of God assembled at the Lord's Table.[32]

Hosted by the American Board, Luthuli visited New York and went on to
speak to youth at various summer camps. To the youth he displayed much
of the oratorical prowess for which he would later become so famous. He
spoke at the Smithfield Congregational Christian Church in downtown
Pittsburgh, Pennsylvania, where he related as well to people one-on-one
as he did to large audiences. In an October 1960 letter to Luthuli, an old
acquaintance, Wilson Minton, vividly recalled an exchange between Luthuli
and himself at the speaker's table on one of these occasions. Luthuli had
said that he and Minton were 'nearer to each other' than many of his own
people could be to him, although their 'skins were of a different colour'.
This comment puzzled Minton and he asked Luthuli what he meant.
Luthuli responded that it was because they 'both were Christians led by
the same Spirit' while those of his people who were not yet Christians
just could not understand his Christian attitude. 'In all my fifty years of
ministry,' wrote Minton, 'I have had no greater compliment than that.'[33]

On 8 October 1948, Luthuli received a Junior Chamber of Commerce
guest speaker award in Columbus, Ohio. In his speech, entitled 'A New
Africa', Luthuli concentrated on issues related to development in rural
Africa and only obliquely addressed racial issues. He said that the future
of Africa, one 'wherein love, brotherliness, righteousness shall abound,
or a reactionary and sour Africa dominated by hate, anger, revenge and
greed, shall depend a great deal on the policies and attitudes secular
agencies, commerce, industries and governments adopt in regulating their
relations with Africa'.[34]

From that point on, Luthuli was hosted by the North American
Missionary Conference. He visited the major cities of Chicago in Illinois,
Minneapolis in Minnesota and Boston in Massachusetts. While in
Massachusetts, Luthuli and Z.K. Matthews, who joined him on the tour,
stayed at the West Newton home of John and Eleanor Reuling.

Though it was not on his itinerary, Luthuli asked to visit the South in
order to learn more about the conditions under which African Americans
lived. His stay was thus extended by three months and it included
Washington DC and Atlanta in Georgia. While in the South, Luthuli
had a relatively impromptu opportunity to speak at Howard University

on behalf of the Mahatma Gandhi Memorial Society, in honour of
Mohandas K. Gandhi (1869–1948) who had been killed by an assassin
earlier in the year. In his speech, Luthuli revealed that he did not
romanticise race relations in the United States, stating that American
'Negroes' still suffered discrimination. He expressed pride that it was when
Gandhi was in South Africa (1893–1914), and after being thrown from a
first-class section of a passenger train in Pietermaritzburg, he devoted
himself to champion the cause of his people's emancipation from
discrimination. In his speech, which survives as a handwritten draft in
the custodianship of the Luthuli Museum, he said he had 'no doubt that
his efforts for his people inspired people such as Dr John Dube and
others to concern themselves with seeking human rights for their people'.
He affirmed the 'dignity of man and the efficacy of non-violence as an
instrument of struggle in seeking freedom for oppressed people', and
prophetically outlined the strategies he would employ as the leader of the
ANC. He praised Gandhi's teaching that 'material wealth must be made
subordinate to spiritual wealth that respects human personality' and
concluded his remarks by pleading that 'those so inspired by [Gandhi's]
philosophy become his undaunted disciples'. Gandhi proved uncompromising in opposition to the use of violence as a means by which to
liberate an oppressed people from colonialism and racism.[35]

A review of Luthuli's sentiments on Gandhi's example illuminates
the roots of Luthuli's tortuous hesitancy to compromise on the use of
violence. In July 1961, Luthuli wrestled with two voices: one of Gandhi's
espousals of satyagraha ('the force that comes from truth, love and non-
violence') and Mandela's persuasive arguments in favour of violence. Those
who disagreed with the resort to violence were primarily inspired by
Gandhi's 1906, 1907 and 1913 satyagraha campaigns. After the perceived
failure of the May 1961 boycott and the intransigent stance of the National
Party government, Mandela argued to Luthuli and others that non-violent
tactics had been exhausted. Writing the epilogue to Johan Wasserman's
short book on Gandhi, *A Man for All Seasons* (n.d.), Mandela said, 'There
came a point in our struggle when the brute force of the oppressor could
no longer be countered through passive resistance alone.'[36] Later we will
see that the ANC and Mandela referenced Gandhi when introducing ethical
qualifications to legitimise the use of violence. For example, in the same
text Mandela wrote:

Gandhi himself never ruled out violence absolutely and unreservedly. He conceded the necessity of arms in certain situations. He said, 'Where choice is set between cowardice and violence, I would advise violence ... I prefer the use of arms in defence of honour rather than remain the vile witness of dishonour ...' Violence and non-violence are not mutually exclusive; it is the predominance of the one or the other that labels a struggle.[37]

The strong impact on Luthuli of his visit to the United States is also confirmed by the testimony of Allison Champion. In an unpublished manuscript entitled 'History in the Making', Champion suggested that the ecclesiastically sponsored trips to India and the United States in part radicalised Luthuli. He said that Luthuli had 'definitely changed his tone' when he arrived back from his nine-month sojourn in the United States. 'He had seen the operation of laws governing black and white in America. He had seen the limitless opportunities granted to the Negroes in the United States.' For Champion, this made Luthuli more susceptible to the influence of the politically ambitious and impatient Youth League.[38]

Upon his return from the United States, Luthuli actually confessed to a state of melancholy to the missioner, John Taylor. 'Spiritually,' he said, 'I wish I [was] still . . . in the United States.'[39] He feared that government repression was only hastening the onset of an aggressive African nationalism and that African leaders were quickly succumbing to extremism. His depression must be seen in the context of the South Africa that he returned to in 1948. It was the year in which the National Party government took power in South Africa on a draconian apartheid platform. His fears for the rise of an aggressive African nationalism came to fruition with the breakaway from the ANC of the Pan-Africanist Congress (PAC) in November 1958 and Mandela's launching of MK in December 1961. His fears that leaders would abandon reason referred to the Youth League and their efforts to have the ANC adopt more radical tactics such as boycotts, strikes, non-cooperation with government institutions and civil disobedience (in what would become the Programme of Action in 1949). In 1948, Luthuli had not yet been courted by the Natal ANC Youth League (1951) or the national ANC Youth League (1952) and thus did not yet subscribe to their more aggressive sentiments and tactics, let alone contemplate being their standard-bearer.

Luthuli's writings document the long-standing influence on him of many American missioners and lecturers, and of his extended ecclesiastic visit to the United States. His education and overseas visit exposed him to, what was in the 1930s and 1940s and what is still to some degree, mythical conceptualisations and idealisations of the founding of the American nation and the seminal role of the Puritan Congregationalists in that founding. In 1960 and 1961, he wrote columns published in the *Golden City Post* and frequently cited American political aphorisms when calling for the 'consent of the governed'. He also quoted Abraham Lincoln's Gettysburg address that was inspired by the Declaration of Independence. For him, there was

> . . . no escaping the fact that the American nation [was] oriented towards a noble goal, that it is bound to the grandest conception there is of human progress and freedom by reason of the heritage which gave it birth . . . We take hope in the fact that the Divine ruler of our destinies has provided for this earth of ours such a nation as the American nation.[40]

Above all, his columns conveyed his desire to see justice done and the dawning of a 'truly democratic Republic of South Africa that [would] provide a true government of the people, for the people and by the people'.[41]

President of the Natal ANC

In *Let My People Go*, Luthuli attributed the awakening of African political awareness to the ruthless apartheid regime, inaugurated by the National Party election victory over Jan Smuts (1870–1950) in 1948. The new dispensation would goad the masses out of 'resigned endurance' and feeble cap-in-hand *hamba kahle* participation in their own governance.[42] Many of the early ANC presidents were detached from the grassroots, reluctant to lose their privileged positions by antagonising the government and were more theoretically than practically inclined.

The 1944 formation of the ANCYL awakened the movement. The Youth League was led initially by Anton Lembede (1914–1947) and supported by Nelson Mandela, Z.K. Matthews's son, Joe Matthews, Walter Sisulu, Ashby Mda, Masabalala 'Bonnie' Yengwa (1923–1987), who was later Natal secretary under Luthuli, Wilson Conco, who was later Natal chairperson under Luthuli, and Oliver Tambo, who was later secretary general under Luthuli. The league was formed in Natal, too, after Manasseh T. Moerane urged Yengwa and other young men to form a local branch. Yengwa argued that the ANC had to move from the abstract to the concrete, from political philosophy to involvement in actual campaigns.

As president general from 1940 to 1949, Dr A.B. Xuma accepted the emergence of the ANCYL and recognised that it was a force with which to be reckoned. He was a cautious man, however, and ultimately the Youth League outgrew his conservatism. Often referred to throughout the ANC's history as the kingmakers, the ANCYL retired Xuma in 1949 and elected James Sebe Moroka as ANC president general with Walter Sisulu as secretary general. Moroka, a Wesleyan *kholwa*, served at the time as the leader of the All-African Convention (AAC). He was compliant with the ANCYL's new militancy where Xuma had been resistant.

In December 1949, the ANC adopted the Programme of Action, inspired by Kwame Nkrumah's example in Ghana, signalling a fundamental change of policy and methods in an uncompromising and final refusal to accept apartheid. The programme urged the adoption of more aggressive tactics such as mass civil disobedience, boycotts, strike action and non-cooperation. It was a radical replacement for what former ANCYL president, Ashby Mda, referred to as the 'dilly-dallying and half-hearted' measures that were the standard course of old guard under Xuma.[43] It spurred the ANC on to demonstrate against the Group Areas Bill (June 1950), to strike in protest against the intention to remove coloureds from the Western Cape's Common Electoral Roll (May 1951) and to launch the Defiance Campaign (June 1952).

When John Dube suffered a stroke in 1945, Allison Champion succeeded him as Natal president after electorally defeating another conservative leader, the Reverend A. Mtimkulu. During the chaos of the meeting that elected him, Luthuli leapt to the stage to establish order and found himself unexpectedly appointed as acting chair of the meeting. Under Champion's leadership, Luthuli served on his executive. Dube had led the ANC Natal region almost independently from the national ANC. Those who elected Champion most likely did so on a mandate to incorporate the ANC in Natal with the national organisation. This Champion did; however, not well enough.

Champion allowed the Natal region to lag behind the national ANC's preparation for the 1952 Defiance Campaign that sought to mobilise the disenfranchised for civil disobedience. Luthuli declined to be re-elected to the executive, feeling that Champion's practice of appointing his own executive was undemocratic. The Youth League in Natal, led by Yengwa, now perceived in Luthuli a new brand of leadership, more radical and more democratic than Champion, and nominated him as president of the Natal ANC. Selby Msimang, who was also a nominee, approved Luthuli's nomination and bowed out of the contest. Winning by a modest majority on 30 May 1951, Luthuli succeeded Champion as president and Msimang was appointed secretary of the Natal ANC.

Champion was crestfallen and felt severely criticised for his failure to accept national ANC policy. He was not the only one displeased with Luthuli's election. A month later, on 14 June 1951, Walter Kamakobosi Dimibar, a sectarian leader who found favour with the government of the day and who enjoyed only tenuous links with the Groutville community, wrote to the secretary of the community committee, Phinehas Mbambo, to express his dismay with and opposition to Luthuli's election. For Dimibar, Chief Luthuli had no business with 'a political organisation, an organisation that is full of strife, full of communistic ideas, full of boycotts against our Government . . . He cannot hold these two [posts.] [H]e has either to keep one and resign the other . . . '[44] Dimibar then suggested that the committee force Luthuli to resign as chief so that another could be chosen as a replacement.

In spite of such criticism, Luthuli did not have many detractors throughout his long career in resistance politics. Charles Hooper, who penned the introduction to the first edition of Luthuli's autobiography, Let My People Go, said of him:

> Assurance and humility stand the Chief and his country in good stead, as do other of his qualities: resilience, youthfulness of spirit, undauntable courage, wisdom, tolerance, charity, a zest for living, patience. If there is one quality, usually associated with leadership, which he lacks, it is ambition. There is behind him no struggle for power, and within him no determination to rule in person.[45]

Defiance Campaign
As the newly elected president of the ANC in Natal, Albert Luthuli had less than one month to prepare for the June 1951 National Conference of the ANC scheduled to be held in Bloemfontein. He and the Natal Executive

Committee were shocked to realise from preparatory materials that the ANC planned to initiate a programme of civil defiance. After having temporarily served as chairperson of the National Conference, Luthuli confessed that the ANC Natal was unprepared for the Defiance Campaign (otherwise known as the Campaign for the Repeal of Discriminatory Legislation). The ANC members did not receive Luthuli's excuses with sympathy and he was even heckled and dubbed a coward. The ANC in Natal agreed to make preparations for the campaign, scheduled for the latter half of 1952, as best they could.

The history of the Defiance Campaign need not be expanded on here. Many other sources, including Luthuli's autobiography, more than adequately document the watershed impact the campaign had on the ANC, and the increasingly antagonistic relationship that developed between the movements for liberation and the National Party government. Suffice it to say, Luthuli's entry into ANC leadership as president of the Natal region was a baptism by fire.

The warm-up to the 26 June 1952 launch of the campaign began from 6 April with mass meetings and demonstrations held throughout the country. Beginning in June, and in three stages gradually increasing in intensity, disciplined and trained volunteers of the ANC and the South African Indian Congress (SAIC), led by Mandela as National Volunteer-in-Chief, began systematically to disobey unjust and oppressive discriminatory laws thus inviting arrest, assault and penalty. Using strategies inspired by Gandhi, the campaign required strict adherence to a policy of non-violence. If the masses acted in concert to defy unjust laws, the oppressed majority and the oppressing minority alike would recognise that the government could not continue to enforce and prosecute petty apartheid restrictions. Furthermore, defiance could educate an otherwise ignorant white electorate about the inhumanity of apartheid. It could engender moral outrage at its insensitivity and brutality. The logistics of protest were announced to the authorities and demonstrators proceeded to flout prohibitions against the use of segregated railway stations, waiting rooms, public toilets, post offices and park benches, in addition to protesting against pass regulations and curfews.

By September of that year, Natal felt ready and able to participate in the campaign. In *The Struggle for a Birthright* (1966), historian Mary Benson speaks of how Luthuli met with his executive in a small ANC office located in a busy Indian shopping centre in Durban and committed himself to crossing South Africa's 'Rubicon'. Luthuli impressed upon his lieutenants that they would 'be calling upon people to make very important demonstrations'. Unless they were 'sure of the road and prepared to travel along it [them]selves', they had no right to call on others to do the same. Together they solemnly pledged to exert all their efforts to meet their objective of securing freedom for the oppressed people of South Africa. Benson records Yengwa's description of what happened next: 'We all said that we were prepared and he said he too was prepared and he asked us to pray.'[46]

During the campaign, the government dispersed the mass meetings organised by the Indian and African congresses. The police arrested Luthuli for the first time though he did not break any laws. As a staff officer, Luthuli's role required him to organise, and not to court arrest. By its climax in October, well over two thousand resisters had participated in the campaign throughout the nation. While the campaign did not persuade the government or the press of the legitimacy of its claims, the protests generated a massive swelling of the ANC's ranks. Between 1951 and 1953, according to Luthuli in Let My People Go, ANC branches increased around the country from fourteen to eighty-seven, and its members in good standing from seven thousand to a hundred thousand.[47]

In October 1952, sporadic incidents of violence broke out unexpectedly in Port Elizabeth, Johannesburg, Kimberley and East London, believed by many, including Luthuli, to be the work of agents provocateurs. Unsurprisingly, the white press and public linked any reported acts of violence to the campaign itself and, in Parliament, the government proceeded to make the Defiance Campaign illegal by passing the Criminal Law Amendment Act and the Public Safety Act. With more and more curfews enforced in some areas of the country, the congresses's leaders decided to terminate the campaign in January 1953.

'The Road to Freedom is Via the Cross'

In August 1952, Albert Luthuli received a communication from the Lower Tugela Native Affairs Commissioner expressing disquiet that he encouraged people to oppose government schemes. This was of concern to the government which employed Luthuli as a chief and authorised him to enforce minor laws within his jurisdiction. Though Luthuli claimed he kept well within the regulations which governed chiefs, the government had a legitimate case against him. As an adjudicator of the law, he simultaneously encouraged people to break some of them. In September 1952, three weeks after his receipt and response to the first expression of concern, Pretoria summoned Luthuli.

The secretary for Native Affairs, W.W.M. Eiselen (1899–1977), the deputy secretary and the Chief Native Commissioner for Natal, met with Luthuli. After some preliminary questions, Eiselen confronted Luthuli with the central grievance that his involvement in the Defiance Campaign contradicted his role as chief. Luthuli defended himself against the charge by making a subtle distinction. He had encouraged the breaking of certain unjust laws. This was, by its nature, *political* and not *criminal*. Secondly, Luthuli declared that he did not conflate his responsibilities as chief and leader in the congress. Thirdly, Luthuli argued that the government recognised congress to be a legal entity and, as long as it was legal, no conflict of interest existed. Luthuli reasoned:

> It was to allow for these wider associations intended to promote the common national interests of the people as against purely local interests, that the government in making rules governing chiefs did not debar them from joining political associations so long as those associations had not been declared 'by the Minister to be subversive of or prejudicial to constituted government'. The African National Congress, its Non-Violent Passive Resistance Campaign, may be of nuisance value to the government but it is not subversive since it does not seek to overthrow the form and machinery of the state but only urges for the inclusion of all sections of the community in a partnership in the government of the country on the basis of equality.[48]

The authorities must have heard this last qualification with a collective wry smile. The ANC clearly intended to subvert the government. The creation of a government on the basis of racial equality would *for the National Party regime* require an overthrow of the form and machinery of the state. Before he walked out of Eiselen's door, Luthuli resolved not to comply with the government's ultimatum.

In October 1952, Luthuli received a letter requesting him to reply to the contradiction still perceived by the Department of Native Affairs. Luthuli replied the same: he saw no contradiction and had no intention of resigning from either the chieftaincy or the ANC. Interviewed in 1993 for the film, *Mayibuye Afrika*, Mangosuthu Buthelezi correctly perceived that 'Luthuli didn't make any choice; he let the government do what it does'.[49] In the same documentary film, Horace Rall, the former magistrate who served the order deposing Luthuli, was quoted as saying that Luthuli had neglected his duties and served 'two masters in opposition' to one another.[50]

From October 1952, Luthuli fathomed fully what was to come. In November, he was deposed by the government. The Groutville community expressed some initial discontent about his removal from office and refused to elect a new chief. In the end, however, a mood of reluctant resignation crept in and nothing was done about the injustice, to Luthuli's disappointment. Though sympathetic with their vulnerability, he was again disillusioned by his own constituency's lack of political activism. From then on, he determined to remain aloof from tribal affairs, seeing chiefs as emasculated by their white supremacist paymasters. He would explore the promise of political liberation in part through the advocacy of a more influential white, Christian and liberal elite.

Shortly after his removal from office on 14 November 1952, Albert Luthuli drafted the personal and biblical statement, 'The Road to Freedom is Via the Cross'. It was released one week later as a joint statement by the ANC and Natal Indian Congress (NIC). Though political in character, documentary evidence proves the statement had a theological, biblical and homiletic genesis and quoted substantive portions of a sermon entitled 'Christian Life: A Constant Venture' that Luthuli had delivered six days earlier at Adams College.[51] The two documents compared illustrate clearly how Luthuli's political perspective in 'The Road to Freedom' statement emanated directly from his theological perspective. Obedience to what Luthuli considered to be the fundamental tenets of his faith was of primary importance and not ultimately the success or failure of any given political tactic or strategy. Luthuli's faith background taught him that success, the 'end', that is liberation, was inevitable, that liberation was not in doubt, precisely because God would ensure that 'might is not right'; therefore, the means were of primary importance.

In the sermon, he explained to his faith community the position he was about to take by providing a biblical rationale for the political statement he would soon issue. Both texts speak the same message, with varied emphases, to different audiences. To his faith-based audience, Luthuli's sermon served as a theological apologia for opting for secular politics rather than ecclesiastic chieftaincy as a means by which to serve the people.

To his political audience, represented by the ANC and the NIC, Luthuli grounded his political statement with a theological foundation. To his political followers, Luthuli communicated that the impetus for politics is a calling from God to serve others. To his faith-based community, Luthuli communicated that through politics, one implements faith. To his ecclesiastic followers, Luthuli proclaimed that one is a mere extension of the other; neither of the two can be separated. He concluded his sermon with the same sentence which formed its title: 'The Road to Freedom is Via the Cross'.

The statement proclaimed that in forfeiting the chieftainship, Luthuli conceived himself to be moving to a larger adventure within the spiritual realm, rather than from the spiritual to the secular realm. Despite choosing the political realm to struggle for the rights of the South African majority, Luthuli was first and foremost motivated by theological, and more specifically, biblical considerations. Because he was the chief of the *abasemakholweni*, his chieftaincy was as theologically premised by the church as it was politically premised by the people of Groutville and the government.

Undoubtedly the most pronounced parallel between the sermon and the statement is the recurring motif: 'launching further into the deep'. To an ecclesiastic audience, this represented a charge; to a political audience, a personal manifesto. However, a far more subtle parallel, though equally significant, is Luthuli's position on tactical and institutional efficacy. Tactical efficacy relates to the utility of methods used based on a record of success, or failure, as the case may be. In particular, the use of militant non-violent methods versus armed revolution was one of many dilemmas that pressed constantly on Luthuli's conscience. Institutional efficacy relates to the utility of a political entity, such as the ANC, as a means by which to achieve liberation for the majority of South Africans.

Luthuli's lamentations from the 'Road to Freedom is Via the Cross' statement are often quoted in nationalists' histories of the period, in clichéd and hackneyed fashion. Luthuli's statement read, in part:

In so far as gaining citizenship rights and opportunities for the unfettered development of the African people, who will deny that thirty years of my life have been spent knocking in vain, patiently, moderately and modestly at a closed and barred door? What have been the fruits of my many years of moderation? Has there been any reciprocal tolerance or

moderation from the government, be it Nationalist or United Party?
No! On the contrary, the past thirty years have seen the greatest number
of [l]aws restricting our rights and progress until today we have reached
a stage where we have almost no rights at all . . .[52]

Those who seek to evince Albert Luthuli's support for the turn to violence
generally quote these questions: ' . . . who will deny that thirty years of
my life have been spent knocking in vain, patiently, moderately at a closed
and barred door? What have been the fruits of my many years of
moderation?' A tone of exasperation is expressed in these words and it
has often been incorrectly interpreted by the ANC to justify its turn to
violence. While the title of the statement proclaimed sacrifice and suffering
as a means to political salvation, portions of the statement have been
manipulated to justify a different, violent, sort of road.

An examination of Luthuli's sermon, 'Christian Life: A Constant
Venture', an immediate source of material for his statement, 'The Road
to Freedom is Via the Cross', reveals that contrary to the nationalist
perspective, the above quote is *not* a rallying call to abandon existing
methods of resistance, but rather a call to continue them *despite* their
seeming inefficacy. The title and the continuing text of the statement
confirm this. Juxtaposed with the sermon, the conclusion that the
statement advocates a continuance of non-violent methods becomes
irrefutable. A key biblical verse upon which the sermon, and thus the
statement, rest relates how despite the apparent futility of previous
strategies, they ought to be continually implemented in faith. The scripture
of emphasis from which Luthuli preached reads as follows:

> When he had finished speaking, he said to Simon, '*Put out into the deep*
> *water* and let down your nets for a catch.' *Simon answered, 'Master, we*
> *have worked all night long but have caught nothing. Yet if you say so, I will let*
> *down the nets*' (Luke 5:4–5; emphasis added).

The biblical text relates that at the time of Jesus' command, Simon Peter
and the disciples were at the 'shore of the lake' (Luke 5:2), cleaning out
their nets. Jesus calls the disciples to '*put out into the deep water*' (Luke
5:3). This is not a change of tactics, but rather a re-doubling of past efforts.
One of Luthuli's themes, as expounded upon above, is that all are called
to a 'larger worthy cause', that is, an intensification of what is currently

being done, for the purpose of establishing the 'kingdom of God'. Simon Peter protests: 'We have been there, done that. And we have nothing to show for it. But, because you are asking, we will continue to do what we believe to be futile. We do so, if not out of faith, then out of obedience'. Luthuli emphasised in his sermon that often humans are 'paralysed or discouraged with [their] failures' and it is only in 'complete obedience' that we are called forward. Understanding this story for himself as a *typological re-enactment*, Luthuli understands that he is to 'launch into the deep', from chieftaincy to full-time ANC leader, from local leader to national leader. The sermon emphasises that neither vocation nor methods are being altered, despite past failures. The statement, directly sourcing the sermon, indicates that only scope or degree of the vocation and methods is being increased, not changed.

The fact that the ANC and the NIC jointly issued Luthuli's statement is not insignificant, for it points to his democratic nature. When questioned by Eiselen in Pretoria, Luthuli stressed that he answered personally and not on behalf of the ANC. He said he did not have its specific mandate to respond on its behalf. Valuing the importance of the collective, however, Luthuli did not issue the 'Road to Freedom' statement in his personal capacity, but rather on behalf of the wider liberation movement. These small acts point to a general pattern where, in his capacity as leader, Luthuli did not act unilaterally or against the majority. It was not his style to do so. Later, after 1962, Luthuli would remain quiet about his opposition to the initiation of violence by the ANC.

President general of the ANC

Dr James Moroka, ANC president general from 1944 to 1952, was among the many thousands of individuals who were arrested and stood trial for their part in the peaceful defiance of apartheid laws. In an unfortunate turn of events, Moroka distanced himself from his co-accused, seeking separate legal counsel, apparently on the pretext that communist lawyers made up part of the defence team. He also took the witness stand to mitigate any legal punishment. It was a humiliating gesture by the leader of a liberation movement.

In December 1952, a month after his dismissal as a tribal chief, Albert Luthuli was elected president general of the ANC on the shoulders of the ANCYL. The membership elected Nelson Mandela as Luthuli's deputy. Potlako Leballo (1915–1986), the future Pan-Africanist leader, formally nominated Luthuli. Moroka's ousting and Luthuli's election brought to the fore the ANCYL's support for a candidate it believed would implement its programmes and objectives. In the past Xuma, Moroka and Champion had all been dispensed with when the ANCYL felt their flexibility had been exhausted. It was not the last time that younger, more militant and increasingly impatient elements in the ANC would manoeuvre their president out of office.

Wider church relations

Despite Luthuli's disappointment in the church's efficacy as an agent of political change, he continued to serve as a leader in various church-based institutions until he was forced by government policy to resign from them. Luthuli served on the advisory boards of McCord Zulu Hospital and the Inanda Seminary (from 1936 to 1959), and on the governing council of Adams College. He also served as the chairperson of the board of the Congregationalist Church of South Africa (Bantu Congregational Church) and, in 1953, as vice chairperson of the executive committee of the Christian Council of South Africa (CCSA), the predecessor of the South African Council of Churches (SACC).

In January 1953, on the heels of his electoral victory, Luthuli attended the executive meeting of the CCSA in the Cape and pressed a reluctant audience to issue what he called a 'non-evasive' statement on the Defiance Campaign. He felt that the 'charge of evasion, where it is made against churches, is not unfounded'.[53] Christians, he felt, should concern themselves with people, not 'disembodied principles', and more importantly, with the conditions under which people live. 'Obviously,' he said, 'we do not expect to see the church organising political movements. But it must be with the people, in their lives.'[54]

Luthuli's belief in the Christian church's responsibility to promote social justice was also adopted by fellow American Congregationalist missioner, Allen Myrick, acting secretary for the American Board Mission. Concluding his 1965 report to the UCBWM, Myrick advocated for a greater prophetic missiological presence and more robust participation by the church in the struggle for justice. He pleaded at length for the American missioners in South Africa to be on the forefront of the fight for racial integration and social justice. These were ideals that Luthuli espoused and had already learned at Groutville and Adams. However, despite his continued loyalty to the church, during the 1950s he was gradually becoming estranged from the work of the mission. His efforts to promote human rights received far more influence in the ANC than it ever could within a hesitant church that practised less enthusiastically what it preached idealistically.

The mission's views on Luthuli and on the political situation in the country were characterised by timidity. It was unwilling to alienate the government and careful not to antagonise the situation further. To some extent, this was understandable. Communications between the mission and the American Board at the time showed that the church experienced long delays and many frustrations in obtaining entry permits for its missioners. Many of Luthuli's contemporaries realistically feared that the government could expropriate mission land, close down additional schools and deny government-sponsored bursaries for continuing education. This had happened to Luthuli's own daughter, Albertinah, whose bursary had been withdrawn as a result of her father's political activities.

The indigenous church leaders and members may have been more prone to inertia than the expatriate-led mission. In a January 1962 letter to Luthuli, John Reuling pointed out that perhaps the church might be more politically outspoken if the American Board had not diluted its power to an even more conservative and unimaginative indigenous leadership.[55] Many African Congregationalists proved even more wary of Luthuli's increasing involvement in politics than their former white American ecclesial paternalists who harboured concerns with the ANC's, and hence Luthuli's, links with communists.

Though resolute in his conviction that the church ought to participate in the fight against injustice in South Africa, Luthuli had moderate expectations of that happening. He acknowledged the pressures and tactics the government deployed to suppress the church in general. Nevertheless, in Let My People Go, he expressed disappointment in the lack of prophetic courage possessed by the church.

> Church sites in African areas are now held on yearly lease at the pleasure of the Minister [of Native Affairs]. The threat is that, if a sermon or a congregation or a bishop displeases the Department, the site will cease to be available. Parsons must not talk politics . . . This threat has many Christian ministers and organisations virtually cowering, as of course the government intends. What is becoming of our Christian witness? I am extreme on this point. Let us lose church sites and keep Christian

integrity. I disagree with those who want to 'save something from
the wreck' because what I see happening is the wreck of Christian
witness . . .[56]

In his autobiography, Luthuli did not deal with the closing of his beloved
Adams College in December 1956. This is surprising given that he served
on the advisory board which had administrative control over the
institution. He did not mention any measures he or the ANC undertook
to object to the forced closure. Paul Rich's 1992 conference paper on
Luthuli and the American Board concluded that Luthuli's ban 'left him
relatively powerless to influence the debates' on the takeover of Adams.[57]
In addition, during much of 1955, when the storm clouds were gathering
over Adams, Luthuli was hospitalised.

Luthuli's claim that the churches did 'almost nothing' in reaction to
the government's withdrawal of support for Christian mission institutions
misleads.[58] According to a document drafted by Adams College principal,
G.C. (Jack) Grant (1907–1978), Alan Paton (1903–1988) was quoted as
saying that the school 'resisted to the end' and exhausted every procedural
possibility to save the school from 'the evil doctrine that has corrupted so
many Christians in a Christian country'.[59] In his narrative of the closure,
Grant speaks of the college being mobilised and receiving 'the blessing
and backing of important and responsible Church organisations in the
country and overseas' – including financial backing.[60] The Action
Committee of the CCSA met personally with the Minister of Native Affairs
who dashed any hopes of Adams College becoming a private school.
F.J. de Villiers, from whom Luthuli learned so much during his days on
the staff at Adams, was now secretary for Native Affairs and authored the
government correspondence, dated 12 July 1956, refusing permission for
Adams College to become a private school. Thus the school was doomed
to the clutches of a grossly inferior Bantu Education.

Luthuli recognised the ambiguities of dependence in which the
mission existed in South Africa. His sympathy with the dilemma faced by
the Congregational church in part explains how he could be critical of
the church and its lack of prophetic action, and yet be loyal to it to his
death. He sensed that the church would not be the vehicle upon which
the majority of South Africans could depend to press for their liberation.
In the first place, it was not inclusive. Prior to the formation of the United
Democratic Front in 1983, the wider church would not work with and

alongside communists, Muslims and black nationalists in a broad-based political movement formed by the congresses as Luthuli did, and did well. During the 1950s and 1960s, whites and insularity dominated the Christian churches, whether Congregationalist or other, Father Trevor Huddleston (1913–1998) and Archbishop Denis Hurley (1915–2004) notwithstanding. In his 25 January 1967 report to the UCBWM, as acting field secretary, Myrick said he felt pastors and laymen alike were 'firmly settled in traditional patterns of life and work. This means that the pastor is primarily a mechanic who keeps the wheels of the church machinery moving and who rarely asks what the machine is for'. The ordinary pastor conformed to stereotypes handed down through the ages, administering the finances and the sacraments, and allowing a 'deep-seated legalism' to infuse the pastorate. 'Add to conservatism and legalism an omnipresent clericalism,' Myrick concluded, 'and one has a powerful bulwark of the status quo.'[61]

In his 1967 year report, Myrick referred to the proposed union of the London Missionary Society (LMS), the Congregational Union of South Africa (CUSA) and the Bantu Congregational Church (BCC) churches.[62] He described the LMS as Botswana's state church, CUSA as dominated by a white minority and the BCC as preoccupied with internal power struggles and provincial and ethnic (Zulu) concerns only. He elaborated on the Natal churches' weaknesses. Predominantly white CUSA members had not formerly worked on an equal basis and in partnership with Africans. Furthermore, its administrative and business practices were Eurocentric. This led to Africans being marginalised from the leadership of the church. Myrick noted that three of the four officers of the Natal regional council were whites, and the one black person, who served as vice chairman, had little influence. Furthermore, despite paying lip service to multiracialism, the local churches remained segregated. Prior to and during Luthuli's meteoric rise to the heights of ANC leadership, none of the three uniting churches poised itself to play a prophetic role in Luthuli's struggle for liberation.

First ban
Soon after taking office of the national ANC presidency, Luthuli began to acquaint himself with his constituency. In February 1953, he visited Alexandra township outside Johannesburg where the Defiance Campaign was called off, Cape Town where he attended the executive of the CCSA

and Port Elizabeth where he met with the impressively organised Cape
branch of the ANC. Luthuli returned home to Natal briefly to address
the Sixth Annual Conference of the NIC in Durban where, in a speech
entitled 'Let Us March Together to Freedom', he extolled those who had
participated in the 'Non-Violent Passive Resistance Campaign' and
emphatically encouraged them to '[k]eep marching on to freedom whatever
the cost and sacrifice'.[63] Luthuli then travelled to the Orange Free State
to visit the ANC there and to strengthen its weak stature within the party
structures.

On 30 May 1953, the government banned Luthuli for a year. The ban
prohibited him from attending any political or public gatherings and from
entering any major city. The legal basis for the ban fell under the Riotous
Assemblies Act and the Criminal Law Amendment Act. It was the first of
four bannings (1953, 1954, 1959 and 1964) that hamstrung Luthuli's
efforts to lead the ANC as president general. The first ban confined him
to small-population centres and to private meetings for the remainder of
1953. He risked arrest even for attending Sunday worship. Refusing to
ask permission to attend regular public worship services, Luthuli only
attended Holy Communion services arguing, questionably, that these were
private occasions in which the minister would serve Holy Communion
only to communicants.

December 1953 saw the ANC National Conference held in the smaller
town of Queenstown. Luthuli and other banned congress leaders attended
by stealth. In his presidential address (not delivered by him), Luthuli
revealed the motivation behind his leadership:

> This annual getting-together of ours may be a most un-welcomed event
> among those whites who mistakenly believe that denying us
> opportunities for free association and free speech will stop us from
> fighting for our rights and so ensure white domination over us. They
> forget that the urge and yearning for freedom springs from a sense of
> *divine discontent* and so, having a divine origin, can never be permanently
> humanly gagged and that human effort to artificially gag it by means of
> harsh discriminatory laws and by threats must result in suspicion, strains
> and tensions among individuals or groups in a nation, as, unfortunately,
> is the state of things in our country, the Union of South Africa (original
> emphasis).[64]

Call for non-violent Freedom Volunteers

In March 1954, Luthuli attended meetings of the NIC in Durban and the Congresses' Joint Executive (CJE) in Tongaat (between Durban and Stanger) to organise the upcoming Congress of the People.[65] Shortly after his ban expired at the end of May, he travelled to Uitenhage where he addressed the annual conference of the Cape Provincial Congress. Immediately thereafter, he travelled to Johannesburg to attend a Resist Apartheid Conference.

During most of his speaking engagements in the winter of 1954, he called for the enrolment of fifty thousand 'Freedom Volunteers', in the spirit of the Defiance Campaign. In a September speech delivered on his behalf to the first Natal Congress of the People held in Durban, Luthuli again called for 'a harmless army of non-violent voluntary organisers and propagandists whose twin task is to be to interest and enrol people for the Congress of the People meetings . . .'[66] The call for Freedom Volunteers harkened back to Gandhi's call for satyagrahis (those committed to using non-violent means and soldiers of truth). In his speech he enjoined people 'to respect the policy of non-violence wisely adopted by our Congresses. Non-violent resistance in any provocative situation is our best instrument. Our strongest weapon is to acquaint our people and the world with the facts of our situation.'[67]

Second ban

On 11 July 1954, less than six weeks after Luthuli had campaigned without restriction, the government imposed a second ban on him. It happened the moment he stepped off the plane on his way to address a group gathered to protest against the planned evictions of Sophiatown, near Johannesburg. Luthuli's first ban at least allowed him to attend meetings in small towns around South Africa. The second ban prevented him from attending public gatherings and confined him to the Stanger magisterial area in the Lower Tugela region for two years. This allowed him to continue to operate as ANC leader, as long as private meetings were held in Stanger. Before returning home from Johannesburg, Luthuli watched the evictions protest from a private home in Sophiatown. His message was delivered in his absence. Again, his speech expressed a call to political action through a Christian theological framework.

Luthuli's second ban also prohibited his attendance at the annual ANC National Conference held at the Bantu Social Centre in Durban, from 16-19 December 1954. In his address, again delivered in his absence, Luthuli expressed his pleasure that the World Council of Churches (WCC) condemned apartheid at their gathering in Evanston, Illinois. 'Clerical opinion,' he said, was 'gradually allying itself with the aspirations of the Africans.'[68] He remonstrated with those Africans who used defeatist arguments to dampen the mood of those fighting for liberation and who believed that 'God in his own time [would] give us freedom without our exertion'. God demands obedience, sacrifice and action, he said. The Freedom Volunteers could be harnessed 'to the noble cause of bringing freedom to all people in Africa'.[69]

Stroke

In early 1955, Luthuli suffered a severe life-threatening health condition that kept him hospitalised and in a virtual comatose state for at least two months. Albertinah Luthuli recalled the time her father fell ill. She said Luthuli 'wasn't accurate about putting the fork in the mouth'. Then Nokukhanya would say, '*Hawu!* What is the matter? Missing the mouth and then getting it in the mouth again.' The condition got worse over the next few days.[70]

The family phoned Dr Mordeciah Gumede in Inanda who visited and examined Luthuli, and confirmed that he had had a stroke. Albertinah Luthuli spoke of the family's efforts to have her father admitted to McCord Zulu Hospital in Durban where Dr Alan Taylor, a good friend of Luthuli's, was superintendent. Upon examination, doctors again determined that Luthuli had suffered a stroke, induced by high blood pressure, and treated him. All was well, until Luthuli's condition suddenly and dramatically deteriorated again. A specialist surgeon was called and diagnosed Luthuli with a coronary attack that he suffered whilst recovering from the stroke.

Luthuli recovered before the opening of the Congress of the People and drafted messages, or at least approved messages written in his name. A Foreign Service dispatch from the Pretoria Embassy in Washington DC to the United States State Department quoted messages from Luthuli that had appeared in *New Age* (19 May 1955) and *Bantu World* (28 May 1955) in which Luthuli said the congress would be taking place at a critical moment when 'the country [was] faced with an impending fascist republic built on apartheid which has been condemned the world over ... This year we shall rededicate ourselves to the struggle for freedom in that great assembly of the people where we shall write a charter of freedom.'[71] The purpose of the government's diplomatic dispatch was to portray the congresses movement as communistic and the ANC as 'communist-penetrated'. Yet it did acknowledge that the 'general membership is not communist-inclined'. It pointed to the 'recently-lowered prestige of the ANC' and suggested that the conference of the congresses would likely fail given government counter-measures. With this expectation, the embassy advised that it need not be banned.

Congress of the People and the Freedom Charter

The Congress of the People took place at Kliptown, Johannesburg, in June 1955. Albert Luthuli did not attend the gathering and the ANC's treasurer general, Arthur Letele (1916–1965), read out a message to the congress on his behalf. In his absence, the congress bestowed upon Luthuli the honour of the Isitwalandwe. The name of the honour is Xhosa in origin, denoting the feathers of the *indwe*, a legendary bird whose feathers are worn only by the bravest warriors. It would be awarded to individuals who distinguish themselves in the struggle for freedom in South Africa. Trevor Huddleston, who wrote *Naught for Your Comfort* (1956), and Yusuf Dadoo (1909–1983), head of the SAIC, also received the Isitwalandwe award. The choosing of an African, a white and an Indian no doubt intended to convey a sense that the struggle against white supremacy was a struggle best fought by a broad multiracial alliance. The selection of *Doctor* Dadoo, who was a communist, along with *Father* Huddleston and *Chief* Luthuli also evinced a broad ideological alliance.

The 1955 Congress of the People at Kliptown is perhaps more famous for its adoption of the Freedom Charter and many historians have described the processes of compiling the charter as well as the seminal importance of its place in the history of the freedom struggle. Though the Freedom Charter was drafted during Luthuli's time as president general, though he participated in the ANC's planning during the latter half of 1953 and though he advertised its drafting in May, he had little to do with its compilation. In fact, he did not even see the Freedom Charter in draft form before it was ratified by the Congress of the People.[72]

In *Let My People Go*, Luthuli gently lamented the prose of the charter, calling it 'uneven', 'vague', at times unnecessarily pedantic and 'open to criticism'.[73] Like a wise statesman, he attributed the poor summation of the people's will to a lack of co-ordination, administration and time management rather than to differences within the alliance. If Luthuli, as leader of the ANC, was marginalised during the drafting of the Freedom

Charter, it would not be the only time that he did not have his hands on the levers of influence when a crucial decision, such as the decision to launch MK, was made.[74]

In October 1955, the Natal ANC gathered to discuss, decide upon and propose redactions to the Freedom Charter before it was ratified by the ANC's annual conference in December. Luthuli and his colleagues prepared a careful resolution from Natal expressing unreserved acceptance of the broad principles enshrined in the Freedom Charter, but also expressing strong concerns about specifics. One of the areas for concern was in the section on equal rights for national groups. Luthuli sympathised with the Africanist perspective that racial groups should not be emphasised. For PAC president, Robert Sobukwe, minority rights could not be recognised because it perpetuated group exclusiveness. 'In the same way as group exclusivism was frowned upon, so was multiculturalism,' according to theological ethicist, Mokgethi Motlhabi. It implied some kind of 'democratic apartheid', or 'racialism multiplied', in effect, safeguarding the interests of whites.[75] Such a condition could only extend the group prejudices and antagonisms of the past into the future. Perhaps for different reasons, Luthuli also favoured a united non-racial, rather than multiracial, nation. A non-racial nation would uphold education, competence, work ethic and merit (not race) as the primary determinants of a person's position or condition in life. Given an equal chance and, without the designations of race, black South Africans would in time earn the same conditions of life as other race groups.

Luthuli and Natal expressed their unease with certain aspects of the Freedom Charter which they believed to be 'good propaganda but . . . not appropriate in a factual document'.[76] They expressed their view that portions of the Freedom Charter were too detailed for a document of universal appeal. For example, references to the length of the work week and various forms of assistance to farmers were felt to be unnecessary. Finally, in a possible stab at the communists, the Natal submission, perhaps influenced by Luthuli's strong Protestant work ethic, stated that lazy persons should expect to go hungry. Luthuli subtly suggested in his autobiography that the presence of outside influences ('principles not previously a part of Congress policy') necessitated the separate adoption of the Freedom Charter.[77]

Despite all of these concerns about the Freedom Charter within the ANC, the ANC working committee, as well as Indians and sympathetic whites in Johannesburg publicised and promoted it as if its ratification by the ANC in December 1955 was a foregone conclusion. At the 19–20 November meeting of the National Executive Committee (NEC) at Luthuli's home, Z.K. Matthews felt much angst because ANC members signed their names, thus endorsing the charter without ANC approval. The members had usurped the ANC's role as the leader of the liberation movement, treating it only as a consultative body.

The same dynamic is observed in 1961. Some viewed the ANC's decision to *initiate* violence as a foregone conclusion after the joint congresses's decision to only *form* MK. In the *formation* of the Freedom Charter and MK, preliminary stages of democratic consensus were met and then prematurely *implemented* as de facto policy by the congresses, primarily based in Johannesburg, and thus circumvented the ANC's procedures and its president general, Albert Luthuli.

With divisions emerging over Africanists' protests to the Freedom Charter, poor planning, the confiscation of important documents by the police in September, a controversial letter from Xuma as well as various accreditation disputes, the 17–18 December 1955 ANC conference in Bloemfontein postponed the decision to ratify the Freedom Charter until a special meeting scheduled for 31 March–1 April 1956 in Orlando, Johannesburg. At the Bloemfontein conference, Luthuli, through Matthews, delivered a special presidential message, in which he made use of his oft-repeated mantra, 'No Cross, No Crown' to encourage Africans to accept the 'gospel of *service and sacrifice for the general and large good without expecting a personal (and at that immediate) reward*' (original emphasis).[78] In his absence, he was elected to serve a second three-year term as president general, with Oliver Tambo as secretary.

Still banned at the time of the Orlando meeting, Luthuli sent a message expressing his views and encouraging delegates to take care in their discussions, particularly on the principle of nationalisation. Complete nationalisation would have been a vision of the communists and trade unionists whose influence and support in the liberation struggle Luthuli welcomed, but to whose political ideology he did not subscribe. Throughout his leadership of the ANC, Luthuli rebuffed those, inside and outside the ANC, who wished to ostracise communists, and felt confident in his ability to contain them within the movement and the ANC. Nevertheless, he remained wary of any inappropriate influence they may have exerted to forward their socio-political and economic aspirations at the expense of liberation, and more specifically, the liberation of the African majority as represented by the ANC.

Despite Luthuli's concerns with the charter, the special meeting in Orlando eventually adopted it without revision, and Luthuli yielded to the democratically concluded motion. Later, in a statement given to the defence in the Treason Trial, he hinted at his disappointment, saying: 'Unfortunately, there was no adequate discussion of the economic clauses of the Charter' as the congress felt it necessary to close ranks against the Africanists' objections.[79] Later, when the ANC decided against his objections to form a military wing and to launch the armed struggle, Luthuli again yielded to a perceived consensus.

In October 1956, Luthuli addressed the SAIC in Johannesburg on the theme 'A Spirit that Refuses to Submit to Tyranny'. As in all his speeches, he expounded on spiritual concepts as much as he did political; his political speeches doubled as homiletic orations. But he was also sensitive to his Indian audience, primarily Hindu and Muslim, and used such phrases as the 'blessings and guidance of the Almighty', 'Noble Divine concepts of man', 'Providence', 'Divine heritage' and 'our honour as created being[s] of God', rather than exclusively Christocentric language.

In Let My People Go, Luthuli speaks of attending an interracial conference in mid-1956, for which the theme was 'The Struggle Must Go On, Bans or No Bans' and in December of that year, he visited Swaziland with Yengwa and Conco. It was upon his return from Swaziland that the government arrested him in Groutville, and charged him with high treason.

Treason Trial

Police arrested Albert Luthuli at his home early on the morning of 5 December 1956 and laid charges against him under the 1950 Suppression of Communism Act. After many papers were confiscated from his home, he was transported to Durban and thereafter, with Yengwa and others, to Pretoria in a Dakota military transport plane. At the Old Fort Prison in Johannesburg, he found dozens of his friends and colleagues similarly charged. Good company comforted Luthuli a great deal during his first experience in jail.

The 1956 Treason Trial in South Africa brought together the brightest and best of South Africa's liberation movement. A total of one hundred and fifty-six were arrested and accused, of whom one hundred and five were African, twenty-three white, twenty-one Indian and seven coloured.

They included G.M. 'Monty' Naicker (1910-1978), Nelson Mandela, Walter Sisulu, Ben Turok, Z.K. and Joe Matthews, Reggie September, Helen Joseph (1905-1992), Lillian Ngoyi (1911-1980), Ida Mntwana (1903-1960), Duma Nokwe, Moses Kotane (1905-1978), Joe Slovo (1926-1995), Oliver Tambo and dozens of others. Luthuli noted in his autobiography that among the trialists were two Anglican priests: Father Walker Stanley Gawe (1900-1980) and Father James Calata (1895-1983). The authorities divided the prisoners into two cells with one priest incarcerated with each group. Calata conducted worship services on Sundays. In his autobiography, Luthuli observed that the experience was an all-expenses-paid meeting of the joint executives of the congresses who 'could at last confer *sine die*, at any level we liked', and Mandela, in his autobiography, almost gleefully called it 'the largest and longest unbanned meeting of the Congress Alliance in years'.[80] Press accounts and cheering crowds showed that the Treason Trial became a new rallying point for the liberation movement. Luthuli, with a smile, gave credit where credit was due, saying: 'I doubt whether we could have devised so effective a method ensuring cohesion in resistance and of enlarging its embrace, as did the government when it set the Trial in motion'.[81]

Despite the delight of the accused at being brought together, none failed to comprehend the gravity of the situation. High treason carried the death penalty. The period covered by the charges was 1 October 1952 to 13 December 1956, embracing the Defiance Campaign, the Sophiatown removals and the Congress of the People. Soon after the preparatory examination started on 19 December 1956, all accused were released on bail for the duration of the trial. Bail payments were funded by the Treason Trial Defence Fund initiated by Bishop Ambrose Reeves (1899-1990), Alan Paton and Alexander (Bob) Hepple (1904-1983). Reeves, particularly, generated a great deal of international sympathy for the liberation movement. Other church figures came to the fore also at this time. The Reverend Arthur Blaxall (1891-1970) visited the trialists in detention. He was especially close to Luthuli whom he had known since their days together on the CCSA and in the Fellowship of Reconciliation.[82] Dominee du Toit, who had led the delegation to Madras, India, in 1938, also visited Luthuli in detention.

The preparatory trial continued until 11 September 1957 during which time the Alexandra bus boycott occurred and rural unrest raged in Zeerust, Sekhukhuneland and the Transkei. Also during the preparatory trial,

Luthuli again fell ill and the court allowed him to be absent for a month. Ambrose Reeves offered him a spiritual retreat at St Benedict's House in Rosettenville in order for him to regain his health.

Luthuli's ability to establish close relationships solidified his influence in the alliance of the congresses. During the Treason Trial, many testified to the fact that those involved in the struggle for freedom undoubtedly viewed Luthuli to be the leader. Those who interacted with him sensed a deep integrity and became loyal to him. Moses Kotane, one-time secretary general of the Communist Party and a treasurer of the ANC, grew very close to Luthuli, becoming perhaps Luthuli's closest political confidant.

The archives uncompromisingly identify Luthuli as the leader of the liberation movement and bear testimony to his strength of character, intelligence and charismatic leadership style. Luthuli firmly held the reins of the ANC and the joint congresses. Tensions were often high and those less secure tended to gravitate and follow those leaders who exhibited a sense of purpose and optimism. While held in detention, Luthuli chaired meetings, led discussions and organised lectures and seminars. He was, according to Ben Turok, 'the obvious leader'.[83] During the following years, as the inefficacy of the ANC's militant non-violent tactics against the violent National Party regime proved apparent, Luthuli's influence waned considerably and his capacity to lead diminished. After the banning of the ANC, and after the government's intransigent response to the May 1961 strike, Luthuli needed to be possessed of substantive influence on the strategic way forward. Without this, his role in the leadership would be a thing of the past.

During the adjournment of the trial in December 1957, charges against sixty-five of the accused were inexplicably dropped. Among the acquitted were Tambo and Luthuli. In August 1958, the Treason Trial proper began with ninety-one of the remaining accused on trial. After an adjournment and reconvening under a revised indictment in January 1959, only thirty accused remained. Yet, throughout the trial until 29 March 1961, Luthuli often had to provide testimony and thus was always indirectly on trial as the president general of the ANC.

Assaulted

After the July 1956 expiry of Albert Luthuli's second ban, his arrest and release from prison in December 1956, and his acquittal from the Treason Trial in December 1957, he experienced a welcome reprieve from any restrictions on his movement or company. On 15 April 1958 (Africa Day), large meetings were held around the country commemorating the first Conference of Independent African States held in Accra. In Durban, Luthuli addressed a sizeable crowd that carried him shoulder high out of the venue. He proceeded to Ladysmith where he addressed another dense gathering.

At around this time, Luthuli began intentionally to court white audiences. In April 1958, he wrote an open letter to white voters inviting them to better understand the aims and objectives of the ANC. The Congress of Democrats organised a whites-only gathering in Johannesburg where he delivered a speech entitled 'Our Vision Is a Democratic Society'.[84] In it, he prophetically challenged South Africans, 'with all [their] diversities of colour and race' to set a 'new example to the world', showing the world 'a new pattern for democracy'.[85] Over three hundred people present at the meeting expressed great appreciation for the sentiments he put forward.

Luthuli also accepted an invitation from the Transvaal Liberal Party to open its conference and speak to more whites who needed convincing, no doubt, to the chagrin of the Africanists who believed that trying to bring whites on board was a waste of time, energy and money – a useless enterprise.

On 22 August 1958, in an incident rarely recalled, six Afrikaner men invaded and violently disturbed a gathering at the St Alban's Hall in Pretoria. The meeting had been initiated by the predominantly Afrikaner Pretoria Political Study Group and Luthuli had been invited to give an address. The attendance of ten Indians qualified the event as 'interracial'. (Though interracial, the Indians were segregated and stood at the back of the venue.)

Diplomats, foreign press correspondents, British social workers, clergy and professors and lecturers from two universities attended the event and witnessed the co-ordinated melee. Chairs were thrown about and the hooligans beat and injured many people, including Luthuli. He was dubbed a 'kaffir' who should not address whites; for such to happen insulted the Afrikaner people. One assailant knocked Luthuli off his chair and assaulted him. Hiding underneath the table and desperately trying to shield himself, Luthuli was repeatedly kicked, receiving numerous blows to the face. As a result of injuries to the jaw, he could not eat for three days. The brutes also attacked the secretary of the study group, Miss M. Schoon, who was thrown from the stage. According to the *Rand Daily Mail*, Schoon 'turned a cartwheel in the air and landed on the floor of the hall'.[86] Police finally arrived, quelled the disturbance and arrested the attackers. With others, the chairperson restrained Hendrik Claassens, the ringleader of the antagonists, and resumed the meeting, 'speaking with a bruise over his forehead and covered with dust'.[87]

Luthuli intended to speak on the theme of racial reconciliation and a peaceful South Africa. Though just brutally beaten, he delivered his prepared speech and theme, unaltered. The *Cape Times* reported:

> Speaking fluently from his notes in a school exercise book, Chief Luthuli said that the Europeans had been sent to Africa by divine purpose to help educate and civilise Blacks. The African was however, becoming confused when he found his helpers were taking advantage of him and exploiting him . . . The sands of time are running out and our amity might change to enmity – I pray God that it doesn't.[88]

The Public Attorney instructed that Claassens and the others be charged with public violence and appear in the Pretoria Magistrate's and Regional Court. They were duly convicted and sentenced, Claassens to a fine of a hundred pounds or four months' imprisonment and an additional three months' imprisonment. In their 1993 documentary film *Mayibuye Africa*, Charlotte Owen and Peter Corbett interviewed Claassens and described him as a 'lonely, old man'. Corbett indicated that he had the sense that Claassens felt no remorse for his actions against Luthuli. 'We are talking about an admirer of Robby Leibbrandt. My impression was that his only regret was having to go to prison for what he did.'[89]

Despite the beating, Luthuli reflected positively on the violent incident, noting in the *Cape Times* report that he saw a glimmer of hope and encouragement provided by the genuine support and willingness of whites to listen to his message. Though the times seemed desperate and even though assaulted, for Luthuli, the non-violent road did not lead to a cul-de-sac. Instead, the incident underscored his desire to let his life demonstrate how to resist injustice. Although he felt increasing frustration with white supremacists for inducing others in the liberation movement to question his non-violent approach, he nevertheless believed in South Africa's bright possibilities.

Exclusive African nationalism versus inclusive South African nationalism

The eighteen months between Luthuli's acquittal and his third ban contained some of the most tumultuous events in the ANC's history. Most notable was the breakaway of the ANC's nationalist camp to form the PAC. Disgruntled about a perceived communist influence, the prominence of multiracialism in ANC tactics and the Freedom Charter as evidence of both, the Africanists withdrew from the Transvaal ANC conference in Orlando and formed their own political party in April 1959. Robert Sobukwe and Potlako Leballo were elected as president and secretary, respectively. The Africanist platform harkened back to the ANCYL-catalysed 1949 Programme of Action inspired by Nkrumah's nascent liberation tactics. Ghana's independence in 1957 and the rapid transition to independence in a number of other African countries fuelled their passions for more radical stances to be taken by the ANC. The PAC's pan-African ideology, symbolised by its own flag, a star's light spreading to the rest of the continent from Ghana, enabled the new party to be attractive to, for example, Nkrumah himself and Tanzania's Julius Nyerere.

The PAC viewed the Freedom Charter as a betrayal of the cause. Because PAC members expressed, on the whole, impatience and militancy, many characterised them to be less disciplined, more impassioned and more spontaneous. More importantly, the PAC wished to carry out the struggle for liberation without (at least visibly) including whites, coloureds or Indians.

The old guard of the ANC, epitomised by Luthuli and Matthews, subscribed to what has been termed 'South African exceptionalism'. This notion conceived of South Africa as a unique African country because it harboured settler, rather than administrative, colonialists. Settlers had become grafted to and thus inseparable from South Africa. The liberation movement, in this view, could not follow or even identify with the rest of the African continent whose colonial overlords would simply retreat to the metropoles. The Freedom Charter's opening words, '. . . [t]hat South Africa belongs to all who live in it, black and white' encapsulated this exceptionalism and, for Africanists, it was deemed political heresy. Though Luthuli sympathised with certain aspects of the Africanists' perspective – their emphasis on individual rights (non-racialism) rather than multiracialism; their concern over communist influence; and the need for radical land reform – he could not sacrifice what he felt was of prime importance: racial unity in the struggle against apartheid.

As leader of the ANC, Luthuli did not see himself as the trailblazer from whose cult of personality the liberation movement would be led; nor did he conceive of himself as one to marginalise opinions at variance with his own in order to homogenise policy to fit with his own perspective. Rather, he conceived himself to be the linchpin holding the liberation movement together. He held together modern and traditional, old and young, black and white, conservative and liberal, capitalist and communist, educated and uneducated, atheist and Christian, Muslim and Jew, rich and poor. Luthuli gauged the unity of the movement to be of paramount importance. He often suppressed his own sentiments on strategic issues so as not to compromise the fundamental aspirations of complete liberation of South Africa's oppressed. He accepted the Freedom Charter despite qualms. He accommodated the Africanist position, provided it did not divide the movement. When the unity of the movement could no longer be guaranteed, his response was to reluctantly allow the Africanists to go. After Sharpeville, the banning of the PAC and the ANC in March 1960 forced both movements north into the continent where they became competitors for independent countries' succour. The more militant members of the ANC adopted aspects of the Africanist position (pan-Africanism, African control of the liberation movement and, later, a willingness to utilise violence).

For Luthuli, 1958 ended with the Forty-Sixth Annual Conference of the ANC held in Durban from 13–14 December and his election to a third term as president general. Oliver Tambo was now deputy president general and Duma Nokwe, general secretary. In his presidential address, Luthuli did not refer specifically to the Africanist breakaway, but rather alluded to and confirmed the ANC's policy of mobilising a democratic rather than a racial majority to govern the country. He dealt with the idea of 'civilisation' that he understood to be a synthesis of the best all cultures have to offer. He reminded his audience also, albeit in a perfunctory manner, of their non-violent methods of struggle. However, the speech concentrated primarily on his increasing confidence in fair-minded whites and his confidence in their ability to join the struggle, thus providing increased impetus for the overthrow of the National Party government. Four times in his speech, Luthuli expressed that 'the manner in which freedom lovers in the white community have come out openly and boldly to champion the cause of making the Union a true democracy for all . . .' encouraged him greatly.[90]

Bantustans

In January 1959, Prime Minister Hendrik Verwoerd announced to Parliament his plans to implement a policy framework for the creation of homelands or Bantustans in the passage of the Promotion of Bantu Self-Government Act (No. 46). Essentially, the proposed legislation extended the objectives of the 1951 Bantu Authorities Act. The National Party government designed territorial constructs called Bantustans during the latter half of the 1950s, to achieve various economic, social and political objectives necessitated by numerous contradictions arising from apartheid ideology that was premised on racial 'separation'. The Act reversed the natural and progressive dying out of that which Luthuli welcomed, the institution of chieftainship.[91] It would institute a system of tribal rule that made African chiefs, contrary to tradition, autocrats and virtually nothing more than instruments of their people's oppression.

In 1956, the Tomlinson Commission for the Socio-Economic Development of Bantu Areas within the Union of South Africa concluded that there was 'no midway between the two poles of ultimate total integration and ultimate separate development' of the racial groups in South Africa. A sustained programme of development of the Bantu areas was needed.[92] The envisioned apex of a Bantustan framework was the perceived 'independence' for black ethnic groups within designated homelands. Apartheid engineered white supremacy, that is, white economic, political, social and economic dominance.

In a report submitted to the Natal People's Conference on 6 September 1959, Luthuli lamented that the Bantustan framework would see between sixty and seventy per cent of peasants thrown off their land, without recourse to new sources of livelihood or employment. Millions of Africans residing and working in white areas (towns and farms) would be rendered stateless and rightless. Nobody wanted the so-called partition of South Africa, so fraudulently advanced. Luthuli put it to the conference:

> In honesty, can it be said that such a Bantustan is in our interest? What is morally wrong in principle cannot be right in practice! So all apartheid laws based as they are on the maxim: 'Separate and unequal' in favour of the Whites can never be in the interests of the non-Whites.[93]

The Act prepared a legislative path for the inauguration in Eshowe of Zululand's first Bantu Regional Authority (Inkanyezi) in October 1959, a significant milestone in the building of the Bantustan framework. Immediately preceding this event, Luthuli published in earnest his grave concerns. In twenty-seven columns written for the Johannesburg-based *Golden City Post*, six articles, all written in September and October 1959, dealt directly with his opposition to Bantustans. In a 20 September 1959 column, Luthuli quoted Paramount Chief Sabata Dalindyebo (1928–1986) of the Abatembu in the Transkei, who had already reluctantly accepted the framework, as saying, 'Half-a-loaf is better than no bread. Before, we had nothing. Now at least we have something.' Luthuli vociferously opposed Chief Dalindyebo's line of thinking.

> Much of our destiny as a people in a scientific age has been placed by the white government in the hands of chiefs and their councillors. *The progress of Bantustans will not be judged on the affluence of a few: chiefs, traders, civil servants and professional people who are hardly 12 percent of the people.* What will matter more is the raising of the general standard of living of the masses of the people to progressively approach civilised standards of living (original emphasis).[94]

In his column published on 4 October 1959, with uncharacteristic passion, he argued that the plan for separate development was fundamentally flawed:

> *Africans Should Categorically Reject the Bantustans Proposals Because*: they purport to meet our demand for direct participation in the government of the country by some pseudo plan of self-government which is falsely acclaimed by the government as conforming to the traditional form of government in African society . . . (original emphasis).[95]

Though Luthuli opposed the Bantustan framework on economic, social and political grounds, he held deep theological objections to it also. In a July 1953 letter to American Board missioner and Inanda Seminary principal, Lavinia Scott, Luthuli condemned the government's lauding of tribalism. He did not shy away from saying that the practice of tribalism was 'unfortunately an embodiment of our traditional culture'. He acknowledged that traditional African culture had some basically good ethical and moral concepts. However, tribalism in its fuller manifestation he pronounced to be '*in practice heathen*' (Rich's and therefore Luthuli's emphasis).[96]

Courting whites

Throughout 1958 and halfway into 1959, while Parliament passed legislation such as the euphemistically named Extension of University Education Act, Albert Luthuli remained openly active as the leader of the ANC. In keeping with the ANC's non-violent methods, he pressed for economic boycotts to be implemented. One such campaign involved the boycott of cigarettes produced by Rembrandt, a tobacco company that supported the National Party. He believed such boycotts would meta-phorically 'punch them in the stomach'.[97]

In his autobiography, Luthuli said that he spoke primarily to white audiences during 1959. He was rapturously received in Cape Town where he met with Anglican Archbishop Joost de Blank (1908–1968), former Chief Justice Albert van de Sandt Centlivres (1887–1966) and Senator Leslie Rubin (1909–2002) with whom he had corresponded for years. One correspondent reported:

> Luthuli's recent visit to Cape Town . . . was an astonishing affair. He stepped off the Orange Express at Cape Town station to be greeted by cheering supporters waiting to garland him. His meeting in the Drill Hall that evening was one of the biggest of its kind ever seen in the Mother City. The next four days went past in a flurry: press conferences, a house party with liberals, clergymen and prominent citizens waiting to shake his hand, a private talk with Black Sash women, an 'inspection' of the demonstration outside Parliament against the university apartheid bill.[98]

One can not underestimate Luthuli's popularity at this time. Multiracial crowds shouted and sang 'Somlandela Luthuli' ('We Will Follow Luthuli'). The city was spellbound. The National Party regime observed that his moderate realism, which had the capacity to mobilise blacks as well as whites, coloureds and Indians, could be far more dangerous than Sobukwe's radical black nationalism.

Luthuli's immense popularity outside the black community made him a potential head of state and the ANC a realistic ruling party, just as thirty years later Nelson Mandela's magnetism and moderate tone with progressive whites enabled him to take the reins of power without the need of a civil war. At the close of the 1950s, in an atmosphere bedevilled by fear and mistrust, only Luthuli captured the imagination and harnessed the hope of many South Africans across the colour bar. Only Luthuli elicited substantial doses of white sympathy, affection and even adoration. In his autobiography, he characteristically said he felt encouraged by the responses of white people he spoke to. 'They seemed to have a real sense of purpose, and a real desire to face and to discuss the issues. Their ignorance was often disturbing – but I must make this partial extenuation for them: it is more and more a government enforced ignorance.'[99]

Where other younger black leaders saw a cul-de-sac in 1961, Luthuli saw for himself a welling up of support for a free and fully democratic South Africa, not only within the black community, but, perhaps more importantly for Luthuli, also within the white liberal community and among Afrikaner intellectuals. A resolved, liberal white community could, in Luthuli's view, with a militant non-violent African majority, constitutionally overwhelm the supporters of apartheid. Something further was needed to inspire and galvanise sympathetic whites to choose democracy – something like a Nobel Peace Prize.

Third ban

On 25 May 1959, seventeen months since his acquittal in the Treason Trial, the government served on Luthuli his third banning order. This order prevented him from being present at and opening a large ANC conference in Johannesburg on 31 May. But it was not necessarily in an effort to prevent him from attending to ANC business that he was banned. Much more importantly, Luthuli had been persuading whites, and many of them. By now, he had something of celebrity status among like-minded whites in South Africa. Perhaps this would explain in part also why Luthuli ultimately could not break with the policy of non-violence: war would inevitably destroy his aspirations for peaceful co-existence between the races. Luthuli's colleagues such as Mandela, Tambo, Sisulu and other prominent African leaders did not at this time have the same mass exposure to white accolades as he did.

In keeping with the progressively harsher nature of each succeeding ban, the 1959 ban prevented Luthuli from attending any meeting anywhere in South Africa and confined him to the Lower Tugela District for five years. Many groups, especially the Liberal Party and the Congress of Democrats protested against the harsh terms of the order. During a members' meeting of the Musgrave Congregational Church in Durban, a statement was passed urging the Minister of Justice to reconsider Luthuli's ban. Published in the press, it proclaimed that the government, and not Luthuli, destroyed 'civil rights and liberties of freedom and conscience', the 'bulwarks of our civilisation'. For them, there was 'no more ardent or sincere upholder of the Christian ideals of brotherly love and the dignity of man than Mr Luthuli'.[100]

Luthuli spent the ten-day hiatus, between his being served the banning on 25 May and 3 June when the geographical portion of it took effect, campaigning. He set off for Johannesburg for the last time on or after 28 May, visiting Oliver Tambo, congress members and, again, his dear friend the Bishop of Johannesburg, Ambrose Reeves. On 1 June a meeting took place at Gandhi Hall in Johannesburg to protest against the banning of the ANC meeting that had been scheduled for the previous day. Despite his being in the area, Luthuli could not attend the meeting and a representative read his statement entitled 'Freedom Costs Dearly'. In it, he reminded his followers that the 'degree to which we of this age are prepared to sacrifice for this freedom is the gauge of our earnestness and sincerity to secure it. It is also the measure of our fitness for it.'[101] Luthuli then flew to Durban on 2 June and began his domestic exile the day before the banning that confined him to Groutville took effect.

A month into his banning, on Freedom Day, 26 June 1959, Luthuli issued a message calling for a boycott of potatoes to protest against the use of slave labour on South African farms. Lasting three months, the boycott also protested against pass laws that rendered thousands of men confined to 'farm gaols'.

Luthuli and the ANC chose the boycott as a means of resisting white supremacy with non-violent methods. In the postscript to his auto-biography, Luthuli said he remained convinced of the moral and tactical rightness of non-violent methods.

> I make it clear that we mean to cling to methods such as this, to non-violence, and we mean increasingly to use these weapons even against such tyrants as South Africa's present government. This is not only a question of morality. As long as our patience can hold out, we shall not jeopardise the South Africa of tomorrow by precipitating violence today.[102]

While banned to Groutville, Luthuli issued public statements following disturbances in June arising from spontaneous women's demonstrations.

He denied that the ANC incited the disturbances and said: 'We have issued statements strongly advising people against violence . . . Violence is not only contrary to our policy, but most inimical to our liberation struggle.'[103]

Luthuli remained quite active in the affairs of the movement. A prolific letter writer, through correspondence with Helen Joseph and others, he assisted in organising the third commemoration of the women's march in August 1959. 'Actually,' he told the *Rand Daily Mail*, 'I am more in touch with affairs than ever before, probably because I have a lot more time for my correspondence.'[104]

The terms of his banning allowed Luthuli to receive visitors, as long as only one visited at a time so as to not constitute a 'gathering'. In September 1959, the American Ambassador to South Africa visited Luthuli at his home. Progressive Party leader, Jan Steytler (1910–1990), also visited, buoying Luthuli's hopes for a peaceful transition to a democratic South Africa as it constituted for him a sign of the gradual opposition of whites to apartheid.

The year ended with the December 1959 ANC conference in Durban. It was the last annual conference the ANC was to have in South Africa for over thirty years. As he had done before, Luthuli issued his presidential message *in absentia*. In it, he advocated that more training be instituted to discipline the rank and file for non-violent actions and warned against 'reckless haste and impatience which would be suicidal and might be playing into the hands of the Government'.[105] It was at this December conference that the ANC decided to co-ordinate an anti-pass campaign that would begin on 31 March 1960.

3

Storm on the Horizon

1960

Can the Africans in South Africa achieve their aims without violence? I hope so. I hope so . . . I do not care so much for the Europeans. They have asked for it. But I do not want my own people to commit national suicide. No, I do not want my people to commit suicide. But will they wait? Will they wait?

— Albert Luthuli, *Daily News*

THE TREASON TRIAL proceeded during 1959 with only thirty defendants. Paradoxically, though the numbers of the accused decreased during the course of the trial, its scope became wider. From an intention to prove that they had intended to act violently against the state, the state now sought to prove that the use of violence was a collective policy of the ANC and its allies. Nelson Mandela and the other accused could, by being found to adhere to such a policy, be guilty of high treason. For this, they faced the death penalty.

Though he had been discharged at the end of the preparatory examination, Albert Luthuli essentially found himself on trial again as the leader of the ANC. The government adjusted his banning order so that he could testify at the trial. Other previously released leaders of the ANC were also called upon to give evidence, among them, M.B. Yengwa and Z.K. Matthews.

While the trial was in progress, Luthuli continued to enjoy the support and succour of liberal whites and he continued to advocate a policy of non-violence while the remaining accused faced the very real spectre of the gallows. It was a time of immense pressure for the leadership of the organisation and the Sharpeville massacre of March 1960 would prove to be the beginning of the end of Luthuli's capacity to lead the liberation movement. Ultimately, it would lead to the ANC's renunciation of the policy of non-violent resistance so close to Luthuli's heart.

Sharpeville

On 18 March 1960, the PAC, under the leadership of Robert Sobukwe, announced the launch of an anti-pass protest to take place ten days before a similar ANC-planned protest action. Duma Nokwe, responding for the ANC, declined to join the PAC protest, not wishing to abandon months of planning for its own incremental campaign, which intended to culminate on 31 March, for one that appeared far more hastily concocted. Sobukwe and a number of others planned to lead PAC volunteers to the Orlando police station where they would submit themselves for arrest in protest against the hated pass laws. The campaign demanded in the strictest terms that protesters used no force or violence in the execution of its strategy.

On 21 March, as Sobukwe and others were duly arrested at the Orlando police station, similar protests were enacted in Evaton, Langa (near Cape Town) and Sharpeville. In Evaton, the protest was broken up by low-flying jets. In Langa, three people were killed and twenty-seven injured in a baton charge by the police. But it was the shooting by the police of sixty-nine protesters, most sustaining injuries in the back, and the wounding of a further one hundred and eight-six at Sharpeville, that sent shockwaves throughout South Africa and the world.

On the same morning, proceedings opened in the Treason Trial with Albert Luthuli in the stand as second witness, after Wilson Conco, for the defence. Owing to Luthuli's high blood pressure, the court agreed to be in session only during the mornings. On that Monday morning, too, many South Africans sipped their coffee or tea, newspaper in hand, and read a relatively submissive appeal in Luthuli's column in the *Golden City Post* arguing that Africans 'cannot manage without the Whites in South Africa. We have accepted your civilisation and we like it, and we are absorbing it as far as we can – despite the effort of your Government to cut us off from it.'[1]

On 26 March, in an effort to stablise the volatile situation, the government suspended the pass laws. It was a tactical decision and did not signal a change of policy. On 27 March, riding the wave of protest prematurely catalysed by the PAC, Luthuli publicly burned his passbook in an effort to capture for the ANC the countrywide feelings of outrage and to launch its anti-pass campaign four days earlier than the scheduled date for the protest on 31 March. Mandela, Nokwe and Walter Sisulu also burnt theirs. The action may have been a game of one-upmanship. PAC supporters who rallied to the called protest only left their passbooks at home on that day.

Events continued at a rapid pace. Sisulu's biography indicates that on the evening of the Sharpeville massacre, Mandela, Sisulu, Nokwe and Joe Slovo resolved to launch a countrywide strike. The four then consulted Luthuli on their decision. Luthuli consented and duly declared 28 March to be a national day of prayer that would include mourning, protest and a stay-at-home. It was to be the biggest strike in the country's history. In custody, Sobukwe responded to the call with a scathing attack on the ANC and its leader. In his biography of Sobukwe, *How Can Man Die Better* (1997), Benjamin Pogrund quotes Sobukwe's explosive attack on their partnerships with liberal whites:

> If evidence of ANC rank opportunism was still required, their call for a day of mourning on 28 March instead of their previously announced coffin-carrying, placard-bearing pass demonstrations of 31 March, provides that evidence. The ANC opposed our campaign. It called it sensational, ill-defined and ill-planned. We showed them and their bosses that we could plan and run the campaign on our own without the advice of sections of the oppressor class. The ANC is now trying to bask in the sunshine of PAC's successes. Luthuli now has the courage which he has lacked for over twelve years to burn his reference book after passes had been suspended. Supported and boosted by the white Press, he has been making one foolish statement after the other, pretending that he has a following in the country . . . Our advice and warning to the ANC and its liberal friends is: Hands off our campaign. We do not need your interference. Go on with your coffin-carrying and other childish pastimes but leave the African people to fight their struggle without you. Tell your bosses you cannot sell the African people because you do not control them.[2]

Sympathetic whites

Albert Luthuli ceremoniously burned his passbook on 27 March 1961 in protest against the massacre at Sharpeville. The event took place in the family home of Tony Brink, chairman of the Liberal Party in Pretoria, where Luthuli was residing while the Treason Trial was underway. Luthuli was photographed holding his burning passbook above an enamel basin and the picture was published. Later, when the Special Branch searched the Brink home for evidence, the enamel bowl was overlooked when it was found to contain a pile of soiled nappies.

For Luthuli, the Brink family home distinguished itself 'by a complete absence of any hint of colour bar'.[3] Tony Brink acted as Luthuli's driver for many days, taking him around many townships to initiate and lead pass-burning protests. It was a relationship that was important to both men. In Let My People Go, Luthuli is expansive in his sentiments for the many benevolent, white, liberal and Christian friends who extended to him so much support, hospitality and solidarity in times of adversity. It was his way of emphasising that the struggle against the apartheid government was multiracial and Christian in nature. Whites, too, had suffered and sacrificed to achieve a democratic South Africa. In his autobiography, he mentioned by name those white persons who were also arrested in the first wave of detentions after the declaration of the State of Emergency: Colin Lang, a prominent member of the Liberal Party; Mark Nye, an ordained minister who provided hospitality to the Treason Trial accused; and Hannah Stanton, warden of the Tumelong Anglican mission at the Lady Selborne township, near Pretoria. He also named other whites who expressed their care and concern: Michael Parkington, a defence attorney had comforted Luthuli with his solicitude during those stressful days; M. de Villiers, a doctor, had diligently attended to Luthuli's health and helped to ease the tensions; Henri Phillipe Junod, a chaplain, had visited Luthuli and those sentenced to death at the Pretoria Central Prison; and Johannes Reynecke, a retired Dutch Reformed Church minister whom Luthuli had known since his days serving on the CCSA, had twice visited Luthuli. In his column of 27 March 1960, Luthuli had affirmed their role when he said: 'Naturally any sympathetic white wants to participate in freeing his countrymen from their present bondage, and to deprive him of this is to make him feel that his stake in the country is questioned.'[4]

Arrests

On the day appointed as a national day of prayer, 28 March 1960, the National Party government tabled the Unlawful Organisations Bill in Parliament, paving the way for the banning of the ANC and other organisations. The very next day the ANC's NEC began making arrangements for the organisation to move underground in the event of its banning. Though Luthuli did not in general approve of sending members of the ANC into exile, he decided with others to mandate Oliver Tambo to escape from the country and represent the ANC internationally.

On 30 March, the government made mass arrests authorised by the State of Emergency declared that day. On the same day, in Cape Town, Philip Kgosana, the twenty-three-year-old PAC regional secretary, led over thirty thousand people in an impromptu march on Parliament at Caledon Square in Cape Town. The government promised Kgosana that if he dismissed the crowd, he would have an audience with the Minister of Justice. It is no exaggeration to say that the history of South Africa rested on this pivotal moment. Kgosana dismissed the crowd peacefully. It was an act of leadership described by Joseph Lelyveld in his Pulitzer prize-winning book, *Move your Shadow* (1985), as holding more power than Luthuli, Mandela and Sobukwe combined. However, when Kgosana and his delegation returned to meet the minister, they were denied an audience. The moment fizzled.

In the early hours of the morning of 30 March, the government rounded up the ANC leadership, among them Mandela, Nokwe and Robert Resha (1920–1973). Police arrested Luthuli at the Brink's home. As they led him away, the Brink family matriarch rushed after Luthuli worried that he had forgotten his slippers and expressed concern that in prison he 'might catch a chill'.[5] No such solicitude was forthcoming from the state. As the detainees were marched into their cells in the early hours, Luthuli was assaulted by a warder. His colleagues were incensed.

The arrests proved to be illegal. The new law had not been fully gazetted. As a formality, the police released them all for a few seconds before re-arresting them under the newly invoked Emergency legislation. It meant that Luthuli was absent from court on 31 March when the Treason Trial reconvened.

At this time, Luthuli was again suffering from poor health. The proceedings in the court tired him physically and emotionally. Faced with charges of incitement while burning his passbook, the court gave him extraordinary permission to remain seated. In his autobiography, he acknowledged that he received 'every consideration and indulgence' from the court.[6] And yet, the authorities sought to seal him off from the other detainees and confine him to a cell where he remained isolated and in bed for most of the day. Whereas during his detention in the preparatory stages of the Treason Trial he had played a politically mobilising role with his colleagues, now he only played a pastoral role, conducting worship services on Sundays. Throughout the five weeks he spent in detention with the other accused in June 1960, he would routinely be returned to isolation after time devoted to exercise or worship. In his autobiography, Luthuli speaks of his 'white-washed cell' as his 'chapel', his 'place of retreat' where he could 'consider the problems of our resistance to bondage'.[7] In time, he was removed to the Pretoria Central Prison's hospital where he remained throughout his detention.

His co-accused fared rather differently. Mandela related in his autobiography, *Long Walk to Freedom*, how his and others' conditions at the Newlands police station and Pretoria Local Prison were primitive, brutal and uncivilised.

> . . . we were taken into a tiny cell with a single drainage hole in the floor which could be flushed only from the outside. We were given no blankets, no food, no mats and no toilet paper. The hole regularly became blocked and the stench in the room was insufferable . . . I do not think that words can do justice to a description of the foulness and filthiness of this bedding. The blankets were encrusted with dried blood and vomit, ridden with lice, vermin and cockroaches, and reeked with a stench that actually competed with the stink of the drain.[8]

From March 1960, while Luthuli and his accused were awaiting trial (separately) on charges arising from the Emergency regulations, a policy rift began to emerge in the ANC on the question of the move from a non-violent to a potentially violent strategy of resistance. Various sources confirm that the preliminary decision to embark upon an armed struggle did not include Luthuli. Certainly his physical isolation from his colleagues must have been a factor in his exclusion from the stream of decision-making. The same four men (Mandela, Sisulu, Nokwe and Slovo) who had met on the night of 21 March to plan a response to the massacre at Sharpeville formed the core of a 'magic circle' that met regularly while they were held in detention between March and August 1960, to plot the way forward and to mobilise the entire country.[9] From these discussions, they eventually resolved that an armed struggle of resistance was an appropriate way forward. But on 1 April, the ANC, through its Emergency

Committee, issued a public statement pledging its commitment to a path of non-violent struggle, even in the event of its banning.

ANC banned

On 8 April 1960, the government banned the PAC and ANC under the Unlawful Organisations Act. The effect of this, coming hot on the heels of the arrests of almost the entire ANC leadership, was to decimate the organisational structure of the movement, thus diminishing further Luthuli's role as its leader. Ben Turok expressed his frustration that respected members of the organisation sat around waiting for the police to pick them up instead of safeguarding their liberty should the ANC need them to step into the leadership.[10] After the arrests of members of the Consultative Committee and the NEC, all who remained were Yusuf Dadoo (who was abroad), Moses Kotane, Michael Harmel (1915–1974) and Turok. Suddenly, the latter three were catapulted into the secretariat of the Consultative Committee, virtually running the organisation and the alliance. Turok and Harmel issued statements, leaflets and policy documents at this time, apparently without Luthuli's knowledge or approval. The truncation of participatory and consensus methods of decision-making removed the ideological and administrative foundation upon which Luthuli always led. As a chief within a highly democratic Christian community, Luthuli was well versed in the leadership practice of democratic consensus. In this, he upheld the example of his uncle, Martin Luthuli, from the days of his youth, as well as the highly democratic ecclesiastic polity of Congregationalism practised in his own faith community. The 1960 State of Emergency had forced the ANC to adopt a more covert, streamlined, efficient and, ultimately, less democratic modus operandi. It was a 'command and control' style of leadership that was needed, one that was antithetical to what Luthuli believed to be appropriate to the ethos of the ANC. His style of leadership in the new dispensation was becoming extinct.

The Treason Trial resumes

The declaration of the State of Emergency had prompted the Treason Trial to enter a period of recess. Resuming on 19 April 1960, Duma Nokwe is said to have commented to activist Helen Joseph: 'This trial is out of date.'[11] The trial had hitherto focused on the ANC and its non-violent strategy. According to Walter Sisulu, long before it was to reach a verdict, planning for the adoption of an armed strategy had begun, inaugurated by the state's violent suppression of non-violent protest tactics.[12] Sisulu, Mandela and others believed the tactics of struggle to be conditional upon the tactics of the antagonist. For Luthuli, violence would only further enrage the antagonist and justify its use of force as 'self-defence' in the court of white and international public opinion. Worse than this, violence initiated by the liberation movement would neutralise, if not reverse, the support given to the liberation movement from domestic and international white, liberal and Christian allies. Luthuli felt that the key to an ultimate democratic victory depended upon the recruitment of allies by moral authority. To the same degree that the apartheid regime became an international pariah, the ANC could become a saint, à la Gandhi. Even the Afrikaans daily, Die Burger, reported that South Africa had become the polecat of the world.

Evidently, the non-violent anti-pass protests at Sharpeville and elsewhere delivered results. The Johannesburg Stock Exchange took a severe blow. International opprobrium followed for the state's resort to violence and isolation from the world community was becoming a real possibility. On 22 March, the United States State Department condemned Pretoria's heavy-handed tactics for the first time. On 1 April, the United Nations Security Council passed a resolution by nine to nil (with the abstaining of Great Britain and France) calling on South Africa to change its policies. In November that year, Luthuli's stance of non-violent political action had brought about his candidacy for the Nobel Peace Prize for 1960. These were no small accomplishments for the anti-pass protests in South Africa.

In their Treason Trial testimony following the Sharpeville massacre, both Luthuli and Z.K. Matthews conveyed their optimism that such pressure would topple white supremacy in South Africa. Matthews cited the example of India. In the Indian fight for liberation from British rule, non-violent tactics used before and following most violent repressive acts perpetrated by the colonial administration earned the movement their greatest international public relations victories. These victories ultimately forced Britain to grant India its independence in 1947. Questioned by Prosecutor Trengove, Luthuli clung firmly to his belief that a sustained campaign of pressure would ultimately bring about the change they were seeking. He said:

My lords, I wouldn't be in Congress if I didn't expect that white South Africa would someday reconsider. That is my honest belief, and one has grounds for it. I think I have already indicated them, but I firmly believe that white South Africa will one day reconsider. When, my lords, I cannot say.[13]

Asked if he was a pacifist, Luthuli replied: 'No, I'm not.' Asked to explain the difference between the non-violence campaign and his not being a pacifist, Luthuli said simply: 'My lords, I merely talk as one feels – I'm not conversant with [the] theory of pacifism, but I am not a pacifist.'[14] The exchange continued:

Court: As far as you personally are concerned, would you be party to violent struggle to achieve your aims?

Luthuli: In the circumstances that obtain in the country – I must say this first – I may have indicated that there might be differences of point of view among different members, but as far as the Congress is concerned, in the circumstances that obtain definitely we are for non-violence. When it comes to a personal level, as to whether at any time one would, I would say that if conditions are as they are, I would never be a party to the use of violence because I think it would be almost national suicide, in the circumstances as they are.

Court: And quite apart from that point of view, what would you say with regard to your own beliefs?

Luthuli: My own beliefs as I have already said are to a certain extent motivated by Christian leanings. Because of my Christian leanings I would hesitate to be a party to violence, my lords. But, of course, I must say in that connection that I am not suggesting that the Christian religion says this and that I am not a theologian, but my own leanings would be in that direction.

Court: Have you at any level of the [ANC] heard a suggestion that the policy [of non-violence] should be changed?

Luthuli: My lords, I've never heard any such suggestion, nor a whisper to that effect.[15]

Court: As far as you personally are concerned, what would be your attitude if such a suggestion were made?

Luthuli: I would oppose it.

Court: Why?

Luthuli: Well, I would oppose it on two grounds really: firstly, from a personal angle, but also because it's not – or it would not be – in the interest of the liberation movement, it would not be a practical thing . . .

Court: . . . Why is it that from time to time, if that is the accepted policy, one finds at meetings reference to your non-violent policy; why should it be necessary to do that?

Luthuli: Well, it is very necessary that we should do so, firstly because in so far as we are concerned we are embarking on something which people may not be fully acquainted with, so that our task is to educate our own members and the African people. Then, of course, the other reason is that we so believe in it that we feel that we should take no chance of anybody not knowing and being tempted to deviate . . .[16]

Was Luthuli evasive in his providing a rationale for his beliefs or was he genuine in intimating his lack of academic or ethical inquiry into pacifism? It is highly unlikely that he would have neglected to investigate the matter given his ecclesiastical upbringing in mission churches and schools, his trip to Madras, India, in 1938 (on the eve of the Second World War), his tour of the United States in 1948 (between the Second World War and the Cold War) and the central place he and the ANC gave to a non-violent approach in the struggle for liberation.

This evidence and other statements to the same effect uphold the ANC's accurate view that Luthuli was not a pacifist. Yet, in his testimony, Luthuli made a distinction between pacifism and non-violent strategy. He reasoned that pacifists refused to use violence in the case of self-defence, whereas adherents to non-violence did not necessarily prohibit violent self-defence in the event of a violent attack.[17]

In August, the Emergency regulations were lifted and, still facing charges related to the burning of his passbook, Luthuli was found guilty. In September, he received a lesser sentence of a £100 fine and six months in jail, suspended for three years, on the condition that he was not convicted of a similar charge during that period. It is likely that the court had regard for Luthuli's serious heart ailment, limited life expectancy and prior detention since March 1960. The authorities released Mandela and the others; they went home for the first time since their arrest five months earlier.

Enriching friendships

Having paid his fine, the white women of the Black Sash took Luthuli to the Anglican St Benedict's retreat house in Johannesburg. The Black Sash saw itself to be a mediator, a peacemaker, an upholder of parliamentary and constitutional democracy and the protection by law of the rights and freedoms of all. It stood for justice in a society which was rapidly becoming brutalised. For Joyce Harris of the Transvaal chapter, the Black Sash supported non-violent direct action. However, a debate was growing in the organisation on whether protest actions by the oppressed majority, even if technically unlawful, should be characterised as 'lawlessness'. Harris vigorously held onto her belief that lawlessness was to be unconditional, saying that it was absolutely imperative that the values for which the organisation stood remained intact. She believed the liberation struggle implied the use of violent means to overthrow the government. The Black Sash could not be party to this. 'In the liberation struggle, we would soon be lost,' she said.[18]

Canon John Collins (1905–1982), Chairman of Christian Action, a major financial supporter of the Treason Trial Fund, reimbursed the Black Sash for the payment of Luthuli's fine. By the end of the trial, Christian Action raised more than £70 000 to obtain the best possible legal defence and aid for the accused and their dependants. It had been doing so since the days of the Defiance Campaign in 1952 with Bishop Ambrose Reeves as founder in Johannesburg and administered by activists Mary Benson (1919–2000) and Bob Hepple. By 1958, the fund had been reconstituted as the Defence and Aid Fund. In all, more than £500 000 was collected and distributed in defence aid.

Luthuli had a high regard for Ambrose Reeves whom he had come to know well during the Treason Trial. He also greatly admired Michael Scott (1907–1983), Trevor Huddleston and Canon John Collins for their contributions to the Christian church as well as to the African people. He also had a warm regard for American Board medical missioner, Alan Taylor, who was superintendent at McCord Zulu Hospital and had offered Luthuli hospitality on his way home from the Treason Trial to resume his ban in Groutville.

Then there was Mary-Louise Hooper, a wealthy white American Quaker widow, who immigrated to South Africa in 1955, bought a home near Durban and worked for two years as Luthuli's secretary and personal assistant.[19] Hooper even donated an Austin car to Luthuli. She became attached to the Luthuli family, and for a year she lived in an outhouse at Ebrahim (E.V.) Mahomed (1916–1981) family's home in nearby Stanger. While there she befriended many other ANC leaders. Hooper boasted an impressive résumé with the ANC. Some sources refer to her as the first white member of the ANC. However, the ANC allowed only black members at the time and, as membership was voluntary rather than elected, it's likely that Hooper's membership status was more honorary than formal. Nevertheless, she was appointed to represent the ANC at three All-African People's conferences in Accra (1958), Tunis (1960) and Cairo (1961).

In 1957, the government arrested Hooper, then imprisoned and deported her from South Africa. She sued the state for unlawful detention and eventually, on a technicality, won and was awarded a sizeable £1 700 in compensation. This sum she donated to a very appreciative ANC.

After returning to the United States in 1958, Hooper served the American Committee on Africa (ACOA), an organisation founded by pacifists to create social change. As a volunteer, she worked full-time as the West Coast Representative of ACOA's Africa Defence and Aid Fund. Her largesse helped to finance not only the ANC, but the Luthuli family for discretionary or emergency purposes. Later, when Luthuli received the Nobel Peace Prize, he personally invited Hooper to join his staff in Oslo, Norway. His close association with Hooper is another link with non-violent allies that he could not disappoint.

All of these friendships and associations Luthuli acknowledged in *Let My People Go*. 'If friendships make a man rich, then I am rich indeed,' he said.[20] Press reports of the day abounded with references to his rubbing shoulders with eminent and liberal, white supporters. But his reputation in other sectors of the liberation movement was deteriorating. Upon being convicted in the pass-burning matter, he chose *not* to read to the court his carefully prepared statement in which he concluded that he believed firmly in the 'duty of all right-thinking people, black and white, who have the true interest of our country at heart, to strive for [the abolition of the pass] without flinching'.[21] He declined to make the statement on the advice of his lawyers and due to concerns for his health, a move that was likely interpreted by many in the ANC as a manifestation of failing resolve. Had he gone soft since the days of his dismissal from his government-conferred chieftaincy when he had issued the powerful 'Road to Freedom' statement? Was he compromised by his fair-skinned ecclesiastical and other liberal supporters?

South African exceptionalism

A doctrine of exceptionalism was all that was holding the ANC back from completing the shift to adopting arms in the struggle for freedom in South Africa. This doctrine drew attention away from the commonality of pan-African historical experience. It argued that both sides of the South African conflict were physically entrenched or permanent. Armed conflict between them would be catastrophic.

Independent African countries had difficulty with the doctrine of exceptionalism. The PAC particularly repudiated it and rushed to fill the 'solidarity niche' in Africa, leaving the ANC isolated. In early 1962, Mandela embarked upon a whirlwind tour of independent African states, hoping to drum up support for the ANC and in so doing thwart the PAC's diplomatic monopoly maintained by its anti-ANC propaganda.

In Ethiopia, Mandela received only eight weeks of military training to qualify him as a commanding officer. During this trip, he felt the ANC's need for pan-African assistance – African support could not be surrendered to the new PAC upstart. He returned to Natal. To Luthuli and the ANC, Mandela proposed a more Africanist stance within the ANC (although in London when trying to convince Yusuf Dadoo, by his own admission, he qualified the proposed change as one of image and not policy). Luthuli brushed the proposal aside, saying that the ANC had chartered a given course for many decades. Africanist leaders around the continent who dismissed the doctrine of exceptionalism were not going to be allowed to dictate ANC policy.

Initially, too, Tambo subscribed to the idea, but over time he aligned his thinking more with pan-African ideology; he had to. Tambo had been sent to establish the ANC-in-exile, preferably in Africa and in the bordering states (later known as the Frontline States). In an interview (2001), Joe Matthews claimed that Tambo was upset by and opposed to the decision to embark upon the use of violence, and even questioned the decision with the leadership in South Africa.[22] Historian Luli Callinicos made the opposite finding: 'Tambo was well aware of the discussions going on inside South Africa and was neither disturbed nor surprised by the turn of events.'[23] Callinicos does not mention Tambo's profound reservations over the ANC's turn to violence. She does, however, concede that Tambo needed Mandela's visit to him in Tanzania to persuade him that the armed struggle made sense in the light of the ANC's banning in South Africa and its isolation in Africa due to the rising popularity of the PAC. Tambo acquiesced. He had converted to an Africanist worldview as a result of his exile. Back in South Africa, on the other hand, Luthuli held fast to a South African exceptionalist understanding. There would be no violence in the struggle to achieve South Africa's liberation if he could help it.[24]

Anton Lembede, a forebear to the Black Consciousness Movement, which Steve Biko later founded and promoted, had influenced the ideology of the Africanist in maintaining that a multiracial approach, such as that adopted by the ANC, only confused the masses and defused their latent nationalist sentiments. Multiracial alliances were perhaps appropriate for the educated and elite blacks, but the masses, having little if any racial esteem for themselves, would never erupt and revolt in the manner that the PAC envisioned if, in their perception, their black leadership was dependent upon white and Indian guidance and trusteeship. Co-operation with other races, constitutional strategies, incremental and compromising goals and a constant harping on non-violent strategies not only lacked sufficient emotional appeal to stir the masses, but anesthetised them, lulled them into a stupor and made them ripe for white supremacists' abuses.

Luthuli's close associations with white Christian liberals did not compromise his political decisions; they did, however, make it exceedingly difficult, if not impossible, to retreat from his political principles. They did not impose on him an indebtedness or obligation. Rather, his personal views concerning the use of violence deeply resonated with the views of his political and spiritual benefactors.

When an opportunity arose to pressure Luthuli into bowing to white, liberal, Christian political concerns in return for political solidarity, funds or friendship, Luthuli firmly declined. For example, in a lengthy letter to Mary-Louise Hooper, Luthuli demonstrated that he would remain steadfast to his convictions. In previous letters, before the Treason Trial, Hooper had suggested to Luthuli that the ANC consider disposing of its attorneys that harboured left-wing or communist sympathies. Hooper suggested that funds for defence lawyers could be better procured if those lawyers were not communists. Not wishing to jeopardise his relationship with Hooper or the funds she raised and donated, Luthuli considered the matter very seriously and laboriously explained the non-viability of changing defence attorneys. He discussed Hooper's proposal confidentially with Yengwa and Lesotho-born, Arthur Letele. All three arrived at an understanding that Luthuli articulated to Hooper. Luthuli carefully explained to her that he 'could bring [his] opinion and weight to bear on the consideration of any new attorneys or advocates if a need arose but the decision would be a majority decision of the Executive or the Working Committee'. He made it clear that a change must be made for 'good reason' and that he knew of no valid reason to create a crisis in either body. In the same letter, Luthuli intimated that since the Defiance Campaign, the ANC had utilised the services of the best attorneys, regardless of their political leanings. He argued that 'only professional ability and sympathy with the cause should be our *criterion*' (original emphasis). In a rare confession, he wrote, 'I do not like communists.' However, 'it would look strange that we work with [the] Congress of Democrats that is predominantly – not wholly – leftist and make an issue of leftism when it comes to a purely professional matter where such consideration should come least'. He argued further that not all their lawyers were communist. Many were liberals, and the legal society in South Africa did not discriminate against leftist or ex-communist members of the bar. Finally, Luthuli explained to Hooper that it was crucial to hire lawyers sympathetic to the cause with a sound political background in the struggle. He hoped Hooper did not make attorneys' political views a condition for the donation of funds. Luthuli closed frankly:

> I hope you are not feeling so strongly on this matter as to make it a condition of your giving us the money you are raising. I would inform you as a friend that I would not refer this matter to colleagues in the Executive until I know what your attitude is after this lengthy explanation. If you should have strings tied to the donation, I am afraid – but in all honesty I must tell you – that the ANC would regretfully decline it. God knows that we appreciate your services very much and we need every penny of the money you may raise but it must not be under conditions that humiliate us and do harm to our panel of defence lawyers in order to qualify for donation from our rightist friends. My policy is that we must make friends from both the West and the East and take from each what is good for us so long as we are not called upon to violate the principles on which we are prosecuting our Freedom Struggle.[25]

An eventful year draws to an end
On 31 August 1960, the government lifted the State of Emergency. September to December proved less climactic after the electrifying events

of March. In September, the ANC's NEC met and resolved to continue
the struggle underground. The government's more repressive laws rendered
the ANC's highly democratic constitution and president general inoperable.
In his autobiography, Nelson Mandela explained that the ANC as a whole
had to be streamlined.[26] Conferences, branch meetings and public
gatherings could no longer be held. The NEC dissolved subordinate entities
such as the Youth League and the Women's League despite their resistance
and even disobedience. The political context forced the ANC to operate
illegally and thus clandestinely. It was agreed that Mandela would operate
full-time underground and activate the M-Plan (Mandela Plan), formulated
in the early 1950s in anticipation of just such circumstances. The plan
depended upon cells of ten households and zones of cells that would
report to local branches. With this organisational structuring, decisions
made by the leadership could be efficiently directed to the constituency.

In October 1960, Z.K. Matthews, the final defence witness, began his
testimony in the Treason Trial. In the same month white South Africans
voted in a referendum to become a republic. In November, the government
declared a State of Emergency in eastern Pondoland and other areas of
the Transkei following an uprising of peasants, later known as the
Pondoland Revolt. The repressive measures in Pondoland were the last
events that Luthuli commented upon in the epilogue of his autobiography.
One can safely conclude that early in 1961, Luthuli completed the dictation
of his autobiography to his amanuenses, Charles and Sheila Hooper.[27]
Luthuli valued his association with the Hoopers. Unrelated to Mary-Louise
Hooper, they added to an already very long list of white, liberal and
ecclesiastical friends. Painstakingly capturing Luthuli's autobiography, the
Hoopers were keenly aware that they were in the presence of a great man.
In his introduction to the 1962 edition of Let My People Go, Charles
Hooper described Albert Luthuli thus:

> His character, his temperament, his qualities and his stature reveal
> themselves discursively, and only as they unfold does one begin to grasp
> the striking wholeness of the man, his coherence and his integrity. A
> mind is at work; but never academically, never without imagination.
> Imagination is at work; but never without restraint and discipline, never
> engaged in fantasy, and never at the expense of truth. Restraint and
> discipline are there; but they issue neither in inflexibility nor in untoward
> austerity.[28]

Also in November 1960, the press began to carry reports on Albert Luthuli's nomination for the Nobel Peace Prize. A wellspring of support from around the world advocated that the prize be bestowed upon him for his staunch non-violent stance against a very violent antagonist. Andrew McCracken of Bronxville, New York, editor of *Advance* magazine, a Congregational publication, was just one of the persons who nominated him. The two men had met in 1948 when Luthuli had lectured in the United States. Particular credit for the nomination, however, should be given to the Swedish Lutheran, Gunnar Helander. Helander, a former South African missioner and later vicar of the Karlskoga parish in Sweden, spoke on the radio, wrote speeches, submitted articles and strongly proposed Luthuli's candidacy to his parliament. He said he had always admired Luthuli for his unswerving position: 'Violence under no circumstances.'[29]

Luthuli had come to know Helander as a friend while serving the Natal Missionary Conference and the Durban Joint Council of Europeans and Africans. Helander served as a missioner in South Africa from 1938 until 1956 during which time he denounced the apartheid system in word and deed. In 1956, he returned to Sweden on furlough and wrote against apartheid in both the Swedish and South African press.[30] In 1957, the South African government denied him a visa to re-enter South Africa. However, he continued to labour in the cause and, through his leadership on the Fund for the Victims of Racial Oppression, Sweden contributed the largest amount of funds to the International Defence and Aid Fund. Like Mary-Louise Hooper, Helander also accompanied Luthuli to Norway.

On his return to Groutville from the Treason Trial, Luthuli set about sending invitations out to various prominent African leaders to attend the Interdenominational African Ministers' Conference to be held on 16–17 December 1960 in Orlando. Those church activists not banned gathered to assess the way forward. Though he was a convenor of the event, Luthuli's banning order did not allow him to be present. Before the police raided the conference and confiscated all documents, it expressed a need for unity among the liberation movements and the need for effective use of non-violent pressures against apartheid. The gathering resolved to sponsor an All-In African Conference scheduled for March 1961 in Pietermaritzburg.

The two meetings proved to be the last dying kicks of the liberation movement's official policy of non-violence. Luthuli feared at this time

that the non-violent character of the resistance movement would expire
altogether. On 13 December 1960, he wrote to Quinton Whyte of the
South African Institute of Race Relations (SAIRR) and three hundred
other prominent whites throughout South Africa, advocating that pressure
be brought to bear on the government to legalise the ANC. He warned
that in a political vacuum, 'anything may take its place: uncontrolled and
undisciplined movements may be formed and terrorism may arise.'[31]

Walter Sisulu, Duma Nokwe and Nelson Mandela, who had provided
crisis leadership during the State of Emergency earlier that year, were
poised in early 1961 to take the ANC decisively into new terrain. Following
a strike in May 1961, they judged that the 'movement's traditional weapons
of protest . . . were no longer appropriate'.[32] Night and day they evaluated
conditions to determine if these were favourable for the launch of an
armed struggle. Elaine Reinertsen, who wrote a scholarly assessment of
MK in 1985, summarised the state of the ANC at the end of 1960, and the
events that led to a quiet coup against Luthuli as follows:

> It is more than likely that the ANC, devastated by police repression,
> the Treason Trial and the State of Emergency, exhausted by extensive
> mass campaigning in the 1950s and taken off guard by its banning in
> 1960, was on the point of collapse. The 'Old Guard' could put up little
> resistance when the initiative was seized by the militant wing of the
> National Executive. The Continuation Committee was dominated by
> youth leaguers and communists; with Luthuli at Groutville, the way
> was open for the implementation of a new revolutionary ideology.[33]

4

The Tempo Quickens
1961

[I]t should be borne in mind that even people involved in the same event remember the details differently, and amnesia is no friend of accuracy.

— Ahmed Kathrada, *Memoirs*

PROSPECTS FOR THE continued use of non-violence in the liberation struggle were steadily dimming in 1961. United Nations general secretary, Dag Hammarskjöld, visited South Africa without calling on Albert Luthuli who was still ANC president general and confined by a banning order to his home in Groutville. The prime minister, Hendrik Verwoerd, announced his intention to withdraw South Africa's application to join the Commonwealth on 15 March and state repression effectively balkanised the liberation movement.

The Treason Trial still loomed. On 23 March, Judge Frans Rumpff interrupted the defence's fourth week of its final argument, led by Bram Fischer (1908–1975), and adjourned. Because Mandela's ban expired on 25 March, he anticipated attending and speaking at the All-In African Conference in Pietermaritzburg during the court recess. Before he departed for Natal, the ANC National Working Committee (NWC) met secretly, presumably in the Transvaal, to discuss strategy. Luthuli could not possibly have been present at this meeting, having long since returned to his home in Groutville following his Treason Trial testimony and after being found guilty and released for burning his passbook.

All-In African Conference
The All-In African Conference, which took place on 24 and 25 March 1961, hosted some fourteen hundred delegates from as many as a hundred

and forty-five organisations, most of which, following the government's culling measures and many of the participants' own boycott of the conference, represented but peripheral and dispersive forces in the liberation struggle.[1] Nonetheless, the conference proved to be the last mass movement gathering organised by a collection of prominent liberation struggle leaders for many decades.

In his book, *Mandela: A Critical Life* (2006), Tom Lodge appropriately entitled his chapter on this period, 'The Making of a Messiah'. With a surprise entrance, an inspiring physical presence, an impassioned keynote address and a stealthy departure, Nelson Mandela sensationalised the conference. Those gathered perceived him as the dynamic new and more militant leader of the liberation struggle. Though participants sang at least one song about the president general, 'Spread the Gospel of Luthuli', one media representative, Benjamin Pogrund, reported that Mandela was the 'star of the show'.[2] Elaine Reinertsen discerned, as others did, that real leadership had passed to Mandela by 1961, although Chief Luthuli remained president general until his death. For some, like Jordan Kush Ngubane (1917–1985), the conference deliberately sidelined Luthuli in favour of Mandela.[3]

The conference resolved to issue an ultimatum to the government through a National Action Council led by Mandela, calling for a national convention of multiracial representatives to determine a new democratic constitution. The conference required the government's response by 31 May, the day South Africa was to be declared a republic. Not expecting the demand to be met, the conference also resolved to stage countrywide demonstrations on the eve of the proclamation of the republic.

Following the conference, Mandela left Pietermaritzburg for Groutville where he reported to Luthuli. He then travelled back to Pretoria for the verdict in the Treason Trial. On 29 March, Judge Frans Rumpff, representing a panel of three judges, announced a unanimous ruling: not guilty. After more than four years in court, the authorities discharged the defendants. The ANC's consistent and passionate teaching and implementation of non-violent strategies had determined the essential basis of the defence's innocence. Luthuli described the verdict as 'a timely upholding of the rule of law in our country'. He added that the ruling gave the lie to 'insistent and malicious propaganda that has presented us as Communists, insurgents and what not, intent on overthrowing the Government by violence when all we wanted was our inherent right to participate fully in governing the country'.[4] In his foreword to *If This Be*

Treason (1963), Helen Joseph's book on the Treason Trial, Luthuli said that the trial had

> been an inestimable blessing because it forged together diverse men of goodwill of all races who rallied to the support of the Treason Trial Fund and to keep up the morale of the accused. What would have been the plight of the accused without our Bishop Reeves, Alan Paton, Dr Hellman, Canon Collins, Bob Hepple, Christian Action, Archbishop de Blank and Archbishop Hurley and all the other loyal men and women [without] whose help and cooperation, chaos would have prevailed in our ranks? We shudder to think even of the prospect of how we would have fared if they had not come forward. In all humility I can say that if there is one thing which helped push our movement along non-racial lines, away from narrow, separative racialism, it is the Treason Trial, which showed the depth of the sincerity and devotion to a noble cause on the white side of the colour line . . .[5]

Since Sharpeville and the State of Emergency, Mandela and Luthuli looked in divergent directions in response to the noose that had been placed around domestic politics. Sympathetic to pan-Africanist sentiments, Mandela discerned that liberation would more likely spring from African nationalist forces represented by organisations such as the Pan-African Freedom Movement of East, Central and Southern Africa (PAFMECSA), the precursor to the Organisation of African Unity (OAU), that had so deeply influenced the PAC at home.[6] Sympathetic to liberal sentiments, Luthuli adhered more to the exceptionalist doctrine that did not exclude like-minded Christian whites from playing a substantive, if not pivotal, part in bringing about liberation. These divergent positions were not necessarily determined by either leader's personal sentiments towards whites. It was a question of tactics, of strategy, of strengths and weaknesses. Mandela was not anti-white and Luthuli was no stooge of white liberals.

In exile, Oliver Tambo formed the South Africa United Front (UF) in 1960 as a coalition of liberation movements that would co-operate to fight the apartheid regime. The UF was described as a way to deal with a

> crisis so overwhelming in character as to demand of those of us abroad the joining of our forces in a united front with a view to seeking the sympathy and support of the peoples and Governments of the world for our struggle, to bring international economic and political pressure

on the South African Government and in general to secure its expulsion
from the world community of nations.[7]

The UF eventually included the PAC, the ANC, the South West Africa
People's Organisation (SWAPO), the SAIC represented by Yusuf Dadoo,
the only non-black organisation, and the South West African National
Union (SWANU), then an up-and-coming movement in South West Africa.
At the All-In Conference Mandela promoted the UF, declaring that future
militant campaigns, which did not include violence, would be aided by
external pressures.

The front was short-lived. The PAC proved to be a difficult ally and a
year later the UF collapsed through what the ANC called the PAC's divisive
actions, particularly during the 1961 strike, and its attempts 'to foist their
organisation's policies on the front itself'.[8] In 1962, Luthuli re-
conceptualised the UF as a multiracial coalition of individual leaders,
many of whom were Christian, white and liberal – and most importantly
– opposed to violence.[9]

Mandela was becoming more critical of domestic, liberal and Christian
calls for moderation and thus non-violence. Liberals and white newspaper
editors often criticised the stay-at-home campaign proposed to coincide
with the celebration of Republic Day and the expected failure of the
government to initiate a national convention. In a March 1961 article
entitled 'The Struggle for a National Convention', Mandela wrote that
the ANC had been 'astonished by the reaction of certain political parties
and "philanthropic" associations which proclaimed themselves to be anti-
apartheid but which, nevertheless, consistently opposed positive action
taken by the oppressed people to defeat this same policy'. Ultimately, this
would only perpetuate white domination and the National Party. He added,
'It also serves to weaken the impact of liberal views amongst European
democrats and lays them open to the charge of being hypocritical.' In
exasperation, Mandela appealed to Sir de Villiers Graaff to declare the
United Party's (UP) stand on a national convention. 'Talk it out, or shoot
it out!' he said bluntly in a letter of 23 May 1961 to the UP leader.[10]

Christopher Gell Memorial Award
In May 1961, the committee of the Christopher Gell Memorial Award for
the Outstanding Contribution to Social Justice in South Africa in 1960
announced that Albert Luthuli would receive the award for his ongoing

and prophetic stand on non-violence in the struggle for justice in South Africa. Christopher W.M. Gell (1917–1958) was an impassioned and eloquent British journalist whose reporting and analysis of the injustices of apartheid were published widely during the last years of his life when, based in Port Elizabeth, he worked energetically while battling enormous odds with his health. Gell had died in 1958. In his memory, the award was created and overseen by a committee comprising liberal whites sympathetic to the goals of the liberation movement. Among them were Norah, Gell's South African-born widow; Bishop Trevor Huddleston; the Archbishop of Cape Town, Joost de Blank; journalist and *Drum* editor, Anthony Sampson (1926–2004); Rabbi Andre Ungar of the Port Elizabeth Progressive Jewish Congregation; Patrick Duncan (1918–1967), a journalist and member of the Liberal Party; and Professor Leo Kuper (1908–1994), an academic and a member of the Liberal Party.

The award was an affirmation of Luthuli's non-violent stance, as was the Nobel Peace Prize, announced later. Between each award's announcement in 1961, the joint congresses met in July where the decision to form MK was made. The Gell announcement prior to, and the Nobel announcement shortly after, the momentous July joint congresses meeting must have weighed on Luthuli's conscience. Both awards affirmed his constant and unswerving stand on non-violence; the decision of the joint congresses meeting asked him to set it aside.

Luthuli applied to the Commissioner of Police for permission to attend the Gell award ceremony in Port Elizabeth, scheduled for 31 May 1961. On 16 May the Minister of Justice, F.C. Erasmus, denied Luthuli's request for permission to travel. The award ceremony had to be postponed.

Only on 22 October, a day before the Nobel committee announced his Peace Prize, did Luthuli receive, *in absentia*, the Christopher Gell award. The publication, *Forum*, printed a copy of his acceptance speech in November 1961, delivered by M.B. Yengwa on his behalf. In it, Luthuli reminded his audience that the government had demonstrated that it was 'arming itself to the teeth against an unarmed people who throughout their struggle have indicated by word and action their desire for a peaceful accommodation of their aspirations by those presently in power'. Neither Sharpeville nor the May strike of 1961 should give cause to be disillusioned, he said. Rather, these events demonstrated that the use of physical force by the authorities was 'a product of fear and not courage'.[11]

May strike

From his base in Johannesburg, Nelson Mandela took command of the proposed 29–31 May 1961 strike, which was scheduled to coincide with the proclamation of the republic. It is a wonder that any success at all could be claimed in the strike, or stay-at-home, given the growing divisions between the PAC and the ANC, the inhibited capacity of the ANC to organise the masses and the profound lengths the state took to counter any form of non-violent protest. The government implemented un-precedented measures, collectively amounting to a preparation for war, to stifle the mass strike action. It prepared itself to use the threat of overwhelming force to quell the protest. Yet, another demonstration of brutal force had the capability to tip the balance of power towards the oppressed masses clamouring for democracy, as it did when the government, albeit briefly, suspended the pass laws after Sharpeville.

After Sharpeville, the United States, the Commonwealth, the United Nations (by a vote of ninety-five to one) and numerous other countries in Asia and Africa unequivocally denounced the apartheid government – all before the Nobel committee announced Luthuli's award of the 1960 Peace Prize. As long as the ANC remained non-violent, South Africa would rapidly become an international pariah. Neither the state nor the liberation movement appeared to consider that another Sharpeville then might very well have spelled the beginning of the end of the apartheid regime. Another Sharpeville would cause the international community to see clearly that the forces of democracy possessed the moral high ground, the *only* moral ground. International solidarity with the oppressed majority would have moved quickly from denunciatory declarations to concrete measures to ostracise South Africa.

On Day One of the strike, 29 May 1961, Mandela told the press that the people's response to the call to stay-at-home was 'magnificent', an unprecedented defiance of state intimidation. Inexplicably and incredibly, however, he called off the campaign on Day Two, 30 May 1961, feeling demoralised and angry with the manner in which some members of the press handled the protest. According to Govan Mbeki (1910–2001), when the reversal came, protesters in Sophiatown were incensed by the decision to call off the campaign and 'descend[ed] on the Executive'.[12] In a statement published by the ANC underground office on 3 June 1961, Mandela claimed that the press and employers throughout the country had played 'a thoroughly shameful role'. He added:

At seven o'clock in the morning of that day, Radio South Africa broadcast news that workers throughout the country had ignored the call for a stay-at-home. The country was told that this news was based on statements made at six o'clock the same morning by Colonel Spengler, head of the Witwatersrand branch of the Special Branch. Similar statements made at approximately the same time by other police officers in different parts of the country were quoted. This means that long before the factory gates were opened and, in some areas, even before the workers boarded their trains and buses to work, the police had already announced that the stay-at-home had collapsed. I cannot imagine anything more fraudulent.[13]

Therefore, if anything, Mandela's call to abandon the strike was premature. Stay-at-homes and strikes required time to gather momentum and careful incremental actions had always been used in the ANC's tradition of protest. Only when public violence had erupted and/or when substantive momentum halted after a prolonged period, such as in the waning months of the Defiance Campaign, did ANC leaders extinguish earlier campaigns. Mandela should not have been disappointed. The stay-at-home had successfully eclipsed the recognition and celebration of Republic Day. The Associated Press reported that ninety per cent of buses in Johannesburg were empty at 9h00 on Monday, 29 May.[14] The *Golden City Post* reported that many thousands of workers registered their protests by staying away from work for three days and forced many businesses to shut down for the period.[15] The overseas press reported that half the city's labour force had stayed away from work. The police later admitted to sixty per cent absenteeism in the Johannesburg area.[16] *New Age* claimed that it was the biggest national strike on a political issue ever staged in South African history.[17]

Events in the Eastern Cape lend credence also to the notion that the May strike was growing in momentum. The protest only began to take effect by the time Mandela called it off as Port Elizabeth experienced a seventy-five per cent absentee rate. In some areas of the Eastern Cape the movement defied the NEC and, for the first time, used petrol bombs to force buses to return to their depots, preventing the transport of workers to their places of employment.

Govan Mbeki recalled being dumbfounded, taking it for granted, not 'seriously', as did Mandela, that the press would issue reports intentionally to dampen the spirit of protest. In his post-strike analysis which appeared in the publication, *Africa South-in-Exile*, Mandela concedes his naivety, saying that '[o]nly after those first tense strike days had passed were more balanced assessments made of the extent of the strike' and that 'the people themselves learnt that they could not trust any verdict on their struggle but their own'. Support was growing stronger every day, he admitted, and 'the demand for a national convention roared and crashed across the country'. The strike was just 'one fighting episode'.[18]

In his autobiography, Mandela recalls speaking to the press on the day he called off the strike, and making a statement for which he was later reprimanded by the NEC.

> That morning in a safe flat in a white suburb I met various members of the local and foreign press, and I once again called the stay at home 'a tremendous success'. But I did not mask the fact that I believed a new day was dawning. I said, 'If the government reaction is to crush by naked force our non-violent struggle, we will have to reconsider our tactics. In my mind we are closing a chapter on this question of a non-violent policy.' It was a grave declaration, and I knew it.[19]

Notwithstanding Mandela's anger and disillusionment at the time of the strike, there was a substantive (if not, as Mandela himself characterised it, 'magnificent') response to the protest; the protest gained momentum and the government committed no horrific acts of violence. If Mandela pronounced the stay-at-home as a success long after the event, his calling-off of the campaign can be considered a tactical blunder. If he determined that the strike infused confidence into the masses of the people, then the justification for the liberation movement to resort to violence (based on an abandoned failed strike) is highly questionable. If the stay-at-home, a supreme form of passive resistance, did not succeed, it was not sufficiently utilised, organised and/or maintained to enable its success. This was the view of Luthuli and other detractors of the move to adopt an armed struggle.

Yet, Mandela and ANC nationalist history narratives universally point to the failure of the May strike to prove that non-violent mass action was ineffective. In their view, therein lay the justification for the turn to violent means. Years later, in a statement to the Truth and Reconciliation Commission in 1996, the ANC claimed that this 'use of police and army troops in May 1961 to defeat the planned national stay-away' justified the movement's turn to violence. However, according to Mandela's own assessment, the May strike in 1961 was prematurely called off despite its partial success. In the event, while the state was poised to use overwhelming force to quell the disturbances, it did nothing of the kind. The strike's success or failure did not constitute the inefficacy of non-violent protest as Mandela and the ANC asserted. And this was a point Albert Luthuli himself made at the time.

In her book, *Chief Albert Lutuli of South Africa* (1963), Mary Benson wrote extensively on Luthuli's thoughts pertaining to non-violence. Written after Luthuli's reception of the Peace Prize, Benson's text conveyed Luthuli's sentiments on violence *after* the May 1961 strike:

> [T]here is no softness in the policy of non-violence; as he has said, it is militant, and he feels, despite government's crushing of non-violent demonstrations such as the three-day stay-at-home in May 1961 that 'the non-violent method, even if unclothing it of any moral consideration – is the most effective and practical in our situation'. He has pointed out that it has never been sufficiently well-organised to prove its efficacy.[20]

The calling-off of the May strike concluded an era of non-violent mass action and ushered in the beginning of a new violent one. In her study on the ANC's turn to violence, Elaine Reinertsen commented that the decision to adopt the armed struggle 'circumvented Luthuli's liberalism', and that 'in all his public utterances after 1961, Luthuli seems to have remained ambivalent toward the existence of Umkhonto'.[21]

The allowance of Umkhonto we Sizwe's formation

Nelson Mandela's autobiography, *Long Walk to Freedom*, stands as a pivot between two divergent understandings of Luthuli's involvement to support the formation and/or launch of MK. Two very different historical memories are evident in texts that pre-date Mandela's autobiography (1995) and texts that post-date it. Texts written prior to Mandela's account cast much doubt about Luthuli's awareness of the decisions and/or whether he supported the decisions to resort to violence. Brian Bunting's *Moses Kotane* (1975), Mary Benson's *Chief Albert Lutuli* (1963) and Joe Slovo's *Unfinished Autobiography* (1995) assert that not only did Luthuli oppose the decision, but he was not privy to its making due to his presumed opposition to it.

Brian Bunting suggests that Luthuli did not even attend the ANC executive meeting or the Congresses' Joint Executives (CJE) meeting that decided to form MK in July 1961.

Lutuli was not involved in the discussions which led to the formation of Umkhonto. For one thing, he was living under restriction at Groutville and able to keep in touch with the ANC leadership in the Transvaal only intermittently. For another, during the crucial months of 1961 when the decision to set up Umkhonto was being formulated, Lutuli was preoccupied with arrangements in connection with his visit to Oslo to receive his Nobel award. A third factor was simply the reluctance of the ANC leadership to engage in a discussion which might result in a Presidential veto before it was necessary.[22]

All three explanations given by Bunting for Luthuli's ignorance of the decision to form MK are very problematic. First, the July 1961 meeting in which the ANC and the alliance of the congresses decided to form MK occurred near Groutville, in Stanger, so Luthuli's restriction in the Lower Tugela region did not, in practice, prohibit the clandestine meetings in which many of the ANC's Transvaal-based leadership also participated. Second, the announcement that Luthuli won the 1960 Nobel Peace Prize did not occur until October 1961. For this reason, Luthuli's preoccupation with arrangements to travel to Norway did not prohibit his presence at or knowledge of the July meetings. Third, given the democratic ethos of the ANC, a presidential veto did not exist. Mandela and others expected opposition from Luthuli who possessed great influence, but he had no veto power over a democratic decision. Only by reason and moral authority could Luthuli persuade the ANC and the congresses not to form MK. Therefore, concerning Luthuli's participation in the decision to form MK, Kotane's testimony through Bunting is inaccurate.

Joe Slovo also contended that Luthuli did not know of the decision to form MK. Slovo wrote in his autobiography:

> Indeed, that grand old man of the ANC, Chief Albert Luthuli, whose presidential leadership had made immeasurable contribution to the radical struggle of the 1950s, was not a party to the decision, nor was he ever to endorse it. It was a measure of his greatness that despite his deep Christian conviction to non-violence, he never forbade or condemned the new path, blaming it on the regime's intransigence rather than on those who created MK.[23]

In her 1986 biography of Mandela, Mary Benson provided no detail as to how the ANC and the congresses decided to form MK. Hence, Benson did not deal with the matter of Luthuli's participation in the decision to form MK. Nevertheless, informed by M.B. Yengwa, Benson implied that Luthuli was unaware of the policy decision to form, and the tactical decision to launch, MK.

> Lutuli raised the question which had long troubled him: Umkhonto's announcement in December 1961 that the policy of non-violence had ended. Aware of Mandela's role, Lutuli criticised the failure to consult [him] and the ANC 'grassroots'. He felt they had been compromised. Although apologetic, Mandela said he thought that, tactically, the action had been correct. Besides, they had wanted to protect Lutuli and the ANC from involvement in the drastic change in policy.[24]

However, Yengwa's unpublished autobiographical manuscript (1976) claimed otherwise.

> Chief Luthuli was still under a banning order and as a result a full [National Executive] Committee was called at Chief Luthuli's magisterial district in secret so that he could attend. This was after everyone in the [Treason Trial] had been discharged. There was a very long heart searching debate, because the ANC's policy of non-violence had been tried since 1952 and after years of action through strikes and other methods they had only [been] met with violence. Some of us were still sceptical about the use of violence, including Chief Luthuli, on the grounds that the people had still to be consulted and we would not be seen to be democratic in changing without consultation from one policy to another. But we had to accept the logic.[25]

Hence, Benson's understanding of Luthuli's ignorance was also not accurate.

A resolute proponent of Luthuli's unwavering support for non-violence was Chief Mangosuthu Buthelezi, president of the Inkatha Freedom Party (IFP) and former chief minister of KwaZulu. Buthelezi is not the only political figure to have used Luthuli's name and prestige to buttress his power and influence, though he perhaps has the longest and most extensive record of such a practice. Several of his statements about Luthuli are on record in speeches made over the years. In 1974, for example, Buthelezi delivered a speech in honour of Luthuli who was given the OAU Merit

Award posthumously. In his speech, Buthelezi made it clear that he viewed Luthuli as his mentor. Buthelezi thus staked a claim to be Luthuli's protégé. To justify his own declared non-violent opposition to apartheid, Buthelezi asserted that Luthuli's 'guiding light was to achieve his ideals through non-violent methods'.[26] Buthelezi accepted the South African exceptionalist paradigm that deemed appropriate, due to South Africa's unique context, only non-violent strategies for overcoming colonialism and white supremacy. In contrast to the 'illegal' ANC, Inkatha could legally pursue a 'composite strategy' involving a number of 'non-violent methods in the struggle that goes on for human rights in South Africa'.[27] Buthelezi conceded that many considered Luthuli's non-violent methods to be naive and his approach to work non-violently to be obsolete. He claimed that methods of violence would compel whites into a laager invoking a backlash that would 'only retard the struggle or complicate it' and that 'Chief Luthuli's non-violence' is the 'only way in which we can contribute toward the avoidance of some catastrophe'.[28] Buthelezi harangued the ANC leadership for breaking away from Luthuli's non-violent stance and for pursuing an unrealistic and almost suicidal violent strategy. He often implied that the mantle of political leadership passed from Luthuli to him.[29]

On the other hand, those texts written after Mandela's book provide accounts that affirm Luthuli's awareness of and support for the decisions to form MK (Ismail Meer's A Fortunate Man [2002], Ahmed Kathrada's Memoirs [2004], Elinor Sisulu's Walter and Albertina Sisulu [2002], Luli Callinicos's Oliver Tambo [2004] and Anthony Sampson's Mandela: The Authorised Biography [1999]). These latter texts cite Long Walk to Freedom extensively and/or can be cross-referenced with it in a way which identifies it as their original source. Most, if not all, other sources accept, comply with or otherwise cite Mandela's recollections. For example, while, in A Fortunate Man, Ismail Meer does not cite Mandela's autobiography, Mandela wrote the foreword. Thus, it is logical to surmise that Meer's version would corroborate Mandela's.[30] And it does. Likewise, Anthony Sampson's book on Mandela would be unlikely to deviate from Mandela's autobiography, thus attaining its 'authorised' status. And it does not. In Long Walk to Freedom Mandela provided the textual gauntlet through which most post-1995 biographers and memoirists funnel their accounts of the ANC's decision to form MK. In Mandela's autobiography one finds an original source, the nationalists' historiographic 'Adam'.[31] To understand the dynamics at work when an emerging nation 'creates' its history, secondary sources must be analysed, interpreted and then compared with primary source evidence. An evaluation of secondary sources must recognise the profound impact that an icon such as Mandela and his corresponding recollection of events has on the formation of South African history. Any accuracy, or more importantly, inaccuracy, in Mandela's account multiplies exponentially as biographies and autobiographies reference Mandela's version. The weight of evidence in favour of Luthuli's cognisance and support of the launch of MK may be premised only upon Mandela's account from which most others, subsequently, merely reference. Therefore, secondary sources derived primarily from a single source when addressing Luthuli's involvement in and possible support of the ANC's decision to incorporate violent methods in its struggle for liberation must be questioned and their veracity viewed with suspicion.

Luthuli was aware of and did participate in the decision not to discipline those who undertook to *form* MK, as Mandela attested in his autobiography. However, Mandela's autobiography was incorrect in implying that Luthuli was made aware of MK's *launch* in December 1961. Elinor Sisulu's book, *Walter and Albertina Sisulu* (2002), also reported Luthuli's involvement in and knowledge of the decision to form MK. Yet, in agreement with the above texts, Sisulu's text affirmed Luthuli's ignorance of and embarrassment by the timing of MK's launch. She reflects that at a meeting to review the launch of MK, Walter Sisulu had said that Luthuli was 'clearly embarrassed about the timing and unhappy about the apparent recklessness that led to the casualties'.[32]

Three crucial meetings

Following the 'failure' of the May strike, Walter Sisulu and Nelson Mandela discussed the question of an armed struggle and resolved to raise the issue at a June 1961 National Working Committee (NWC) meeting. It was not the first time that the two men had debated the matter. In his autobiography, Mandela disclosed that they had first mentioned the idea as far back as 1952. By June 1961, Mandela was convinced of the need for an armed wing.

He tabled the idea at the June 1961 meeting of the NWC. Moses Kotane argued vociferously against Mandela's proposal, accusing him of not having thought it through carefully. Kotane worried, according to Mandela in *Long Walk to Freedom*, that embarking on this course would expose 'innocent people to massacres by the enemy'. There was still room for the old methods 'if we are imaginative and determined enough'. Kotane wondered if Mandela was resorting to revolutionary talk in desperation after having 'been outmanoeuvred and paralysed by the government's actions' in the May strike. Mandela chided Sisulu, he says, for not coming to his rescue.[33] Elinor Sisulu reports that for her father, Walter, Kotane was a formidable fellow. Sisulu thought it better to retreat quietly, believing the matter would be better handled by Mandela and Kotane, one on one.[34] Mandela tells us that later, in a private all-day meeting, he told Kotane bluntly that his (Kotane's) mind was 'stuck in the old mould of the ANC's being a legal organisation'. On their own, people were forming armed units. They were way ahead of the ANC. 'The only organisation that had the muscle to lead them was the ANC.'[35]

Later, Mandela privately persuaded Kotane, who said he would not contest the motion if it were made at the next NWC meeting to be held a week later. And it was at this meeting, on the second attempt, that Mandela persuaded the NWC to agree that the proposal be brought to the NEC that would meet in Durban in July 1961.

While contemplating the adoption of violence, Nelson Mandela worried that the ANC had just emerged from a four-year trial wherein its consistent and clear non-violent policy had thwarted the prosecution's efforts to have the trialists found guilty of high treason. He confessed in his autobiography that the ANC had contended in the Treason Trial that non-violence was an 'inviolate principle', adding that he personally believed that the tactic should be abandoned when it no longer worked. Mandela had good reason to be concerned about the upcoming NEC meeting. Here he would face Luthuli's 'moral commitment to non-violence', and he expected it to cause difficulties.[36] It did.

Albert Luthuli consistently and unconditionally opposed any move towards violence, before, during and after the decision to form MK. In 2002, the Committee for South African Solidarity co-founder and president, Narainsamy Thumbi (N.T.) Naicker (1922–2003), highlighted a discussion he had with Luthuli regarding his suspicions of a turn to violence. Naicker said:

> He entertained us for a while and then he told us, 'Why don't we get into the car and go away from here?' He drove around into the bamboos behind his residence. He said, 'Since it was getting a little dark and

late, there's no likelihood of the Security Branch (the apartheid political police) getting in here – at least we would know beforehand, if they do.' When we got there he had a flashlight that he turned on and we were able to converse. All he wanted to know was, whether we had any knowledge that there were any steps being taken to move from one aspect of the movement into violence. I said as far as we are concerned we are non-violent and there's no way we will become violent and if the ANC is with us it should be happy. Chief was happy with that it and it seems to cut some measure with his association with organisations that are non-violent. So he was non-violent to the utmost.[37]

The date of this poignant meeting Naicker had with Luthuli is not indicated. However, the context reveals that it took place shortly before the July 1961 NEC meeting.

At the July 1961 NEC meeting, Mandela took an adamant position on the need to resort to violence. Seeking the moral high ground, he argued that the movement had no other alternative: 'It was wrong and immoral to subject our people to armed attacks by the state without offering them some kind of alternative.'[38] Many in the movement felt rudderless. Sporadic attacks, he argued, had already begun to take place, or were imminent, by the African Resistance Movement (ARM), by the PAC's Poqo and in rural uprisings such as those in Pondoland and Tembuland. The ANC's moral and strategic responsibility would be to control and direct that violence that had become inevitable. It was a matter of principle, just as the commitment to non-violence methods had been. Violent campaigns or acts could be directed at symbols of the state, of oppression, rather than against human beings.

Luthuli resisted these arguments. For him, the use of non-violence was not only premised on strategic grounds. Ethical, theological and relational considerations also heavily predisposed him to oppose the use of violence. He also argued that the ANC received its mandate from the grassroots; the ANC could not make such a massive policy alteration (strict non-violence to an armed movement) without the consultation and re-training, ideologically speaking, of the membership. They worked all night to convince Luthuli, and eventually the physical vigour and the rhetorical tenacity of the young lions must have fatigued the older man.

Mandela's autobiography suggested that Luthuli proposed an ambiguous compromise in the NEC meeting. After what must have been for Luthuli a thoroughly exhausting night, he recommended that 'a military movement should be a separate and independent organ, linked to the ANC and under the overall control of the ANC, but fundamentally autonomous'.[39] 'Independent', yet 'linked'? 'Autonomous', yet 'under the overall control'? These contradictions carried into the CJE's meeting held the following evening.

A further indication of Luthuli's objection to the decision to form a military movement was his warning not to neglect 'the essential tasks of organisation and the traditional methods of struggle', as they were primary.[40] There is little, if any, evidence that Mandela heeded this warning following the decisions to form MK. Mandela spent the rest of 1961 constituting an 'army' and testing its munitions. Little time could be spent on political organisation for Mandela had only six months to prepare his army before launching it, unbeknownst to Luthuli, at the close of the year.

Mandela perceived that Luthuli had to accede to the arguments that a military campaign was inevitable. However, Luthuli only agreed that the matter be referred to a more representative body where he would have more allies. Though the NEC formally endorsed the NWC's decision to form an armed movement, Luthuli suggested that the meeting resolve to have never discussed the matter.[41]

Mandela stated that Luthuli requested that meeting 'treat the new resolution as if the ANC had not discussed it' so that the legality of the other congresses in the alliance was not jeopardised. Yet, it was at a *secret* meeting that the *banned* ANC resolved to prepare for *illegal* violence. Therefore, given this context, it is hard to conceive that any decision taken by the ANC could further jeopardise the other member congresses. In addition, not documenting or not announcing the resolution would not protect other groups should they have needed protection. To consider the matter 'not discussed' is a different matter from not having the matter documented or announced. Therefore, as Meer suggested, Luthuli requested that the matter be considered not to have been discussed so that, the following evening, at a meeting of the Congresses' Joint Executive (CJE), he could (re-)open the debate as if it had never happened and invite those in the ANC who were opposed to violence to ally themselves with other members of the congresses who also opposed violence. This would allow those in the ANC with non-violent inclinations to argue in solidarity (and thus strength) with like-minded leaders at the CJE meeting to be held the following night. Luthuli proved to be a very astute and clever chairperson. He clearly did not agree with the decision but his Congregational ethos predisposed him against imposing his will as the chairperson. He was not the sort of leader, as Natal MK Commander, Curnick Ndlovu (1932–2002), put it, 'who believed in dictating'.[42]

Opening the CJE meeting the following evening, Luthuli called for particularly careful consideration of this difficult matter. He had also called for caution before with the ANC's ratification of the Freedom Charter which, too, was a disputed process. Presiding as chairperson over the meeting, he called for the matter to be discussed afresh. In *A Fortunate Man*, Meer remembered that Luthuli wanted members of the NEC 'to feel free to participate and express their own individual views in the debate'.[43] It was, for Mandela, an inauspicious opening to the meeting.

Mandela had argued against Moses Kotane in the first NWC meeting and against Luthuli in the NEC meeting. The Indians of Natal, political disciples of Gandhi and followers of satyagraha, proved the most difficult to convince at the CJE's meeting, which was held at the Bodasinghs' beach house near Stanger. From 20h00, the argumentation raged all night. Yusuf Cachalia, J.N. Singh (vice president of the SAIC) and 'Monty' Naicker (president of the SAIC) proved to be worthy adversaries. Singh countered Mandela charging that 'Non-violence has not failed us. We have failed non-violence'.[44]

In light of the disunity evident in the democratic movement prior to the All-In African Conference and Mandela's inexplicable and rash calling-off of the May strike, Singh argued a valid point. Mandela retorted that non-violence had failed, for it had 'done nothing to change the heart of the oppressors'.[45] Luthuli again voiced his misgivings. He optimistically dreamed that if the hearts of the international community, white liberal democrats and faithful Christians could be changed to struggle non-violently, together with the unified mass action sponsored by African, coloured and Indian political movements, then the oppressors would be forced to capitulate. He reasoned that non-violent methods would foment far more political and economic pressure on a heavily armed, sophisticated and brutal regime than would an untrained, unequipped and isolated army.

As with the previous night's discussions, it was likely that complete exhaustion rather than carefully reasoned consensus allowed a resolution to be accepted at dawn. The members of CJE agreed that Mandela and others would not be disciplined for forming a new military organisation separate from the ANC, which itself would remain non-violent.

Mandela said in his autobiography that the military organisation 'would not be subject to the direct control of the mother organisation'.[46] The contradictions apparent in the NEC resolution were not clarified in the resolution taken by the CJE. No one made clear the distinction between 'direct' and 'indirect' control. Mandela inferred that the distinction between 'direct' and 'indirect' were 'operational' and 'political', respectively, or 'tactical' (short term) and 'strategic' (long term), respectively. In his 1964 Rivonia Trial statement, Mandela testified that he would 'at all times subject [MK] to the political guidance of the ANC and would not undertake any different form of activity from that contemplated without the consent of the ANC'.[47]

MK's ambiguous status also led to what Joe Slovo referred to as the 'necessary fiction' that it was initially not the armed wing of the ANC.[48] The NWC, NEC and CJE meetings had allowed Mandela to get his proverbial foot in the door. To placate Luthuli, the CJE resolved to keep the organisations separate. Robert Resha was the first to publicly dispel the myth that the ANC and MK were not synonymous and, at its October 1962 consultative conference at Lobatse, Bechuanaland (Botswana), the ANC dispensed with Luthuli's 'compromise'. Mandela had orchestrated the change he intended for the ANC. Despite acknowledging in his autobiography that the meeting agreed the ANC would remain non-violent, Mandela contradicted himself by confiding only four sentences later that '[h]enceforth, the ANC would be a different kind of organisation . . . embarking on a new and more dangerous path, a path of organised violence, the results of which we did not know and could not know'.[49]

The ANC has claimed since Luthuli's death in July 1967 that Luthuli supported the move to initiate violence. In an article which appeared in *Sechaba* in August 1967, it stated:

> There is a wrong and unfortunate impression that Chief Lutuli was a pacifist, or some kind of apostle of non-violence. This impression is incorrect and misleading. The policy of non-violence was formulated and adopted by the national conferences of the African National Congress before he was elected President-General of the organisation. The policy was adopted in 1951 specifically for the conduct of the 'National Campaign for Defiance of Unjust Laws' in 1952. What is correct, however, is that as a man of principle and as a leader of

unquestionable integrity, Chief Lutuli defended the policy entrusted
to him by his organisation and saw to it that it was implemented. When
that policy was officially and constitutionally changed, he did not falter.[50]

Luthuli's support for the changed policy is more than implied in these
words. In that he would not and did not condemn the use of violence,
the ANC can claim that he 'did not falter' in accepting the shift. However,
Luthuli's refusal to condemn the changed policy does not justify the
assertion that he agreed with it and subsequently supported it. Such a
position obscures the real dilemma in the ANC, the disputation between
Luthuli and Mandela in 1961, and avoids a critical assessment of the turn
to violence.

Sechaba, the official media organ of the ANC, printed the above
statement in a special supplement dedicated to Luthuli following his death.
It was subsequently published verbatim in an issue of Spotlight on South
Africa.[51] It was again published verbatim in Lutuli Speaks: Statements and
Addresses by Chief Albert Lutuli President of the African National Congress of
South Africa,[52] and yet again in a publication entitled 'The Road to Freedom
is Via the Cross', published as the third volume of South African Studies.[53]
The same statement can still be found verbatim on current ANC internet
websites.[54] The above oft-repeated claim by the ANC that Luthuli adopted
the new position on violence should no longer be publicised.

By disregarding Luthuli's theological foundation, commentators and
historians risk distorting the 'faith-based' motivations behind his political
principles and decisions. Luthuli did not subscribe to the ANC as his god
or hold himself seminally accountable to the ANC. The ANC was not the
primary entity to which he had held an allegiance. ANC nationalist
interpreters of Luthuli's life erroneously understand Luthuli to have been
political before being spiritual. For Luthuli, the opposite held true. In his
autobiography, Luthuli declared that which took priority in his life when
he professed, 'I am in Congress precisely because I am a Christian'.[55]
Furthermore, Luthuli revealed, 'My ambitions are, I think, modest – they
scarcely go beyond the desire to serve God and my neighbour, both at full
stretch.'[56]

The theological motivations in many of the Mahatma Gandhi's
utterances were also often similarly overlooked. Luthuli admired and
emulated Gandhi's use of strictly non-violent methods of resistance. His
speeches contain hundreds of quotations advocating a 'strategic pacifism',
which are strikingly similar to Gandhi's. Both men were given at times to

speaking in hyperbole to emphasise a point. Gandhi stated he preferred violence to cowardice when he wrote:

> Where the choice is set between cowardice and violence I would advise violence . . . This is because he who runs away commits mental violence; he has not the courage of facing death by killing. I would a thousand times prefer violence than the emasculation of a whole race. I prefer to use arms in defence of honour rather than remain the vile witness of dishonour. [57]

Not being a pacifist, Luthuli also preferred violence to cowardice. Yet, those perspectives, in and of themselves, do not support a thesis that Gandhi or Luthuli supported violence within the South African context. Luthuli and Gandhi did not consider those who fought utilising non-violent means to be cowards. In fact, the opposite was true. Gandhi and Luthuli believed that to fight not using violence – to sacrifice and die while fighting non-violently – was in fact the bravest of options. In the same statement, Gandhi articulated their mutually shared perspective when he argued, 'I praise and extol the serene courage of dying without killing. Yet, I desire that those who have not this courage should rather cultivate the art of killing and being killed, than to basely avoid danger.' The ANC and Mandela were both disingenuous when utilising the above statement by Gandhi to justify their own stance on violence. Likewise, the ANC and Mandela are disingenuous when they claimed Luthuli supported the turn to violent methods.

While accepting his Peace Prize in Oslo, Norway, for his stance on utilising non-violent methods, Luthuli expressed his courage when he reasoned that as a Christian he could not 'look on' while 'systematic attempts' were made to 'debase the God-factor in man or set a limit beyond which the human being in his black form might not strive to serve his Creator to the best of his ability'.[58]

Nobel Peace Prize announced

Gunnar Helander, who motivated so strongly for Luthuli's eligibility to win the Nobel Peace Prize, was successful in convincing thirty-four members of the Swedish Parliament and also Albert Schweitzer (1875–1965), himself a former Peace Prize winner, of Luthuli's worthiness, and they subsequently recommended him. In February 1961, Norwegian socialist members of Parliament added their support to the Swedish nomination. Many others are known to have motivated for Luthuli to be given the award, among them the Reverend Arthur Blaxall, his old friend and colleague. Ronald Segal, editor of *Africa South-in-Exile*, also proposed Luthuli as a candidate before the International Union of Socialist Youth (IUSY). The IUSY unanimously passed a resolution in support of Luthuli at a 1960 conference in Vienna.

On 23 October 1961, a month or two after the crucial CJE meeting and almost two months before the launch of MK, the Nobel committee formally announced the news that Luthuli was to be awarded the 1960 Nobel Peace Prize. The following day, the *Daily News* in Durban acknowledged Luthuli's Nobel credentials:

> [His] long career of struggle has been marked by a constant faith in the common humanity of all peoples in this land. He has steadfastly refused to compromise while eschewing all violence in the pursuit of his ideal of non-discrimination. He has suffered for his principles but seldom allowed words of bitterness to cross his lips or emotion to blur his vision.[59]

It was E.V. Mahomed, Luthuli's very close friend, who, at around 17h30 on 23 October, told him that he had won the prize.[60] One of the first to congratulate Luthuli was Arthur Blaxall. Luthuli told Blaxall that he thought Mahomed was playing a trick on him. Just the day before, he had received *in absentia* the Gell Memorial Award. Luthuli ribbed Mahomed for confusing the two awards.

Mahomed could arguably be considered Luthuli's closest friend. He had joined the Liberal Party, founded a branch in Stanger and, in time, became the party's national treasurer and secretary. In his deposition to the Truth and Reconciliation Commission (1996), Mahomed's son, Yunus, testified that Luthuli was in their home daily. Much of Luthuli's secretarial work was carried out at Mahomed's office, and if special needs or circumstances arose, Mahomed would drop everything to serve Luthuli. After Luthuli won the Peace Prize, Mahomed did just this. The office handled phone calls, telegrams and all correspondence. And in addition to serving as Luthuli's bookkeeper, Mahomed often acted as his chauffeur too.

Admirers swamped Luthuli with congratulations. On the night of the announcement, he did not rest until three in the morning and the phone rang continuously from as early as six the following morning. Luthuli's diary was crammed with booked interviews. Mary Benson also worked alongside Mahomed doing secretarial work, handling the great bulk of correspondence flooding into Stanger from all over the world. When she left to travel overseas, Mahomed asked Jean Hill to take over as Luthuli's personal secretary.[61]

Alan Paton, too, responded in the *Gazette* that the award was 'wonderful news'. That 'one of her sons had been chosen to receive such an honour' instilled pride in South Africans, he said.[62] Political accolades and recognition for Luthuli did not only come from the Liberal Party. Jan Steytler, leader of the Progressive Party, also reacted warmly to the news.[63] The Most Reverend Joost de Blank, Archbishop of Cape Town and Metropolitan of the Church of the Province of South Africa, congratulated him on behalf of the Episcopal Synod.

Those who knew Luthuli intimately testify that after hearing that he won the Peace Prize, he sequestered himself in his home for several hours in deep thought, prayer and meditation. In an interview with the *Daily News*, Luthuli spoke of the added burden of responsibility the Peace Prize engendered. 'God help me live up to it,' he said.[64] During this time, Luthuli determined his strategy so that the reception of the award fostered the maximum possible coverage, and thus sympathy, for the liberation struggle. The award presented a window of opportunity that required bold leadership. He had to speak to, argue for and declare the use of non-violence consistently and resolutely. It was no time for an ambiguous, confusing and contradictory avowal of both violent *and* non-violent methods.

Many suspected, both then and now, that the Nobel committee awarded Luthuli the Peace Prize with the intention to reinforce his and the liberation movement's non-violent stance, thus pushing them farther away from the 'violent' precipice all feared was on the horizon. In *Africa Today* Ezekiel Mphahlele, for example, suggested that the Nobel Prize 'may have been interpreted as implying that the Scandinavians were investing in non-violence in South Africa'. The July decision to form MK meant that 'this would be expecting too much'. He suggested that Luthuli felt 'awkward' investing in 'a prize for a religious-political creed his organisation now found irrelevant'.[65] Ranjith Kally, in *The Struggle: Sixty Years in Focus* (2004), commented that with violence being seriously considered, 'peace loving people, needed to boost Chief Albert Luthuli for they feared that South Africa was on the brink of bloodshed'.[66] They were convinced that he had been able to stave off any mass conflict.

The *Sunday Tribune* editorial of 29 October 1961, entitled 'Let Him Go', suggested that it was now impossible for Luthuli to be anything but 'moderate' and a 'man of peace'. Three days after the announcement that Luthuli had won the Peace Prize, the *Tribune*'s Michael Lloyd mused that he was the 'umpteenth newsman' to interview him at Groutville. Luthuli told Lloyd that he was a 'militant', but that his militancy consisted in prosecuting the struggle along peaceful lines, with 'as few scars as possible'.[67]

Luthuli told Mary Benson that they gave him the prize because, 'quite correctly', they believed him to be 'the leader of a liberation movement that pursued non-violence'.[68] He recognised that some would suspect the prize was intended to manoeuvre for a non-violent approach by the liberation movement. This Luthuli refuted, telling the *Sunday Tribune* that there was no ulterior motive in the award. 'I'm sure the award was given . . . because I have always worked for peace. It is not trying to buy me for peace.'[69]

Nevertheless, the decision of the Nobel committee cemented Luthuli's past and present position on non-violence for the future and, from the time of the announcement in October 1961, he argued prolifically for non-violent methods. The award, he said, stiffened his resolve to advocate only non-violent means despite the ANC and the joint congresses's decision in July. It was a stand that distanced him from the leadership in the ANC. By April 1962 his appeals had grown to become embarrassing to the liberation movement that had long since changed policy. Ultimately, the Nobel committee failed to influence the ANC to remain non-violent. Luthuli's influence had weakened. Mandela's had strengthened.

Upon his arrival at the Johannesburg airport while connecting to London, the Liberal Party presented Luthuli with a wrist watch. Luthuli regarded this gift as an expression of the deep bond between the party and himself despite any 'differences of opinion on tactics in our common fight for freedom'.[70] Many in the Liberal Party at the time were practising Christians who espoused a theology based on non-violence. Bill Bhengu, a prominent African member of the party, emphasised that Luthuli's non-violent stance was the reason for the Liberal Party's support of him. Charles Hill (1920–2002), in an unpublished report on a protest meeting, expressed much the same sentiments, contrasting Luthuli's Christianity with (state president) C.R. Swart's presumption that Luthuli advocated violence.[71]

[I] had heard Luthuli on many occasions, but [I] do not remember a single occasion where Luthuli ever deviated from the basic preachings of Christianity. However, Mr Swart revealed to Parliament a tremendous discovery that Luthuli had spoken to the Overseas BBC network that the non-Europeans will not seek their goals always by meek submission. Was not this proof enough that Luthuli preached violence? asked Mr Swart.[72]

The Liberal Party, like the Black Sash and white middle-class progressive Christians, found in Luthuli a kindred soul. Their shared belief in non-violence superseded any differences they may have had. If the Liberal Party, the Black Sash and white progressive Christians did not explicitly state non-violence was a central tenet of their creed, it was because non-violence was assumed and, for all intents and purposes, non-debatable.

Forestall through the press

After the announcement, Albert Luthuli issued a stream of public statements in the press advocating a strategic pacifism. The Nobel Prize bolstered his non-violent stance, if it did not lead him to question his earlier yielding to democratic decisions arrived at by beleaguered and exhausted majorities within the July 1961 NEC and CJE meetings. By now his leadership of the ANC was more symbolic. Perhaps he thought it was more than this, for he believed he could forestall through the press any possible plans to activate MK.

In gracious acceptance statements, Luthuli said again and again that the Peace Prize had not been awarded to him alone. Rather, in his view, the Nobel committee had also awarded the Peace Prize *to the* ANC and even to the continent of Africa. He viewed himself as a representative only. On 24 October 1961, the *Daily News* reported his expressed sentiments: 'This is an honour for the whole of Africa. If I falter, the whole people will suffer a setback.'[73] By accepting the award as president general of the ANC, he hoped to send a message to ANC members not to make the turn to violence.[74] Both the *Cape Argus* and the *Star* of 24 October 1961 reported him as saying:

I think I won the [Nobel Peace Prize] because I was leader of the African National Congress and generally of our liberation movement here. The ANC and its allies had decided to carry out its struggle along non-violent lines. It was my happy task to help implement that decision, and I think, because I was leader of the movement, I became a symbol of the people and their peaceful actions. I must say that I would not pigeon-hole myself as a pacifist. I would not hesitate to give my hand if my country went to war. But on practical consideration it would be suicidal in the circles today to abandon our policy of non-violence.[75]

The ANC has repeatedly said that Luthuli 'did not falter' when it officially and constitutionally changed its policy on violence. Yet, the timing of the 'official' policy change is unclear. Does the ANC's claim refer to the July 1961 agreement not to discipline those who were given permission to form a new violent organisation? Or, does it refer to the Lobatse Conference, when the ANC acknowledged MK as its own?[76] Because the government declared the ANC illegal in 1960, the ANC could not officially and constitutionally change its policy, at least not within South Africa; that is, it could not consult and receive a domestic mandate from the grassroots through its democratic structures.

For two reasons, the decisions taken by the NEC and the CJE to not discipline those who endeavoured to form MK did not restrain Luthuli in advocating for non-violence. First, the meetings decided to allow the formation, but not launch, of MK. Second, Luthuli continued to make the important qualification that the ANC and MK were separate (though linked) organisations. Whether one considers, for the sake of argument, the July 1961 NEC and CJE meetings or the 1962 Lobatse Conference, the answer remains the same: Luthuli did not agree with, nor did he consider that the ANC supported, an armed movement from October 1961 (when the Nobel committee announced his award) to at least 1964 when, in his Rivonia statement, he indicated that the ANC had 'never abandoned its method of a militant, non-violent struggle'.

By indicating that Luthuli 'did not falter', the ANC can only *imply* that he did not condemn the use of violence. It could not have meant that Luthuli himself made the switch to violence, since he did nothing but advocate for the use of non-violent methods. With these qualifications, Luthuli continued to assert his *and* the ANC's non-violent stand. In the ensuing months, these qualifications would prove for Luthuli to be integrity-saving loopholes.

Days after the announcement, Theo Greyling of the South African Broadcasting Corporation (SABC) prepared a ten-minute radio documentary that questioned Luthuli's credentials and worthiness to win the

Peace Prize. In response, Alan Paton of the Liberal Party, Jan Steytler of the Progressive Party and much of the liberal South African public vigorously protested against what was described as a 'vicious' attack on Luthuli. Luthuli then fired off an angry letter to the *Rand Daily Mail* stating, 'All I can say is that I will continue to stand for the prosecution of our freedom struggle along peaceful lines'.[77] In a limp defence of the broadcast, the SABC responded that its documentary had been 'factual'.

Luthuli continued to use his columns in the *Golden City Post* to make impassioned appeals to South Africans across the racial spectrum. He pleaded with whites for a change of heart. At the same time, he was well aware that many of the oppressed were becoming impatient and more militant. With the independence of Ghana in 1957, and many more African countries to follow suit, an excited air was sweeping the continent. In two August 1961 columns in the *Golden City Post*, Luthuli warned that time was running out for South Africa. In October, he pleaded with fellow Africans to 'stand for the realisation of friendship among all people of South Africa' and 'to exercise patience and forbearance, even in a situation that provokes a spirit of enmity'.[78]

Luthuli spoke with many well-known and credible journalists in November and December 1961, consistently advocating for the continued use of non-violent methods. In an interview with Benjamin Pogrund of the *Rand Daily Mail* on 14 November 1961, he stressed:

> Africans dare not forsake the path of non-violence. To do so would lead to disaster both for themselves and for South Africa. It is true that we have not had great success in the past in the achievement of our aims by following non-violent methods. But this does not mean that the methods have failed us – only that we have failed the methods . . . It is my hope that the successful application by Africans of non-violent methods will exert sufficient pressure on white South Africa to cause Whites to say, 'We can't go on like this. Let us sit down and discuss our mutual problems'. It is the task of the Africans to organise and discipline themselves so as to make the fullest use of non-violent methods to bring this about.[79]

Pogrund went on to explain that methods Luthuli had in mind included stay-at-homes, demonstrations and general non-collaboration – all of which were accepted throughout the civilised world as democratic and peaceful ways of registering protest against government policy. He reported Luthuli's view that, until then, these methods had not been exploited to the fullest. Even what Luthuli called the 'highest form' of protest, the stay-at-home, had not been fully supported and the government did nothing for the spirit of non-violent protest by constantly talking and acting through force. 'Despite this,' Luthuli told Pogrund, 'we shall continue to exert pressure through non-violent means. We will continue to be the legitimate kind of pressure used all over the world.'[80]

Press reports from this period reveal that at every opportunity Luthuli declared that non-violence was not just a method, but The Method. In a conversation on 23 November 1961 with Canadian Ambassador J.J. Hurley, Luthuli affirmed 'that it would in his opinion be "suicidal folly" to try to overthrow the government by force'.[81] A seven hundred-word cabled report by Daniel McGeachie to his paper, the *Daily Express* in London, was intercepted by the South African postal service and withheld, producing a storm of outrage over the attack on press freedom from white, black, liberal and nationalist journalists. The *Cape Times* of 20 November 1961 carried an article on the matter, quoting from McGeachie's article Luthuli's fears:

> Non-violent agitation will win and I still think that the majority of black South Africa is behind me. Stories that there are plans of violence may be government propaganda. The government wants a show-down. They want us to fight so that they have an excuse to mow us down.[82]

If one incorrectly understands that the NEC and CJE decisions authorised MK's formation and launch, then Luthuli's hypothesis printed in the *Cape Times* that 'stories' of impending violence derived from 'government propaganda' suggest that he did not participate nor was informed about decisions made by the July 1961 meetings. Talk of violence from the government, Luthuli told Pogrund, was purely propagandistic: it was a ploy to goad Africans into force which could be met by force. However, all evidence suggests that the July 1961 NEC and CJE meetings authorised the formation of MK by not discipling those who chose to do so. So, how does one explain Luthuli's comments regarding the claim that violence was not being planned? The answer is that for Luthuli the July 1961 decisions did not authorise MK's launch. In Luthuli's mind an organisation was permitted to be formed to prepare for the possible event of violence; but, as far as Luthuli was aware, no violence was actually planned. Three months later, the Peace Prize intercepted the passage from formation to launch, dramatically extending the road previously thought to be a policy cul-de-sac. Luthuli re-assessed the now promisingly effective non-violent tactics in light of the international publicity and sympathy and, as the president general, re-doubled his advocacy for an exclusively non-violent struggle. From October to December (and into 1962 until the introduction of the Sabotage Act), he repeatedly emphasised through the public domain a desperate need to cancel, revisit and/or postpone any implementation of plans by the newly formed organisation. With the intensity of government repression, what better place to issue imperatives than through the media?

Yet, Luthuli must have been nervous. He recognised the frustrations he believed the 'young people', that is Mandela and others, were facing. Benson, in her biography on Luthuli, quotes his fears:

> You would expect people to start questioning and asking, 'How long would these white men take advantage of our seeming docility?' It would not be surprising to find some, particularly young people, beginning to question the efficacy of non-violence when they face so aggressive a government. If the oppressed people here ever came to indulge in violent ways that would be a reaction against the policy of government in suppressing them. 'However much you may disagree with them, you cannot *blame* them. But the leadership', he added, 'stand by the non-violent method' (original emphasis).[83]

To Oslo

Many newspaper editors and political commentators debated the pros and cons of Luthuli's Nobel Peace Prize as one drama after another unfolded between the announcement of the prize on 23 October and its reception in Oslo on 10 December 1961. What would be the reaction of the South African government? Would the government grant Luthuli a passport? Would he be allowed to travel outside of Oslo? Universal opinion seemed to have it that the government would do far more harm than good if it denied him a passport and prevented him from travelling, even though he remained under banning orders. For the government, the decision was a lose/lose proposition. If allowed to attend, Luthuli would effectively denounce the South African government's policy of apartheid. If they denied him permission to travel, the government would have the rather ironic privilege of accepting it on his behalf through a representative with diplomatic or consular status.[84]

The government bitterly disputed Luthuli's worthiness to receive the Peace Prize and in doing so incriminated itself. Instead of remaining silent, it issued petty and condescending vitriol through the Minister of the Interior and F.W de Klerk's father, Senator Jan de Klerk (1903–1979). On 27 October, Luthuli applied to the Ministry of the Interior for the lifting of his travel ban and a passport. If the government refused to grant it, Luthuli said he would apply for a Rhodesian passport on the basis of his Rhodesian birth.

Luthuli's application was short-sighted in that it requested only a few days and included a trip to Tanganyika (Tanzania) to celebrate that country's independence. Rather than Tanganyika (for which permission was denied anyway), Luthuli should have applied to visit Sweden, England or even the United States after receiving news of winning the Peace Prize as invitations would likely be received to visit these countries.[85] Later, and well into his sojourn on 11 December, Luthuli and the Swedish government applied to the South African legation in Oslo for permission for him to visit Sweden as was customary for Nobel Peace Prize winners. The belated application was unsuccessful.

Meanwhile, the Minister of Justice, B.J. Vorster (1915–1983), turned down an application from Luthuli for permission to attend a celebratory gathering on 28 October in Stanger. Over nine hundred people turned up to honour Luthuli on this occasion, including Alan Paton who read out a song of praise for Luthuli.

> You there, Luthuli. They thought your world was small.
> They thought you lived in Groutville.
> Now they discover it's the world you live in.
> You there, Luthuli. They thought your name was small.
> Luthuli of Groutville, now they discover your name is everywhere.
> You there, Luthuli. They thought you were chained like a backyard dog.
> Now they discovered they are in prison but you are free.
> You there, Luthuli. They took your name of chief. You were not worthy.
> Now they discover you are more chief than ever.
> Go well, Luthuli. May your days be long. Your country cannot spare you.
> Win for us also, Luthuli, the prize of peace.[86]

Many accounts of this period erroneously state that the government delayed and/or initially refused to grant Luthuli a passport until the last minute. In fact, the government, having received the application late on 31 October, announced on 6 November that Luthuli and his wife, Nokukhanya, could travel. The Luthulis received the passports on 23 November. Furthermore, the government granted Luthuli more days abroad than requested in his application, realising that for 'practical reasons', he would need more time. The government felt that Luthuli's request did not take into consideration travel delays, connecting travel and 'time to relax after a long journey before such an important event'.[87] Though efficient in its approval, the government's granting of a passport was nonetheless begrudging, ungracious and included many loosely defined restrictions. Luthuli was not permitted, for example, to make any political statements, nor tarnish South Africa's image. Restrictions also forced the cancellation of a meeting planned in London between Christian Action, the Anti-Apartheid Movement and Luthuli.

Luthuli was inconsistent in his willingness to be obedient to the government's conditions for travel. He indicated that he would abide by government decisions that would limit his speaking 'at functions other than at the official Peace Prize ceremony', but clearly did not abide by its directive to refrain from making political statements that might tarnish South Africa's image. Luthuli wrote to De Klerk on two occasions: once to ask if he could attend social gatherings and once to ask if he could travel to places in Norway outside Oslo. The minister responded to the former in the affirmative while the latter query was left unanswered. In the event, Luthuli felt obliged to turn down an invitation to address a religious meeting in Norway's oldest cathedral, Stavanger, because his passport conditions confined him to Oslo.

On 10 November, over ten thousand people attended a rally at Currie's Fountain Sports Stadium in Durban. Needless to say, Vorster denied Luthuli permission to attend. In a statement read out on his behalf, Luthuli again tried to re-address the decisions made in July by saying that the award was an 'encouragement to continue by non-violent means the struggle for freedom and justice for all'.[88]

Also in November, Luthuli assembled his staff that would accompany him while in Norway at their own expense. They included Mary-Louise Hooper, Oliver Tambo and Robert Resha. During the fortnight immediately before his departure for Norway, Luthuli devoted most of his time in Groutville to composing his acceptance speech and Nobel lecture. Few, if any, interviews were granted.

After a prayer service on the morning of 5 December, E.V. Mahomed drove Luthuli and his wife in a convertible coupé from Groutville to Durban, arriving at 10h30 for lunch at the Himalaya Hotel in Durban's Indian quarter, and then in convoy to Louis Botha Airport for a 15h00 flight to Johannesburg. Upon his arrival in Durban, thousands swarmed in the streets to greet Luthuli. At the airport, the authorities asked Luthuli to instruct the crowd to clear out of the whites-only hall. This he did, inviting the crowd outside where he joined them in song.

The flight from Durban to Johannesburg was delayed for forty-five minutes due to a technical hitch. Yet another delay occurred when, after take-off from Johannesburg, the aircraft had to return to the airport because of mechanical problems related to its pressurisation system. This second delay must have caused Luthuli great distress. Surprisingly, no press reports conveyed the suspicion that the government may have orchestrated both delays to examine Luthuli's luggage contents or to frustrate itineraries that included meetings with anti-apartheid organisations. One article, carried in the London *Times*, reported, oddly, that as the aircraft returned to Jan Smuts airport, 'the engineer of the Comet fell ill . . . and has been taken to a nursing home'.[89] The flight to London was delayed until the following morning. The Luthulis ate their supper in the upstairs airport lounge while the white passengers ate at the ground floor restaurant. They rested in the multiracial terminal transit sleeping quarters while the other white passengers lodged at a local Johannesburg hotel.

Arriving in London at 3h15 on the morning of the 6 December, some eighteen hours later than expected, the Luthulis were unable to enjoy a planned sightseeing tour of the capital and to visit the home of Canon John Collins before travelling on to Oslo. Despite their late arrival, over two hundred people were patiently waiting to greet them, among them, Oliver Tambo and Robert Resha.

Tambo served as Luthuli's manager and secretary for the European visit. From London, the party departed for Copenhagen, Denmark, with a brief stop in Gothenburg, Sweden, meeting dignitaries all along the way. In Gothenburg, Luthuli's old friend, Gunnar Helander, boarded the plane to Oslo. On this flight, Helander asked Luthuli if he did not wish to seek political asylum in Norway or Sweden. Luthuli responded firmly in the negative saying that his place was among his own people in South

Africa. Luthuli's response proved consistent with his stance discouraging those in the struggle from fleeing the country into exile.[90]

Immediately, on his arrival in snow-laden Oslo on 7 December, Luthuli gave his first broadcast interview, emphasising his non-violent principles and saying 'even today it would be possible for white and coloured people to live peacefully together in South Africa'.[91] Tambo, very concerned about Luthuli's health, sent him straight to bed after dinner, disappointing many members of the press.[92]

On 9 December, King Olav of Norway received Luthuli at the Royal Palace. Luthuli commented that his conversation with the king was very pleasant, but avoided controversial discussion about conditions in South Africa. At a press conference that evening, Luthuli proclaimed his position on non-violence, but subtly warned that the threat of violence increased each day that political suppression lasted. He made no mention to the press that Mandela and others had already converted to the violent option. More appeals to hold the non-violent line would be made to his political colleagues in South Africa in the days ahead.

Luthuli received the Peace Prize on Sunday afternoon, 10 December 1961, and gave his Nobel address the following day. Perhaps the best account of Luthuli's acceptance of the Peace Prize came from John Reuling, Luthuli's mentor and friend since their days at Adams, who dictated a seven-page letter to the American Board in the Rome airport after departing from Norway for Salisbury, Rhodesia. Reuling provided an engaging personal account of his efforts to be present on the occasion that Albert Luthuli, a product of the American Board Mission, was to receive one of world's most notable awards. He was a wonderful storyteller, making even his rental of a tuxedo and purchase of inexpensive cufflinks for the award ceremony seem intriguing. Reuling had difficulty securing a pass for even one of the public events arranged for the award. After his last unsuccessful attempt to obtain a pass, a door suddenly opened and Luthuli, accompanied by Nokukhanya, appeared in the passage. Instantly, the two men were joyfully reunited and exchanging, in Zulu, news of family and old missionary friends. Reuling then received from the organisers special cards with his name inscribed on them. He encountered few difficulties afterwards though he regretted that in order for him to be given a dinner pass, someone likely had to stand down.

A university auditorium was filled to capacity on the afternoon that Luthuli received the award. Speaking only in Norwegian and without translation, the Nobel committee's chairperson, Gunnar Jahn (1883–1971), gave a detailed overview of Luthuli's life, tracing his association with the American Board Mission, Adams College, his Christian training and quoting from some of his speeches and writings. Jahn emphatically commented upon Luthuli's stance on violence.

> Never has he succumbed to the temptation to use violent means in the struggle for his people. Nothing has shaken him from this firm resolve, so firmly rooted in his conviction that violence and terror must not be employed . . . Well might we ask: will the non-whites of South Africa, by their suffering, their humiliation and their patience, show the other nations of the world that human rights can be won without violence, by following a road to which we Europeans are committed both intellectually and emotionally, but which we have all too often abandoned? If the non-white people of South Africa ever lift themselves from their humiliation without resorting to violence and terror, then it will be above all because of the work of Luthuli, their fearless and incorruptible leader who, thanks to his own high ethical standards, has rallied his people in support of this policy, and who throughout his adult life has staked everything and suffered everything without bitterness and without allowing hatred and aggression to replace his abiding love of his fellow men. But if the day should come when the struggle of the non-whites in South Africa to win their freedom denigrates into bloody slaughter, then Luthuli's voice will be heard no more. But let us remember him then and never forget that his way was unwavering and clear. He would not have had it so.[93]

What was Luthuli thinking as he heard these words (perhaps through private translation), prior to his being called forward to accept the Nobel Peace Prize? Popular South African history would have one believe that Luthuli, as president of the ANC since 1952, had supported the formation of MK just five months prior to receiving the Nobel Peace Prize, and had, following the award, sanctioned the initiation of violence. In his autobiography, Mandela admitted the incongruencies, saying that the award had come at 'an awkward time for it was juxtaposed against an announcement that seemed to call the award itself into question. The day after Luthuli returned from Oslo [16 December 1961], MK dramatically announced its emergence.'[94]

If the assumption that Luthuli sanctioned violence is true, what raced through Luthuli's mind as Jahn declared that Luthuli was 'unwavering and clear' on his objection to violence? If Luthuli's position was not resolutely against violence, surely he would have experienced a sense of panic and existential angst as he listened to Jahn declare that 'if the liberation movement is to resist the temptation to use violence, it will be due to Luthuli's influence'. If Luthuli's position was not resolutely against violence, undoubtedly he would have bristled as Jahn concluded that 'if the liberation movement ever resorted to violence, it will be due to an abandonment of Luthuli's voice'. Did Luthuli support the massive ethical and strategic change in the liberation movement's policy? If we assume the answer is 'Yes, Luthuli sanctioned the violence', did Jahn's introduction engender a profound dilemma for Luthuli?

John Allen, author of *Rabble-Rouser for Peace* (1997), Desmond Tutu's authorised biography, provided a glimpse of the confusion that this book clarifies.

> The Norwegians appear to have learned after the Prize was announced but before it was conferred that violence had become likely: Luthuli told at least one Norwegian in Oslo that notwithstanding his own feelings on the issue, he had felt bound at a meeting with the ANC's leaders some months earlier to accept a decision to embark on sabotage. The Norwegians did not know when sabotage would begin and, given the operational autonomy of MK, it is unlikely that even Luthuli knew.[95]

At the conclusion of Jahn's speech, Luthuli walked to the podium, received a scroll, bowed to the king and handed it to Nokukhanya. Luthuli accepted the prize in, for him, uncharacteristic attire. He had borrowed from Mangosuthu Buthelezi the partial regalia of a Zulu warrior king, complete with leopard skin and claw necklace. Only twice before in his life, after one of his daughter's (Hilda Thandeka) weddings and another during a photo shoot in the United States, had Luthuli been photographed wearing and/or carrying traditional accoutrements. By wearing the regalia at the ceremony in Oslo, Luthuli risked disapproval by some within the ANC and his Congregationalist church.[96] Luthuli was not a traditional hereditary chief, he was an *amakholwa* chief. Some who disapproved mistakenly interpreted the wearing of traditional attire as nostalgia for 'heathenism' or as a display of Zulu nationalism. For others, such as Tambo and other ANC leaders, the *amakhosi* were government minions, stooges and vestiges of the apartheid government's efforts to stunt the development of Africans. Luthuli also subscribed to this judgement. His choice of dress can therefore be perplexing. One can conclude that he did not wear the adornments of an African king so as to represent Zulu nationalism or traditional leadership. Rather, he wore the regalia of an African leader to represent the continent of Africa in front of the world press. Luthuli recognised that, as the leader of the longest existing and largest liberation movement in Africa, he represented the aspirations of the emerging African continent and his remarks while accepting the Nobel prize demonstrated this conclusion.

Luthuli delivered a short, fifteen-minute acceptance speech after receiving the award. Humorously, he reminded the audience that the South African government did not feel that he was worthy of such an esteemed honour. Therefore, the award, he said, had managed for the first time in history to produce an issue on which they agreed. The primarily Norwegian audience was enraptured with his self-deprecating humour.

That same evening John Reuling attended a very private and formal dinner at which Luthuli was also present. In a brief speech, Luthuli focused upon the importance of Africa to the world today, the need for arriving at peaceful solutions, his own ideals and his determination to avoid violence. Reuling's letter also spoke of his having been present as an observer the following day when Luthuli was interviewed for a BBC *Panorama* current affairs programme. Asked how long people would respond to his 'Bible-punching' appeal or whether they would fall prey to the 'rabble-rousers', Luthuli responded that *despite* the fact that the National Party government exhibited no intention to ease its apartheid policies thus far, 'militant non-violence in South Africa was still a valid weapon that could be most effective, and that it was better than resorting to violence to gain one's freedom'.[97] To resort to any other method 'might bring bloodshed', he added. 'To gain freedom without bloodshed is a much better way.'[98]

Though Luthuli's statements were moderate, Reuling admired the frank and courageous manner in which he firmly critiqued the South African government. Reuling surmised that Luthuli 'went far beyond the bounds of what they had permitted him to do, and there is every possibility that he may suffer for it upon return'.[99]

On Monday, 11 December 1961, Luthuli, despite all the harassment and complications arising from the government's cantankerous response to his award, delivered a seventy-minute Nobel lecture and continued to emphasise the movement's non-violent methods. Dressed this time in a suit, Luthuli stated:

> Through all this cruel treatment in the name of law and order, our people, with few exceptions, have remained non-violent. If today this (Nobel) peace award is given to South Africa through a black man, it is not because we in South Africa have won our fight for peace and human brotherhood. Far from it. Perhaps we stand farther away from victory than any other people in Africa. But nothing we have suffered at the hands of the government has turned us from our chosen path of disciplined resistance. It is for this, I believe, that this award is given.[100]

Luthuli devoted the first twenty minutes of his lecture to creating 'a picture of the African continent in a state of [relative] peaceful revolution'. For the remaining fifty minutes, he criticised apartheid for being 'a museum piece, a relic of an age which everywhere else is dead or dying'.[101]

In Norway, Luthuli played the role of a pacifist, though he was not one. Contrary to Sechaba's claim in August 1967 that once the ANC decided to opt for military methods, Luthuli 'did not falter', in Norway, without explicitly saying so, he pleaded that there be no decision taken to launch the new organisation. Receiving the Peace Prize, and as a possible retort to Nelson Mandela, Luthuli stated he believed non-violence was 'the only correct form' the struggle could take. From both 'the moral and the practical point of view the situation of the country demands it. Violence disrupts human life and is destructive to perpetrator and victim alike . . . To refrain from violence is the sign of the civilised man.'[102]

At this time, Luthuli was not just preaching non-violence to western audiences in Norway. He also issued a statement for domestic consumption that reiterated the same themes. Those in MK's newly formed leadership structures must have paid attention to the audio and print news on Luthuli saturating the media at the time. He was, after all, officially still leading the liberation movement as the president general of the ANC. His statement to the Rand Daily Mail on 12 December 1961 was blunt: 'There are no responsible persons among us in the African National Congress who advocate violence as a means of furthering our cause.'[103] Could Luthuli have been more clear?

The Peace Prize must have caused embarrassment to some within in the NEC and CJE. A November 1961 Congress[es] Bulletin issued by the National Consultative Committee defensively qualified the meaning of Luthuli's award:

> We care not a rap for those [Africanists] who throw mud by sneering at this award because it is a 'Peace' award. Of course we stand for peace! . . . But let it not be misunderstood. Peace for us, is not peace in bondage . . . Let the world, and our government, therefore know: our oppressors are turning to the most savage repression in order to safeguard their miserable privileges and to prevent the people stretching out their hands for the fruits of our modern age. This we can no longer tolerate, and we will summon all our brain and brawn . . .[104]

If not embarrassed by the award, then many in the ANC were ignorant of its significance. Whereas Luthuli viewed the award as a public relations weapon against the National Party regime, others undervalued it. In a 1995 interview, Walter Sisulu confided that they had not attached importance to the Nobel Peace Prize itself. 'But from that time on we began to analyse it and realise its significance.'[105]

Luthuli's last public event in Oslo was a religious and personal farewell gathering at the Oslo cathedral hosted by the Bishop of Stavanger, Fridtjov Søiland Birkeli (1906–1983). Here, Luthuli did not shy away from confronting his ecclesiastical soulmates with constructive criticism. While he was a product of Christian evangelisation and hence deeply respected and had participated in the Christian mission, the cultural imperialism that accompanied it did not escape his reproach. Luthuli admired and emulated many aspects of western culture; however, he opposed western philosophical efforts to denigrate African culture. In the Oslo cathedral, he attacked Rousseau's concept of the 'noble savage' as insulting, derogatory and abhorrent. Having first-hand knowledge of Norwegian missions in Natal, as close as thirty kilometres from Groutville in Maphumulo, Luthuli commented specifically on their mission's record. The Norwegian Lutherans had good reason to be proud. Nonetheless, he soberly criticised the mission for not having aggressively enough established schools and universities, and not ordaining indigenous clergy into the ministry in sufficient time. Luthuli then comforted his audience by commending them for recent corrective measures.

The Luthulis departed from Oslo on 14 December for Johannesburg via Hamburg, Zurich, Athens and Khartoum on Scandinavian Airlines. On 15 December they flew on to Durban where E.V. Mahomed was waiting to meet them and return them to their home in Groutville.

The prize

In 1961, the Nobel Peace Prize would have awarded Albert Luthuli around R31 000. Before departing for Norway, he had little time to contemplate how he would use it and needed time to discern a manner in which the funds would be put to good use to forward the liberation struggle non-violently.

Eventually, he used the prize money to purchase two farms in Swaziland. On these farms he hoped to offer humanitarian relief to refugees. No evidence exists to suggest that the farms served as military bases, training centres or launch sites for armed incursions. Nokukhanya Luthuli told her biographer, Peter Rule, that M.B. Yengwa and Wilson Conco visited a few times. Other than that, not many refugees stayed there.

Many clues reveal that the venture failed. Nokukhanya purchased the farms and supervised all the work. Rule speaks of her spending long periods away from home (six months a year) and experiencing 'the hardships of life as a woman on her own in a strange country'.[106] She joined the workers in the field and ran a farm store to 'earn a bit more money', but life was hard:

> I had to tolerate a lot from some men who were very troublesome. They could not understand why I, a woman, was there on the farm. For them it was a man's job. This is the kind of attitude I had to put up with. Because I was alone and vulnerable they tried to intimidate me ... At night I was all alone because the workers did not want to stay in the farm compound and they all went away to their farms.[107]

Rule suggests that any profit made on the farms went towards helping the ANC in London. If their purpose was to support the armed movement or refugees of the armed movement, then the ANC would have supported and used them. The ANC would also have felt obligated to assist its ailing president general's wife, not tolerating her sacrificial and solitary toiling. In accordance with Luthuli's will, the money from the sale of the farms after his death contributed to the Luthuli Educational Trust to fund scholarships and to assist schools with libraries and books. All things considered, it is reasonable to conclude that Luthuli intended that the farms purchased with the Nobel Peace Prize money contribute to non-violent methods of resistance.

MK's launch

On 16 December 1961, a series of explosions around the country dramatically announced the activation of MK. Simultaneously, MK published its manifesto declaring that 'the government has interpreted the peacefulness of the movement as weakness; the people's non-violent policies have been taken as a green light for government violence. Refusal to resort to violence has been interpreted by the government as an invitation to use armed force against the people without any fear of reprisals.'[108]

MK's first day of violent attacks resulted in the death of one of its own, two aborted arsons and a blown-up manhole containing telephone cables.[109] Petrus Molefe (1938–1961) was killed in the vicinity of his target by a premature explosion. His partner in the failed act, Benjamin Ramotse, sustained burns on his hands and face. Ramotse's hospitalisation later led to his arrest as forensic experts linked the residue on his clothes to the explosion. In a 1986 article for the twenty-fifth anniversary edition of the MK journal *Dawn*, Joe Slovo narrated his aborted attempt to burn down the Johannesburg Drill Hall. The chairs and wooden floor that were meant to catch on fire from a homemade incendiary device were being cleaned by workers. His next target of administrative offices was spared because an official unknowingly caught him in the act of attempting to burn them down.[110] Ben Turok unsuccessfully tried to set alight the Native Divorce Court located in a Durban post office, having placed an incendiary device in a drawer that he then closed, asphyxiating the fuse. The police found the device intact, with fingerprints linking it to Turok thus leading to his arrest and imprisonment.[111] Jack Hodgson (1910–1977) and Lionel 'Rusty' Bernstein (1920–2002) succeeded in the destruction of some telecommunication cables.

Eric Mtshali related how he and Bruno Mtolo, later to be state witness 'Mr X.' who incriminated many in the Rivonia Trial, Billy Nair (1929–2008), Curnick Ndlovu and Ronnie Kasrils, all members of MK Natal Regional Command, suffered the same anticlimactic operations that characterised most of the inaugural sabotage efforts. On Ordnance Road in Durban, Mtshali and others planted a bomb at a door of the Durban pass office. Due to either sabotage within their ranks or to inexperience, it did not explode properly and caused very little damage. Although on their second operation they succeeded in felling a pylon, the team concluded that both operations were 'then not what we wanted them to be'.[112]

Ebrahim Ismail Ebrahim, a founding member of MK in the Natal Regional Command, narrated how his small unit had stolen a great deal of dynamite. In doing so, they threw away the blasting caps, not knowing what they were. Ebrahim later carried out relatively successful operations that knocked out power in much of Durban and delayed trains after impairing lines with explosives. Yet, Ebrahim also told of an unsuccessful pipe-bomb attack that caused no damage at all to the targeted telephone cables. In other unsuccessful operations, thick canvas covering goods trains proved impervious to petrol bombs hurled from above.[113]

Bobby Pillay explained how he, David Perulam (later turned state witness), Ebrahim and a fourth unnamed comrade planned to destroy the offices of an informant named Ahmed Sadeck Kajee. The first attempt using a fire-bomb was aborted when they were spotted by a guard. Their fast footwork in retreat was all that allowed them to escape. Following this failure, they intended to burn down the municipal bus depot. Again, they aborted this mission also because of the presence of guards. Next, they decided to bomb a train. Somehow, they had placed a bomb underneath the seat on which an old African man was sitting. 'Thanks God it did not go off (sic),' Pillay wrote, relieved. Apparently, one of the saboteurs improperly constructed the timing device. Pillay acknowledged in his narrative that his team acted against instructions not to cause loss of life. A second operation to blow up the Kajee business proved more successful when the premises suffered severe damage. Another operation destroyed three tracks and a signal box below the Victoria station bridge. Pillay's last operation failed to destroy an electric pole with a pipe-bomb. He said the charge had failed to ignite. The following morning he noticed it still 'attached to the pole'.[114]

The media rushed to report on the acts of sabotage and Luthuli sensed MK's involvement. In his biography of Moses Kotane, Brian Bunting reports that Luthuli 'demanded an explanation of what was going on'.[115] The news of the loss of life and the amateurishness of the acts had infuriated him. The ANC headquarters delegated prominent leaders, one after the other, to liaise with him. No one satisfactorily explained the situation to Luthuli. Finally, Luthuli summoned Moses Kotane. In defiance of his banning order, Kotane travelled to Groutville to meet Luthuli. The two huddled in a sugar cane field and clarified matters. According to Bunting, Luthuli told Kotane that he would not advocate the use of violence to any member of the ANC. Yet, Luthuli confided that he would not forbid or condemn the acts of sabotage for it was ultimately the government's fault. Nonetheless, Bunting related that Luthuli felt the question of sabotage should have been discussed by the ANC through the 'usual channels', and said: 'When my son decides to sleep with a girl, he does not ask for my permission, but just does it. It is only afterwards, when the girl is pregnant and the parents make a case, that he brings his troubles home.'[116]

The liberation movement's inability to carry out effective sabotage and the degree that such violence would antagonise the state caused Luthuli and Kotane to predict that it would not be an effective means by which to prosecute the struggle for liberation and to argue against it before MK's formation and initiation. Kotane gauged the initiation of violence to have 'ruined the movement'. After the initiation, Kotane severely chastised Ben Turok, saying: 'What the hell's wrong with you, why did you do stupid things like this? . . . If you throw stones at people's windows they're going to come out and break your neck, so don't do it unless you know what you are doing.'[117]

In his autobiography, Slovo confided that the plans for violence were 'utterly unreal', calling the initiation of violence 'at best, an heroic failure' that left the liberation movement 'abysmally weak in the years that followed'.[118] He reflected that among the factors which influenced their approach was a failure to assess the situation properly. 'We did not sufficiently realise,' he said, 'that the beginnings of armed struggle would lead to the very steps which the enemy took.'[119]

The purpose of reviewing the initial failures of MK is not to denigrate or dishonour those who sacrificed their lives for South Africa's liberation. To avoid any concerns that this brief account reflects pejoratively upon the ANC or its decision to adopt the armed struggle, only narratives sanctioned and published by the ANC are quoted. Most of these appeared in the 1986 publication, Dawn, MK's twenty-fifth anniversary commemorative publication. In most of the narratives contained in this account, MK veterans themselves acknowledged that the turn to violence was disastrous for the movement. The ANC's own published narratives demonstrate that the initiation of violence was ill-conceived, inept, haphazard and ultimately a fast-track strategy to derailing the liberation movement in the short and medium term. In the long term, MK appeared to be successful in keeping alive the psychological impetus through its armed campaign against the apartheid state. However, it is doubtful whether the turn to violence in the early 1960s advanced the day of South Africa's liberation. Instead, given the context of the Cold War, it likely postponed it.

It remains undisputed that the first MK operatives were untrained, ill-equipped and naive about the implications of their actions. The ninety-day detention laws and the use of torture to extract information from operatives could not be foreseen in the early days of MK activities. In another narrative which also appeared in the *Dawn* commemorative publication, Steve Tshwete recollected how the regime tortured one operative and how it understood the significance of the ANC's leadership change from Luthuli to Mandela.

> The police knew it too. I remember an instance when one cadre was told by one of the most famous torturers: 'Look here! I used to understand the old Congress of Luthuli, not this thing of Mandela. This is not an organisation but a bloody f[. . .] army. You are therefore a soldier and I am going to *bliksem* you like is done to a captured soldier.'[120]

Luthuli felt that his plan for using militant non-violent strategies (economic sanctions, international diplomacy and mass civil disobedience) would preserve the leadership of the liberation movement and advance the cause of liberation more effectively than sabotage and guerrilla warfare. The inexperience and ineffectiveness of MK's assaults very quickly led to the incarceration of most of the ANC's leadership, including Mandela, thus decapitating the movement. Slovo himself soberly confessed that in the years following the Rivonia Trial 'all the heroic efforts made by the movement to reconstitute in the underground failed. And for all practical purposes the internal movement as an organised structure had been destroyed.'[121]

The narratives contained in the 1986 commemorative edition of *Dawn*, written by those who initiated armed conflict on 16 December 1961, bear testimony to the short and medium-term failure of the armed struggle, notwithstanding the bravery of those who participated and the moral legitimacy of the cause. In the same publication Albie Sachs and Ronnie Kasrils highlighted the arrests, detentions, executions and betrayals of many MK cadres in the opening months and years of armed conflict: Denis Goldberg, Nelson Mandela, Curnick Ndlovu, Billy Nair, George Naicker (1919–1998), Eleanor Anderson and Bruno Mtolo.[122] MK cadres also recalled the arrests of Vuyisile Mini (1920–1964), Wilson Khayingo (1926–1964) and Zinakile Mkhaba (1929–1964).[123] With most if not all of the ANC leadership in jail or in exile, there was no one left to whom Luthuli could advocate militant non-violent strategies, and no one to carry out the organisation's laborious administration.

Luthuli's ban is often rightly blamed for limiting his leadership. However, MK cadres' narratives reflect that it was not primarily Luthuli's banning that limited his leadership (he still assisted in the organisation of the Pietermaritzburg conference and still met clandestinely with many ANC officials and Kotane). Two other circumstances primarily amputated Luthuli's leadership. First, the sudden imprisonment and exile of most of the other leaders of the movement limited Luthuli's pool of human resources and thus his capacity to lead. Second, the ANC's ideological and thus strategic policy changes required a different 'command and control' mould of leadership, and hence Luthuli's marginalisation. Though his influence had waned since Sharpeville, the initiation of violence made certain that the levers of leadership fell from his hands altogether. As Mandela announced, the non-violent movement had ended.

More important than revealing the non-efficacy of the initial strikes is the absence of any documentation of Luthuli's leadership at the time: the silence.[124] Narratives dealing with the launch of MK fail to state whether Luthuli participated in or assented to the initiation of violence. The silences in the narratives, especially from operatives in Natal, reveal that Luthuli was not involved, directly or indirectly, in the strategic implementation of violence. In her study on MK, Elaine Reinertsen also identified this silence saying: 'History is more richly textured if its pages can bring to life some of the silent moments surrounding high points of activity. These silences are very often full of conflicts, dissension and procrastination of real human beings . . .'[125]

In the narratives cited above, none of the MK cadres ever mentioned receiving instructions, advice, counsel, affirmation or support from

Luthuli, privately or publicly. No one mentioned Luthuli. Not even the Natal cadres expressed a single sentiment about or revealed a single instruction from Luthuli. The reason for this is clear: all of the Natal MK members belonged to the Communist Party and only one, Curnick Ndlovu, was also a member of the ANC. Bruno Mtolo's book, *Umkhonto we Sizwe: The Road to the Left* (1966), revealed a great deal of contestation at the time between the ANC and the Communist Party in Natal. Mtolo concluded that 'after the sabotage attempts it became clear that the local officials of the ANC in our province were not consulted', though MK designated Ndlovu to serve as its liaison with the ANC.[126] As 'Mr X.' and as an author, Mtolo is a problematic source. By providing testimony and writing a book, Mtolo intended to reflect negatively on the ANC to the state's benefit. Mtolo's concluding chapter, entitled 'Lalela [Listen], Chief Luthuli!' is absurd. The chapter is a personal appeal to Luthuli to accept the Bantustan framework. Possibly, Mtolo did not even write it; or, if he did, the state likely compelled him to do so. For example, Mtolo contradicted the above and below mentioned contents of his book when he stated, 'Remember, Chief, that the police could have acted against you at the time of Umkhonto we Sizwe. Those things were done in your name. We were the "military wing" of the ANC, and the Head Committee members were careful to obtain your approval for their actions.'[127]

Nonetheless, there is little reason to suspect that sharp disagreement did not exist between many within the ANC and the Communist Party over the use of violence and this does not necessarily reflect poorly on the ANC from the state's perspective. Mtolo also disclosed that the division existed within the Communist Party itself. His book asserted that MK did not involve the ANC in its formation or plans for launch, and purposefully so.

> We were all convinced Communists who would have nothing to do with the ANC unless it was prepared to toe the Communist line . . . We even managed to get recruits for military training overseas without approaching the ANC . . . [SACTU members] were also told that it was time that they should know their true leaders who were prepared to fight to the bitter end, and had to realise that leaders who were against Umkhonto we Sizwe were leading them nowhere . . . We could not trust some of the people who made up the ANC leadership. We could not let the dangerous underground movement be controlled by

the leaders of a mass organisation which included people who had different views from us as far as sabotage was concerned . . . Curnick told us that Walter [Sisulu] had given him strict instructions that we were not to give in to the ANC under whatever pressure.[128]

Some of those within the ANC, some communists such as Rowley Arenstein (1918–1996) and some from the SAIC applied three points of pressure on MK. Firstly, as seen in the July NEC and CJE meetings, most members of the Natal ANC opposed the use of violence and, like Luthuli, still actively opposed it. Secondly, the ANC wished to know who in the ANC also served MK. Thirdly, the ANC wished to authorise approval for any violent action. MK would not compromise on any of these three pressures. While MK believed it possessed operational autonomy from the ANC, the ANC believed it had political suzerainty over MK. MK considered its tactics, membership and launch to be operational considerations whereas the ANC considered them to be political. A clash proved inevitable as ANC leaders, according to Mtolo, voiced their suspicions that MK was an organisation 'led by irresponsible people'.[129]

MK's newly formed hierarchy, composed of a high command led by Mandela and regional commands, ignored Luthuli's leadership in the months following the announcement of the Peace Prize. The 16 December bombings were, at best, reckless, and, at worst, insubordinate. The December bombings (and more specifically their timing) exceeded the allowance given to a high command to constitute an organisation only, that is, not activate it. This rendered moot its mandate to remain under the political supervision of the ANC and, if anything, displayed its leaders' immaturity. In the same way that the M-Plan was formulated in anticipation of the possible and future need to implement it, and then implemented when circumstances deemed it necessary, MK could have been formed and not launched until a political cul-de-sac had been reached. For Luthuli, the ANC's looking the other way while Mandela led the formation of MK implied holding in abeyance plans for the initiation of armed actions.

If Luthuli did not agree with the initiation of violence, why did he not specifically denounce MK and its tactics? Three reasons stand out. Firstly, Luthuli could not blame 'brave just men' for choosing a violent course. It was a phrase that Benson quoted from her 1961 interviews with Luthuli and it was a phrase he used in his statement at the conclusion of the Rivonia Trial to describe those who resorted to violence in order to seek justice. It is also a phrase that has been much used and abused ever since. It does not say that he agreed with them. Luthuli only sympathised with his lieutenants and blamed the National Party regime. Secondly, a democratic process within three meetings agreed to form MK. In a public denunciation, Luthuli would be unable to differentiate his reluctant yielding to a democratic decision to turn a blind eye to ANC members forming MK before the Nobel Prize announcement, and his opposition to MK's launch and tactics after the Nobel Prize announcement. A denunciation of MK and its tactics would only appear hypocritical despite the fact that Luthuli did not support the decision to form or know of MK's launch. Thirdly, once Mandela launched MK, there was no turning back for the liberation movement. What was done was done.

Luthuli believed that refutation of the intractable course chosen could only harm the liberation struggle. It would never contribute to it. Though he never denounced the launching of MK activities, he continued to publicly discourage violent strategies until April 1962 and exclusively advocate for non-violent methods until his death.

Disconcerting conversation

Nelson Mandela testified in his autobiography that he visited Albert Luthuli in Groutville before departing for North Africa in January 1962.

> Before leaving [for the PAFMECSA conference in Addis Ababa in February 1962], I secretly drove to Groutville to confer with the chief. Our meeting – at a safe house in town – was disconcerting. As I have related, the chief was present at the creation of MK, and was as informed as any member of the National Executive about its development. But the chief was not well and his memory was not what it had once been. He chastised me for not consulting with him about the formation of MK. I attempted to remind him of the discussions that we had in Durban about taking up violence, but he did not recall them. This is in large part why the story has gained currency that Chief Luthuli was not informed about the creation of MK and was deeply opposed to the ANC taking up violence. Nothing could be farther from the truth.[130]

Mandela mistakenly remembered over forty years later Luthuli's displeasure at this meeting to be caused by Luthuli's inability to recall two momentous all-night meetings he had chaired just five months earlier. Did Luthuli fall victim to the historical amnesia described by Kathrada?

Portrait of Albert Luthuli by Gerard Bhengu from a newspaper photo taken early in Luthuli's life, late 1960s (Howard Trumbull).

Mabulasi Makhanya, the first indigenous convert of the American Board, 1847 (Wider Church Ministries, United Church of Christ).

Images commonly juxtaposed to justify the missiological project, date unknown (Wider Church Ministries, United Church of Christ).

Pastor (left) and deacons at the Umvoti (Groutville) church, Natal, 1900 (Harvard University, Houghton Library, American Board Collection).

Indigenous American Board ministers of religion, Natal, date unknown (Harvard University, Houghton Library, American Board Collection).

Worshippers gathered at a mission outstation, Natal, date unknown (Wider Church Ministries, United Church of Christ).

Z.K. Matthews (left), Robbins B. Guma (centre) and Albert Luthuli (right) at Adams College, late 1920s (Killie Campbell, K.R. Brueckner Collection).

Albert Luthuli, the first African teacher-trainer instructor in South Africa, at Adams College, about 1930 (Killie Campbell, K.R. Brueckner Collection).

First Advisory Board of Inanda Seminary, 1936. From left to right: Miss L. Scott, Mr R. Guma, the Rev. W. Ndawonde, Mrs G. Sivetye, Chief A.J. Luthuli, Mrs S.S. Ndlovu, Mr N. Luthuli, Dr J.L. Dube, Mr Charles Dube, Miss M. Carter, Miss M. Walbridge (Inanda Seminary Archives).

Visiting chiefs at a meeting of the Zulu Society, 1946 (Durban Local History Museum).

Drs John Reuling (seated) and Lavinia Scott (speaking) in the Inanda Seminary chapel, 1958 (Inanda Seminary Archives).

Albert Luthuli's handwritten speech on Gandhi at Howard University, Washington DC, 1948 (Luthuli Papers).

MAHTMA GAHDI
MEMORIAL ON THE
OCCASION OF THE
CENTENRI CEMTENARY
CELEBRATIONS OF THE
WASHINGTON UNIVESTI
UNIVERSITy, U S. A

I am happy to join
the thousands who are
congratulating the
washington University die on
reaching a century of
Meritorius Serice in the
interest of Higher Education
, uplift among the
American Negros to
setting them to effectively
challenge discrimination
from which they still suffers
from which they still suffer

Albert Luthuli's modest home, Groutville (Durban Local History Museum).

Mrs Nomhlatuzi Ntuli (left) and Mr K.E. Masinga (right) with Luthuli (centre) speaking at Inanda Seminary's eightieth anniversary, 1949 (Inanda Seminary Archives).

Congregationalist ministers Posselt Gumede (left) and
John Dube (right) with Albert Luthuli (centre) at Inanda
Seminary, 1936 (Mwelela Cele).

Mary-Louise Hooper (centre), Albert Luthuli, M.B. Yengwa and others, date unknown
(Luthuli Museum, Yengwa Collection).

Albert and Nokukhanya Luthuli at Inanda Seminary, date unknown (Killie Campbell, K.R. Brueckner Collection).

Albert Luthuli being congratulated by E.V. Mahomed and Rolfes Robert Reginald Dhlomo for the Nobel Peace Prize award in Stanger, 1961 (Durban Local History Museum).

Prayer service at home before Luthuli's departure for Oslo, Norway, 1961 (Durban Local History Museum).

Crowd waiting to greet Albert Luthuli on his return from Oslo, Norway, 1961 (Luthuli Museum, Yengwa Collection).

Painting of *The Black Christ* by Ronald Harrison, 1962.

Albert Luthuli and Americal Board missioner, Howard Trumbull, about 1965 (Howard Trumbull).

Telegram inviting Albert Luthuli to New York to receive the Family of Man award, 1964 (Luthuli Papers).

CPD AJG 0900.

DURBAN

1964 OCT 17 AM 9 03

TACL405 LOG345 NB236 NEWYORK 110 16 1522EDT

LT.LUTHULI CARE ABM 66 BEATRICE STREET DURBAN.

THIS IS OFFICIAL INVITATION FOR ATTEND FAMILY OF MAN DINNER NEWYORK OCTOBER 28TH TO RECEIVE HUMANITIES AWARD BEING GIVEN YOU PRESIDENT KENNEDY GUEST OF HONOR LAST YEAR. GENERAL EISENHOWER THIS YEAR LARGEST EVENT OF ITS KIND IN US YOUR EXPENSES OUR OF 5000 DOLLAR GRANT HAVE SENT FULL INFORMATION TO SOUTH AFRICAN AMBASSADOR IN WASHINGTON THEY SAID INFORMATION HAS BEEN SENT TO THEIR GOVERNMENT AS THEY AWAIT YOUR FORMAL APPLICATION BEFORE THEY CAN ACT PLEASE ADVISE REV DR ARTHUR LEE KINSOLVING PRESIDENT PROTESTANT COUNCIL HONORABLE JOHN HAY WHITNEY, CHAIRMAN DINNER COMMITTEE MR WHELLOCK H BINGHAM CHAIRMAN SOCIETY FOR THE FAMILY OF MAN

5000.

Bridge upon which Albert Luthuli was killed while crossing, 1967 (Durban Local History Museum).

Train passing over bridge demonstrating the overlap of the locomotive into the footplate, 1967 (Durban Local History Museum).

Post-mortem Serial No.(*)_____

Exhibit No.(*) __C.__

- Case Inq. 76/67.

REPORT ON A MEDICO-LEGAL POST-MORTEM EXAMINATION.

To the Magistrate of (*)____ **Stanger**

I, (*) __Jacobus Johannes van Zyl_____, do hereby certify—

I. that at (*)____ **Stanger Mortuary**

on the __21__ day of _____ **July** ___19 67__ commencing at __4.0__ . ~~a.m.~~/p.m.,

I examined the body of ____ **Bantu** _____(*) __Male__ _____(*) __Adult__ _____(*);

II. that this body was identified to me(*)—

(a) by __Eric Chili_____ of __Groutville_____; and

(b) by _____ of _____

as being that of (**)__Albert John Luthuli_____ whose reputed age was __+ 70 yrs__ .

III. that this body was also identified to me (**)—

(a) by __Peter Papayya_____ of __Stanger Hosp._____

as being that of __the body conveyed from the scene of the accident to
Stanger Hosp._____; and

(b) by __Dr. Gregersen_____ of __Stanger Hosp._____

as being that of __the patient attended in casualties Stanger Hosp.__

IV. that the chief post-mortem findings made by me on this body were (**):—____

1. // base scull' - blood oozing from (R) ear.
2. Multiple lacerations scalp - sutured.
3. Laceration (R) shin.
4. // ribs (L) & (R) side.
5. // (L) Ulna proximal end. Puncure mark for I.V. drip (R) cubital vein.
6. Multiple bruises (L) & (R) hand - dorsal aspect.

; and

V. that, as a result of my observations a schedule of which follows, I concluded—

(a) that death had occurred (**) __+ 1½ hrs_____ prior to my examination; and

(b) that the cause/~~times~~ of death was/~~were~~(**) __Cerebral haemorrage & contusion brain.__

Dated at ____ **Stanger** _____ this __21__ day of __July__ _____ 19 67

Signature____ J.J. van Z~~yl~~

Designation (**) __D/S.__

Sgd C.B.P.Lewis Det.Serg.V. No.149

21st July 1967.

Albert Luthuli's Medico-Legal Post-Mortem Examination, 1967 (Luthuli Papers).

Arial view of Albert Luthuli's funeral service at the Groutville Congregational Church, 1967 (Durban Local History Museum).

Local Congregational pastor, the Reverend Nimrod G. Ngcobo, and family at Albert Luthuli's graveside service, 1967 (Luthuli Museum).

"Albert would have rejected today's violence..." Mrs Albert Lutuli.

Chief M G Buthelezi sharing a happy moment with Mrs Albert Lutuli.

The widow of ANC President Chief Albert Lutuli, Mrs Nokukhanya Lutuli, 81, says her husband would never have identified with the present policies of the External Mission of the ANC.

In an interview with the *Durban Daily News* at her Groutville home, Mrs Lutuli, 81, added that he also would not have condoned the violence which exists in South Africa today.

"Like my husband, I am sick and tired of violence. Albert worked towards a better South Africa by negotiation, not by the barrel of a gun which the ANC of today is doing. It makes me very sad indeed. I am glad my husband has not lived to see what's happening to the present-day ANC."

Chief Lutuli was awarded the Nobel Peace Prize in 1960 and died in 1967 when he was hit and killed by a train near his home. His funeral was attended by dignitaries from many parts of the world.

Chief M G Buthelezi, who was advised by Chief Lutuli and assisted him for many years, was asked to deliver the funeral oration. Later, when the OAU made a posthumous award to Chief Lutuli, Mrs Lutuli asked Chief Buthelezi to accompany her to the ceremony in Maseru, Lesotho.

In her interview Mrs Lutuli said she was now waiting to die.

"I'm tired of seeing the violence that exists in the world," she said. A once-dynamic woman, she played an active role in her husband's affairs.

Mrs Lutuli added that State President P W Botha should ". . . stop fighting to maintain apartheid. Its silly and it involves the loss of lives of innocent people."

Excerpt from an interview with Nokukhanya Luthuli in the *Durban Daily News*, 1985 (Durban Local History Museum).

Launch of the Chief Albert Luthuli Legacy Project, 2004. From left: The Reverend Dr Bruce Theron shaking hands with President Thabo Mbeki, the Reverend Dr Bonganjalo Goba, KwaZulu-Natal Premier Sibusiso Ndebele and Albertinah Luthuli (Scott Couper).

The author, Scott Couper, and captain of the amaButho (Soldiers of Christ), Themba Alexander Mgobhozi, at the Groutville Congregational Church, UCCSA, 2008 (Scott Couper).

Albert Luthuli's gravesite at the Groutville Congregational
Church, UCCSA, 2008 (Scott Couper).

Groutville Congregational Church, UCCSA, 2008 (Scott Couper).

Luthuli was indeed angry with Mandela. However, his anger did not arise because he felt he was not involved in or informed about the allowance of MK's formation. Certainly, he had presided over the critical meetings which arrived at the decision, and more importantly, he remembered being present. Instead, it was MK's launch without his knowledge, on the heels of the receipt of the Nobel Peace Prize, that angered Luthuli.

Following the failed May 1961 strike, Mandela had held a press conference with western journalists at which he spoke of 'closing a chapter on this question of a non-violent policy'. The NEC reprimanded him for making such a statement public without first consulting with the movement. Luthuli felt that Mandela had again acted unilaterally by issuing the manifesto announcing MK on 16 December 1961. Although the manifesto qualified that MK would use violence as a 'complement to previous actions' and, although it stated that 'repression and violence will no longer be met with non-violent resistance only', the overall tone declared: 'We are striking out on a new road for the liberation of the people of this country.'[131] It implied the abandonment of non-violent methods, violating the NEC and CJE meetings' agreements to continue traditional methods of resistance. By authorising the formation of an armed movement, the NEC and CJE intended to prepare for, at most, a parallel strategy, and more realistically, a secondary strategy. Luthuli warned that the formation of MK must not be at the expense of the continuance of political methods. In unpublished autobiographical fragments dating back to his period of imprisonment in the 1970s, Nelson Mandela reflected that he and others 'had made exactly that mistake, drained the political organisations of their enthusiastic and experienced men [and] concentrated our attention on the new organisation'.[132]

By forming and launching MK, the ANC abandoned its political work. Having not educated, informed or trained the grassroots for a new form of struggle, the sabotage operations rendered most ANC members spectators. The MK manifesto contradicted the joint congresses's covenant with MK when it stated: 'The time comes in the life of any nation when there remain only two choices: submit or fight.' From Mandela, this constituted a political statement that equated Luthuli's militant non-violent methods with 'submission' and violence with 'fighting', and declared boldly, 'We shall not submit . . .'[133]

Some evidence suggests that rather than complement the ANC's non-violent strategies, the launch of MK intentionally sought to undermine them. Mohamed Meghraoui of Algeria's National Liberation Front (FLN) proposed in an unpublished article of August 1967, shortly after Luthuli's death, that the timing of MK's launch aimed specifically to diminish the anesthetising effect the Nobel Prize would have on the South African majority. He said that it became important for the oppressed people of South Africa to demonstrate to the world that no amount 'of respectable titles could stop the struggle of the African people'.[134] Meghraoui suggested outrageously that Luthuli intended to return to South Africa from Oslo to launch MK the following day.[135] In the article, which was submitted to, but not published by the ANC publication, *Sechaba*, Meghraoui refuted the distorted 'Western press' descriptions of Luthuli 'as a pacifist, a Ghandi [sic] of South Africa'. He described Luthuli as a 'revolutionary', a 'fighter' and a 'militant' and concluded that Luthuli 'constantly stood for the overthrow of the racist regime by the use of the most orthodox method of our times, i.e. the armed struggle'.[136]

Mary Benson, in her biography of Mandela, points to the central problem in Luthuli's position. It was not his marginalisation from the decision to allow for the formation of MK that was the issue. Rather, he felt disturbed by the unilateral political statements that accompanied the premature commencement of the new organisation's methods. According to Benson, Luthuli was aware of the role of Mandela and 'criticized the failure to consult himself and the ANC "grassroots"'. For Luthuli, 'they had been compromised'.[137]

The manifesto stated that 'Umkhonto we Sizwe fully supports the national liberation movement and our members, jointly and individually, place themselves under the overall political guidance of that movement'.[138] Though the new organisation would be separate from the ANC, the two entities would be linked and MK would come under the ANC's formal control. M.B. Yengwa stated the same in his unpublished draft autobiography. While it is true that due to the political climate the precise relationship between the ANC and the armed movement was nebulous and often characterised oxymoronically, Luthuli felt that the 16 December implementation of the new methods and the rationale for justifying them were intrinsically political rather than operational. Because no one had consulted him about the planning, impending occurrence and the timing of the December bombings, Mandela violated the spirit, if not the letter, of the CJE meeting's compromise.

The entire manifesto essentially indicted and rebuked the 'former' non-violent strategies, not only viewing them as obsolete, but as fuelling continuing oppression by the state. Mandela had himself said that the government viewed the non-violent policies of the liberation movement as a green light for government violence. He was willing to be the 'tail that wags the dog', as he did previously during the interview with foreign journalists following the May 1961 strike. In his autobiography, he stated: '. . . sometimes one must go public with an idea to push a reluctant organization in the direction you want it to go'.[139] This Mandela did, not just in word, but also in deed. Luthuli was helpless to stop it.

5

Brave Just Men

1962–1966

There are many unanswered prayers. We forget that the answer
to prayer may be 'No!' because God knows what we should have!
— Albert Luthuli's notes from a radio broadcasted sermon by
the Congregational minister, The Reverend Noel Tarrant

IN DECEMBER 1961, the ANC received an invitation from the Pan-
African Freedom Movement for East, Central and Southern Africa
(PAFMECSA) to attend a conference in Addis Ababa, Ethiopia, which
would take place in February 1962. Meeting on 3 January 1962, the ANC
NEC meeting resolved to ask Nelson Mandela to lead the ANC delegation
to the conference. The ANC underground and Luthuli insisted that
Mandela go. Given the ANC's need to secure outside political, financial,
moral and military support for the new phase of its struggle, it hoped to
use the PAFMECSA conference as a means to network throughout the
continent and communicate with allies in exile. A whirlwind tour by
Mandela of west, north and east Africa would connect the rather insular
ANC with the wider continent.

Divergent objectives
As established at the end of Chapter 4, prior to his departure for the
PAFMECSA conference, on 8 January 1962 Nelson Mandela drove covertly
to Groutville to liaise with Albert Luthuli. Two sources offer information
about their meeting, both authored by Mandela. In his biography on
Mandela, Tom Lodge points to three discrepancies between Mandela's
autobiographical account of this meeting and his January 1962 diary
entries. Firstly, Mandela's 8 January diary entry mentioned that 'Luthuli
was in high spirits' when he met with him.[1] In and of itself, this does not

represent a contradiction with Mandela's autobiographical recollection thirty years later of a 'disconcerting' conversation.

A second and more pertinent discrepancy is whether Luthuli approved of the military objective of Mandela's sojourn throughout Africa. In his 1964 Rivonia Trial statement, Mandela indicated that in addition to attending the conference, the purpose of his visit was to 'obtain facilities for the training of soldiers' and to 'solicit scholarships for the higher education of matriculated Africans'.[2]

Luthuli may have only been aware of the educational rather than the military purpose of the trip. One recalls Mtolo's earlier testimony that members of the ANC were not consulted on the objectives of obtaining military training. Arranging support and, more importantly, training, for the new military force may have been the intention of the trip for Mandela, Sisulu and other members of the NEC, but that may not have been articulated to Luthuli on 8 January. In his 1964 Rivonia Trial court statement, Mandela contradicted himself regarding the intended objectives of his trip. First he stated that prior to his departure the purpose of his trip would include military objectives. However, later Mandela stated that a military objective went against an original ANC decision:

> I also made arrangements for our recruits to undergo military training. But [in north Africa] it was impossible to organise any scheme without the cooperation of the ANC offices in Africa. I consequently obtained the permission of the ANC in South Africa to do this. *To this extent then there was a departure from the original decision of the ANC, but it applied outside South Africa only* (emphasis added).[3]

A third discrepancy is that Mandela's 8 January diary entry neglects to comment that Luthuli expressed anger about the decision to follow an armed course. Perhaps Mandela did not wish to record Luthuli's disagreement in his diary. Tom Lodge eruditely speculates that in his autobiography Mandela interpolated into his telling of the 'disconcerting meeting' later debates about Luthuli's views.[4] Also in his autobiography, Mandela failed to explain how on 3 January Luthuli approved of Mandela's exiting the country to arrange training, finances and political support for MK, and then, five days later, on 8 January, chastised Mandela for not consulting him about MK's formation. Mandela also failed to explain how Luthuli eventually arrived at his support of MK's formation after,

according to Mandela, forgetting about his participation in its formation
and his subsequent anger about being marginalised. Such discrepancies
suggest Luthuli did not know of the military objectives for Mandela's trip
and that he never supported the turn to violence.

African sojourn

Mandela's autobiography gave a detailed chronicle of his sojourn
throughout Africa. On 10 January, he drove to Lobatse, Bechuanaland
(Botswana), illegally exiting South Africa. After travelling to Kasane in
northern Bechuanaland, he flew to Mbeya, Tanganyika (Tanzania).
Proceeding to Dar es Salaam, Mandela met the independent country's
first president, Julius Nyerere (1922–1999), who advised him to postpone
the armed struggle. Next, Mandela travelled via Khartoum, Sudan, to
Accra, Ghana, where he met Oliver Tambo for the first time in nearly two
years. In February, Mandela travelled to Addis Ababa to attend the
PAFMECSA conference. At the conference, Mandela's speech proclaimed
the opposite of that which Luthuli and (according to Luthuli in his Rivonia
statement) the ANC believed: '[A]ll opportunities for peaceful struggle
had been closed to us', hence the need to launch MK.[5] If, as Benson
asserted, Luthuli chastised Mandela after his return from north Africa,
Mandela's speech gave Luthuli good reason to be upset. Mandela said at
the PAFMECSA conference, 'A leadership commits *a crime* against its own
people if it hesitates to sharpen its political weapons where they have
become less effective . . . On the night of 16 December last year, the whole
of South Africa vibrated under the heavy blows of Umkhonto we Sizwe'
(emphasis added).[6] For Luthuli, Mandela's ethical accusation and
hyperbole could easily be interpreted as insubordinate and insulting.

Mandela continued to Cairo and Tunis and on to Rabat, Morocco,
where, he records in his autobiography, the head of the Algerian mission
advised him not to neglect the political side of war saying, 'International
public opinion is sometimes worth more than a fleet of jet fighters'.[7]
Mandela then travelled to Bamako in Mali, to Guinea and to Sierra Leone
where he was mistaken for Luthuli. Next, Mandela journeyed to Liberia,
back to Ghana and back to Guinea where he met Ahmed Sekou Touré
(1922–1984). In Dakar, Mandela conversed with President Léopold Sédar
Senghor (1906–2001) and then proceeded to London were he had a
disconcerting conversation with Yusuf Dadoo. Mandela records that Dadoo
objected to his view that the ANC must seek to be more pan-Africanist in

nature and that within the alliance of the congresses the ANC (blacks) 'had to appear to be the first among equals'.[8] Upon Mandela's return to South Africa, Luthuli expressed these same objections to him.

Mandela then travelled a second time to Addis Ababa to receive six months of military training. Training was rudimentary, but included drill marches, firing with an automatic rifle and pistol, demolition and mortar firing. He learned to make and avoid bombs and mines. He spent much of his time being trained in military science and tactics by an Ethiopian officer. After only eight weeks, the ANC urgently requested Mandela return home as the 'internal armed struggle was escalating and they wanted the commander of MK on the scene'.[9] Again, the fact that the ANC, and not the MK high command, requested Mandela's return is very confusing. The ANC remained non-violent by agreement. What had the ANC to do with an escalating internal armed struggle? More than likely, Mandela had to return home early because his 'army' was being arrested, tried and imprisoned very quickly as a result of the initial failings of MK's launch. Lodge speculated that Sisulu recalled him, worried that a prolonged absence would demoralise the MK rank and file as anxieties regarding whether Mandela would return to South Africa increased. After only eight weeks of training, on 24 July, Mandela had to lead his army in defeating the most powerful military force on the African continent.

On his return Mandela immediately reported to the National Working Committee (NWC) on the lessons learned during his journeys. During his trip to north and west Africa, he had frequently became frustrated by the PAC's propaganda against the ANC. Recently decolonised Africa identified with a militaristic outlook and sympathised with a racial divide, and the ANC's non-violent and multiracial policy failed to impress or inspire, if it was understood at all. Luthuli did not necessarily desire to impress Africa. His objective was the long-term acceptance and support of the western world and Africa's fusion, not separation, with it as a free and equal partner. In December 1961 during the events celebrating his reception of the Peace Prize, Luthuli wooed the west. Beginning in January 1962, Mandela sought to woo Africa.

History suggests that Luthuli's approach may have been more pragmatic than Mandela's. By 1990, the support of the Frontline States and MK's incursions into South Africa had not succeeded in effecting a regime change. Rather, regime change was precipitated by a combination of non-violent internal pressures from churches, trade unions, the mass democratic movement drawn together in the United Democratic Front and the pressure of economic sanctions fuelled by widespread international condemnation of the apartheid regime. The fall of the Berlin wall and the collapse of communism atrophied the eastern bloc's support of African liberation movements. For western democracies, gone was the communist bogeyman, and thus gone was their support for Pretoria.

The PAC eventually became irrelevant outside and inside South Africa. Its pro-Africanist stance may have appealed to the newly emerging African states, but it was a stance that undermined the organisation's efforts to generate support outside Africa. Countries like Sweden and Norway, long time supporters of the ANC, did not support the PAC because of its expressed racial character. Tor Sellström, author of several texts on the anti-apartheid struggle in Scandinavia, reflected that while the PAC was recognised by the Organisation of African Unity (OAU), it never received assistance from the Swedish government or tangible support from the Swedish non-governmental organisation (NGO) community. From the outset, Swedish support went to the ANC.

While Mandela was away, contention had arisen over the nature of the ANC and its leader's recently published autobiography, *Let My People Go*. If Luthuli's Nobel Peace Prize did not embarrass Mandela enough, then Luthuli's autobiography did.

Let My People Go

When William Collins published Albert Luthuli's autobiography on 18 January 1962, Nelson Mandela was preparing to address the PAFMECSA gathering in Addis Ababa. While the autobiography proclaimed: 'We do not struggle with guns and violence, and the supremacist's array of weapons is powerless against the spirit', Mandela told the conference in Ethiopia that it was a 'crime' for the leadership to hesitate to change tactics when those tactics proved futile.[10] The autobiography caused much embarrassment to Mandela and others. Mandela wrote in a 24 July report to the ANC Working Committee that some of Luthuli's statements in his autobiography 'have been extremely unfortunate and have created the impression of a man who is a stooge of the whites'.[11]

Luthuli's choice of a title for his autobiography was a fundamentally biblical (rather than political) act and it provides a clue to understanding the life and leadership of the man. To understand the role of the biblical Moses, is to understand Luthuli. Using the hermeneutical lens of a typological re-enactment, one perceives that Luthuli saw himself as obedient rather than successful, an ethical as much as (if not more than) a political leader, non-violent rather than militarist and even a tragic rather than a triumphant character in his inability to reach the Promised Land.

In choosing the title *Let My People Go* for his autobiography, Luthuli invoked the prophet Moses' divinely inspired biblical refrain to the Egyptian Pharaoh who oppressed the Hebrew nation.[12] As with 'The Road to Freedom is Via the Cross', the choice of title strongly suggested that he perceived himself to be a spiritual leader as much as, if not more than, a political leader. He may well have understood his life and life's work along the lines of a typological re-enactment, by which is meant a method or lens of biblical hermeneutics whereby one discerns one's context, calling or life direction, by identifying with personalities in the biblical narrative. Typological re-enactment encourages one to emulate faithful biblical personalities or, conversely, to learn from them if they failed in some way. If Luthuli understood his life's purpose to be a re-enactment of the role of Moses in the Bible, it would have provided for him a framework for both understanding the past and discerning the will of God for the future. His emulation of Moses became a simple method of making relevant the biblical text to his life.[13]

Though Luthuli did not receive formal theological training that would prepare him specifically for the vocation of ministry, his strong faith, adequate education, innate intelligence and Christian upbringing made him a formidable lay minister. If he had opted for the ordained ministry, he would have succeeded admirably. While he had sufficient formal and self-education to articulate the fundamentals of Christianity, and arguably do so more proficiently than his peers who did enter the ministry, Luthuli did not study theology formally and could not develop for himself a 'systematic' theology, a theology that, to the extent that it is possible, is comprehensively logical, doctrinal and integrated. As a layperson, Luthuli's theology would have been parochial rather than systematic. Rather than doctrine, philosophy or direct revelation, typological re-enactment relies on narratives to convey various descriptive and proscriptive themes. The narratives may be in the form of myth, parable or actual historic personalities and occurrences.

The biblical Moses waged a political struggle utilising non-violent methods. The divine interventions that convinced the Pharaoh to allow the Hebrews to leave Egypt were undeniably forceful, even deadly.[14] Nevertheless, they were neither the direct result of Moses' hand nor the result of a Hebrew army.[15] For Moses, the means to liberation were fidelity and obedience to God (Exodus 4:21a, 7:2 and 12:24). Pharaoh's heart would be hardened and his kingdom would suffer catastrophe due to its own leader's intransigent position (Exodus 4:21b, 7:2, 8:15, 8:19, 8:32, 9:7, 9:12, 9:34–35, 10:20, 10:27 and 11:10).

Luthuli did not envision himself as a Joshua, Saul, David or Solomon who, through military might, would build a great nation. Rather, he looked to Moses who humbly led in obedience despite all his inadequacies.[16] Time after time, Moses' obedience resulted in failure as the Pharaoh repeatedly rescinded his mercy. Yet, Moses continued to confront Pharaoh and repeated God's refrain, 'Let my people go!'[17]

Even following the Hebrews' liberation, Moses' role as a moral leader coincided with his role as a political leader for he provided the Hebrew people with the Ten Commandments and the Torah (The Law) (Exodus 20). Luthuli perhaps even foreshadowed his inability to see the Promised Land of his own people's liberation when he predicted in his 1952 'The Road to Freedom is Via the Cross' statement:

> What the future has in store for me I do not know. It might be ridicule, imprisonment, concentration camp, flogging, banishment and even death. I only pray to the Almighty to strengthen my resolve so that none of these grim possibilities may deter me from striving, for the sake of the good name of our beloved country, the Union of South Africa, to make it a true democracy and a true union in form and spirit of all the communities of the land.[18]

And like Moses, Luthuli would not reach the Promised Land (Deut. 32:48–52; 34). Like Moses, who led the Chosen People that were to be a light to all nations, Luthuli saw himself leading South Africa as 'a new example to the world'.[19] In a 1958 speech entitled 'Freedom is the Apex', Luthuli told a meeting of the Congress of Democrats held in Johannesburg that he personally believed that South Africa, with all its 'diversities of colour and race' would one day 'show the world a new pattern for democracy. I think there is a challenge to us in South Africa to set a new example for the world. Let us not side-step that task.'[20]

Handwritten notes of Luthuli's dating back to 8 January, the first Sunday morning of 1967, when he tuned in to a radio sermon preached at a Congregationalist church in Cape Town, highlight the teaching that

God's response to one's prayers is often 'No'. This sermon would have resonated with Luthuli's re-enactment of Moses. Moses desired to enter the Promised Land. God told Moses that he would not; he would only see it from a distance (Exodus 32:52). Luthuli also wished to see that for which he strove so obediently. Concluding his autobiography, he prayed that God would give him strength and courage enough to die for the struggle if necessary. He did not want to die, however, until he had 'seen the building begun'.[21]

Luthuli's request was not granted. Even with the companionship of Nokukhanya, the final years of Luthuli's life were lonely. Government restrictions, his own adherence to non-violence and his aging body marginalised him from the ANC and the world. Luthuli had fought for a South Africa that would belong to all who lived in it, irrespective of colour. As his life waned, white South Africans who were resistant to change retreated farther into their laager, 'armed to the teeth', as Luthuli put it in his speech to acknowledge his receiving of the Christopher Gell memorial award. MK's launch unleashed the state's wrath, resulting in the imprisoning and/or exiling of other leaders of the liberation movement. In such a move, the ANC turned away from him as its leader, though he continued to hold the office of president general. Luthuli's people had let *him* go.

For six months after its initial publication, copies of Let My People Go were sold in South Africa. The Minister of Justice, B.J. Vorster, allowed the sale of unsold books in stock already imported from England into South Africa. In August 1962, however, Vorster put a stop to the import of any further copies. The book was banned under the General Law Amendment (Sabotage) Act.

Embarrassment to the congresses

Albert Luthuli found a kindred spirit in the Durban attorney, Rowley Arenstein, who had gone so far as to describe the armed struggle 'totally uncalled for' and had said that it had failed.[22] Arenstein left the Communist Party over its decision to initiate an armed struggle prior to the ANC and joint congresses's decision to do the same. He felt betrayed by the Communist Party because he felt that it intentionally excluded him when making the decision to opt for violence. After expressing these objections, the Communist Party, for its part, expelled him.

At a meeting of the Congresses' Joint Executive (CJE) in January 1962, after Mandela had launched MK in December 1961, Arenstein had argued vociferously against the creation of an armed wing and questioned under whose control the military wing would fall. He adamantly maintained that Luthuli had never agreed to the shift in policy.

In the course of his work, Arenstein frequently provided legal representation for those who became entangled with the law for political reasons.[23] In 1958, he strategised with Luthuli on how to increase the active membership of the ANC by focusing on grassroots issues. For their efforts, membership grew from one thousand in 1958 to twenty thousand in 1959. According to Arenstein, he ran the Durban branch of the ANC during the 1960 State of Emergency. After the government banned the ANC, Arenstein suggested they rename the organisation the 'African National Council' and continue to work to achieve the *objectives* of the ANC that, according to a then-recent Supreme Court ruling, had not been banned with the organisation. The ANC refused, and, according to Arenstein, resigned itself to the fact that the government had closed all avenues of non-violent methods.

At least with the wider and international public, Luthuli was not a spent political force as 1962 began and he continued to use the media as a forum to promote his views. In February, African Americans' Chicago-based *Ebony* magazine published an article by Luthuli entitled, 'What I Would Do If I Were Prime Minister' wherein he laid out his political manifesto.[24] Another American magazine, *Atlantic Monthly*, reprinted the article shortly thereafter.[25] In this article, Luthuli provided broad perspectives on land reform, trade union rights, democratic polity, housing, education and foreign policy. The 1 February issue of *New Age* published a statement entitled, 'We Don't Want Crumbs'.[26] In this article, his autobiography and his many columns on the subject in the *Golden City Post*, Luthuli expressed his perspectives on democracy, society and civilisation as he intoned against the government's proposed homeland policy.

Luthuli's incessant harping on non-violence long after MK's launch deeply disturbed many of his more militant colleagues following MK's launch. His publicised views directly contradicted Mandela's views found in MK's manifesto. For example, on 25 March 1962, Luthuli's regular column published in the *Golden City Post* read:

When we strive for the same goal through non-violent methods, the government visits us with more and harsher laws to suppress – if not completely destroy – our liberation efforts. *Is this not inviting the oppressed to desperation? Nonetheless, I would urge our people not to despair over our methods of struggle, the militant, nonviolent techniques. So far we have failed the methods – not the methods us* (original emphasis).[27]

In the same month the *Golden City Post* published the above column excerpt, a report of a CJE meeting recorded that Luthuli's columns were 'frequently so mutilated that the policies expressed there were on occasion distorted, thus being of some embarrassment to the Congresses'.[28] The minutes of that meeting record that the matter would be 'taken up'.

The suggestion is that Luthuli was reprimanded by his own movement. Apparently, it was felt that Luthuli had overreached himself in his advocacy for non-violent methods and had come dangerously close to condemning the turn to violence. This breach could not be tolerated. Luthuli needed to be counselled not to embarrass the movement. Following the matter's resolution, much of the leadership felt assured that such sentiments from Luthuli would no longer be heard or read. In resolving the matter, the ANC very possibly advised Luthuli to stop advocating a policy of strict non-violence. Before his death, the ANC refrained from making any assertion that Luthuli supported the armed movement.

The index of seventy-six articles itemised by Bailey's African Photo Archives (BAPA) indicates that Luthuli's last column for the *Golden City Post* was published on 27 May 1962, two months after the matter was recorded in the minutes of the CJE. A comparison of the published columns with unpublished drafts shows that the *Golden City Post* did little, if any, editing of Luthuli's submissions. In published form, the length and style of the columns are uniform and characteristic of Luthuli's pen. Further, besides his opposition to violence, there is no evidence of Luthuli 'distorting' any of the ANC's stated policies. After the 25 March column appeared, virtually nothing further is heard from Luthuli on the subject of non-violence, save for a 29 April column article claiming that the 'mood of white South Africa forces on us the use of militant efforts – on non-violent lines – in the prosecution of our struggle'.[29]

How and when the ANC, through the CJE, advised Luthuli to curb his statements advocating non-violence is unknown. The archives are silent on this issue. Luthuli and the ANC likely established a covenant that committed him to refrain from criticising or questioning the turn to violence. In March 1963, soon after his escape from South Africa, the ANC's secretary general, Duma Nokwe, travelled to Sweden, where he delivered a militant speech at the launch of a national consumer boycott campaign held in Stockholm. Also at this launch, Nokwe read a message telephonically transmitted by Oliver Tambo in London encouraging a boycott of South African goods. The message was said to be authorised by Luthuli. During his visit, Nokwe spoke in regard to the methods of struggle, indicating that the ANC had no choice but 'to abandon its policy of non-violence', that 'there no longer [were] any peaceful ways left' and that the South African people would 'not get its [sic] freedom without a [sic] bloody chaos'. Notably, Nokwe ominously emphasised, 'And I assure you that our leader, Albert Luthuli, will not condemn that.'[30]

Sabotage Act

Albert Luthuli could have continued to contribute columns to the Golden City Post until at least 24 June 1962, the date of his last domestic publication in New Age. If those within the liberation movement did not pressure Luthuli to refrain from making 'embarrassing' statements, then the government did. When the General Law Amendment Bill became the Sabotage Act of 27 June 1962, it 'prohibited the reproduction of any statement made anywhere at any time (including any time in the past) by a person who was banned from attending gatherings'.[31] The Act also prescribed the death penalty for a wide range of offences and allowed the government to commit people to house arrest. Some viewed the legislation tantamount to 'civil death' for those on whom it fell. With this piece of legislation, the government silenced Luthuli within South Africa's borders until his death. Fully aware of the impact the legislation would have, Luthuli wrote against it in New Age, three days before it became law.[32] The illegality of quoting Luthuli may have been a relief to many who thought that his continued advocacy of non-violent methods was tantamount to, in Mandela's words, 'committing a crime' against his own people.

Regarding historical memory, Luthuli's prolonged silence within South Africa, neither for nor against the violent movement, transcends the relatively short period of time from 16 December 1961 when MK launched until 29 April 1962 when, for the last time, Luthuli advocated strict non-violence in his Golden City Post column. What seems apparent is that by not recognising this brief and forgotten slice of time, the ANC disingenuously claims that once the decision had been made to initiate the armed movement, 'Luthuli did not falter'.

Internationally, Luthuli could not be silenced. Before the Act became law, he wrote a statement for publication in England's *Guardian* newspaper opposing it. On 8 July 1962, the *Guardian* published Luthuli's statement soon after its reception. In it, Luthuli communicated his characteristically buoyant and optimistic outlook despite contemplating the draconian legislation. He did not doubt the fall of tyranny. Doubt only existed regarding liberation's timing and cost. His statement related that, unlike Mandela, he had never concluded that the non-violent path led to a cul-de-sac. Luthuli perceived the Sabotage Act as a sign of the National Party's desperation and indicative of the foundational weakness of the apartheid system. He declared that the oppressive legislation stood as a governmental admission of the 'effectiveness of our freedom and of its latent potentialities'.[33] Non-violent international political and economic pressure on the apartheid regime was to be the key to liberation.

In July 1962, the *Cape Times* asked the Minister of Justice for permission to publish quotations by Luthuli. The request was denied. The *Cape Times* wished to ask Luthuli if the government had granted him a passport to an upcoming Cultural Conference in Copenhagen, Denmark, to which he had received an invitation. In denying the request, the Minister of Justice indicated that he need never be asked again to lift Luthuli's restriction.[34]

Luthuli as the 'The Black Christ'

At the young age of twenty-two, Roland Harrison, the artist who painted *The Black Christ*, had the fortune to meet Luthuli in 1962, under clandestine circumstances. Harrison painted the figure of Christ, crucified on a cross, with Luthuli's features. With the permission of Archbishop de Blank, St Luke's Anglican Church in Salt River unveiled the painting. It drew a storm of controversy. Not only did Christ appear as a black man, but the two Roman soldiers resembled Prime Minister Hendrik Verwoerd, and the Minister of Justice, John Vorster. Jan de Klerk, then Minister of the Interior, ordered that the painting be taken down and the young artist appear before the Censorship Board.[35] The board subsequently banned the painting, ruling that it offended religious sensibilities. Following a documentary on the painting aired on the American television network CBS, the government ordered the painting to be destroyed. Danish and

Swedish allies of the Anti-Apartheid Movement then smuggled it to Great Britain where, under Canon John Collins's care, its display raised a substantial sum of money for the Defence and Aid Fund.[36] Harrison suffered arrest and torture at the hands of the Special Branch who through their interrogations aimed to discover with whom Harrison collaborated to paint, display and smuggle *The Black Christ*.

Knowing about the painting and its significance, Luthuli expressed a desire to meet Harrison. With the help of the Norwegian Embassy and at great risk, a clandestine meeting was arranged. Harrison was smuggled from Cape Town to Durban, driving slowly through the night, taking advantage of the cover of darkness. Harrison met Luthuli in Groutville under a corrugated iron shack designated to be the rendezvous site. Harrison documented the meeting in his book, *The Black Christ* (2006). It was a memorable encounter:

> A deep strong voice said 'Hello, my son.' I stammered some greeting in return, and as he grasped my hands with his, a distinct energy seemed to course through my body . . . Then, suddenly, like a newborn baby entering the world for the first time, I burst into tears. I cannot explain whether it was the magic of that moment, or sheer magnetism of the occasion, but the next thing I knew two strong arms had wrapped themselves around me and once again a strong comforting voice said, 'It's alright to cry, my son . . . It's okay . . . I can see that you have already endured so much . . . It's okay . . .' I felt the strength of his compassion flow into my trembling body and fill my soul.[37]

In a 2006 interview, Harrison stated that during this secret, private meeting Luthuli had said to him that violence was not and would never be 'the answer to our problems'. He added:

> And this is, this is what he says to me, 'The road that lies ahead, is very, it's going to be very very . . . it's a stormy road . . . you have to travel soberly.' He says to me, 'You've done something that's very dangerous.' He says, 'But, you were very very brave. You should feel very proud,' he says. 'What you have done is something that was non-violent. You have spoken in a non-violent manner.' And, he was so sweet to me. 'You know,' he says, 'you caused such a fervour.' He says to me that, 'what you have actually done', he says, 'you have highlighted the plight of the blacks now with this, this is what you have done.'[38]

Rector of Glasgow University

In October 1962, students in South Africa and Scotland honoured Luthuli. On 7 October, Luthuli accepted the offer of the National Union of South African Students (NUSAS) to become their honorary president. On 22 October 1962, students at the University of Glasgow elected Luthuli as Lord Rector in recognition of his 'dignity and restraint' in a 'potentially inflammatory situation'.[39] The rectorship of the university was purely honorary. As rector, Luthuli's role would have been to be the chair of the University Court, the chief executive body of the university that met monthly. Students elected Luthuli for the position knowing that he would serve in *absentia*. Technically, this obstacle did not prevent Luthuli's candidacy as it was customary that very important rectors were not expected to attend any meetings; nonetheless, his unavailability became a campaign issue among students. Due to Luthuli's unavailability to chair, an assessor needed to be chosen, with his consent, to represent him.[40]

Luthuli's election cannot be described as insignificant as he was the first foreigner and 'non-white' to be nominated for rector. Though he accepted nomination and agreed to stand for election, he did not campaign against the other candidates.[41] Students campaigned in his favour, easily obtaining Luthuli's electoral win. The students themselves inappropriately marred the election, with rival factions contesting each other; a melee erupted and some thirty-four students were arrested for breach of the peace and forming part of a disorderly crowd.[42]

Aside from taking one phone call from a student representative soon after his election, Luthuli never acted as rector.[43] Print media reports at the time indicate that after an initial correspondence informing Luthuli of his election, no other correspondences from the university reached him.[44] In Parliament, Helen Suzman questioned the apparent interception of mail. The government denied the allegation. E.V. Mahomed, who received Luthuli's post on his behalf, indicated that Luthuli did not even receive the invitation to Scotland to be installed or the request to nominate an assessor. In mid-1963, Luthuli applied for a passport to attend the long-postponed installation. After a significant delay, the government finally rejected the application in January 1964.[45] A very disappointed David Holmes, president of the Students Representative Council, indicated that Luthuli's complete absence from the rectorship would render him the first not to attend an installation.[46] The ceremony never took place.[47]

Martin Luther King Junior

While Albert Luthuli was the first African Nobel prize-winner, in 1964 Martin Luther King Junior became the youngest. For both men, the prizes recognised their non-violent stance in the struggle against white supremacy in South Africa and the United States, respectively. Both held relatively similar theological views and they were in accord on the strategic and ethical rationale for non-violent methods of resistance. Both men denied being pacifists. Yet, it was not King's, but only Luthuli's, legacy of non-violent resistance that received a reversal, with ANC veterans using his disavowal of pacifism as evidence of his support for the ANC's turn to violent forms of resistance.

Indeed, Luthuli's stance on the use of violence was deceptively contradictory, and it is Martin Luther King's theological perspectives that can help illuminate Luthuli's position. King was more articulate and nuanced than Luthuli when conveying his religious convictions, a consequence of his having studied theology formally. He received a Ph.D. in Systematic Theology from Boston University. He was also an ordained minister. On the other hand, Luthuli's formal education was constrained by economic circumstances and the need for him to work as a teacher so that he could support his mother financially. He turned down a scholarship to Fort Hare where he would have at least received a Bachelor's degree. Nevertheless, the Christian faith no less influenced Luthuli than King; Luthuli represented the quintessential *kholwa*: born, raised and educated in the bosom of American Congregationalism transplanted to Natal by the American Board. As such, a theological view of Luthuli allows historians to better understand him and his fundamental place in South Africa's politics.

Only two months before the alliance of congresses agreed to form MK, a column appeared in the 28 May 1961 issue of the *Golden City Post* entitled 'Why I Believe in Non-Violence'. It could serve as a veritable treatise on Luthuli's rationale of pacifism, had Luthuli been a pacifist. The column began:

> I firmly believe in non-violence. It is the only correct form which our struggle can take in South Africa. Both from the moral and the practical point of view the situation in our country demands it . . . To refrain from violence is the sign of the civilised man . . . Non-violence gives us a moral superiority . . . we pledge ourselves to non-violent activity because our better natures and our consciences demand this of us . . .

My hope and prayer is that any activity on our part now or in the future time will be on peaceful lines.[48]

The statement does not hint at a context or provocation that might warrant or justify violence. Pacifist assertions riddled the column.

If we are to be sincere when we advocate non-violence, we must see to it that we do not create situations where others, rightly or wrongly, for whatever reason, will declare it necessary to use violent methods against us . . . let it be remembered that to create situations where violence becomes inevitable makes one a sponsor – intentional or not – of violence.[49]

Then, bluntly and out of the blue, Luthuli ended the column by declaring: 'I am no pacifist but a realist.' Luthuli possessed solid pacifist credentials, both in word and deed. Yet, he refused to identify with it. In *South Africa's Nobel Laureates* (2004), Kader Asmal related that Luthuli once observed 'that anyone who thought he was a pacifist should try to steal his chickens'.[50]

Luthuli's public and private rejections of pacifism are consistent. In a letter to the editor printed in the *Rand Daily Mail* and reprinted by *Sechaba* in October 1967, Charles Hooper wrote quite clearly about Luthuli's stance, saying that Luthuli's condemnation of violence had been 'conditional' and 'qualified'. While 'he advocated only non-violence and dialogue because they were what he passionately wanted South Africans to believe in', it was his (Luthuli's) 'privately maintained' view that 'Stauffenberg was right in trying to destroy Hitler'.[51]

Hooper is a credible source as he and his wife, Sheila, spent many hours in discussion with Luthuli, in the dictating and drafting of *Let My People Go*. The opportunity to discuss the nuances of theology and ethics regarding the issue of violence could only have been irresistible for Hooper. Luthuli dictated much of his autobiography during the months preceding the July 1961 decision to form MK and hence the issue of violence was foremost in his mind when working with Hooper.

The rationale behind Luthuli's claim to be a realist centres on his belief that at home and abroad, it was benevolent, white, liberal and Christian advocates in league with the oppressed majority who would be the key to South Africa's liberation. In his May 1961 column, he suggested that a non-violent path was a 'high call to peaceful duty and action'. Straying from this path would only result in the loss of outside support and sympathy for the cause. 'We must widen our area of cooperation and friendship,' he said, 'and not drive away millions of potential friends and supporters by taking the wrong, evil road.'[52]

This justification for the use of non-violence is the smoking-gun evidence that proves Luthuli could not and did not support the formation and launch of MK. His sentiments also explain why: his domestic and international constituency bound him to never countenance the loss of the moral high ground.

The most prominent rejection of pacifism occurred during Luthuli's testimony at the Treason Trial. In response to the judge's direct question, Luthuli declared he was not a pacifist and said that, although he was not conversant with the theory of pacifism, he knew he was not a pacifist. This statement is surprising, coming from a man who had pacifists as some of his closest allies (for example, Mary-Louise Hooper and George Houser). The statement becomes somewhat less surprising when Luthuli stated he was not knowledgeable about communism, nor had he ever read Marx, but that he regarded Moses Kotane as his closest political confidant.

In a *Cape Argus* interview following the announcement of his being awarded the Nobel Peace Prize, Luthuli said, 'I must say that I would not pigeon-hole myself as a pacifist'.[53] He then confessed that his faith was primary to his thinking in all matters. His 'Christian leanings' inclined him to hesitate 'to be a party to violence'.[54]

Perhaps Luthuli lacked the theoretical tools acquired in higher education to further qualify his beliefs. He apologised for not being a theologian that would be able to discern an authoritative Christian position (should one have ever existed). In *Voices of Liberation*, Volume 1, Gerald Pillay stated in his comments on the Rivonia Trial that Luthuli often spoke of ' "militant non-violent struggle" where "militant" is used to mean what Martin Luther King Junior meant by direct non-violent action. This is quite consistent with [Luthuli's] claim not to be a pacifist yet choosing non-violence as the best option for political struggle'.[55]

Luthuli and Martin Luther King Junior were contemporaries. When Luthuli travelled to the United States in 1948, King was only nineteen and studying theology at Crozer Seminary. Though any direct collaboration between the two was unlikely, they jointly issued an 'Appeal for Action against Apartheid' on 10 December 1962 under the American Committee on Africa (ACOA). The archive shows that they held each other in high regard. In a December 1959 letter, King commended Luthuli for his reputation and regretted 'that circumstances and spacial divisions have made it impossible for [them] to meet'. He spoke of his admiration for Luthuli's 'great witness' and for his 'dedication to the cause of freedom and dignity'. He said: 'You have stood amid persecution, abuse and oppression with a dignity and calmness of spirit seldom paralleled in human history. One day all of Africa will be proud of your achievements.'[56]

In King's powerfully brief two-page acceptance speech at his Nobel Peace Prize award ceremony in 1964, Luthuli is the only person mentioned by name. He said that the Nobel committee 'honours, again, Chief Luthuli of South Africa, whose struggles with and for his people, are still met with the most brutal expression of man's inhumanity to man'.[57]

King never joined a pacifist organisation. Yet he thought, spoke and acted as a pacifist. His advocacy of a strict non-violent stance is well documented, and his rationale for adopting pacifist strategies echoes Luthuli's. He famously believed:

> Violence as a way of achieving racial justice is both impractical and immoral. It is impractical because it is a descending spiral ending in destruction for all. The old law of an eye for an eye leaves everybody blind. It is immoral because it seeks to humiliate the opponent rather than win his understanding; it seeks to annihilate rather than convert. Violence is immoral because it thrives on hatred rather than love. It destroys communities and makes brotherhood impossible. It leaves society in monologue rather than dialogue. Violence ends by defeating itself. It creates bitterness in the survivors and brutality in the destroyers.[58]

Though he advocated pacifist strategies, King was not a pacifist. And neither was Luthuli. The work of American public theologian, Reinhold Niebuhr, provided King with a framework into which he could place his understanding. It hung on the idea of 'realistic pacifism', a conviction that avoided the false idealism and superficial optimism embraced by pacifist organisations. In his autobiography, King explains:

> Niebuhr's great contribution to theology is that he has refuted the false optimism characteristic of a great segment of Protestant liberalism.

Moreover, Niebuhr has extraordinary insight into human nature, especially the behaviour of nations and social groups. He is keenly aware of the complexity of human motives and of the relations between morality and power. His theology is a persistent reminder of the reality of sin on every level of man's existence. These elements in Niebuhr's thinking helped me to recognise the illusions of a superficial optimism concerning human nature, the dangers of false idealism. While I still believe in man's potential for good, Niebuhr made me realise his potential for evil as well. Moreover, Niebuhr helped me to recognise the complexity of man's social involvement and the glaring reality of collective evil. Many pacifists, I felt, failed to see this. All too many had an unwarranted optimism concerning man and leaned unconsciously toward self-righteousness. It was my revolt against these attitudes under the influence of Niebuhr that accounts for the fact that in spite of my strong leaning toward pacifism, I never joined a pacifist organisation. After reading Niebuhr, I tried to arrive at a realistic pacifism. In other words, I came to see the pacifist position not as sinless but as the lesser evil in the circumstances. I felt then, as I feel now, that the pacifist would have greater appeal if he did not claim to be free from the moral dilemmas that the Christian non-pacifist does.[59]

King's explanation allows one, first, to understand Luthuli's jarring conclusion, 'I am not a pacifist, I am a realist', found in his 28 May 1961 *Golden City Post* article and, second, to understand why Luthuli denied the pacifist label yet advocated and lived out its tenets. King's sympathetic disavowal of pacifism conveys why Luthuli can best be described as a 'strategic pacifist' rather than an 'ideological pacifist'. The distinction is important. An ideological pacifist is one who believes that resorting to violence or war to sort out conflicts is always unjustifiable. Disputes should be always resolved through peaceful means. A strategic pacifist is not a pacifist, but one who believes that in a given situation, pacifist methods can be the most efficacious. According to King, if Luthuli identified himself as an ideological pacifist, he would be uninformed, naive and even oblivious to reality as pacifist strategies are blinded, not contextually implemented and serve as a panacea. By proclaiming himself a realist, Luthuli denied being a pacifist. As a strategic pacifist, Luthuli comprehended the full dimensions of the struggle he led and chose freely the strategy to adopt. He chose pacifist methods, being fully cognisant of the forces arrayed against him and the ramifications of any actions taken. Luthuli, like King, denied being a pacifist, yet chose to implement its tenets. King discerned that pacifists failed to possess a realistic understanding of human nature. When Luthuli declared that he was a realist, not a pacifist, he proclaimed the South African context warranted pacifist methods and that the extent of the National Party's intransigence did not elude him.

George Houser and the American Committee on Africa

The 'Appeal for Action against Apartheid' statement was the result of many years of co-operation and partnership between Mary-Louise Hooper, South African clerics such as Joost de Blank, Ambrose Reeves (who served the ACOA as an international sponsor), Martin Luther King Junior and George Houser, a pacifist and founder and executive secretary of the ACOA.

Albert Luthuli and Houser first met in 1954. Born to Methodist missioner parents, Houser was imprisoned for a year in 1940 for protesting against mandatory registration for the United States military draft. After receiving ministerial training at the Chicago Theological Seminary, Houser founded in 1942 an organisation that pursued non-violent direct action against racial segregation. In 1953 Houser founded the ACOA to support anti-colonial struggles throughout Africa and to assist in the abolition of apartheid in South Africa. By 1957, Houser had been declared a prohibited immigrant in the British territories of Northern Rhodesia (Zambia), Tanganyika (Tanzania), Uganda and Kenya.

Primarily working through E.V. Mahomed as an intermediary, Houser and Luthuli corresponded in 1956, discussing means by which the ACOA would assist the ANC to print its own publication using a press in Phoenix administered by M.K. Gandhi's grandson, Arun Gandhi (1892–1952). In 1958 and 1959, their correspondence dealt with the ACOA's efforts to raise funds to defend those charged in the Treason Trial through the Africa Defence Fund, for which Houser requested Luthuli to serve as adviser. Again in 1960, Luthuli and Houser (with Alan Paton and the Bishop of Johannesburg) co-operated in the establishment of the South African Committee for Higher Education that assisted disadvantaged students with domestic and international scholarships. Co-operation continued into 1961 as the ACOA sponsored annual events to celebrate Africa Freedom Day. And it was Houser who, in October and November 1961, extended the invitation to Luthuli to speak in the United States as part of his Nobel Peace Prize acceptance tour.

In February 1962, Houser introduced Luthuli to the ACOA's 'Appeal for Action'. It was intended to follow on from the 1957 Declaration of Conscience in which more than a hundred leaders from every continent sought to appeal to the South African government to bring its policies into line with the Universal Declaration of Human Rights. Houser envisioned that Martin Luther King Junior, Albert Luthuli and Eleanor Roosevelt (1884–1962) would be the three 'sponsors' whose chief role was to lend their names and authority to the invitation requesting international figures to sign the appeal. The substance of Luthuli's correspondence with Houser and the Americans underscores the importance that Luthuli attached to the need to cultivate international solidarity. Strict adherence to non-violent methods was the key to securing international support. In September 1962, Luthuli wrote to various foreign leaders that South Africans, faced with the new Sabotage Act, risked the death penalty if they challenged segregation. 'Up to twelve million of my people look to you,' he said, *'for we cannot win equality without the help of the outside world'* (original emphasis).[60]

The international support network, dominated by white, Christian and liberal advocates of human rights, inextricably bound Luthuli to non-violent methods of resistance, placing him in opposition to the shift to the use of violence made by the ANC. In the same general letter to various foreign leaders, Luthuli feared a 'cataclysm that would destroy our movement':

> *Appeal for Action against Apartheid* is projected to bring pressure on South Africa on an international scale – pressure for change before it is too late . . . before we are caught in a bloody revolt which would necessarily polarise along racial lines and blot out all hope of justice in South Africa. Such a cataclysm would destroy our movement here; it would endanger hard-won progress everywhere, including America. That is why Martin Luther King joins me as an initiating sponsor for this *Appeal for Action* . . . As you write your check, I am sure you will make a sacrifice – not for the recognition accorded by the Nobel Prize, but for the cause we share: that interracial amity shall not perish (original emphasis).[61]

The actual appeal, issued jointly by Luthuli and King, is even more explicit in its advocacy of non-violent methods. They presented two possibilities for the future. The first was that government intransigence would lead to a possible liberation brought about by violence and armed rebellion; the second was that a transition to a society based upon equality for all without regard to colour would be brought about by a global quarantine of apartheid South Africa. The first scenario would result in violence and armed rebellion once it was clear that 'peaceful adjustments' were no longer possible.[62] At the time of writing both men considered non-violent options still to be viable, although to a decreasing degree. However, they expressed their fear that 'large scale violence would take the form of a racial war'. Such a supposed liberation may be successful. But, at what cost? 'Mass racial extermination will destroy the potential for interracial unity in South Africa and elsewhere.'[63] Mandela reluctantly risked such a scenario. Luthuli could not. The government also would not risk such a scenario and moved quickly to extinguish Mandela's 'army'.

There was still time to adopt the non-violent method, according to Luthuli. To do so would give the ANC public support and the moral high ground, especially in their appeal to Christians and international human rights advocates. But, with the launch of MK, and the ANC's looking for succour to communist countries during the Cold War, the support of western governments, representing predominantly Christian and democratic nations, was quickly evaporating. As long as western governments perceived the ANC to be a proxy of the Soviet Union, the liberation movement's efforts to institute effective sanctions were always doomed to fail. Such was the situation until the collapse of communism in the late 1980s.

In September 1963, Luthuli received a request from Houser to offer a few words in support of the ACOA on the occasion of its tenth anniversary. Luthuli's greeting to the ACOA affirmed his deep respect and admiration for the organisation.

> We are partners with you in your mission, and I could assure you in the name of my people that when our day of deliverance comes, you will most assuredly not find us wanting in the responsibility which the forging of a suitable government acceptable to all ranks of our multiracial population will entail. Long live the American Committee on Africa! And may Africa always live up to the trust that you have reposed on her!![64]

Martin Luther King Junior's support for the Anti-Apartheid Movement continued through the auspices of the ACOA. In December 1962, in consultation with Houser, King and other African American leaders met with President John Kennedy (1917–1963) to discuss United States foreign policy concerning Africa. On 10 December 1965, at a Human Rights Day rally organised by Houser, King pronounced that continued United States' economic support of South Africa amounted to a 'shame' for the nation and called for an economic boycott of South African goods as a demonstration of the 'international potential of non-violence'.[65]

The Rivonia and Ngakane trials

On 26 July 1962, Nelson Mandela again travelled to Natal to meet with Luthuli and members of the Natal MK Regional Command. In this meeting, Mandela advised that the ANC should be seen as dominant within the alliance of the congresses to appease potential Africanist allies throughout the continent. Luthuli disagreed and said he would deliberate on the matter further by consulting others. On 5 August, while leaving Natal, police arrested Mandela outside Howick, near Pietermaritzburg. The following day, he was charged with incitement (for the May 1961 strike) and leaving South Africa illegally (for his January 1962 north, east and west Africa trip). He was held at the Johannesburg Fort during his trial and later at the Pretoria Central Prison. Following the imposition of a three-year sentence, the authorities transferred Mandela to Robben Island. It was May 1963. By mid-July Mandela again stood trial, this time on a charge of sabotage, alongside Walter Sisulu, Ahmed Kathrada, Govan Mbeki, Raymond Mhlaba, Billy Nair, Bob Hepple, Denis Goldberg, Lionel Bernstein, Arthur Goldreich and Harold Wolpe (1926–1996). Later police arrested Elias Motsoaledi (1924–1994) and Andrew Mlangeni. Two escaped from custody (Goldreich and Wolpe), one agreed to testify for the prosecution (Hepple) and one was found not guilty (Bernstein).

The charges arose from a police raid on the alleged MK headquarters situated on the Communist Party-owned farm, 'Lilliesleaf', at Rivonia, near Johannesburg. In the course of the raid police found Mandela's diary written during his Africa tour and a document entitled 'Operation Mayibuye', a plan for the launch of a guerrilla war. Justice Quartus de Wet found that there was sufficient evidence to convict those tried for sabotage for which the death penalty was a likely possibility.

At the time of the trial Albert Luthuli continued to espouse the view that a non-violent solution for the problems in South Africa was still possible. On 9 March 1964, before sentencing in the Rivonia Trial (judgment was handed down on 4 March), he wrote to the General

Secretary of the United Nations, (Pantanaw) U Thant (1909–1974), to appeal to the international community to 'act promptly and with firmness' to bring pressure to bear on the apartheid government given the very real possibility of capital sentencing for the accused. The death sentence 'would have disastrous results for any prospects of a peaceful settlement of the South African situation and could set in motion a chain of actions and counter-actions which would be tragic for everyone in South Africa as they would be difficult to contain'.[66]

On 12 June 1964, the court sentenced Mandela, Sisulu and six other accused to life imprisonment. Luthuli proceeded to issue a statement, much quoted since and frequently used to support the claim that he supported the initiation of violence in the formation of MK.[67] In the statement Luthuli did not critique the move to armed tactics. Indeed, he argued, no one could 'blame' those who resort to a military option given the circumstances. Yet, he began his statement saying that the militant non-violent option was still valid:

> The African National Congress never abandoned its method of a militant, non-violent struggle, and of creating in the process a spirit of militancy in the people. However, in the face of the uncompromising white[s'] refusal to abandon a policy which denies the African and other oppressed South Africans their rightful heritage – freedom – no one can blame brave just men for seeking justice by the use of violent methods; nor could they be blamed if they tried to create an organised force in order to ultimately establish peace and racial harmony . . . They represent the highest in morality and ethics in the South African political struggle; this morality and ethics has been sentenced to an imprisonment it may never survive.[68]

Nationalistic commentaries rarely state categorically that Luthuli supported the initiation of violence, though they frequently *imply* that he did. For example, in a public lecture on 2 August 2004, then Deputy President Jacob Zuma recollected:

> Another highlight of Luthuli's leadership of the ANC is that it was during this period that the armed struggle was launched. He clearly articulated this ANC policy in a statement issued on 12 June 1964, when Nelson Mandela, Walter Sisulu and six other leaders were

sentenced to life imprisonment in the Rivonia Trial . . . He said, 'The
African National Congress never abandoned its method of a militant,
non-violent struggle . . . However . . . no one can blame brave just men
for seeking justice by the use of violent methods . . .'[69]

Zuma and others who use Luthuli's 1964 statement to justify a 1961
decision to launch MK, with no intermediate justification, fail to explain
how Luthuli 'clearly articulated' the ANC's armed strategy while
simultaneously indicating that the ANC never abandoned the non-violent
struggle. Indeed, it could be argued that Luthuli clearly articulated his
inaccurate understanding of ANC policy when he said, 'The ANC never
abandoned its method of a non-violent struggle.' His 'No one can
blame . . .' statement was not the ANC's policy, but his personal sentiments,
and these personal sentiments conveyed an understanding of, not
agreement to, a given course of action. A closer reading of the tortuously
crafted statement suggests quite the opposite of that which Zuma claimed.

Luthuli's first assertion, that the ANC never abandoned its non-violent
methods is problematic. M.B. Yengwa, in his draft biography, said that
the proceedings of the Lobatse Conference in October 1962 were 'used as
evidence of the ANC's support for the armed struggle'. Yet, he said, at
Lobtase '[s]urprisingly, the subject of sabotage was not very controversial
and the conference unanimously agreed to embark on the armed struggle'.[70]
Brian Bunting, in his biography of Moses Kotane, reports that 'no specific
decisions about the use of violence were taken' at Lobatse. 'However, the
delegates were briefed in private by Kotane and others at talks held outside
the conference hall, and the conference resolutions made it plain that the
delegates were all very aware that violence was an inescapable reality of
the political scene, and they accepted it.'[71]

Luthuli appears to make a distinction between himself, who
represented the ANC, and those convicted, who represented MK. An
argument can be made that the ANC decided to pursue *both* non-violent
and violent means. Yet, to have 'never abandoned' non-violent means
while simultaneously opting to utilise violent means is a contradiction.
Technically, it could be argued that Luthuli held that, prior to the ANC's
legal ban in 1960, the organisation never abandoned its method of militant,
non-violent struggle. Yet, this perspective would render Luthuli
disingenuous given that he considered the ANC an entity in 1961 when
he insisted that MK must be separate from the ANC. For years he had
repeatedly warned in his columns for the *Golden City Post* that time was

running out and that people were desperate and impatient. He could not argue convincingly in July 1961, when the decision to permit the formation of MK was made, that violence was not inevitable given the intransigent position of the National Party government. Before the Nobel committee announced that Luthuli won the Peace Prize, he, with others of similar ilk, such as Z.K. Matthews, yielded to those justifying a resort to violence because they had very persuasive, if not convincing evidence, based on precedent, to validate their claims. Hence, Luthuli declared, '. . . no one can blame brave just men . . .' Yet, Luthuli was not one of those brave just men who resorted to violence in order to seek justice. He had always characterised an initiation of violence as reckless. Bravery is not necessarily intelligent, discerning, wise or pragmatic. Luthuli intentionally made a subtle, but important, distinction between 'sympathy' and 'support'. Sympathy or solidarity with Mandela and the others does not assume support or agreement with their methods. Luthuli also made a subtle, but important, distinction between the ANC organisation he led as president general and the 'brave just men' who could not be blamed if their patience became exhausted.

Perhaps more difficult to explain is Luthuli's declaration that Mandela and others possessed '. . . the highest in morals and ethics within the liberation struggle'. Luthuli clearly implied that he was not a pacifist when he lauded those sentenced. By doing so, Luthuli was, in King's words, wary of perceiving himself as 'self-righteous' and not 'free of the moral dilemmas' faced by Mandela and the others who also had lost patience. If Luthuli felt that Mandela and the others were not morally or ethically culpable for resorting to violence, why could he not advocate and support violence. After all, he was the leader of a liberation movement that effectively agreed to allow those within its ranks to form an organisation that would be prepared to initiate violence. The reasons are as simple as they are complex. Luthuli's strong Christian leanings (his ecclesiastic upbringing and his theological foundation), combined with his belief that a violent solution would be suicidal for oppressed and oppressors alike and the advent of new strategic opportunities afforded by his reception of the Nobel Peace Prize persuaded him against supporting the initiation of violence by MK.

Ironically, the greatest typical distortion of Luthuli's position on violence came not from an ANC politician, but from the Swedish cleric and primary advocate of his reception for the Nobel Peace Prize, Gunnar

Helander. As a Christian in solidarity with Luthuli and the anti-apartheid struggle during the 1960s, Helander espoused a unique stand on the ANC's turn to violence. 'I had no objection to it,' he said. He admired Luthuli whose 'line had been "violence under no circumstances"'.[72] Yet, in a 1996 interview, Helander seemed to imply the contradiction that Luthuli changed his stance on violence. Amalgamating Luthuli's 1952 'Road to Freedom' statement and his 1964 Rivonia Trial statement, he quoted Luthuli saying: 'I have been knocking on a closed door for year after year. I could not use violence myself, but I cannot any longer condemn those who advocate the use of violence.'[73]

In his statement on the Rivonia Trial, Luthuli expressed support for, but not agreement with those convicted. He did not, as an individual, nor as the ANC president general, ever advocate or justify violence prior to or after the 1961 decision to form MK, to which he had been party. And he did not agree with the path chosen by the convicted, despite sympathising with them and understanding their frustration with the National Party regime's perpetually intractable behaviour. The Rivonia statement is the epitome of balanced and reasoned diplomacy. Nevertheless, it remains confusing that in Luthuli's May 1961 declarations in the *Golden City Post* he described the path of violence as the 'evil road' and path of non-violence as a sign of 'civilisation' and 'moral superiority', and in his Rivonia statement he held that those convicted represented 'the highest in morality and ethics in the South African political struggle'.[74]

Some sources suggest that the state had sufficient evidence to arrest and presumably convict Luthuli in the Rivonia Trial. This claim is unfounded. During the trial, the most damaging evidence had been produced by the state's star witness, 'Mr X.', or Bruno Mtolo. Joel Joffe, an attorney acting for the accused, described Mtolo as a 'recidivist criminal' and an 'old hand' in the witness box whose testimony was a 'skilfully "interwoven mixture of fact and fiction"'.[75] However, Mtolo did testify about Luthuli's waning influence in the ANC, describing it as a 'slight but definite swing from the leadership of Chief Luthuli towards Mandela'.[76] Songs sung at meetings lauding Luthuli were now replaced by songs lauding Mandela. Communists were behind the swing, Mtolo claimed.

If the state had evidence to indict and convict Luthuli on charges of sabotage, it would have done so. Reminiscent of the Treason Trial, the state was unable to present sufficient evidence to show that Luthuli had ever supported the use of violence. Indeed, the state would have found no end of evidence to demonstrate the opposite. Luthuli's moderate and persuasive position would place the ANC on the moral high ground. Instead, Mandela's diaries, his PAFMECSA speech and the testimony of the accused allowed the state to claim the moral high ground to a credulous white South African public whereas Luthuli's moderate and persuasive position would place the ANC on the moral high ground.

In February 1964, the South African government detained Pascal Ngakane, Albertinah Luthuli's husband and thus Luthuli's son-in-law, under the Transkei Emergency Regulations. These regulations allowed him to be held indefinitely without being charged and without access to legal advice. In July 1964, the state charged and tried Ngakane on four counts of violating the Sabotage Act and Suppression of Communism Act (for belonging to and furthering the aims of the ANC), departing from the Republic and defeating the ends of justice. During his trial, another state witness, also known as 'Mr X.', presented evidence that Luthuli opposed MK's operations and even offered to resign from the ANC. Mr X.'s testimony, to some degree, is questionable as he allowed himself to be used as a witness for the state against those with whom he formerly served. The veracity of his testimony is especially questionable if it agreed with the state's desired portrayal of Luthuli as a leader of an armed revolutionary movement. Evidence from a questionable witness is usually probative if it in some way contradicts the state's case as Mr X.'s did. Therefore, Mr. X's claim that Luthuli offered to resign from the ANC is plausible, if not likely.

In his testimony against Ngakane, Mr X. said he had first heard of MK in March 1962 when M.B. Yengwa had reported that Luthuli had spoken of resigning if the ANC resorted to violence. After the meeting, Mr X. testified, Yengwa had told him Luthuli did not want to be a 'stumbling block' in this matter.

Though Mr X.'s testimony may be seen as suspect given the fact that he gave evidence for the state, nothing in the archival record contradicts the assertion that Luthuli offered to resign from the ANC. Mr X.'s testimony in Ngakane's trial and other archival evidence leads to a conclusion that as a result of Luthuli's objections to violence, he reluctantly yielded to others' convictions for its required use while continuing to advocate for non-violent methods.

Family of Man award

Late in his life, Albert Luthuli continued to receive accolades and successfully maintain the close ties with sympathetic whites allied to the ANC's struggle, in large part because he did not renounce the non-violent path and was never heard to support the initiation of violence. The acceptance of the Gell, Nobel and Family of Man awards displays the degree to which Luthuli embedded himself with the liberal cause that assumed only non-violent tactics to be permissible within the South African context, and thus never divorced himself from the ANC's similar historic stance.

In 1964 Luthuli received at his home in Groutville a telegram from the New York City Protestant Council announcing that he had been given the Family of Man award and inviting him to be present to receive the honour on 28 October 1964 at the Astor Hotel in Manhattan. The Council, representing seventeen hundred Protestant churches in the New York metropolitan area, bestowed four awards: Human Relations, World Peace, Education and Communications. Luthuli received the Human Relations award for 'leading the fight against the apartheid policy of the South African government and always advocating firm and continued opposition by non-violent means'.[77] The award attached a US$5 000 grant. It was not an insignificant honour. The guest of honour at the 1963 award ceremony was United States president, John Kennedy. The scheduled guest of honour at the 1964 ceremony was former president, Dwight Eisenhower (1890–1969).

As with the Nobel award, it is highly improbable that Luthuli would have considered receiving the Family of Man award if he had at any time advocated or countenanced violence. On 17 October, Luthuli posted two letters, one to the local magistrate in Stanger and one to the Minister of Justice in Pretoria, requesting permission to attend. For Luthuli to receive the award in person, he would have to depart by 26 October. Luthuli's attendance seemed remote. He would be required to obtain travel bookings, income tax clearance, passport photos and a passport from Pretoria, all while being confined to Groutville, and thus banned from Stanger and Durban. Luthuli would first need to obtain blanket permission to break his banning restrictions.

In documents stamped 'Secret', the South African Embassy in Washington DC advised the Secretary of Foreign Affairs in Pretoria on 14 October 1964 that the award 'may reflect a desire in certain chiefly

Methodist and Presbyterian quarters in New York to make political mischief for South Africa'.[78] Groups hostile to South Africa, including the United Nations, would surely 'seize on Luthuli should he come to New York'. The embassy therefore advised that applications for passports be denied. Luthuli did not attend.

Mphiwa Mbatha, an Adams College alumnus, received the award for Luthuli and spoke on his behalf. John Reuling of the American Board communicated with Luthuli in early November informing him of the occasion and discussed the means by which the American Board could facilitate the transfer of the grant money from New York to Durban on Luthuli's behalf.

American Board links with Luthuli continued in late 1964 and correspondence confirms that Luthuli possessed a diminished influence within the ANC and continued to neither support nor condemn the turn to violence. One American Board missioner, Edward Hawley, met Oliver Tambo in Dar es Salaam in November of 1964, and agreed to carry a typed, unaddressed and unsigned letter to Luthuli in Groutville.[79] Hawley's visit was facilitated by American Board missioner, Howard Trumbull, and the local Congregational minister in Groutville. In an interview, Hawley confided the following discussion with Luthuli.

> Luthuli talked freely about his experiences under the banning orders and explained that this current one had banned him from going to church . . . One of the most moving parts of that conversation came when I asked him about how he dealt with the increasing pressure to use force in combating apartheid. His response was, and I can remember this almost verbatim, 'I have never been a violent man. And I could never be one . . . The young men still come out to see me. When they tell me that non-violence has always been met by violence, I have no words left'. It was clear to me that he still wished that justice might be obtained non-violently. But, he no longer could find arguments to convince them that this was possible.[80]

Luthuli must have known that his arguments for a non-violent approach were wearing thin. Charles Hooper, in his introduction to the 1962 edition of Let My People Go, asked for how long the African majority could continue to strive for freedom in a situation which showed 'no signs of abating'. 'How long,' he asked, 'before the Union's African people are seeking a new embodiment of new wishes? How long before, out of the depths, they cry, "If the man of peace does not prevail, give us men of blood"?'[81]

Swedish links

The South African government also prohibited Luthuli from accepting an invitation to Sweden. Concerned about reports of Luthuli's deteriorating health, Sweden's Minister of Foreign Affairs to South Africa, Hugo Tamm, visited Luthuli at his home in Groutville in early 1965.[82] Alarmed by a report that the South Africa's security police questioned Luthuli about this visit, the Stockholm branch of the ruling Social Democratic Party invited him to Sweden to speak at May Day demonstrations in Stockholm, making the invitation through the South African government. In an abrasive reply on 3 June 1965, the South African envoy to Sweden, Anthony Hamilton, denied Luthuli the opportunity to travel to Sweden. Hamilton claimed that despite restrictions placed upon him, Luthuli

> . . . continued meeting with Communists and well-known agitators, both openly and in secret. He abused the privileges accorded to him and defied and provoked the authorities and the government at every turn.
>
> Mr Luthuli has therefore only himself to blame for the restrictions and prohibitions still imposed upon him. These are unavoidable if all the peoples of South Africa are to be protected against the violence which would accompany a Communist-inspired coup d'état. The restrictions on Mr Luthuli have been imposed only as a last resort . . . In the past, when passport facilities were granted to Mr Luthuli, the promises he gave were not fulfilled. Since his last visit abroad [to accept the Nobel Peace Prize] there has been no change in his attitude. In the circumstances, the South African government cannot, therefore, allow Mr Luthuli to undertake the proposed visit.[83]

Despite the banning of the ANC, the imposition of the Sabotage Act, the imprisonment of many of the liberation struggle leaders after the Rivonia Trial and the exile of other ANC leaders, the outside world's contact with Luthuli continued on a limited basis. Though such contact continued, the South African government struggled hard to effect Luthuli's 'civil death'. Contrary to the ANC nationalists' inference that Luthuli continued to lead the liberation movement by having secret meetings in cane fields,

Swedish activist, Tor Sellström emphasised that banning restrictions made communication with Luthuli almost impossible and limited the degree to which he could continue to lead the movement. Often ecclesiastic rather than political links facilitated what limited contact Luthuli had with the outside world. In a June 2008 interview, Sellström related that Ronnie Kasrils often contacted the Swedish legation in Pretoria. They then established contact with Luthuli through the Church of Sweden Mission in order to hear news about him and publish that information on behalf of the ANC. Even at the October 1962 Lobatse Conference, where the ANC 'officially' decided that MK be affiliated with the ANC, the ANC received no information about Luthuli, let alone leadership from him. In addition, judging by Luthuli's Rivonia statement, Luthuli was not even informed that the ANC officially changed its policy in Lobatse.[84] Such tenuous links with the ANC reveal that although Luthuli held the position of president general, the position held only titular status with the ANC-in-exile. In her study of MK, Elaine Reinertsen confirms that Luthuli's role had diminished to that of a figurehead. Her statement that Luthuli 'did not, and indeed would not, as a recipient of the Peace Prize, echo the sentiments of Umkhonto we Sizwe' provides 'the strongest evidence of the declining role of the President-General'.[85]

Robert Kennedy's visit

Only Luthuli's Nobel Peace Prize surpassed the degree to which the June 1966 visit to South Africa of Senator Robert Kennedy (1925–1968), brother of the recently slain United States president, J.F. Kennedy, embarrassed the apartheid regime. The *Rand Daily Mail* called the Kennedy visit 'the best thing that has happened to South Africa for years'. The editor-in-chief commented that '[i]t is as if a window has been flung open and a gust of fresh air has swept into a room in which the atmosphere had become stale and foetid. Suddenly it is possible to breathe again without feeling choked.'[86]

During a whirlwind visit from 4–9 June, Bobby Kennedy electrified the South African press, youth and public. The frazzled press corps that tried to keep pace with him nicknamed him the 'human dynamo'. In all of his speeches, Kennedy brilliantly critiqued white South Africa's racism, materialism, increasing totalitarian leanings and paranoia of communism by speaking about the successes and mistakes of the American project to realise a 'more perfect union'. Speaking indirectly to South Africa by speaking directly about the United States, Kennedy gave a stinging evaluation of apartheid as the abandonment of all that western civilisation holds sacred. Advocating 'peaceful and non-violent change', his speeches beautifully captured Luthuli's philosophical, theological and political understandings.[87]

At dawn on the 7 June, Bobby Kennedy flew via helicopter to Grout-ville to visit Luthuli. The two met privately for about an hour. During the visit, Luthuli and Kennedy took a stroll down the road, listened to speeches of former US president, John Kennedy, on a record player that he presented to Luthuli as a gift, and they had tea. Luthuli expressed his fear that the black majority in South Africa would be driven by despair to violence. What seemed clear was that the black majority in South Africa had an ally in Washington DC. Flying over the Valley of a Thousand Hills back to Johannesburg, Kennedy gave a press conference describing Luthuli as one of the most impressive men he had ever met. The significance of the visit to Luthuli could not be underestimated. The *Rand Daily Mail* summarised it thus:

> Think, also, what this visit has meant to the non-Whites of South Africa
> – his acceptance of them as people who count as much as anyone else,
> as people to be greeted and sought out and talked to as friends. In this
> sense his meeting with ex-Chief Albert Luthuli was not merely a valuable
> personal contact but a symbol of recognition of the African people as
> part of our community.[88]

Bobby Kennedy had also said the chief seemed 'thin'. The man who was rendered irrelevant domestically by the liberation movement itself, and by the government through the Sabotage Act, was ailing. At this time, much of Luthuli's energy was consumed by farming. He tilled the fields with his workers. He did not wage or support the armed struggle in secret meetings under the cover of cane, although there is no doubt that the cane fields were at times able to offer a measure of secrecy for meetings. But, Luthuli was not well and his health problems were fast becoming chronic. Even a mild stroke could disorient him enough to result in a tragic death on a precarious railway bridge. When it came, however, it was a death widely purported to have been the work of the apartheid government.

6

Alone on the Tracks

1967

Albert Lutuli – the man many people would have loved to see as Prime Minister – was crushed to death by a train this week. He could not have died a happy man. Few of his dreams – not for himself but for his people who meant so much to him – were realised during his lifetime.

— 'Luthuli, the Leader, Started Dying Years Ago',
unknown publication, July 1967

PRIOR TO THE 24 May 1964 expiry of Luthuli's five-year banning order, a close confidant of his told Dennis Royle, a *Natal Witness* reporter:

Luthuli's way of life has recently undergone a complete change. The 66-year-old former Zulu Chief (he gave up his chieftainship when he went into politics) is no longer a bustling politician but a quiet retiring farmer . . . Luthuli who cannot talk for publication, is still dedicated to the concept of a multiracial society gained by non-violent means. But his banning from public life offers him little chance of furthering these aims.[1]

Effective 31 May 1964, the Minister of Justice, B.J. Vorster, imposed on Luthuli an even more severe banning than the one he received in 1959. Unlike his 1959 banning order, the new one would prevent Luthuli from travelling even to the next closest town, Stanger, until 31 May 1969. The Minister of Justice felt confident that Luthuli's activities furthered the cause of communism and warned him not to publish any statements, address any meetings or make contact with any banned people. The Liberal Party, the National Union of South African Students (NUSAS) and the

International Confederation of Free Trades Unions all publicly protested Luthuli's banning.

Luthuli's health

Evidence suggests that Luthuli's political and physical life were winding down considerably. From October 1964 until his death in July 1967, thirty-three months, the only known archival documents produced by Luthuli's hand are sermon notes and some medical reminders. Microfilm images of these documents are held today in archives at the University of Cape Town and the University of South Africa. Other than one letter and one declaration of congratulations, the 'documents' are in fact scraps of paper on which Luthuli scratched notes.[2] These reveal that the last six months of Luthuli's life were perhaps insular and almost exclusively focused on religious matters. Dates of services, scripture readings and notes on sermons that Luthuli listened to over the radio comprised the bulk of his written attention. Notes not related to religious matters were reminders of dates and times for medical appointments. The scribblings on various scraps of paper, magazine articles and even product advertisements or labels are dated 8 January, 22 January, 5 February, 16 February, 26 February, 3 March and 5 March 1967. Scripture readings, for example, are found inscribed upon a *Forward Africa* newsletter. By no means can a conclusion be based solely on these jottings; nonetheless, it appears that Luthuli's mental state deteriorated. The latter writings can scarcely be deciphered. His deteriorating penmanship, never particularly neat, and the absence of any archival records during his last two years of life bring into serious doubt that he was active as the president general of the ANC, or that he posed a political threat to the government.

In their biography, *Nokukhanya: Mother of Light* (1993), Peter Rule, Marilyn Aitken and Jenny van Dyk record that Nokukhanya Luthuli confirmed that in 1966 she knew Luthuli's health was deteriorating:

> He was already weak when I returned to Groutville [from the farms in Swaziland] in 1966. And he was very touchy. He got depressed when something went wrong in the house. His feelings had run high because of the treatment he received from the police. They often used to come and take him away from the house, even at that stage. I decided not to go back in 1966 because things had deteriorated so much at home that I needed time to work up the fields and crops.[3]

In January 1966, McCord Zulu Hospital in Durban admitted Luthuli for hypertension. The American Board Superintendent of the hospital at the time, Howard Christofersen, specifically recalled visiting Luthuli's room to bid him farewell prior to returning to the United States. In an emailed correspondence, Christofersen reminisced:

> It was there that [Luthuli] quoted Professor Aggery who had visited African educational institutions in the early 1920s. 'Like the black and white keys on the piano, the whites need the blacks and the blacks need the whites.' That was the first time that I had heard that expression and it stuck by me because it was so impressive that he would say that after the way in which he had been persecuted.[4]

On 15 March 1967, only ten days after the last inscribed piece of paper mentioned above, Luthuli signed his Last Will and Testament bequeathing all his immovable property to his wife and all of his children save his first born son, Hugh, who was omitted.[5] The Will appointed Edward Mzoneli, Mordeciah Gumede and Eben Ntuli as the executors. On 16 March, Luthuli signed a codicil bequeathing a piece of land to his nephew, Norman Luthuli. One can only speculate that those close to Luthuli and/or Luthuli himself began to be aware of his physical decline. Yet, in later oral testimonies, the family has always maintained that Luthuli possessed good health until the time of his death.

The scraps of paper found in the Luthuli Papers confirm accounts in newspaper articles published in mid-1967 that Luthuli was not able to do much reading or writing and spent most of his time listening to the radio. For one thing, his eyes troubled him. On 2 April 1967, the *Sunday Times* reported that Luthuli had recently undergone delicate surgery to his left eye at the McCord Zulu Hospital. For this treatment, Luthuli was granted a suspension of his banning orders. The eye had troubled him for many years and had been 'virtually useless' ever since his stroke in 1955. It caused Luthuli considerable, constant pain, to the extent that doctors discussed with him the possibility of removing it. Thulani Gcabashe, Luthuli's son-in-law, was quoted in the report saying that there was a fear that the other eye might also be affected. The medical spokesman at McCord also told the *Sunday Times* that Luthuli 'had not been cured yet and that he would not be "for a very long time . . . He has a very nasty eye and that is all I can say".'[6]

Other newspaper articles suggest that more than an eye may have troubled Luthuli. He remained in the McCord Hospital for as many as four weeks, other health factors (such as high blood pressure) very likely prolonging his admission. The drafting and signing of Luthuli's Will immediately preceding his four-week hospitalisation again casts doubt on the long-held conviction that Luthuli benefited from good health at the time of his death. One of the last publicised visits to Luthuli came in July 1967, shortly after a Swedish newspaper interviewed him, leading Tor Sellström, in his book on Sweden's involvement in the liberation movement, to describe Luthuli as 'an old and tired man'.[7]

The primary sources of information describing the events immediately preceding and following Luthuli's death are found in the interviews with Nokukhanya Luthuli in Rule's biography of her, in interviews found in newspaper clippings and in sworn statements submitted to the inquest held after Luthuli's death. From these sources, we are able to piece together a sequence of events leading to the death of Albert Luthuli.

The death of Albert Luthuli

On Wednesday, 19 July 1967, two days before Luthuli's death, Nokukhanya and her husband walked together from their home in Groutville to the land he rented to cultivate sugar cane. From the fields, Luthuli proceeded to his shop at Gledhow, just a few minutes' walk away, while Nokukhanya remained behind. Between the field and shop were two bridges. Members of the local community had walked across one well-known bridge daily for many decades. The other bridge, slightly to the west (inland), was under construction. During this walk and visit to the field, Nokukhanya told her husband to use the new bridge to cross over the Umvoti River to his shop to the north. Luthuli followed his wife's suggestion and used the new bridge that day. Approximately one week after her husband's death, in a sworn statement for the inquest report, Nokukhanya lamented, 'For what reason my late husband crossed over [the old] rail bridge on this occasion when he was struck by a train I do not know.'[8]

On Thursday, 20 July, a day before her husband was killed, Nokukhanya had a disagreement with him. Rule records that many years later, she recalled:

He said that [tomorrow] he wanted to go and see how the cane workers were progressing . . . I protested: 'But you were there yesterday. You get so exhausted and you look so tired. I will go myself, either tomorrow or on Monday, when I come back from Durban. There is no hurry.' But he insisted saying, 'No, I'll go.'[9]

Also on the same day, Luthuli, as was his custom, conducted a short devotional service at his home. Luthuli's son, Christian, described in a publication known as *The Post* how, after concluding, Luthuli said that the following day he would not lead the prayer meeting. Rather, he appointed Nokukhanya for this task. None of the family members took any notice of the comment, despite its break with family tradition.[10]

The following day, Friday 21 July 1967, after a hurried breakfast with his wife, Luthuli left his home at about 8h30 informing her that he would be walking to his general dealer's store near the Gledhow train station. That day, Nokukhanya also left home for Durban to purchase seed potatoes. Luthuli stood, as he usually did, at the bus stop on the corner of the Main Road (R102), waiting alone for a benevolent lift from a passing vehicle to his general dealer's store about a mile-and-a-half away. Roughly an hour later, at 9h30, Luthuli arrived at his shop where he delivered a package to Eness Mfeka, an employee at the store. In April 1964, *Drum* magazine carried a story about Luthuli, describing the store as 'a tumble-down old building with crude sign-writings in front. To lend some brightness to the otherwise drab surroundings are coloured trade advertisements adorning paint-starved walls.'[11]

Luthuli walked from his home to his store every day. From his home or his store, he travelled to and from the trust land he leased to grow sugar cane, to supervise his few workers. The cane field was about a half a mile away from the Umvoti River railway bridge, or three hundred yards, by Nokukhanya's estimation, on the south side of the river, slightly west (inland) of the bridge that he crossed to reach his fields. Since 6h30 that morning, two men (Mbuyeseni and Mpanza) and a woman (Ziphi Gumede) were busy cutting cane in Luthuli's field at a place where the bridge was visible.[12]

At approximately 10h00, Luthuli left the store, having declined a cup of tea, and informed Mfeka that he was going to his fields, but that he would be returning. Detective Charles Lewis of the South African Railways Police in Durban reported that he interviewed the people working on Luthuli's land and that none had seen or met with Luthuli that morning. In her testimony, Ziphi Gumede also mentioned that Luthuli did not meet her and the two men as expected.

Almost forty minutes later, Luthuli decided to re-cross the river to return to his store without having fulfilled his objective. He could have verified their progress visually from afar. But, having walked across the bridge to the fields, one would assume that he would stop to converse with the field labourers. In the April 1964 *Drum* feature, G.R. Naidoo recorded that the labourers treated Luthuli as their father, respecting him as a chief. Luthuli would not only supervise their work, but he would listen to their problems.[13] However, no one is known to have seen Luthuli during the thirty-eight minutes following his departure from the store. On his way back to the store, tragedy struck.

At 10h29, a goods train pulled by a locomotive left Stanger (now KwaDukuza), southbound for Durban. The day was bright and clear. Aboard the train were the driver (Stephanus Lategan), the conductor or 'guard' (Pieter van Wyk) and the boilerman or 'fireman' (Daniel Greyling). The train, running engine first, consisted of sixty axles (that is, fifteen carriages) with a tonnage of seven hundred and sixty-seven tons, loaded with syrup and sugar. At 10h36 the train passed Gledhow station, where Andries Pretorius was the station master, without stopping. At 10h38, two minutes after passing the Gledhow station, the train began to cross the Umvoti River railway bridge that was situated about a thousand yards away. At this point, Luthuli must have begun to re-cross the bridge having not met his workers in the field. Anyone entering the bridge from the south would have passed a sign that read, 'Umvoti River / Persons / Cross This Bridge at Their Own Risk' in English and Afrikaans. The driver, Stephanus Lategan, consistently indicated in his testimony before the inquest, and in cross-examination, that he blew the whistle from the time he noticed a pedestrian walking towards the train from the south end of the bridge until the train reached him. In his sworn statement, he said:

> This Bantu however did not appear to me to take any notice whatsoever of my train but just continued walking along the side of the bridge in the direction of the approaching locomotive. He had walked about the distance of about fifteen or sixteen paces along this bridge when my engine commenced to overtake him . . . he made no attempt to step towards the side or turn his body sideways to the moving train but continued to walk in the same manner . . .[14]

The driver then exclaimed to the boilerman that the train 'knocked someone'. Lategan continued:

> In my estimation the front right hand side of the buffer beam missed this Bantu by a fraction that I would have estimated at about two inches and the engine moved past him up to the place where the front end of the cab of the locomotive is situated and I saw the corner of the cab strike him on the right shoulder and this caused him to be spun around and I saw him lose his balance and fall between the right hand side of the bridge and the moving train.[15]

The driver then immediately applied the brakes at the southern end of the bridge, bringing the train to a standstill. Upon looking to the rear, the conductor noticed a man lying on the side of the bridge by the footplate. The conductor, Pieter van Wyk, disembarked. In his sworn statement, he said he

> noticed that it was an elderly Bantu man with a white goatee dressed in a khaki shirt, pants and a coat with a similar colour and he wore a pair of brown shoes. To me it seemed as if this Bantu was either dead or unconscious and I saw blood oozing out of his mouth. I did not know this Bantu man.[16]

The boilerman and the driver disembarked from the train and found the man lying just alongside the western (right) leg of the line with his head hanging between the side of the rail and the sleepers. Though the injured man was alive and breathing, the boilerman presumed he had received head injuries as he could see blood flowing from his mouth and he appeared to be unconscious. Also noticed by the driver was the severe laceration on the top/middle portion of the head. The man's face was streaming with blood. The boilerman and the driver placed him, particularly his head, in a more comfortable position. The driver testified that the conductor requested the station foreman (Steyn) and station master, Andries Pretorius, to summon an ambulance.

After phoning Stanger for an ambulance to come, the station master and foreman immediately departed on foot for the bridge. They found the conductor and the driver standing at the south end of the bridge next to Luthuli who was lying on the track and on the steel plate that is used to walk across the bridge. Andries Pretorius said in his sworn statement:

> This Bantu was lying on his back and I saw that he had sustained severe
> head injuries which were bleeding profusely and he was unconscious at
> the same time. Immediately I saw this elderly Bantu[.] I recognised him
> as being ex-Chief Albert Luthuli from Groutville.[17]

The Senior Medical Superintendent of Stanger Hospital, Gwendoline
Mary Gregersen, had an excellent reputation and her integrity was
unquestioned. Her obituary stated that she was 'scrupulously careful to
ensure the patients' rights were adequately protected and would fight
furiously to see that they were'.[18] According to Gregersen's sworn statement,
Luthuli was found in the following condition when she first saw him in
the casualty department five minutes after his arrival at the hospital, at
approximately 11h50:

> He was shocked. His pulse was 120, his blood pressure was 130/80, he
> had a fracture [undecipherable] base of the skull and he was bleeding
> freely from injuries to this head; he was semi-conscious. The patient
> had a jagged laceration at the base of the skull on the left hand side;
> this injury was about four to five inches in length from the outer ends.
> There was a three-inch laceration on the centre of the occiput [sic], on
> the right parietal region he had an abrasion and a laceration an inch
> long. He was bleeding freely from the right ear; and he had fractured
> ribs on both sides; he had a fractured left elbow; he had a bruising
> [undecipherable] Fracture of the left hand; he had a laceration to the
> right lower leg.[19]

From 11h50 to 14h20, two-and-a-half hours, the doctors treated Luthuli
for his wounds. The staff first gave him a blood transfusion and his
lacerations were sutured. Next, Luthuli was X-rayed and given oxygen. At
some time, Luthuli was administered the heart stimulant, Coramine. At
12h15, Luthuli's second son, Christian, arrived at the Luthuli home and
was informed by the station master that his father had been struck by a
train. At 13h05, while visiting her son-in-law, Thulani Gcabashe, and
daughter, Hilda Thandeka, at St Aiden's Hospital, Durban, (where she
was a nurse), Nokukhanya was told her husband had been involved in an
accident. She also received the news from a second daughter, Eleanor
S'mangele (who was a nurse at McCord Zulu Hospital in Overport,
Durban).

Christian Luthuli arrived at the Stanger Hospital with two sisters-in-law shortly before 13h00 and saw his father. He recalled the occasion in an article published in *The Post* and in an interview in November 2005, thirty-eight years later. Luthuli was conscious.

> My father looked so peaceful. His head was heavily bandaged. He tried
> to smile at me. I asked him how he was feeling, and he replied that he
> could feel nothing. These were his only words he spoke. I was too
> overcome with emotion and I walked out of the room.[20]

Nokukhanya received news through Christian of Luthuli's possible transfer for brain surgery, and proceeded with her daughters to King Edward VIII Hospital in Durban where they searched for him in vain. In Stanger, Luthuli's condition deteriorated despite resuscitative measures being performed. It was decided to not transfer him to King Edward because he was not stable. Instead, a decision was made to send for a neurosurgeon from Durban to come to Stanger. Upon hearing this news at King Edward, Nokukhanya proceeded north to Stanger.

At about 13h30, Christian was joined by two family relations and the Reverend Gideon Sivetye, a Congregational minister, brother-in-law and close friend of Luthuli, at the Stanger hospital. There they saw Luthuli, who was having trouble breathing. At about 14h15, Sivetye led a prayer around Luthuli's bedside with his family and members of the hospital staff in attendance. Christian feared speaking to his father, lest he strain him and cause him to die. He remembered:

> When I saw him, I knew then that the sun was setting for my father. I
> knew then that the thin threads of life were breaking. The Reverend
> Sivetye led a prayer at my father's bedside in which my cousin, sister-in-
> law and the sister in charge and I joined. It was a simple prayer, said by
> a friend who was choking with emotion. My father appeared to be
> peaceful when the prayer was said. His breathing was hardly noticeable
> but perhaps he was conscious that we were praying for him and his last
> moments must have been happy ones.[21]

Immediately following the prayer, a neurological surgeon from St Augustine's Medical Centre in Durban, Mauritius Joubert, arrived at Stanger Hospital at 14h20. Joubert reported in his sworn statement that upon his arrival he found Luthuli to be in a deep coma and not responding to any stimulation. Joubert confirms that X-rays determined that extensive skull fractures were present as well as a fracture of the left elbow and right ninth rib.[22] The senior medical superintendent of Stanger Hospital, Gregersen, was present for the entirety of Joubert's examination. Five minutes later, at 14h25, Luthuli died. By Christian's account, exactly five minutes later, at 14h30 Nokukhanya arrived at the hospital. Joubert and/ or a nurse confided the news of her husband's death to Nokukhanya, who had missed by only moments the opportunity to say goodbye to her husband. The first words Nokukhanya uttered after being told the news was, 'I want to see my husband'. For fifteen minutes, she cried alone, quietly, over her husband. That evening, in keeping with her husband's last wishes for her to lead the family service from this day, Nokukhanya prayed a simple prayer.

Perhaps the most pertinent question is: What was Luthuli doing for almost forty minutes from the time he left his store to the time of the accident, if not visiting those whom he intended to see in his field? Did he not feel well? Was he suffering a mild stroke and thus not thinking clearly? This is possible given Luthuli's four-week admittance to McCord Hospital just three months prior to his accident. Why did he not take the alternative way, either through the cane fields, or over the new bridge, as his wife suggested earlier in the week? While suffering a stroke, did he then revert to his daily habitual pattern and path toward the store? Did he become disorientated as he had during his 1955 stroke? In 1955, his stroke was perceptible only over time; his cognitive and physical abilities were only gradually, but substantively, impaired. A stroke, disorienting him sufficiently to be hit by a passing train with a cab that overlaps the bridge's very narrow footplate, is the most obvious explanation for the accident. Luthuli had a long history of hypertension, hospitalising him in 1955, 1961, 1966 and 1967. The overall state of his health, chronic high blood pressure condition and history of strokes are all factors that point to the cause of Luthuli's death.

Shrouded in suspicion?
After learning of the death of Albert Luthuli, people across the world understandably suspected foul play on the part of the apartheid state. To this day, speculation remains alive as to the 'mysterious' cause of the ANC leader's death. Words like 'suspicious', 'mysterious circumstances' and

'shrouded in controversy' are ubiquitously used to describe the death despite the fact that a formal inquest concluded otherwise, and that neither Nokukhanya Luthuli nor the family's legal representative, Andrew Wilson, contested the findings at the time.

In interviews with those who knew Luthuli, suspicion abounds. Rhona Mzoneli, who lives near the Luthuli home remembered, 'We were all shocked to hear about his death. We are still not too sure how he died. Official reports said he died from a train accident, nobody knows how it happened.'[23] Thabani Mthiyane, a retired lecturer from the University of Zululand, on a visit to Luthuli's grave once questioned, 'Who really knows the spot where Luthuli died in a so-called train accident?'[24] Nearly forty years after Luthuli's death, the *Weekend Witness* re-iterated the perception saying that although Luthuli was said to have been killed by the train at Groutville, 'many have suspected that this could have been a more sinister plot and nearly forty years later the true facts still have not emerged'.[25]

Immediately after receiving news of his death in 1967, the ANC and its allies suspected the South African government killed Luthuli. Members of the ANC stoked suspicions by secretly distributing pamphlets countrywide that alleged apartheid death squads killed Luthuli. Further north, ZAPU also alleged murder in an August 1967 statement, re-printed in *Sechaba*:

> The sudden death of Chief Albert Luthuli is a great loss not only to the people of South Africa but to all of us who come from Southern Africa. It was during his term of office that an impetus was given to the African nationalist movements in Lesotho, Botswana, Swaziland, Mozambique, Southern Rhodesia, Tanganyika, Zambia and Malawi. His murderers will be dismayed by the immortality of his noble ideas.[26]

Elsewhere in the region, the Tanganyika African National Union (TANU) described the circumstances of Luthuli's death as 'dubious'.[27] In South West Africa (Namibia), on 24 July 1967, Jacob Kuhangua, secretary general of the South West Africa People's Organisation (SWAPO), cried:

> The treacherous act of brutality, the train that knocked him down, 'The *Nobel Peace Prize Winner*' inspired by the hatred and fanaticism against which he fought so hard, has struck down in the flower, a life full of determination, a life full of great achievement, a life full of promise

for his country and people and indeed a Son who died for human respect (original emphasis).[28]

Students at Lincoln University in the United States characterised Luthuli's death as 'shrouded in mystery'. In a July 1967 letter to the ANC, the vice president of the Mozambique Liberation Front, Uria T. Simango, doubted 'the information that he was killed by a train. His death, we believe, was a premeditated one'.[29] Mohamed Meghraoui of the Algerian National Liberation Front nonsensically stated in a draft article that Luthuli 'was assassinated, before having fulfilled his mission: the launching of the armed struggle of liberation'.[30] In the July 1968 issue of *Sechaba*, N.G. Maroudas submitted a number of poems commemorating Luthuli's death. One piece cast serious doubt on the accidental nature of Luthuli's death and, with rather poor poetic imagery, implied the train was the apartheid state.

> Chief, when that train knocked you
> down (Was it really an accident? –
> 'He had been going blind for some time' –
> Were you really so blind that you
> could not see it coming?
> Or so deaf that you could not hear
> it coming?
> Or so senile that you didn't have
> enough sense
> To stay out of its way?
> Never mind:
> However blind or deaf you
> might or might not have been then
> You are dead now),
> When your body was finally broken by
> that huge machine,
> That juggernaut of a police state,
> howling along its one way track,
> And your life dripped into the ground,
> Could you, in your last agony, still
> bear to think
> How insolently love had been met with hate:

> The hot grinning hate of masterful men
> Intent on subduing to their lust and
> greed
> The tender human spirit
> Behind the barbed wire of Law and Order.[31]

A year after Luthuli's death, an article entitled '*Somlandela uLuthuli*' ('We Will Follow Luthuli') stated that Luthuli was 'murdered by the vile system of apartheid and fascism that stalks our country today'.[32]

Other sources report the theories of conspiracy, yet cast doubt on their validity. The *Dictionary of South African Biography* stated:

> On 21/7/1967 [Luthuli] received multiple injuries when he was struck from behind [sic] by a train as he was crossing a railway bridge between his shop and his home; he died the same day in hospital. It is almost certain that he did not hear the train. This may have been due to defective hearing, or to the fact that he was walking into a strong wind. Some people including members of his family, have suspected foul play, but there is no firm evidence for this whatsoever.[33]

The inquest report contains a sworn statement by Nokukhanya Luthuli, dated 1 August 1967 and signed eleven days after her husband's death on 21 July 1967. The conclusion of her statement reads, 'In my own mind and that of my family we are satisfied that he met with his death as a result of pure accident'.[34] Less than ten years later, in a March 1975 *Trust* article entitled, 'My Life with Chief Luthuli', Nokukhanya stated:

> I fear I'm going to die before I'm satisfied . . . I don't want to live very long. I want to die as I am – nice and strong. The years are running out, and I badly want to satisfy myself about the Chief's death. If I don't it will be the greatest disappointment of my life. When people ask me how the Chief died, all I can say is that I don't know. When we recovered the body we found that his ribs were not broken and his body had no injuries. When a train hits a man his body is badly injured.[35]

Many members of the Luthuli family believe that someone intentionally killed Luthuli.[36] In Rule, Aitken and Van Dyk's biography, Nokukhanya mentioned that she thought Luthuli had a premonition that he was going to die. She also had her premonitions. On the day before his death, when she argued with her husband not to visit the cane workers by himself, she feared he may be attacked. Indeed, her dealings with the security police had caused her to fear for her husband's life. She related how they would pick him up from home and try to pressure him to leave the ANC. Nokukhanya knew neighbours were spying on her husband, reporting on his and others' arrivals and departures. She feared it would be all too easy to plan an attack. Nokukhanya stated that people in Natal were being killed in cane fields and then carried to the train tracks.[37] Ten days before his death, Nokukhanya recollected that a white man, who upon meeting Luthuli, had called him a 'communist'. Such an aspersion had been cast on him for decades. Presumably by 1967, it may well have amused rather than depressed Luthuli. It must be noted that Nokukhanya only articulated her suspicions, and they were not backed by evidence, even circumstantial, of foul play.

Albertinah Luthuli, Luthuli's eldest daughter and, today, a member of the national parliament, understandably feels that her father was murdered. She disputed Mandela's perception that in 1961 Luthuli could not remember important meetings he chaired, and the accusations of apartheid government officials that Luthuli's senility possibly caused his collision with the train at Gledhow. She confided her suspicions about the manner of her father's death.

> The world was [unintelligible] and they know that he wasn't senile, exactly. And then also, I don't like it [Mandela's characterisation of Luthuli's health] myself because it kind of fits into this thing what the people who we believe killed him want the world to believe. Ya. We believe that he, you know, he was killed by the apartheid system, by the apartheid regime, at Gledhow. It wasn't an accident. And they gave the same reasons, when they say he was senile, he couldn't hear, he couldn't see. Now, you ask anybody, they will tell you . . . He could hear. He could hear. And he could see also. One eye was not good. The other one was good. He could see. That is why he could walk on his own all the way, and all that kind of thing. So, you know that kind of thing is, which, obviously, really isn't [a] true reflection of the state of Albert, my father, at that particular time, at that time. That he was senile and all that kind of thing.[38]

Though he is now deceased, preserved are the suspicions of Edgar Sibusiso Luthuli, one of Luthuli's sons. In *Nokukhanya*, Rule, Aitken and Van Dyk quote Edgar's suspicions:

> I don't think my father was struck by the train. He used to cross the bridge often. When I was home, I would walk with him, and one thing I noticed was that he was very, very, careful. When a train was coming he would stand, not even walk, and hold onto the railings tightly. The space was big enough for the train to pass you on the bridge. My suspicions were confirmed one day in 1983 or 1984, when I was shopping at Checkers in Stanger. An elderly man, recognising me as Luthuli's son, came up to me and said he knew how my father had died. If I was interested I should come to his house and he would tell me. He told me he had been working somewhere near Gledhow Station for the Railways when the accident happened. But I decided not to follow it up. It was a time of severe political repression and I was very suspicious of his motives.[39]

Interviewed for *The Legacy of a Legend*, a documentary film produced by Amandla Communications in 2005, Thandeka Gcabashe, maintained as her mother had, that a train did not strike her father. Rather, another instrument struck him, presumably wielded by his murderer.

> On post-mortem when he was examined, there were no multiple injuries like you would find in a train accident. There was only one large gash of a wound at the back of his head as well as swelling of the wrist which indicated that after he was probably hit with a blunt instrument and as he was getting weak and life was waning out of him he held on to a rail and he twisted his wrist and so our view and the view of many people is that it was a game of dirty tricks.[40]

Thandeka's interview and Nokukhanya's conclusions about Luthuli's lack of injuries contradicted both the post-mortem, and consequently the District Surgeon/Examiner (Van Zyl) and the Stanger Hospital Superintendent's (Gregersen) sworn testimony. According to the post-mortem, extensive injuries were diagnosed. It is unknown if the actual X-rays were ever presented as evidence. The medical attendants reported that a blood transfusion was given and the wounds were sutured.

Bernard Magubane doubted Luthuli crossed the rail bridge, even with an oncoming train approaching. In *The Legacy of a Legend*, he said there must have been a conspiracy involved in the incident:

> He had travelled that route daily. He knew when the trains pass. You know, he was an intelligent man. How would he just walk on the rails? It just doesn't make any sense. It doesn't add up. Some sinister thing must have happened. You know? This was a very critical time. I mean, in South Africa, in the history of this country. Nineteen-sixty-seven was really a very critical time. I mean, and the symbolism of Luthuli was probably just too important – his presence, was just too important. If you wanted to create dissension within the movement, how else could you do it? By eliminating him under circumstances in which you could not point at the person who was actually responsible for his death.[41]

As previously indicated, Edgar Luthuli witnessed and testified that his father crossed the bridge on previous occasions. Luthuli was, he said, 'very, very careful' when a train came. Indeed Andries Pretorius, the Station Manager at Gledhow, indicated in his statement that the bridge 'had become a common means' by which to cross the river and that he himself had once been on the bridge when a train had passed. Eness Mfeka, the woman who tended Luthuli's shop affirmed that 'he normally walked over the rail bridge'. The possibility that Luthuli, whose fields and shop lie on either side of the bridge, crossed the bridge when a train might pass is not as preposterous as Magubane judged it to be. Furthermore, according to Edgar's testimony, it was not uncommon for Luthuli to encounter a train on the bridge while crossing it without undue concern. It was a dangerous business, but it was possible to avoid collision with an oncoming train by leaning towards and firmly gripping the railings. This was illustrated in a *Sunday Tribune* picture carried on 30 July 1967 showing a man (Mataba) standing on the same footplate upon which Luthuli had walked adjacent to a passing train.

Magubane's vague reference to some kind of 'dissension' that would be created within the liberation movement by Luthuli's death is counterintuitive. In July 1967, the Sabotage Act silenced Luthuli, at least publicly. If there was any dissension in the movement previous to Luthuli's death, it likely concerned the issue of violence, though the ANC deliberated and planned for it in July 1961 and Mandela implemented it in December

1961. Despite the ANC's resort to violence, Luthuli never advocated violence and continued to consistently argue for militant non-violent resistance. Luthuli's death would not likely create any dissension in the liberation movement. Conversely, Luthuli's death enabled the ANC to consolidate and homogenise a narrative justifying the rationalisation of its decision to embark on an armed strategy. There was ANC dissension *before* the accident. *After* the accident, with a homogenised history, there could be ANC cohesion.

In a press statement issued on 21 July 1967 (also entitled 'July 21'), Oliver Tambo used the occasion of Luthuli's death to serve as a call to arms. In the statement he vigorously defended the ANC's policy on violence, making frequent use of the word 'revolutionary' to refer to and assume the implementation of a violent strategy, quite unlike Luthuli's paradigmatic use of the same word in his Nobel lecture. Contrary to Luthuli's death causing dissension within ANC ranks, the statement reveals that dissension already existed within the ANC *before* Luthuli's death. 'The enemies of our revolutionary struggle,' Tambo said, 'were bent on fanning divisions inside the ranks of the ANC whilst at the same time making futile attempts to isolate Chief Albert Luthuli from the mainstream of the revolutionary movement, came forth with allegations that Chief Luthuli never approved the change-over from emphasis on non-violent struggle to the present phase.'[42]

From 1961 to his death, Luthuli never refuted the so-called 'enemies of the revolutionary struggle' who alleged that he did not support the use of violence. This is because Luthuli did not support the violent movement. However, neither did he condemn the use of violence as per Nokwe's assurance in Sweden. That had been taken care of by the ANC and the government. Until April 1962, Luthuli remained constant in his non-violent stance in the public sphere. From April 1962 until his death in July 1967, he was for the most part silent on the ANC's use of violence. And while Luthuli never publicly advocated violence, he certainly never participated in its planning or implementation.

What motive, therefore, did the apartheid government have in eliminating a very parsimonious presence, already smothered by restrictions? Luthuli's banning rendered him politically impotent. He could not meet people in groups. With other banned individuals, he could meet only with great risk and subterfuge. The government effectively silenced him. With the imposition of the June 1962 Sabotage Act's prohibition on quoting banned individuals, Luthuli could only issue by stealth a few international statements during the remaining five years of his life. There was little, if any, motive for the government to murder an old, partially blind and partially deaf man who could not effectively lead a liberation movement (with whom, on the use of violence, he did not agree) under the strict terms of his banning order.

Those who conclude that Luthuli's death was a mystery or the result of a political conspiracy have not formally investigated his murder and/or have not interrogated, and thus cited, the inquest report in detail. The exceptions are Rule, Aitken and Van Dyk's biography of Nokukhanya and Charlotte Owen and Peter Corbett's audio-visual documentary on Luthuli, *Mayibuye Afrika*. Rule, Aitken and Van Dyk extensively referred to the official inquest report and even pictured its first page in their book. Though they referred to the inquest, they conveyed as findings of the inquest conclusions contrary to its contents. For example, they wrote that the inquest found Luthuli to have been dragged when there was no testimony to that effect in the inquest.[43] Owen and Corbett carefully studied the inquest and interviewed Andrew Wilson who had represented the Luthuli family; they also concluded that it almost certainly was an accident. The family's claim that Luthuli was a victim of foul play deserves the utmost attention and respect. However, to make such claims historians and other professional commentators must be held to a higher standard of evidence than the family.

Historians have not hitherto exhausted all the circumstantial evidence surrounding the death of Albert Luthuli. On the day before his death, Nokukhanya argued she should go to the fields on her husband's behalf because just the previous day he was 'so exhausted' and 'looked so tired'. A review of Luthuli's medical condition, further, renders it not impossible to determine that a mild stroke, such as he had experienced before, may have been sufficient to momentarily disorient, unbalance and generally discombobulate Luthuli. In such a state, he would more likely than not have been unable to evade the ten to ten-and-a-half inch overlap of the passing train and the footplate on which he was standing.

Luthuli had a long history of hypertension, high blood pressure and strokes. He had been hospitalised as early as 1952 and as late as 1967. In the final months of his life, his penmanship deteriorated, the number of archival records he produced plummeted, he became half blind and deaf and, before an unusually long hospitalisation for an eye operation, he prepared his Last Will and Testament. On 21 July, Luthuli went from his shop to visit his workers in the field. They never saw him. He returned to his shop across a rail bridge's narrow footplate. Photographic evidence shows that any misstep or failure to balance appropriately to avoid an approaching train with cab that extended over the footplate would prove catastrophic.

The myth that Luthuli was killed, like the myth that he supported the turn to violence, leads to inaccurate interpretations of Luthuli. To say that Luthuli was mysteriously killed is to understand that he still had a vital role in the struggle for liberation at the time of his death, that he was a threat to the apartheid regime. Sadly, Luthuli had long since been considered obsolete by leaders of his own movement and he had little contact with those imprisoned, banned or exiled. Since Sharpeville, through the State of Emergency and upon the launch of MK, Luthuli served only as the honorary, emeritus, titular leader of the ANC and thus no motive existed for his death. A martyr inspires the oppressed, not the oppressor.

Postscript

AS RECENTLY AS JULY 2008, the Nelson Mandela Foundation sponsored an exhibition at the University of Fort Hare's ANC archives focusing on and drawing parallels between the lives of the two towering figures of the struggle for liberation in South Africa – Nelson Mandela and Albert Luthuli. The exhibition explored various themes such as 'Modernisers', 'Speaking to Power', 'International Legitimacy' and 'Armed Struggle' to establish the parallels – often stretching the facts to make them fit.

The exhibition's interpretative notes stated, for example, that both men hailed from 'powerful traditional families' and that they 'continued to embrace the traditional roles into which they were born [while] . . . both wrestled with the idea of accepting chieftainship'. In extension of this, the exhibition intimated that Luthuli and Mandela (though, for Mandela, vicariously through his father) 'were stripped of their chieftainships because they refused to act as puppets for the authorities'. The elected chieftaincy of the *amakholwa* in Groutville cannot be described as 'traditional' or 'powerful'. Albert Luthuli was certainly not born into an inherited traditional role. He identified himself in his autobiography as a 'commoner'.[1] It was only Mandela who issued from a royal lineage.

Perhaps the most alarming statement of all in the exhibition notes was that 'Approached by Mandela, Luthuli agreed to the armed struggle'. This is a very terse distortion of what actually occurred. Again, relying on Mandela's autobiography, the exhibition read:

> In June 1961 when Nelson Mandela introduced the idea of the armed struggle at an ANC meeting he was concerned that, because Chief Luthuli was committed to non-violence, he might be reluctant to agree. After listening to hours of motivation Luthuli finally agreed that armed struggle was inevitable. Luthuli opened the debate again at a meeting with the Indian Congress, the Congress of Democrats, the South African Congress of Trade Unions and the Coloured People's Congress. At the

204

end of the meeting Mandela was mandated to form a military
organisation, separate from the ANC.

The above is simply not true. Luthuli's 1962 column in the *Golden City
Post* and his 1962 collaboration with Martin Luther King, Junior, prove
that he did not believe that armed struggle was unavoidable. Inevitably,
the exhibition went on to quote from Luthuli's speech at the Rivonia
Trial, 'no one can blame brave just men' in solidarity with the ANC leaders
convicted to life sentences three years later in 1964. As is argued in this
book, Luthuli's statement is a carefully crafted statement of solidarity,
not agreement, for those who initiated MK.

If anything, this review of the life of Albert Luthuli has shown that he
most reluctantly yielded to the congresses's joint, democratic decision to
not discipline Mandela should he form a military organisation that would
be prepared to fight in the event that armed conflict became inevitable.
Because Luthuli objected to this decision, he insisted the military
organisation not be directly affiliated with, yet subject to, the ANC that
he led as president general.

The exhibition juxtaposed quotations alongside each other to give
the impression that Mandela and Luthuli possessed coterminous
philosophies on the role of violence. It strategically placed Mandela's
May 1961 'we will have to reconsider our tactics' statement with a July
1961 quotation of Luthuli in which he denied being a pacifist. Such
obfuscation homogenises the contexts in which the statements were made
and hides the very real and robust interaction between Mandela and
Luthuli on what was so vexed and urgent an issue.

Many nuanced misconceptions exist within the above ANC nationalist
version of history. First, it can be argued that rather than mandating
Mandela to form an armed organisation, the alliance of congresses and
the ANC 'permitted' or 'allowed' this, without the threat of disciplinary
action. Second, the relentless argumentation by Mandela over two long
nights sufficiently disillusioned and exhausted Luthuli to concede the
possible future inevitability of violence. It does not follow that Luthuli
supported the decision. The grand old man of the ANC, as Joe Slovo
called Luthuli, yielded to intense motivations and a compromise decision,
democratically derived to form, not launch, MK. For Luthuli, any thoughts
of the inevitability of violence derived from Mandela's resolute and sharp
mind rather than from the political context.

Mandela always respected Luthuli. Always. Serving a life sentence on Robben Island at the time of Luthuli's death in 1967, Mandela speaks in his autobiography of his distress at the reaction of one of their number to the news:

> [W]e also learned of Chief Luthuli's death at home in July 1967 . . . Luthuli's death left a great vacuum in the organisation; the chief was a Nobel Prize winner, a distinguished, internationally known figure, a man who commanded respect from both black and white. For these reasons, he was irreplaceable . . . We organised a small memorial service for the chief in section B and permitted everyone who wanted to say something to do so. It was a quiet, respectful service with only one sour note. When Neville Alexander of the Non-European Unity Movement rose to speak, it was apparent that he had come not to praise the chief but to bury him. Without even perfunctory regrets at the man's passing, he accused Luthuli of being a stooge of the white man, mainly on the ground that the chief had accepted the Nobel Peace Prize.[2]

In time, Mandela would also earn the Nobel Peace Prize. Mandela befriended his warders, led a Government of National Unity in partnership with a party that imprisoned him for over two decades, wore the Springbok rugby jersey, had tea with the widow of apartheid's architect and orchestrated a miracle by leading a political and social revolution without civil war. Luthuli would have been proud, very proud, of his lieutenant in 1994.

Despite their political differences in July 1961, Mandela never forgot the lessons Luthuli taught. Yet, Mandela and Luthuli were not the same. By articulating their differences, the purveyors of history can best accurately remember them and honour the reasons for which they fought. For both fought honourably.

Appendix 1

'Christian Life: A Constant Venture'

Handwritten outline of a sermon preached at the Adams College morning worship service, Sunday, 9 November 1952, by Albert John Luthuli.[1]

"CHRISTIAN LIFE A CONSTANT VENTURE"

Text: St Luke 5:4. "And when he had ceased speaking he said to Simon: 'Put out into the deep and let down your nets for a catch.'" Launch out into the deep.

I. CHRISTIAN LIFE SHOULD BE ADVENTUROUS.

1. We remain spiritually and morally dwarfed when we could be spiritual and moral giants

2. We remain paralysed or discouraged with our failures when we ...

Scripture Readings   Old Testament
                             New Testament: St. Luke 5:1–11

Hymns	I Am Not Ashamed	507
	Who is on the Lord's Side?	519
	A Closer Walk with God	457
	Take My Life	512

---

1. University of Cape Town, Manuscripts and Archives Department, Legal Collections, Luthuli Papers (BCZA 78/46–7), CAMP MF 2914, microfilm, Reel no. 2.

Hymns already chosen by Mr Grant:

O Worship the King	9
Lead Us Heavenly Father	653
Who Is One the Lord's Side	519
Jesus Through Joy of Loving Hearts	420 (is very good.)

'Christian Life: A Constant Venture'

Text: St Luke 5:4: 'AND when he had ceased speaking he said to Simon: "Put out INTO THE DEEP AND LET DOWN YOUR NETS FOR A CATCH"': LAUNCH OUT INTO THE DEEP

CHRISTIAN LIFE SHOULD BE ADVENTUROUS:

We remain SPIRITUALLY and MORALLY dwarfed when we could be SPIRITUAL AND MORAL giants.

We remain paralyzed or discouraged with our failures / when at the master's

AS to SIMON PETER and his partners by the lake of Gennesaret the mater calls to VENTURE INTO THE UNKNOWN. Venture into the deep – LAUNCH OUT INTO THE DEEP AT CHRIST'S bidding.

> so that from being
> mere teachers, we become effective Christian Teachers.

Mere Farmers, Doctors, and ARTISANS, become effective Christian Farmers, ARTISANS, Doctors who seek to lead others to Christ.

N.B. Peter and his friends – from fishing fish to fishing men.

'I will make you fishers of men', Christ says.

ST PETER AS AN EXAMPLE OF AN ADVENTUROUS SOUL IN THE CHRISTIAN LIFE.

Simon Peter, the centre figure of the story OF our TEXT who grew through venturing into the deep in the Christian way to merit the title of 'Saint Peter', says else where in his writings

N.B. 2 Peter 3:18: 'But grow in the grace and knowledge of our Lord and Savior Jesus Christ.'

N.B. SIMON PETER CERTAINLY GREW THROUGH EVER LAUNCHING INTO THE DEEP SINCE THAT FIRST CALL BY THE MASTER TO VENTURE INTO THE DEEP BY THE SEA OF GENNESARET.

from a cowardly follower of his master at the crucifixion he
became the bold Peter of the Acts of the Apostles.

(ii.)   from a disciple with narrow spiritual conception which tended to
confine Christian heritage to Jews, he gained a wider and rich conception of
the Universality of the Christian Gospel.

To Samaria with John
To Cornelius the Italian official in Caesarea
Acts 10:27, 28, 34, 35, etc

What was the secret of Peter's success?

SECRET OF PETER'S SUCCESS AS SEEN IN HIS EXPERIENCE
THAT WAS DESTINED TO CHANGE THE WHOLE COURSE OF PETER'S
LIFE.

came to him at his work: CALLED TO A HIGHER CALL – Something greater;
a higher kind of fishing – fishing men. He was at but work: Lazy
[undecipherable] [undecipherable] good for God's [walk?].
N.B. Sometimes we may feel called upon to use the rich experience in the
same work we may have been doing.

Complete obedience to master. 'Master we toiled all night and we took
nothing! But at your word, I will let down the nets.

Utter humility – Depart from me, for I am a sinful man, Oh, Lord.

OTHER EXAMPLES

HISTORY ABOUNDS WITH HELPFUL EXAMPLES OF ORDINARY MEN AND
WOMEN WHO THROUGH 'LAUNCHING INTO THE DEEP' IN OBEDIANCE
[TO THE] DIVINE CALL BECAME OUTSTANDING AND EFFECTIVE MEN OF
GOD.

HEROES OF FAITH AS HEBREWS SO FITTINGLY DESCRIBES THEM.

N.B. In varying and may be even lesser degrees we too can be daring
ventures in the deep [sic].

1.   Enoch – High degree of personal spiritual and moral life.

Hebrews 11:5, Enoch was taken up so that he should not see
death, and he was not found because God had taken him. Now
before he was taken he was attested to [undecipherable] pleased God.

Abraham – Venturing into new religious concepts of God. So became father of a nation with a NEW RELIGION which became the foundation of Christianity.

Moses – Nation liberator and builder on godly principles. Left princely comforts to venture into the deep at God's command.

St PAUL – BUILDING A Christian Universal Church with New Concepts of Christian ethics and principals to accommodate people of different races: Jews and gentile.

N.B. His venturous spirit is so well shown in these words. Philippians 3:
             'But one thing I do . . .

Martin Luther
David Livingstone:

helped destroy slavery and so became outstanding Christian liberator of Africa.

EXAMPLES OF MEN WHO FAILED GOD BY FAILING TO LAUNCH INTO GOD'S DEEP.

even with special talents God forbid that we be like –

Saul – disappointed God and God had to say 'he regrets he made him kin
Samson – used his power finally to destroy himself. Even with talent.
Jonah – ran away from a mission: Narrow vision of God['s] purpose

GOD'S PURPOSE FOR YOU

God made you for

a life of fellowship with him and DESTINED TO BE A BLESSING.

To be a blessing in the world: as he said to Abraham, 'Thou shall be a blessing
– indeed God meant your life in some way to be a blessing, not a curse in the world.

N.B. THE Deepeth OF Your LAUNCHING INTO THE Deep SEA of Christian Experience will be the measure of the quality and effectiveness of your being a blessing to humanity, as with Peter in our story.

THE DEMANDS OF A VENTUROUS CHRISTIAN LIFE

Obeying and FoLLoWING JESUS: Peter said, 'Master, we toiled all night and took nothing! But at your word, I will let down the nets

- implicit trusting obedience, Humility, Humility

Following Jesus means launching out into the deep ———

Ridding ourselves of TIMID HESITANCIES
ridding ourselves of the urge to give paramouncy to ensuring EARTHLY SECURITY AND COMFORT at the expense of SPIRITUAL AND MORAL GROWTH

Someone has so effectively state this truth.

N.B. 'Let the Soul respond to this adventurous call to launch itself upon the deeps of God. It is at the point of utter commitment, where we cut the anchor rope that binds us to all earthly pleasures and reluctance, that the full experience of grace comes upon us.

This divine recklessness, This holy foolishness, is the beginning of salvation.

'Put out into the deep!' What a reproach this is to our little earth-bound loyalties, our timid clinging to shallow waters!
Narrow – Petty Jealous   N.B.   Incidentally, shallow water [indecipherable] –
– bickerings –   [indecipherable] narrow, petty [indecipherable] –
away in Christ [ventures?]   Jealousness.

CHRISTIAN INSTITUTION A GOOD ENVIRONMENT AND CLIMATE FOR CREATING AND DEVELOPING THIS URGE IN you.

Forget self and so find yourself in a LARGER WORTHY CAUSE

N.B. Pray to God never to be content with your Second-Best

GOD DOES WONDERS with small things

You may never be an Enoch, a St Peter, a St Paul, but even as a One TALENT MAN
Two [TALENT MAN]
Aaron's [indecipherable]   Aaron's rod
Turn to [indecipherable]   – use it – more will come

            But your seemingly humble daily work
student work ·
your clean room as teacher
your desk as carpenter etc

N.B. Your simple boat could be [indecipherable] used by Christ to supply teachers of the multitude right here at Adams, first

These daily avenues of your can be made a place from which Christ can be heard.

3.   CALL TO LARGER VENTURE   RESPOND

If a call should come to follow Christ to larger ventures in his cause, dare all for Him.

<u>End of Life</u>
So that at the end of your life, like that Christian Hero AND ADVENTURER ST PAUL

NRSV LUKE 5:1–11; CALLING THE FISHERMEN
Text Verse: Luke 5:4

Once while Jesus was standing beside the lake of Gennesaret, and the crowd was pressing in on him to hear the word of God, he saw two boats there at the shore of the lake; the fishermen had gone out of them and were washing their nets. He got into one of the boats, the one belonging to Simon, and asked him to put out a little way from the shore. Then he sat down and taught the crowds from the boat. **When he had finished speaking, he said to Simon, 'Put out into the deep water and let down your nets for a catch'** (emphasis added). Simon answered, 'Master, we have worked all night long but have caught nothing. Yet if you say so, I will let down the nets.' When they had done this, they caught so many fish that their nets were beginning to break. So they signaled their partners in the other boat to come and help them. And they came and filled both boats, so that they began to sink. But when Simon Peter saw it, he fell down at Jesus' knees, saying, 'Go away from me, Lord, for I am a sinful man!' For he and all who were with him were amazed at the catch of fish that they had taken; and so also were James and John, sons of Zebedee, who were partners with Simon. Then Jesus said to Simon, 'Do not be afraid; from now on you will be catching people.' When they had brought their boats to shore, they left everything and followed him.

NRSV ACTS 10:27–28 and 34–35; PETER AND CORNELIUS

And as he talked with him, he went in and found that many had assembled; and he said to them, 'You yourselves know that it is unlawful for a Jew to associate with or to visit a Gentile; but God has shown me that I should not call anyone profane or unclean.

Then Peter began to speak to them: 'I truly understand that God shows no partiality, but in every nation anyone who fears him and does what is right is acceptable to him.'

NRSV HEBREWS 11:5; THE EXAMPLE OF ENOCH

By faith Enoch was taken so that he did not experience death; and 'he was not found, because God had taken him'. For it was attested before he was taken away that 'he had pleased God'.

NRSV PHILIPPIANS 3:13–14; BREAKING WITH THE PAST

Beloved, I do not consider that I have made it my own; but this one thing I do: forgetting what lies behind and straining forward to what lies ahead, I press on toward the goal for the prize of the heavenly call of God in Christ Jesus.

Appendix 2

'The Road to Freedom is Via the Cross'

A public statement made by Albert Luthuli immediately after he was dismissed from his position as chief by the government in November 1952. It was issued jointly by the African National Congress and the Natal Indian Congress.[1]

I have been dismissed from the Chieftainship of the Abase-Makolweni Tribe in the Groutville Mission reserve. I presume that this has been done by the Governor General in his capacity as Supreme Chief of the 'Native' people of the Union of South Africa save those of the Cape Province. I was democratically elected to this position in 1935 by the people of Groutville Mission Reserve and was duly approved and appointed by the Governor General.

---

1. Albert Luthuli, *Let My People Go: The Autobiography of Albert Luthuli, Nobel Peace Prize Winner* (Cape Town: Tafelberg, 2006), pp. 232–236.

Path of moderation

Previous to being a chief I was a school teacher for about seventeen years. In these past thirty years or so I have striven with tremendous zeal and patience to work for the progress and welfare of my people and for their harmonious relations with other sections of our multiracial society in the Union of South Africa. In this effort I always pursued what liberal-minded people rightly regarded as the path of moderation. Over this great length of time I have, year after year, gladly spent hours of my time with such organisations as the church and its various agencies such as the Christian Council of South Africa, the Joint Council of Europeans and Africans and the now defunct Native Representative Council.

In so far as gaining citizen rights and opportunities for the unfettered development of the African people, who will deny that thirty years of my life have been spent knocking in vain, patiently, moderately and modestly at a closed and barred door?

What have been the fruits of my many years of moderation? Has there been any reciprocal tolerance or moderation from the government, be it Nationalist or United Party? No! On the contrary, the past thirty years have seen the greatest number of Laws restricting our rights and progress until today we have reached a stage where we have almost no rights at all: no adequate land for our occupation, our only asset, cattle, dwindling, no security of homes, no decent and remunerative employment, more restrictions to freedom of movement through passes, curfew regulations, influx control measures; in short we have witnessed in these years an intensification of our subjection to ensure and protect white supremacy.

A new spirit

It is with this background and with a full sense of responsibility that, under the auspices of the African National Congress (Natal), I have joined my people in the new spirit that moves them today, the spirit that revolts openly and boldly against injustice and expresses itself in a determined and non-violent manner. Because of my association with the African National Congress in this new spirit which has found an effective and legitimate way of expression in the Non-Violent Passive Resistance Campaign, I was given a two-week limit ultimatum by the Secretary of Native Affairs calling upon me to chose between the African National Congress and the chieftainship of the Groutville Mission Reserve. He alleged that my association with Congress in its Non-Violent Passive Resistance Campaign was an act of disloyalty to the state. I did not, and do not, agree with this view. Viewing non-violent passive resistance as a non-revolutionary and, therefore, a most legitimate and humane political pressure technique for a people denied all effective forms of constitutional striving, I saw no real conflict in my dual leadership of my people: leader of this tribe as chief and political leader in Congress.

Servant of people

I saw no cause to resign from either. This stand of mine which resulted in my being sacked from the chieftainship might seem foolish and disappointing to some liberal and moderate Europeans and non-Europeans with whom I have worked these many years and with whom I still hope to work. This is no parting of the ways but a 'launching farther into the deep'. I invite them to join us in our unequivocal pronouncement of all legitimate African aspirations and in our firm stand against injustice and oppression.

I do not wish to challenge my dismissal, but I would like to suggest that in the interest of the institution of chieftainship in these modern times of democracy, the government should define more precisely and make more widely known the status, functions and privileges of chiefs.

My view has been, and still is, that a chief is primarily a servant of his people. He is the voice of his people. He is the voice of his people in local affairs. Unlike a Native Commissioner, he is part and parcel of the Tribe, and not a local agent of the government. Within the bounds of loyalty it is conceivable that he may vote and press the claims of his people even if they should be unpalatable to the government of the day. He may use all legitimate modern techniques to get these demands satisfied. It is inconceivable how chiefs could effectively serve the wider and common interest of their own tribe without cooperating with other leaders of the people, both the natural leaders (chiefs) and leaders elected democratically by the people themselves.

Must fight fearlessly

It was to allow for these wider associations intended to promote the common national interests of the people as against purely local interests that the government in making rules governing chiefs did not debar them from joining political associations so long as those associations had not been declared 'by the Minister to be subversive of or prejudicial to constituted government'. The African National Congress, its Non-Violent Passive Resistance Campaign, may be of nuisance value to the government but it is not subversive since it does not seek to overthrow the form and machinery of the state but only urges for the inclusion of all sections of the community in a partnership in the government of the country on the basis of equality.

Laws and conditions that tend to debase human personality – a God-given force – be they brought about by the state or other individuals, must be relentlessly opposed in the spirit of defiance shown by St Peter when he said to the rulers of his day: 'Shall we obey God or man?' No one can deny that in so far as non-Whites are concerned in the Union of South Africa, laws and conditions that debase human personality abound. Any chief worthy of his position must fight fearlessly against such debasing conditions and laws. If the government should resort to dismissing such chiefs, it may find itself dismissing many chiefs or causing people to dismiss from their hearts chiefs who are indifferent to the needs of the people through fear of dismissal by the government. Surely the government cannot place chiefs in such an uncomfortable and invidious position.

Even death

As for myself, with a full sense of responsibility and a clear conviction, I decided to remain in the struggle for extending democratic rights and responsibilities to all sections of the South African community. I have embraced the Non-Violent Passive Resistance technique in fighting for freedom because I am convinced it is the only non-revolutionary, legitimate and humane way that could be used by people denied, as we are, effective constitutional means to further aspirations.

The wisdom or foolishness of this decision I place in the hands of the Almighty.

What the future has in store for me I do not know. It might be ridicule, imprisonment, concentration camp, flogging, banishment and even death. I only pray to the Almighty to strengthen my resolve so that none of these grim possibilities may deter me from striving, for the sake of the good name of our beloved country, the Union of South Africa, to make it a true democracy and a true union in form and spirit of all communities in the land.

My only painful concern at times is that of the welfare of my family but I try even in this regard, in a spirit of trust and surrender to God's will as I see it, to say: 'God will provide.'

It is inevitable that in working for freedom some individuals and some families must take the lead and suffer. The Road to Freedom is via the CROSS.

MAYIBUYE!
AFRIKA! AFRIKA! AFRIKA!

Appendix 3

Nobel Peace Prize Acceptance Speech

Albert Luthuli's Acceptance Speech, on the occasion of the award of the Nobel Peace Prize in Oslo, 10 December 1961.[1]

Your Majesty, Mr President, Ladies and Gentlemen, here present!

On an occasion like this words fail one. This is the most important occasion not only in my life, but in that of my dear wife, Nokukhanya, who shares with me this honour. For, friends, her encouragement, not just mere encouragement but active support, made me at times fear that she herself might end in jail one day. She richly shares with me this honour.

I will now, Mr President, humbly present my speech of acceptance of this great honour. A significant honour which I feel I least deserve, Sir.

I have committed into writing what I have to say, I will proceed to read that.

This year, as in the years before it, mankind has paid for the maintenance of peace the price of many lives. It was in the cause of his activities in the interest of peace that the late Dag Hammarskjöld lost his life. Of his work a great deal has been written, but I wish to take this opportunity to say how much I regret that he is not with us to receive the encouragement of this service he has rendered mankind. I might here pause and interject, friends, to say as I was thinking of this unfortunate occasion that brought about the passing of Dag Hammarskjöld. I remember that many lives have been lost in Africa, starting with Livingstone of old to this day. Lives worthily lost to redeem Africa. It is significant that it was in Africa, my home continent, that he gave his life. How many times his decisions helped to avert a world catastrophe will never be known. But there are many of such occasions, I am sure. But there can be no doubt that he steered the United Nations through one of the most difficult phases in its history. His absence from our midst today should be an enduring lesson for all peace-lovers, and a challenge to the nations of the world to

---

1. G. Liljestrand (ed.), *Le Prix Nobel en 1960* (Stockholm: Nobel Foundation, 1961). Found at: <http://nobelprize.org/nobel_prizes/peace/laureates/1960/lutuli-acceptance.html> accessed 18 July 2010.

eliminate those conditions in Africa, nay, anywhere, which brought about the tragic and untimely end to his life. This, the devoted Chief Executive of the world.

As you may have heard, when the South African Minister of Interior announced that subject to a number of rather unusual conditions, I would be permitted to come to Oslo for this occasion, conditions, Mr President, made me literally to continue a bad man in the free Europe. He expressed the view that I did not deserve the Nobel Peace Prize for 1960. Such is the magic of a peace prize, that it has even managed to produce an issue on which I agree with the Government of South Africa. I don't think there are very many issues on which we agree. Although for different reasons.

It is the greatest honour in the life of any man to be awarded the Nobel Peace Prize, and no one who appreciates its profound significance can escape a feeling of inadequacy, and I do so very deeply, when selected to receive it. In this instance, the feeling is the deeper, not only because these elections are made by a committee by the most eminent citizens of this country, but also because I find it hard to believe that in this distressed and heavily laden world I could be counted among those whose efforts have amounted to a noticeable contribution to the welfare of mankind. I recognize, however, that in my country, South Africa, the spirit of peace is subject to some of the severest tensions known to men. Yes, it is idle to speak of our country as being in peace, because there can be no peace in any part of the world where there are people oppressed. For that reason South Africa has been, and continues to be, the focus of world attention. I therefore regard this award as a recognition of the sacrifice made by many of all races, particularly the African people, who have endured and suffered so much for so long. It can only be on behalf of the people of South Africa, all the people of South Africa, especially the freedom-loving people, that I accept this award, that I acknowledge this honour. I accept it also as an honour not only to South Africa, but for the whole continent of Africa, to this continent, Mother Africa! To all its people, whatever their race, colour or creed might be, and indeed, friends, I like to say, quite long ago my forefathers extended a hand of friendship to people of Europe when they came to that continent. What has happened to the extension of that hand only history can say, and it is not time to speak about that here, but I would like to say, as I receive this prize of peace, that the hand of Africa was extended. It was a hand of friendship, if you read history.

It is an honour for the peace-loving people of the entire world and an encouragement for us all to redouble our efforts in this struggle for peace and friendship, or indeed we do need in this world of ours at the present moment peace and friendship. These are becoming very rare commodities in the world. For my part, I am deeply conscious of the added responsibility which this award entails. I have the feeling that I have been made answerable for the future of the people of South Africa, for if there is no peace for the majority of them there is no peace for any one. As I said it is idle to speak of peace anywhere where there are people still suffering under oppression. I can only pray, friends, that The All Mighty will give me the strength to make my humble contribution to the peaceful solution of South Africa's, and indeed, the world's problems, for it is not just South Africa, or Africa, there are other parts of the world where there are tensions, and those places are sorely in need of peace, as we are in my own continent, as we are in my own area of South Africa.

Happily, I am only one among millions who have dedicated their lives to the service of mankind, who have given time, property and life to ensure that all men shall live in peace and happiness, and I like to here say, that there are many in my country who are doing so.

I have already said I have noticed this award on behalf of all freedom-loving peoples who work day and night to make South Africa what it ought to be. It is appropriate, Your Majesty, Mr President, at this point, to mention the late Alfred Nobel to whom we owe our presence here, and who, by establishing the Nobel Foundation, placed responsibility for the maintenance of peace on the individual. It is so easy sometimes to hide under groups when you do very little for a cause. Here the stress is on the individual, so making peace, no less than war, is the concern of every man and woman on earth, whether they be in Senegal or Berlin, in Washington or in the shattered towns of South Africa. However humble the place, it can make its contribution also, it is expected to make its contribution to peace. It is this call for quality in the late Nobel's ideals which have won for the Nobel Peace Prize the importance and universal recognition which it enjoys. For indeed it enjoys deservingly this universal recognition. In an age when the outbreak of war would wipe out the entire face of the earth, the ideals of Nobel should not merely be accepted or even admired, they should be lived, with a stress on, they should be lived!

It is so easy to admire a person, to admire what he or she stood for or stands for, and yet shrink from cutting off the mission of the present. The challenge, friends, is for us to live the ideals that Nobel tried to uphold in the world as enshrined in the Nobel Peace Prize and other prizes which he bequeathed to mankind. Scientific inventions, at all conceivable levels should enrich human life, not threaten existence. Science should be the greatest ally, not the worst enemy of mankind. Only so can the world, not only respond to the worthy efforts of Nobel, but also ensure itself against self-destruction. Indeed the challenge is for us to ensure the world from self-destruction. In our contribution to peace we are resolved to end such evils as oppression, white supremacy and race discrimination, all of which are incompatible with world peace and security. There is indeed a threat to peace.

In some quarters it is often doubted whether the situation in South Africa is a threat to peace, it is no doubt that any situation where men have to struggle for their rights is a threat to peace. We are encouraged to know, by the very nature of the award made for 1960 that in our efforts we are serving our fellow men in the world over.

May the day come soon, when the people of the world will rouse themselves, and together effectively stamp out any threat to peace in whatever quarter of the world it may be found. When that day comes, there shall be 'peace on earth and goodwill amongst men', as was announced by the Angels when that great messenger of peace, Our Lord came to earth.

Nobel Lecture, 11 December 1961[1]

Africa and Freedom

In years gone by, some of the greatest men of our century have stood here to receive this award, men whose names and deeds have enriched the pages of human history, men whom future generations will regard as having shaped the world of our time. No one could be left unmoved at being plucked from the village of Groutville,[2] a name many of you have never heard before and which does not even feature on many maps – to be plucked from banishment in a rural backwater, to be lifted out of the narrow confines of South Africa's internal politics and placed here in the shadow of these great figures. It is a great honour to me to stand on this rostrum where many of the great men of our times have stood before.

The Nobel Peace Award that has brought me here has for me a threefold significance. On the one hand, it is a tribute to my humble contribution to efforts by democrats on both sides of the colour line to find a peaceful solution to the race problem. This contribution is not in any way unique. I did not initiate the struggle to extend the area of human freedom in South Africa; other African patriots – devoted men – did so before me. I also, as a Christian and patriot, could not look on while systematic attempts were made, almost in every department of life, to debase the God-factor in man or to set a limit beyond which the human being in his black form might not strive to serve his Creator to the best of his ability. To remain neutral in a situation where the laws of the land virtually criticised God for having created men of colour was the sort of thing I could not, as a Christian, tolerate.

On the other hand, the award is a democratic declaration of solidarity with those who fight to widen the area of liberty in my part of the world. As such, it

---

1. F.W. Haberman (ed.), *Nobel Lectures: Peace 1951–1970* (Amsterdam: Elsevier, 1972). Found at: <http://nobelprize.org/nobel_prizes/peace/laureates/1960/lutuli-lecture.html> accessed 18 July 2010.
2. Groutville, Luthuli's home village of some five hundred population on the Natal coast about fifty miles north of Durban, is the centre of the Umvoti Mission Reserve that supports about five thousand Zulus.

is the sort of gesture which gives me and millions who think as I do, tremendous encouragement. There are still people in the world today who regard South Africa's race problem as a simple clash between black and white. Our government has carefully projected this image of the problem before the eyes of the world. This has had two effects. It has confused the real issues at stake in the race crisis. It has given some form of force to the government's contention that the race problem is a domestic matter for South Africa. This, in turn, has tended to narrow down the area over which our case could be better understood in the world.[3]

From yet another angle, it is welcome recognition of the role played by the African people during the last fifty years to establish, peacefully, a society in which merit and not race would fix the position of the individual in the life of the nation.

This award could not be for me alone, nor for just South Africa, but for Africa as a whole. Africa presently is most deeply torn with strife and most bitterly stricken with racial conflict. How strange then it is that a man of Africa should be here to receive an award given for service to the cause of peace and brotherhood between men. There has been little peace in Africa in our time. From the northernmost end of our continent, where war has raged for seven years, to the centre and to the south there are battles being fought out, some with arms, some without. In my own country, in the year 1960, for which this award is given, there was a state of emergency for many months. At Sharpeville, a small village, in a single afternoon sixty-nine people were shot dead and 180 wounded by small arms fire;[4] and in parts like the Transkei,[5] a state of emergency is still continuing. Ours is a continent in revolution against oppression. And peace and revolution make uneasy bedfellows. There can be no peace until the forces of oppression are overthrown.

Our continent has been carved up by the great powers; alien governments have been forced upon the African people by military conquest and by economic domination; strivings for nationhood and national dignity have been beaten down by force; traditional economics and ancient customs have been

---

3. In one of his extemporaneous insertions, Luthuli here points out that the race issue in South Africa is not just a 'clash of colour', but a 'clash of ideas', oppression versus democratic rights for all.
4. The result of police reaction to anti-pass tactics used by the Pan-Africanist Congress, which supported an Africans-only resistance as opposed to the African National Congress idea of working with all races; this action circumvented an ANC anti-pass campaign scheduled for a few days later.
5. In the Eastern Cape Province of South Africa.

disrupted, and human skills and energy have been harnessed for the advantage of our conquerors. In these times there has been no peace; there could be no brotherhood between men.

But now, the revolutionary stirrings of our continent are setting the past aside. Our people everywhere from north to south of the continent are reclaiming their land, their right to participate in government, their dignity as men, their nationhood. Thus, in the turmoil of revolution, the basis for peace and brotherhood in Africa is being restored by the resurrection of national sovereignty and independence, of equality and the dignity of man.

It should not be difficult for you here in Europe to appreciate this. Your continent passed through a longer series of revolutionary upheavals, in which your age of feudal backwardness gave way to the new age of industrialisation, true nationhood, democracy, and rising living standards – the golden age for which men have striven for generations. Your age of revolution, stretching across all the years from the eighteenth century to our own, encompassed some of the bloodiest civil wars in all history. By comparison, the African revolution has swept across three quarters of the continent in less than a decade; its final completion is within sight of our own generation. Again, by comparison with Europe, our African revolution – to our credit – is proving to be orderly, quick, and comparatively bloodless.

This fact of the relative peacefulness of our African revolution is attested to by other observers of eminence. Professor C.W. de Kiewiet, president of the University of Rochester, USA, in a Hoernlé Memorial Lecture for 1960, has this to say: 'There has, it is true, been almost no serious violence in the achievement of political self-rule. In that sense there is no revolution in Africa – only reform . . .'

Professor D.V. Cowen, then professor of comparative law at the University of Cape Town, South Africa, in a Hoernlé Memorial Lecture for 1961, throws light on the nature of our struggle in the following words: 'They (the whites in South Africa) are again fortunate in the very high moral calibre of the nonwhite inhabitants of South Africa, who compare favourably with any on the whole continent.' Let this never be forgotten by those who so eagerly point a finger of scorn at Africa.

Perhaps, by your standards, our surge to revolutionary reforms is late. If it is so – if we are late in joining the modern age of social enlightenment, late in gaining self-rule, independence, and democracy, it is because in the past the pace has not been set by us. Europe set the pattern for the nineteenth and twentieth-century development of Africa. Only now is our continent coming into its own and recapturing its own fate from foreign rule.

Though I speak of Africa as a single entity, it is divided in many ways by race, language, history, and custom; by political, economic, and ethnic frontiers.

But in truth, despite these multiple divisions, Africa has a single common purpose and a single goal – the achievement of its own independence. All Africa, both lands which have won their political victories but have still to overcome the legacy of economic backwardness, and lands like my own whose political battles have still to be waged to their conclusion – all Africa has this single aim: our goal is a united Africa in which the standards of life and liberty are constantly expanding; in which the ancient legacy of illiteracy and disease is swept aside; in which the dignity of man is rescued from beneath the heels of colonialism which have trampled it. This goal, pursued by millions of our people with revolutionary zeal, by means of books, representations, demonstrations, and in some places armed force provoked by the adamancy of white rule, carries the only real promise of peace in Africa. Whatever means have been used, the efforts have gone to end alien rule and race oppression.

There is a paradox in the fact that Africa qualifies for such an award in its age of turmoil and revolution. How great is the paradox and how much greater the honour that an award in support of peace and the brotherhood of man should come to one who is a citizen of a country where the brotherhood of man is an illegal doctrine, outlawed, banned, censured, proscribed and prohibited; where to work, talk, or campaign for the realisation in fact and deed of the brotherhood of man is hazardous, punished with banishment, or confinement without trial, or imprisonment; where effective democratic channels to peaceful settlement of the race problem have never existed these three hundred years; and where white minority power rests on the most heavily armed and equipped military machine in Africa. This is South Africa.

Even here, where white rule seems determined not to change its mind for the better, the spirit of Africa's militant struggle for liberty, equality, and independence asserts itself. I, together with thousands of my countrymen have in the course of the struggle for these ideals, been harassed and imprisoned, but we are not deterred in our quest for a new age in which we shall live in peace and in brotherhood.

It is not necessary for me to speak at length about South Africa; its social system, its politics, its economics, and its laws have forced themselves on the attention of the world. It is a museum piece in our time, a hangover from the dark past of mankind, a relic of an age which everywhere else is dead or dying. Here the cult of race superiority and of white supremacy is worshiped like a god. Few white people escape corruption, and many of their children learn to believe that white men are unquestionably superior, efficient, clever, industrious, and capable; that black men are, equally unquestionably, inferior, slothful, stupid, evil, and clumsy. On the basis of the mythology that 'the lowest amongst them is higher than the highest amongst us', it is claimed that white men build everything that is worthwhile in the country – its cities, its industries, its mines, and its agriculture and that they alone are thus fitted and entitled as of right to own and control these things, while black men are only temporary sojourners in these cities, fitted only for menial labour, and unfit to share political power. The prime minister of South Africa, Dr Verwoerd,[6] then minister of Bantu Affairs, when explaining his government's policy on African education had this to say: 'There is no place for him (the African) in the European community above the level of certain forms of labour.'

There is little new in this mythology. Every part of Africa which has been subject to white conquest has, at one time or another and in one guise or another, suffered from it, even in its virulent form of the slavery that obtained in Africa up to the nineteenth century. The mitigating feature in the gloom of those far-off days was the shaft of light sunk by Christian missions, a shaft of light to which we owe our initial enlightenment. With successive governments of the time doing little or nothing to ameliorate the harrowing suffering of the black man at the hands of slave drivers, men like Dr David Livingstone[7] and Dr John Philip[8] and other illustrious men of God stood for social justice in the face of overwhelming odds. It is worth noting that the names I have referred to are still anathema to some South Africans. Hence the ghost of slavery lingers on to this day in the form of forced labour that goes on in what are called farm prisons. But the tradition of Livingstone and Philip lives on, perpetuated by a few of their line. It is fair to say that even in present-day conditions, Christian missions have been in the vanguard of initiating social services provided for us. Our progress in this field has been in spite of, and not mainly because of, the government. In this, the church in South Africa, though belatedly, seems to be awakening to a broader mission of the church in its ministry among us. It is beginning to take seriously the words of its founder who said: 'I came that they might have life and have it more abundantly.'[9] This is a call to the church in South Africa to help in the all-round development of man in the present, and not only in the hereafter. In this regard, the people of South Africa, especially those who claim to be Christians, would be well advised to take heed of the conference decisions of the World Council of Churches held at Cottesloe, Johannesburg, in 1960, which gave a clear lead on the mission of the church in

---

6. Hendrik Frensch Verwoerd (1901–1966), National Party leader and prominent advocate of apartheid in the Union of South Africa; Native Affairs minister (1950–1958); prime minister (1958–1966).
7. David Livingstone (1813–1873), Scottish missionary and explorer in Africa.
8. John Philip (1775–1851), British missionary in South Africa; was influential in gaining rights for the natives but had to abandon his plan for independent native states.
9. John 10:10.

our day.[10] It left no room for doubt about the relevancy of the Christian message in the present issues that confront mankind. I note with gratitude this broader outlook of the World Council of Churches. It has a great meaning and significance for us in Africa.

There is nothing new in South Africa's apartheid ideas, but South Africa is unique in this: the ideas not only survive in our modern age but are stubbornly defended, extended, and bolstered up by legislation at the time when, in the major part of the world, they are now largely historical and are either being shamefacedly hidden behind concealing formulations or are being steadily scrapped. These ideas survive in South Africa because those who sponsor them profit from them. They provide moral whitewash for the conditions which exist in the country: for the fact that the country is ruled exclusively by a white government elected by an exclusively white electorate which is a privileged minority; for the fact that eighty-seven percent of the land and all the best agricultural land within reach of town, market, and railways are reserved for white ownership and occupation, and now through the recent Group Areas legislation non-whites are losing more land to white greed;[11] for the fact that all skilled and highly paid jobs are for whites only; for the fact that all universities of any academic merit are exclusively preserves of whites; for the fact that the education of every white child costs about £64 per year while that of an African child costs about £9 per year and that of an Indian child or coloured child costs about £20 per year; for the fact that white education is universal and compulsory up to the age of sixteen, while education for the non-white children is scarce and inadequate; and for the fact that almost one million Africans a year are arrested and jailed or fined for breaches of innumerable pass and permit laws, which do not apply to whites.

I could carry on in this strain and talk on every facet of South African life from the cradle to the grave. But these facts today are becoming known to all the world. A fierce spotlight of world attention has been thrown on them. Try as our government and its apologists will, with honeyed words about 'separate development' and eventual 'independence' in so-called 'Bantu homelands',[12]

---

10. Meeting from 8–14 December 1960, the Council delegates lived and worked together without regard for the colour bar and in their final report included criticism of the Union government's racial measures.
11. Legislation permitting the division of residential land in South African cities into sections, each for one racial group.
12. Under the apartheid or 'separate development' policy, Bantu 'homelands' or Bantustans are areas set aside for Africans only, where, the theory goes, they can preserve their own culture and traditions.

nothing can conceal the reality of South African conditions. I, as a Christian, have always felt that there is one thing above all about 'apartheid' or 'separate development' that is unforgivable. It seems utterly indifferent to the suffering of individual persons, who lose their land, their homes, their jobs, in the pursuit of what is surely the most terrible dream in the world. This terrible dream is not held on to by a crackpot group on the fringe of society or by Ku Klux Klansmen,[13] of whom we have a sprinkling. It is the deliberate policy of a government, supported actively by a large part of the white population and tolerated passively by an overwhelming white majority, but now fortunately rejected by an encouraging white minority who have thrown their lot with non-whites, who are overwhelmingly opposed to so-called separate development.

Thus it is that the golden age of Africa's independence is also the dark age of South Africa's decline and retrogression, brought about by men who, when revolutionary changes that entrenched fundamental human rights were taking place in Europe, were closed in on the tip of South Africa – and so missed the wind of progressive change.

In the wake of that decline and retrogression, bitterness between men grows to alarming heights; the economy declines as confidence ebbs away; unemployment rises; government becomes increasingly dictatorial and intolerant of constitutional and legal procedures, increasingly violent and suppressive; there is a constant drive for more policemen, more soldiers, more armaments, banishments without trial, and penal whippings. All the trappings of medieval backwardness and cruelty come to the fore. Education is being reduced to an instrument of subtle indoctrination; slanted and biased reporting in the organs of public information, a creeping censorship, book banning, and blacklisting – all these spread their shadows over the land. This is South Africa today, in the age of Africa's greatness.

But beneath the surface there is a spirit of defiance. The people of South Africa have never been a docile lot, least of all the African people. We have a long tradition of struggle for our national rights, reaching back to the very beginnings of white settlement and conquest 300 years ago. Our history is one of opposition to domination, of protest and refusal to submit to tyranny. Consider some of our great names: the great warrior and nation builder Shaka, who welded tribes together into the Zulu nation from which I spring; Moshoeshoe, the statesman and nation-builder who fathered the Basuto nation

---

13. Founded in 1915 in Georgia, the 'modern' Ku Klux Klan, an anti-Negro, anti-Catholic, anti-Semitic organisation, reached its peak of power in the US in the mid-twenties; is now moribund.

and placed Basutoland beyond the reach of the claws of the South African whites; Hintsa of the Xhosas, who chose death rather than surrender his territory to white invaders.[14] All these and other royal names, as well as other great chieftains, resisted manfully white intrusion. Consider also the sturdiness of the stock that nurtured the foregoing great names. I refer to our forbears, who, in trekking from the north to the southernmost tip of Africa centuries ago, braved rivers that are perennially swollen; hacked their way through treacherous jungle and forest; survived the plagues of the then untamed lethal diseases of a multifarious nature that abounded in Equatorial Africa; and wrested themselves from the gaping mouths of the beasts of prey. They endured it all. They settled in these parts of Africa to build a future worthwhile for us, their offspring. While the social and political conditions have changed and the problems we face are different, we too, their progeny, find ourselves facing a situation where we have to struggle for our very survival as human beings. Although methods of struggle may differ from time to time, the universal human strivings for liberty remain unchanged. We, in our situation, have chosen the path of non-violence of our own volition. Along this path we have organised many heroic campaigns. All the strength of progressive leadership in South Africa, all my life and strength, have been given to the pursuance of this method, in an attempt to avert disaster in the interests of South Africa, and [we] have bravely paid the penalties for it.

It may well be that South Africa's social system is a monument to racialism and race oppression, but its people are the living testimony to the unconquerable spirit of mankind. Down the years, against seemingly overwhelming odds, they have sought the goal of fuller life and liberty, striving with incredible determination and fortitude for the right to live as men - free men. In this, our country is not unique. Your recent and inspiring history, when the Axis powers overran most European states, is testimony of this unconquerable spirit of mankind. People of Europe formed resistance movements that finally helped to break the power of the combination of Nazism and Fascism, with their creed of race arrogance and Herrenvolk mentality.

Every people has, at one time or another in its history, been plunged into such struggle. But generally the passing of time has seen the barriers to freedom going down, one by one. Not so South Africa. Here the barriers do not go

---

14. Shaka [also Chaka] (?-1828), the 'Black Napoleon', built the Zulu nation by conquest between 1816 and 1828, when he was assassinated. Moshoeshoe [also Moshesh] (c. 1780-1870) fought off the Zulus and later signed an agreement with the British, under whose protection and guidance Basutoland had been developing self-government. Hintsa of the Gcaleka Xhosas, a tribal chief, was killed when trying to 'escape' the English in 1835.

down. Each step we take forward, every achievement we chalk up, is cancelled out by the raising of new and higher barriers to our advance. The colour bars do not get weaker; they get stronger. The bitterness of the struggle mounts as liberty comes step by step closer to the freedom fighter's grasp. All too often the protests and demonstrations of our people have been beaten back by force; but they have never been silenced.

Through all this cruel treatment in the name of law and order, our people, with a few exceptions, have remained non-violent. If today this peace award is given to South Africa through a black man, it is not because we in South Africa have won our fight for peace and human brotherhood. Far from it. Perhaps we stand farther from victory than any other people in Africa. But nothing which we have suffered at the hands of the government has turned us from our chosen path of disciplined resistance. It is for this, I believe, that this award is given.

How easy it would have been in South Africa for the natural feelings of resentment at white domination to have been turned into feelings of hatred and a desire for revenge against the white community. Here, where every day, in every aspect of life every non-white comes up against the ubiquitous sign 'Europeans Only' and the equally ubiquitous policeman to enforce it – here it could well be expected that a racialism equal to that of their oppressors would flourish to counter the white arrogance toward blacks. That it has not done so is no accident. It is because, deliberately and advisedly, African leadership for the past fifty years, with the inspiration of the African National Congress, which I had the honour to lead for the last decade or so until it was banned, had set itself steadfastly against racial vaingloriousness. We know that in so doing we passed up opportunities for an easy demagogic appeal to the natural passions of a people denied freedom and liberty; we discarded the chance of an easy and expedient emotional appeal. Our vision has always been that of a non-racial, democratic South Africa which upholds the rights of all who live in our country to remain there as *full* citizens, with equal rights and responsibilities with all others. For the consummation of this ideal we have laboured unflinchingly. We shall continue to labour unflinchingly.

It is this vision which prompted the African National Congress to invite members of other racial groups who believe with us in the brotherhood of man and in the freedom of all people to join with us in establishing a non-racial, democratic South Africa. Thus the African National Congress in its day brought about the Congress Alliance and welcomed the emergence of the Liberal Party and the Progressive Party, who to an encouraging measure support these ideals.

The true patriots of South Africa, for whom I speak, will be satisfied with nothing less than the fullest democratic rights. In government we will not be satisfied with anything less than direct, individual adult suffrage and the right to stand for and be elected to all organs of government. In economic matters we will be satisfied with nothing less than equality of opportunity in every sphere, and the enjoyment by all of those heritages which form the resources of the country, which up to now have been appropriated on a racial 'whites only' basis. In culture we will be satisfied with nothing less than the opening of all doors of learning in non-segregated institutions on the sole criterion of ability. In the social sphere we will be satisfied with nothing less than the abolition of all racial bars. We do not demand these things for people of African descent alone. We demand them for all South Africans, white and black. On these principles we are uncompromising. To compromise would be an expediency that is most treacherous to democracy, for in the turn of events, the sweets of economic, political, and social privileges that are a monopoly of only one section of a community turn sour even in the mouths of those who eat them. Thus apartheid in practice is proving to be a monster created by Frankenstein. That is the tragedy of the South African scene.

Many spurious slogans have been invented in our country in an effort to redeem uneasy race relations – 'trusteeship', 'separate development', 'race federation' and elsewhere, 'partnership'. These are efforts to sidetrack us from the democratic road, mean delaying tactics that fool no one but the unwary. No euphemistic naming will ever hide their hideous nature. We reject these policies because they do not measure up to the best mankind has striven for throughout the ages; they do great offense to man's sublime aspirations that have remained true in a sea of flux and change down the ages, aspirations of which the United Nations Declaration of Human Rights[15] is a culmination. This is what we stand for. This is what we fight for.

In their fight for lasting values, there are many things that have sustained the spirit of the freedom-loving people of South Africa and those in the yet unredeemed parts of Africa where the white man claims resolutely proprietary rights over democracy – a universal heritage. High among them – the things that have sustained us – stand the magnificent support of the progressive people and governments throughout the world, among whom number the people and government of the country of which I am today guest; our brothers in Africa, especially in the independent African states; organisations who share the outlook we embrace in countries scattered right across the face of the globe; the United Nations Organisation jointly and some of its member nations singly. In their defence of peace in the world through actively upholding the quality of

---

15. Adopted by the General Assembly on 10 December 1948; for details, see presentation speech for René Cassin and his Nobel lecture in Haberman (ed.), *Nobel Lectures*, pp. 385–407.

man, all these groups have reinforced our undying faith in the unassailable rightness and justness of our cause. To all of them I say: Alone we would have been weak. Our heartfelt appreciation of your acts of support of us we cannot adequately express, nor can we ever forget, now or in the future when victory is behind us and South Africa's freedom rests in the hands of all her people.

We South Africans, however, equally understand that, much as others might do for us, our freedom cannot come to us as a gift from abroad. Our freedom we must make ourselves. All honest freedom-loving people have dedicated themselves to that task. What we need is the courage that rises with danger.

Whatever may be the future of our freedom efforts, our cause is the cause of the liberation of people who are denied freedom. Only on this basis can the peace of Africa and the world be firmly founded. Our cause is the cause of equality between nations and peoples. Only thus can the brotherhood of man be firmly established. It is encouraging and elating to remind you that, despite her humiliation and torment at the hands of white rule, the spirit of Africa in quest for freedom has been, generally, for peaceful means to the utmost.

If I have dwelt at length on my country's race problem, it is not as though other countries on our continent do not labour under these problems, but because it is here in the Republic of South Africa that the race problem is most acute. Perhaps in no other country on the continent is white supremacy asserted with greater vigour and determination and a sense of righteousness. This places the opponents of apartheid in the front rank of those who fight white domination.

In bringing my address to a close, let me invite Africa to cast her eyes beyond the past and to some extent the present, with their woes and tribulations, trials and failures, and some successes, and see herself an emerging continent, bursting to freedom through the shell of centuries of serfdom. This is Africa's age – the dawn of her fulfilment, yes, the moment when she must grapple with destiny to reach the summits of sublimity, saying: Ours was a fight for noble values and worthy ends, and not for lands and the enslavement of man.

Africa is a vital subject matter in the world of today, a focal point of world interest and concern. Could it not be that history has delayed her rebirth for a purpose? The situation confronts her with inescapable challenges, but more importantly with opportunities for service to herself and mankind. She evades the challenges and neglects the opportunities, to her shame, if not her doom. How she sees her destiny is a more vital and rewarding quest than bemoaning her past, with its humiliations and sufferings.

The address could do no more than pose some questions and leave it to the African leaders and peoples to provide satisfying answers and responses by their concern for higher values and by their noble actions that could be

Footprints on the sands of time.
Footprints, that perhaps another,
Sailing o'er life's solemn main,
A forlorn and shipwrecked brother,
Seeing, shall take heart again.[16]

Still licking the scars of past wrongs perpetrated on her, could she not be magnanimous and practice no revenge? Her hand of friendship scornfully rejected, her pleas for justice and fair play spurned, should she not nonetheless seek to turn enmity into amity? Though robbed of her lands, her independence, and opportunities – this, oddly enough, often in the name of civilisation and even Christianity – should she not see her destiny as being that of making a distinctive contribution to human progress and human relationships with a peculiar new Africa flavour enriched by the diversity of cultures she enjoys, thus building on the summits of present human achievement an edifice that would be one of the finest tributes to the genius of man?

She should see this hour of her fulfilment as a challenge to her to labour on until she is purged of racial domination, and as an opportunity of reassuring the world that her national aspiration lies not in overthrowing white domination to replace it by a black caste but in building a non-racial democracy that shall be a monumental brotherhood, a 'brotherly community' with none discriminated against on grounds of race or colour.

What of the many pressing and complex political, economic, and cultural problems attendant upon the early years of a newly independent state? These, and others which are the legacy of colonial days, will tax to the limit the statesmanship, ingenuity, altruism, and steadfastness of African leadership and its unbending avowal to democratic tenets in statecraft. To us all, free or not free, the call of the hour is to redeem the name and honour of Mother Africa.

In a strife-torn world, tottering on the brink of complete destruction by man-made nuclear weapons, a free and independent Africa is in the making, in answer to the injunction and challenge of history: 'Arise and shine for thy light is come.'[17] Acting in concert with other nations, she is man's last hope for a mediator between the East and West, and is qualified to demand of the great powers to 'turn the swords into ploughshares'[18] because two-thirds of mankind is hungry and illiterate; to engage human energy, human skill, and human

---

16. From 'A Psalm of Life' by Henry Wadsworth Longfellow (1807–1882), American poet.
17. Isaiah 60:1.
18. Isaiah 2:4.

talent in the service of peace, for the alternative is unthinkable – war, destruction, and desolation; and to build a world community which will stand as a lasting monument to the millions of men and women, to such devoted and distinguished world citizens and fighters for peace as the late Dag Hammarskjöld, who have given their lives that we may live in happiness and peace.

Africa's qualification for this noble task is incontestable, for her own fight has never been and is not now a fight for conquest of land, for accumulation of wealth or domination of peoples, but for the recognition and preservation of the rights of man and the establishment of a truly free world for a free people.

Appendix 5

The Rivonia Statement

The following statement was issued by Chief Lutuli on 12 June 1964, when Nelson Mandela, Walter Sisulu and six other leaders were sentenced to life imprisonment in the Rivonia Trial. It was read at the Security Council meeting on the same day by the representative of Morocco.[1]

Sentences of life imprisonment have been pronounced on Nelson Mandela, Walter Sisulu, Ahmed Kathrada, Govan Mbeki, Dennis Goldberg, Raymond Mhlaba, Elias Motsoaledi and Andrew Mlangeni in the 'Rivonia trial' in Pretoria.

Over the long years these leaders advocated a policy of racial co-operation, of goodwill, and of peaceful struggle that made the South African liberation movement one of the most ethical and responsible of our time. In the face of the most bitter racial persecution, they resolutely set themselves against racialism; in the face of continued provocation, they consistently chose the path of reason.

The African National Congress, with allied organisations representing all racial sections, sought every possible means of redress for intolerable conditions, and held consistently to a policy of using militant, non-violent means of struggle. Their common aim was to create a South Africa in which all South Africans would live and work together as fellow-citizens, enjoying equal rights without discrimination on grounds of race, colour or creed.

To this end, they used every accepted method: propaganda, public meetings and rallies, petitions, stay-at-home-strikes, appeals, boycotts. So carefully did they educate the people that in the four-year long Treason Trial, one police witness after another voluntarily testified to this emphasis on non-violent methods of struggle in all aspects of their activities.

But finally all avenues of resistance were closed. The African National Congress and other organisations were made illegal; their leaders jailed, exiled or forced underground. The government sharpened its oppression of the

---

1 . Found at: <http://www.anc.org.za/ancdocs/history/lutuli/lutuli4.html> accessed 18 July 2010.

peoples of South Africa, using its all-white Parliament as the vehicle for making repression legal, and utilising every weapon of this highly industrialised and modern state to enforce that 'legality'. The stage was even reached where a white spokesman for the disenfranchised Africans was regarded by the Government as a traitor. In addition, sporadic acts of uncontrolled violence were increasing throughout the country. At first in one place, then in another, there were spontaneous eruptions against intolerable conditions; many of these acts increasingly assumed a racial character.

The African National Congress never abandoned its method of a militant, nonviolent struggle, and of creating in the process a spirit of militancy in the people. However, in the face of the uncompromising white refusal to abandon a policy which denies the African and other oppressed South Africans their rightful heritage – freedom – no one can blame brave just men for seeking justice by the use of violent methods; nor could they be blamed if they tried to create an organised force in order to ultimately establish peace and racial harmony.

For this, they are sentenced to be shut away for long years in the brutal and degrading prisons of South Africa. With them will be interred this country's hopes for racial co-operation. They will leave a vacuum in leadership that may only be filled by bitter hate and racial strife.

They represent the highest in morality and ethics in the South African political struggle; this morality and ethics has been sentenced to an imprisonment it may never survive. Their policies are in accordance with the deepest international principles of brotherhood and humanity; without their leadership, brotherhood and humanity may be blasted out of existence in South Africa for long decades to come. They believe profoundly in justice and reason; when they are locked away, justice and reason will have departed from the South African scene.

This is an appeal to save these men, not merely as individuals, but for what they stand for. In the name of justice, of hope, of truth and of peace, I appeal to South Africa's strongest allies, Britain and America. In the name of what we have come to believe Britain and America stand for, I appeal to those two powerful countries to take decisive action for full-scale action for sanctions that would precipitate the end of the hateful system of apartheid.

I appeal to all governments throughout the world, to people everywhere, to organisations and institutions in every land and at every level, to act now to impose such sanctions on South Africa that will bring about the vital necessary change and avert what can become the greatest African tragedy of our times.

Notes

Introduction

1. K. Kaunda, no title, and T. Mbeki, 'The Tempo Quickens', in D. Chetty and D. Collins (eds), *The Deepest International Principles of Brotherhood and Humanity: The Albert Luthuli Memorial Lecture* (Durban: Public Affairs and Corporate Communications, University of KwaZulu-Natal [UKZN], 2005).
2. Birth and death dates have been provided at first mention for individuals who are no longer living and whose death dates are known. Birth and death dates have not been provided at all for those still living and for those whose death dates are unknown.
3. Kaunda, no title, in Chetty and Collins (eds), *The Deepest International Principles*, p. 22.
4. J. Chissano, 'Keynote Address by H.E. Joaquim Alberto Chissano, Former President of the Republic of Mozambique and Chairperson of the Africa Forum at the Albert John Luthuli Memorial Lecture' (Pretoria: Africa Forum, 2007), p. 2.
5. UKZN, Alan Paton Centre and Struggle Archives (APC&SA), PC80/1/1/2, Alpheus Zulu, Inaugural Address of the Albert Luthuli College, 15 March 1977, p. 1.
6. Order of Mendi for Bravery, citation, Profile of the Luthuli Detachment. Found at: <http://www.thepresidency.gov.za/orders_list.asp?show=368> accessed 2 May 2010.
7. 'Nelson Mandela Would Like to See Definitive Biography of Chief Luthuli', *Daily News*, 14 October 1991.
8. Here, as in some other sources, 'Luthuli' is spelled 'Lutuli'. Albert Luthuli often signed his letters 'Lutuli'. Other members of Luthuli's family have always spelled their surname 'Luthuli' and found it peculiar, then and now, that Luthuli omitted the h. Most secondary sources include an h. In this account, historical variations in the spelling of names and place names have been preserved.
9. S. Ndebele, 'Inkosi Albert Luthuli Debate', KwaZulu-Natal (KZN) Provincial Government, 19 July 2007, p. 2. Found at: <http://www.polity.org.za/article.php?a_id= 113159> accessed 4 January 2008.
10. Rhubarb Productions film, *Servant of the People: A Commemorative Tribute to Chief Albert Luthuli*, sponsored by the KZN premier's office, February 2007.

Chapter 1: The Home of my Fathers

1. The contemporary term 'missioner' seeks to evade the pejorative stereotype associated with the term 'missionary'.

2. Perhaps this is because when Luthuli wrote, he often wrote for an international and, more importantly, ecumenical audience. Therefore, he likely refrained from identifying himself and his faith tradition in 'sectarian' or denominational terms.

3. Some sources indicate that Albert Luthuli was born on 18 December 1898. Albert and Nokukhanya Luthuli's ecclesiastical marriage certificate, kept safely in the family Bible, indicates Luthuli's birth date as 21 December 1898. Because Luthuli only 'calculated' that 1898 was the year of his birth, he could not have known the day. Also, if his father, John Luthuli, died in mid-1898 when Luthuli was six months old, Luthuli could not have been born in December 1898. If the December dates for Luthuli's birth are accurate, he may have been born in December 1897.

4. N. Gordimer, *The Essential Gesture: Writings, Politics and Places*, S. Clingman (ed.) (Johannesburg: Taurus, 1988), p. 32.

5. D. Briggs and J. Wing, *The Harvest and the Hope: The Story of Congregationalism in Southern Africa* (Johannesburg: United Congregational Church of Southern Africa [UCCSA], 1970), p. 291.

6. S. Couper, 'Luthuli's Conceptualisation of Civilisation', *African Studies*, Vol. 70, No. 1, March/April 2011, page numbers unknown at time of publication.

7. G. Atkins and F. Fagley, *History of American Congregationalism* (Boston: The Pilgrim, 1942), p. 230.

8. E.S. Reddy (ed.), *Luthuli: Speeches of Chief Albert Luthuli 1898–1967* (Durban: Madiba, 1991), p. 13.

9. Briggs and Wing, *The Harvest and the Hope*, pp. 291–292.

10. Although, Esther Johnson indicates 1822 as the date Philip accepted the pastorate. E. Johnson, 'Cape Town: The Establishing of Congregationalism in Southern Africa', in S. de Gruchy (ed.), *Changing Frontiers: The Mission Story of the UCCSA* (Gaborone: Pula, 1999), p. 20.

11. K. Asmal, D. Chidester and W. James (eds), *South Africa's Nobel Laureates: Peace, Literature and Science* (Johannesburg: Jonathan Ball, 2004), p. 25.

12. F. Welsh, *South Africa: A Narrative History* (New York: Kodansha International, 1999), p. 109.

13. A. Ross, *John Philip (1775–1851): Missions, Race and Politics in South Africa* (Aberdeen: Aberdeen University, 1986), p. 2; see also p. 299 note 1.

14. A. Sillery, *John Mackenzie of Bechuanaland, 1835–1899: A Study in Humanitarian Imperialism* (Cape Town: A.A. Balkema, 1971), p. 4.

15. V. Khumalo, 'Head Rings or Top Hats? An Inquiry into the Shifting Meaning of Body Coverings in Nineteenth Century KwaZulu-Natal', *Chicago Art Journal*, Spring 2001, pp. 41–42 and note 15.

16. N. Etherington, *Preachers, Peasants and Politics in Southern Africa, 1835–1880: African Christian Communities in Natal, Pondoland and Zululand* (London: Royal Historical Society, 1978), p. 275.

17. Cited in E. Smith, *The Life and Times of Daniel Lindley, 1801–1880* (England: Epworth, 1949), p. 160.

18. KZN Archives Depository (KZNA), Pietermaritzburg Archives Repository (PAR), American Board Mission (ABM), 'The Female Boarding School in Foreign Missions', (Boston, 1866), p. 1.

19. Grout's colleague, George Champion, also graduated at Andover Seminary. Today, the seminary is known as Andover Newton Theological Seminary and is a United Church of Christ-affiliated theological school.

20. A.E. Cubbin, 'Origins of Empangeni: Revd Aldin Grout's Mission Station Inkanyezi on the Mpangeni River, May 1841–25 July 1842, *Contree*, Vol. 31, 1992, p. 26. Shula Marks used the term 'ambiguous dependency' to refer to the divided loyalties of early African leaders. See her work, *The Ambiguities of Dependence in South Africa: Class, Nationalism and the State in Twentieth Century Natal* (Johannesburg: Ravan, 1986).

21. Smith, *Daniel Lindley*, p. 220.

22. L. Grout, *Zulu-land or Life Among the Zulu-Kafirs of Natal and Zulu-land South Africa* (Philadelphia: Presbyterian Publication Committee, 1864), p. 225.

23. N. Gordimer, 'The Man Who Burned His Pass', in *Heroes of Our Time* (New York: E.P. Dutton and Company, 1961), p. 88.

24. A. Luthuli, *Let My People Go: The Autobiography of Albert Luthuli* (Johannesburg: Collins, 1962 with an introduction by Charles Hooper; Cape Town: Tafelberg, 2006 with an introduction by Kader Asmal). All citations are from the 2006 edition; p. 5.

25. Luthuli, *Let My People Go*, p. 8.

26. R. Houle, 'The American Mission Revivals', in B. Carton, J. Laband and J. Sithole (eds), *Zulu Identities: Being Zulu, Past and Present* (Pietermaritzburg: University of KwaZulu-Natal Press, 2008), p. 224; see also pp. 235–236 note 7.

27. V. Robinson, *The Solusi Story: Times of Peace, Times of Peril* (Washington DC: Review and Herald, 1979), p. 58.

28. Robinson, *Solusi Story*, p. 59.

29. Robinson, *Solusi Story*, p. 65.

30. Luthuli, *Let My People Go*, p. 11.

31. W. Madikizela-Mandela, 'A Person of Immense Dignity and Noble Bearing', *Umrabulo: Special Edition, A Tribute to Chief Albert Luthuli*, August 2007, p. 28.

32. J. Guy, *The View across the River: Harriette Colenso and the Zulu Struggle against Imperialism* (Cape Town: David Philip, 2001), p. 127.

33. S. Marks, *Reluctant Rebellion: The 1906–8 Disturbances in Natal* (Oxford: Clarendon, 1970), p. 122.

34. UKZN, Killie Campbell Africana Library (KCAL), Book and Manuscript Collections, Martin Luthuli before the South African Native Affairs Commission 1903–05, 28 May 1904, Minute of Evidence, Vol. III, p. 868.

35. Marks, *Ambiguities of Dependence*, p. 49.

36. V. Khumalo, '"A Great Invitation": Publics, Assemblies and Opinion Formation in Natal, 1900–1910', University of KwaZulu-Natal, May 2010, p. 10.

37. UKZN, KCAL, Book and Manuscript Collections, Martin Luthuli before the South African Native Affairs Commission 1903-05, 28 May 1904, Minutes of Evidence, Vol. III, p. 860.

38. In an interview with Nokukhanya Luthuli, Tim Couzens and Annica van Gylswyk expressed an interest in knowing more about Ngazana. Nokukhanya confirmed that Ngazana was of the same line as Luthuli and that he lived in Groutville, yet she did not say whether he was one of Luthuli's father's brothers. University of South Africa (UNISA), Library, Archives, Documentation Centre for African Studies (DCAS), Albert Luthuli Files (ACC 135), taped interview with Nokukhanya Luthuli, 5 June 1978.

39. T.D. Mweli Skota, *The African Yearly Register: Being an Illustrated National Biographical Dictionary (Who's Who) of Black Folks in Africa* (Johannesburg: R.L. Esson and Company, n.d.).

40. J.W. Hofmeyr and G. Pillay (eds), *A History of Christianity in South Africa*, Vol. 1 (Pretoria: HAUM Tertiary, 1994), p. 185.

41. W. Marable, 'African Nationalist: The Life of John Langalibalele Dube' (Michigan: UMI Dissertation Services, 1976), p. 94.

42. P. Isaka ka Seme, 'The Regeneration of Africa', *Journal of Royal African Society*, Vol. 5, 1905-1906, pp. 404-408.

43. T. Couzens, 'Discovering Seme', p. 8. Found at: <http://www.anc.org.za/ancdocs /history/people/seme.html, pp. 1-27> accessed 1 April 2006.

44. Luthuli, *Let My People Go*, p. 16.

45. Luthuli, *Let My People Go*, p. 28.

46. Owing to the illness of a missionary who headed the school, the school was closed between 1856 and 1865.

47. UKZN, KCAL, Book and Manuscript Collections, *Iso Lomuzi: Amanzimtoti's Students' Magazine*, Vol. 1, No. 1, September 1931, inside cover. This publication was in print from September 1931 to November 1956.

48. Luthuli, *Let My People Go*, p. 24.

49. Unsourced document, p. 67.

50. University of Cape Town (UCT), Manuscripts and Archives Department (MAD), Luthuli Papers, BCZA 89/46-47, (CAMP) 2914, microfilm reel No. 1, Albert Luthuli to Mary-Louise Hooper, 8 June 1956.

51. Luthuli, *Let My People Go*, p. 25.

52. Luthuli, *Let My People Go*, p. 27.

53. Luthuli, *Let My People Go*, p. 27.

54. Luthuli, *Let My People Go*, pp. 27-28.

55. Luthuli, *Let My People Go*, p. xxvi.

56. Briggs and Wing, *The Harvest and the Hope*, p. 282.

57. UKZN, KCAL, Book and Manuscript Collections, Inanda Seminary Papers, KCM 52609, John Reuling to Albert Luthuli, 6 January 1962.

58. Reuling's personal papers document with photos his relationship with Luthuli at Adams College as early as 1932-1933, Luthuli's visit to the United States in

1948 (West Newton, Massachusetts) and even his attendance at Luthuli's Nobel Peace Prize acceptance events in 1961.

59. Maphitha can also be spelt 'Maphita'. Dhlokolo can also be spelt 'Ndlokolo'.
60. Reddy, *Luthuli*, p. 38.

Chapter 2: The Christian Mode

1. A. Luthuli, 'Natal Native Teachers' Union', *Natal Teachers' Journal*, Vol. 12, No. 2, January 1933, pp. 96-97.
2. Luthuli, *Let My People Go*, p. 20.
3. An American Board missioner adopted Champion's father; hence the surname, Champion. Mhlongo was Champion's father's original surname.
4. UNISA, Library, Archives, DCAS, Collection: A.W.G. Champion, Accession No. 1, File no, 3.1.1.15, Albert Luthuli to the ICU *yase* Natal, 30 September 1930.
5. Luthuli, 'Natal Native Teachers' Union', January 1933, p. 98.
6. Luthuli, *Let My People Go*, p. 23.
7. S. Marks, 'Patriotism, Patriarchy and Purity: Natal and the Politics of Zulu Ethnic Consciousness', in L. Vail (ed.), *The Creation of Tribalism in Southern Africa* (Berkeley: University of California Press, 1989), p. 217.
8. LM, Dr Mordecai Gumede, 'Memorial Service to Pay Tribute to the Late Chief Albert Luthuli', Groutville, 29 August 1982.
9. Couper, 'Luthuli's Conceptualisation of Civilisation', *African Studies*, Vol. 70, No. 1, March/April 2011, page numbers unknown at time of publication.
10. Marks, *Ambiguities of Dependence*, p. 71.
11. Confusingly, in *Let My People Go*, Luthuli indicated that he ran against three other candidates (p. 42).
12. LM, Albert Luthuli to the Native Commission in Stanger, 24 June 1940.
13. Luthuli, *Let My People Go*, p. 43.
14. Luthuli, *Let My People Go*, p. 42.
15. Luthuli, *Let My People Go*, p. 44.
16. Luthuli, *Let My People Go*, p. 44.
17. Luthuli, *Let My People Go*, p. 48-49.
18. Luthuli, *Let My People Go*, pp. 55, 58.
19. University of the Witwatersrand (UW), William Cullen Library (WCL), South African Institute of Race Relations (SAIRR), AD843B (Part I), 100.4, Unknown to Albert Luthuli, 8 April 1941.
20. A glebe was a church property bequeathed to various missions by the British colonial government.
21. Luthuli, *Let My People Go*, p. 70.
22. International Missionary Council, *The World Mission of the Church: Findings and Recommendations of the International Missionary Council, Tambaram, Madras, India, 12-29 December 1938* (London: International Missionary Council, 1939), p. 7.
23. A. Boesak, *Black and Reformed: Apartheid, Liberation and the Calvinist Tradition* (Johannesburg: Skotaville, 1984), p. 135.
24. Luthuli, *Let My People Go*, p. 69.

25. UKZN, KCAL, Book and Manuscript Collections, KCP 5319, 276, LUT 8832, A. Luthuli, 'Evangelism for Educated Bantu Youth', *South African Outlook*, (October 1940), reprinted by Lovedale Press, p. 2.
26. Luthuli, 'Evangelism for Educated Bantu Youth', pp. 1-3.
27. In his autobiography, Luthuli records that his formal inclusion in the ranks of the ANC did not happen until 1945 or 1946 (*Let My People Go*, p. 90).
28. Luthuli, *Let My People Go*, p. 94.
29. Mzala (J. Nxumalo), *Gatsha Buthelezi: Chief with a Double Agenda* (London: Zed, 1988), p. 81. Mzala itemised other arguments criticising Buthelezi's participation as leader of the KwaZulu homeland and his use of Luthuli and Matthews's service on the NRC to validate it (pp. 45-47). See also LM, Buthelezi, Mangosuthu, 'A Tribute by Prince Mangosuthu Buthelezi' at the funeral of Dr Eliachim Thabani Zibusisoziyeza Mthiyane, 'ETZ', Noodsburg Congregational Church, UCCSA, 10 January 2007.
30. Luthuli, *Let My People Go*, p. 97. See also S. Couper, 'Chief Albert Luthuli and the Bantustan Question', *Journal of Natal and Zulu History*, Vols. 24 and 25, 2006-2007, pp. 240-268.
31. Luthuli, *Let My People Go*, p. 74.
32. American Congregational Association Archives (ACAA), Albert Luthuli to Frank Loper, 29 June 1948, reprinted in *Missionary Herald*, December 1948, pp. 32-33.
33. LM, Charlotte Owen and Peter Corbett Papers (COPCP), Wilson Minton to Albert Luthuli, 27 October 1960.
34. LM, COPCP; ABM Archives, A. Luthuli, 'A New Africa: An Address Given to the Junior Chamber of Commerce', Columbus, Ohio, 8 October 1948.
35. LM, A. Luthuli, '[Mahatma Gandhi] Memorial on the Occasion of the Centenary Celebrations of [Howard University]', original handwritten draft, pp. 3-4.
36. J. Wassermann, *A Man for All Seasons: Mohandas Gandhi* (Pretoria: Voortrekker Museum, Series No. 2, n.d.), p. 22.
37. Wassermann, *A Man for All Seasons*, p. 22.
38. UW, WCL, Champion, A922, A8, 'History in the Making', unpublished manuscript dated 23 November 1952. George Champion was perhaps the only person to paint an unfavourable portrayal of Luthuli, describing him as highly malleable and inexperienced, and as a 'politician in the Indian pocket'. His contempt for Luthuli reflected his own vindictive nature and his embarrassment over Luthuli's dramatic electoral win for the presidency of the ANC's Natal branch in November 1951. Champion also resented the ANC Youth League's radical support of the 1949 resolution defying the Unjust Laws of the Union, and their subsequent ousting of Dr A.B. Xuma in favour of Dr J.S. Moroka.
39. P. Rich, 'Albert Luthuli', in H. Bredekamp and R. Ross (eds), *Missions and Christianity* (Johannesburg: Wits University Press, 1995), p. 200 note 57.
40. Bailey's African Photo Archives (BAPA), A. Luthuli, 'Declaration of Independence', *Golden City Post*, 16 July 1961.
41. BAPA, A. Luthuli, 'It's Up to White South Africa', *Golden City Post*, 30 April 1961.

42. Luthuli, *Let My People Go*, p. 99.

43. South African Democracy Education Trust (SADET), *The Road to Democracy in South Africa (1960-1970)*, Vol. 1 (Cape Town: Zebra, 2004), p. 30.

44. UNISA, Library, Archives, DCAS, Allison Wessels George Champion (AWGC), No. 1, 19.7.2.1, Luthuli Memorial Foundation Correspondence, W. Kamakobosi Dimibar to the Secretary of the Groutville Committee, Phinehas Mbambo, 14 June 1951.

45. Luthuli, *Let My People Go*, 1962 edition, introduction, p. 11.

46. M. Benson, *The Struggle for a Birthright* (Middlesex: Penguin Books, 1966), p. 144.

47. Luthuli, *Let My People Go*, p. 118.

48. This statement appeared in the draft and final versions of A. Luthuli, 'The Road to Freedom is Via the Cross', *South African Studies*, Vol. 3 (London: Publicity and Information Bureau of the African National Congress, n.d.), and in *Let My People Go*, pp. 232-236. See also Appendix 2.

49. UCCSA Head Office Archives, Interview, Mangosuthu Buthelezi, in audio-visual documentary, *Mayibuye Afrika: Chief Albert John Lutuli, His Story*, Charlotte Owen and Peter Corbett (Anglo American Corporation of South Africa, Shell and Durban Arts Association, 1993).

50. UCCSA Head Office Archives, Interview, Horace Rall, in audio-visual documentary, *Mayibuye Afrika*, 1993. Rall's claim may have legitimacy. One of Lavinia Scott's regular reports to Reuling stated: 'We have heard that there had been some criticism of Chief Luthuli at Groutville – perhaps for being away too much, or perhaps just for not favouring certain people. I do not know. But we have heard recently that the people there say they do not want any other chief and that if they can't have him they will get along with none.' UKZN, KCAL, Book and Manuscript Collections, Lavinia Scott to John Reuling, December 1952, p. 3.

51. UCT, MAD, A. Luthuli, handwritten sermon, 'Christian Life: A Constant Venture', 9 November 1952. See also Appendix 1.

52. Luthuli, *Let My People Go*, p. 233.

53. Luthuli, *Let My People Go*, pp. 130-131.

54. Luthuli, *Let My People Go*, p. 131.

55. UKZN, KCAL, Book and Manuscript Collections, KCM 52609, John Reuling to Albert Luthuli, 6 January 1962; quoted in Rich, 'Albert Luthuli', p. 201.

56. Luthuli, *Let My People Go*, pp. 131-132.

57. P. Rich, 'Albert Luthuli and the American Board Mission in South Africa', presented at the Conference on People, Power and Culture: The History of Christianity in South Africa, 1792-1992 at the University of Western Cape (UWC) Great Hall and Genadendal Mission Museum, from 12-15 August 1992, by the UWC Institute for Historical Research. Found at the St Joseph's Theological Institute, Hilton, KwaZulu-Natal.

58. Luthuli, *Let My People Go*, p. 131.

59. UKZN, APC&SA, AP 370.968 GRA, G. Grant, 'The Liquidation of Adams College', p. 6.

60. Grant, 'The Liquidation of Adams College', p. 43.
61. UCCSA Head Office Archives, United Church Board for World Ministries (UCBWM) Field Secretary Correspondence, A. Myrick, 'Report of the Acting Field Secretary, South African Mission, for the Year 1966, to the UCBWM', 25 January 1967, p. 1.
62. UCCSA Head Office Archives, UCBWM, Field Secretary Correspondence, A. Myrick, 'Report of the Acting Field Secretary, South African Mission, for the Year 1967 to the UCBWM', 30 January 1968.
63. UNISA, Library, Archives, DCAS, South African Indian Congress (SAIC), 105, 7.1.8, A. Luthuli, 'Let Us March Together in Freedom', opening address at the Sixth Annual Provincial Conference, Durban, 21-22 February 1953, p. 5.
64. A. Luthuli, 'Presidential Address' at the ANC Annual Conference of 18-20 December 1953, quoted in T. Karis and G. Carter (eds), *From Protest to Challenge: A Documentary History of African Politics in South Africa 1882-1964*, Vol. 3 'Challenge and Violence, 1953-1964' (Stanford: Hoover Institution, 1977), pp. 115-116.
65. The CJE comprised the ANC, the SAIC, the Congress of Democrats and the South African Coloured People's Organisation (SACPO).
66. A. Luthuli, 'Let Us Speak Together of Freedom', speech presented at the Natal Congress of the People's Congress, 5 September 1954, reprinted in *Fighting Talk*, Vol. 10, No. 10, October 1954, pp. 4-5.
67. G. Pillay (ed.), *Voices of Liberation, Albert Luthuli*, Vol. 1 (Pretoria: Human Sciences Research Council, 1993), p. 80.
68. 'Luthuli "Addresses" Congress Conference in Durban', *Ilanga lase Natal*, 25 December 1954.
69. Karis and Carter (eds), *From Protest to Challenge*, Vol. 3, p. 138.
70. LM, Albertinah Luthuli, Interview with the author, 6 January 2006.
71. ANC, Luthuli House, Johannesburg, Archives Division, 'Foreign Service Dispatch No. 304 from the Pretoria Embassy (Washington DC) to the United States State Department', 2 June 1955.
72. In the days before the Congress of the People (22 June), only the ANC's Working Committee saw the draft (including Walter Sisulu, Nelson Mandela and Joe Matthews). On the day of the congress (25 June), only the ANC's National Executive (including Wilson Conco) reviewed the draft.
73. Luthuli, *Let My People Go*, pp. 151, 153.
74. Some of the correspondence between Luthuli and his intimate circle of lieutenants, relating to the more controversial clauses and suggested amendments to the charter before it was passed at the Kliptown Congress, are among papers which, according to members of the family, were removed without permission to the United States where they remain in the possession of an unknown party.
75. M. Motlhabi, *The Theory and Practice of Black Resistance to Apartheid: A Social-Ethical Analysis* (Johannesburg: Skotaville, 1984), p. 81.
76. Karis and Carter (eds), *From Protest to Challenge*, Vol. 3, p. 66.
77. Luthuli, *Let My People Go*, p. 154.

78. Document 13a: Albert Luthuli, 'Special Presidential Address', ANC Annual Conference of 17-18 December 1955, in Karis and Carter (eds), *From Protest to Challenge*, Vol. 3, p. 213.

79. 'Statement taken from Chief Albert Luthuli' for the defence in the Treason Trial. Cited in Karis and Carter (eds), *From Protest to Challenge*, Vol. 3, p. 71; see also p. 95 note 225.

80. Luthuli, *Let My People Go*, p. 160; N. Mandela, *Long Walk to Freedom: The Autobiography of Nelson Mandela* (London: Abacus, 1995), p. 234.

81. Luthuli, *Let My People Go*, p. 165.

82. Founded in 1914, the Fellowship of Reconciliation is an international, interfaith and interdenominational organisation that seeks to replace violence, war, racism and economic injustice with non-violence, peace and justice.

83. UWC, Robben Island Mayibuye Archive (RIMA), MCH 07, 8.4.5, Interview, Ben Turok, October 1974, p. 3.

84. UCT, MAD, Thornton Collection (BC 930), ANC (A5); also under the title: 'Freedom is the Apex: Chief A. Luthuli Speaks to White South Africans'.

85. Pillay (ed.), *Voices of Liberation*, Vol. 1, p. 126. Also found in Karis and Carter (eds), *From Protest to Challenge*, Vol. 3, pp. 456-463.

86. 'She Did Cartwheel When Hit - Witness', *Rand Daily Mail*, 28 October 1958.

87. 'Riot at ANC Meeting - Roughs Kick Women, Assault Luthuli', *Cape Times*, 22 August 1958.

88. 'Riot at ANC Meeting', *Cape Times*, 22 August 1958.

89. UCCSA Head Office Archives, Charlotte Owens and Peter Corbett, Interviews for *Mayibuye Afrika*.

90. UCT, MAD, Luthuli Papers, BC 930, A5, Albert Luthuli, Presidential Address to the Forty-Sixth Annual Conference of the ANC, 13-14 December 1958, 2 (also 1, 4 and 9).

91. Luthuli, *Let My People Go*, p. 129.

92. *Summary Report of the Commission for the Socio-Economic Development of the Bantu Areas within the Union of South Africa*, UG 61-1955 (Tomlinson Commission). Cited in William Beinart, *Twentieth-Century South Africa*, revised edition (Oxford: Oxford University Press, 2001), p. 161.

93. LM, A. Luthuli, 'An Examination and Appraisal of the Political Import of the African Woman's Demonstration in Natal', a report for the Natal People's Conference on 6 September 1959 in Durban (Bantu Social Centre), drafted 31 August 1959, pp. 4-5.

94. BAPA, A. Luthuli, 'Answer These Posers, Bantustan Supporters', *Golden City Post*, 20 September 1959.

95. BAPA, A. Luthuli, 'Bantustans Plan is Not for Us!', *Golden City Post*, 4 October 1959, p. 6.

96. Rich, 'Albert Luthuli', p. 202. Rich cited American Board Mission A/2/13, Albert Luthuli to Lavinia Scott, 6 July 1953.

97. Karis and Carter (eds), *From Protest to Challenge*, Vol. 3, p. 292; see also p. 367 note 69. Karis and Carter cited 'Report of the National Anti-Pass Council',

signed by Duma Nokwe, secretary general of the ANC, submitted to the Mass National Conference of 30 May 1959.

98. 'Ex-Chief Luthuli's Influence on White Opinion', *Forum*, July 1959, p. 12.

99. Luthuli, *Let My People Go*, p. 209.

100. 'Luthuli Ban Criticised by Church', publication unknown, 8 June 1959.

101. UW, WCL, ANC, AD2186, Ga84, A. Luthuli, 'Freedom Costs Dearly', handwritten draft, 28 May 1959 at the Groutville Mission, Natal. See also Luthuli, *Let My People Go*, p. 213.

102. Luthuli, *Let My People Go*, p. 218. See also 'African's Call for Non-Violence', *Times*, 26 August 1959, p. 7, and a joint press release from Luthuli (ANC) and Peter Brown (Liberal Party) to the *Rand Daily Mail*, signed 20 February 1960 and released 1 March 1960, UKZN, APC&SA, PC2/4/11/3. Found also at LM.

103. 'Luthuli Denies ANC Part in Disturbances', *Star*, 25 August 1959.

104. 'Banished Chief Still in Touch with ANC', *Rand Daily Mail*, 17 December 1959. Luthuli, *Let My People Go*, p. 215.

105. A. Luthuli, 'The Presidential Address', 47th Annual ANC Conference, Durban, 12-13 December 1959, in Karis and Carter (eds), *From Protest to Challenge*, Vol. 3, p. 296; see also p. 368 note 81.

Chapter 3: Storm on the Horizon

1. BAPA, A. Luthuli, 'A Message to White SA', *Golden City Post*, 20 March 1960. Excerpts from the article were republished the next morning in: 'Leader's Pledge to Whites: "Nothing to Fear"', *Times*, 21 March 1960, p. 9, and 'Whites Need Not Fear Africans – Luthuli', *Natal Mercury*, 19 March 1960.

2. Benjamin Pogrund, *How Can Man Die Better: The Life of Robert Sobukwe* (Johannesburg: Jonathan Ball, 1997), p. 141. It is unlikely that Sobukwe would chastise and ridicule Luthuli in this manner. I suspect that it was drafted by an underling.

3. Luthuli, *Let My People Go*, p. 222.

4. BAPA, A. Luthuli 'A Message for Black SA', *Golden City Post*, 27 March 1960.

5. UCCSA Head Office Archives, Audio-visual documentary, *Mayibuye Afrika*.

6. Luthuli, *Let My People Go*, p. 223.

7. Luthuli, *Let My People Go*, p. 224.

8. Mandela, *Long Walk to Freedom*, pp. 283, 284.

9. SADET, *The Road to Democracy*, 1, p. 72.

10. UWC, RIMA, MCH 07, 8.4.5, Interview, Ben Turok, October 1974, pp. 9-10.

11. E. Sisulu, *Walter and Albertina Sisulu: In Our Lifetime* (Cape Town: David Philip, 2002), p. 141.

12. W. Sisulu, Interview, cited in SADET, *The Road to Democracy*, Vol. 1, pp. 70-71.

13. Quoted in M. Benson, *The African Patriots: The Story of the African National Congress of South Africa* (London: Faber and Faber, 1963), p. 283.

14. Pillay (ed.), *Voices of Liberation*, Vol. 1, p. 157, quoting excerpts from Luthuli's evidence at the Treason Trial (August 1958–March 1961).

15. Luthuli may be contradicting himself here as earlier he stated, 'there may be differences of point of view [regarding violent struggle] among different members'.

16. Pillay (ed.), *Voices of Liberation*, Vol. 1, pp. 152, 163. Pillay identified 'the records of the Treason Trial' as his source for these excerpts. Indeed, that for which Luthuli expressed fear in his Treason Trial testimony would happen: leaders would be 'tempted to deviate' shortly thereafter or unbeknownst him, were already 'tempted to deviate'.

17. Mandela, *Long Walk to Freedom*, p. 277.

18. UCT, MAD, Jo Macrobert Papers, BC 1165, C2, J. Harris, 'The Black Sash: Discussion Paper', n.d., p. 2.

19. The ANC elected secretaries (for example, M.B. Yengwa and Selborne Maponya) to administer Luthuli's affairs in the congress. Mary-Louise Hooper, Jean Hill and Mary Benson are also identified as Luthuli's personal secretaries. Oddly, Yengwa rarely, and Maponya almost never, appear in documentary archives. Ebrahim Mahomed and Goolam Suleman served as his personal accountant and secretary, respectively.

20. Luthuli, *Let My People Go*, p. 227.

21. Luthuli, *Let My People Go*, p. 246.

22. J. Matthews, Interview, cited in SADET, *The Road to Democracy*, Vol. 1, p. 90.

23. L. Callinicos, *Oliver Tambo: Beyond the Engeli Mountains* (Cape Town: David Philip, 2004), p. 281.

24. The ANC in the later 1960s grudgingly accepted the South African exceptionalist doctrine: 'South Africa's social and economic structure and the relationships which it generates are perhaps unique . . . What makes the structure unique and adds to its complexity is that the exploiting nation is not, as in the classical imperialist relationships, situated in a geographically distinct mother country, but is settled within the borders.' ANC, *Forward to Freedom: Documents on the National Policies of the African National Congress of South Africa* (Morogoro: ANC, n.d.).

25. UCT, MAD, Luthuli Papers, BCZA 78/46–47, Albert Luthuli to Mary-Louise Hooper, 2 July 1956, pp. 2–3.

26. Mandela, *Long Walk to Freedom*, p. 301.

27. Charles Hooper, an Anglican priest, served a parish near Zeerust and wrote the very moving book *Brief Authority* (New York: Simon and Schuster, 1960) about the apartheid regime's oppression of indigenous people. He wrote the book in the same spirit as Trevor Huddleston's *Naught for Your Comfort* (Johannesburg: Hardingham and Donaldson, 1956), which followed the forced removals from Sophiatown.

28. Luthuli, *Let My People Go*, 1962 edition, introduction, p. 8.

29. Gunnar Helander, Interview, Västerås, 12 February 1996, in Tor Sellström (ed.), *Liberation in Southern Africa – Regional and Swedish Voices: Interviews from Angola, Mozambique, Namibia, South Africa, Zimbabwe, the Frontline and Sweden*, second edition (Uppsala: Nordiska Afrikainstitutet, 2002), p. 286.

30. From 1949 until 1959, Helander published on average one anti-apartheid novel per year, the first being *Zulu Möter Vit Man* (Stockholm: Sv. Kryrkans Diakonnistyrelses Bokförlag, 1949).
31. UW, WCL, SAIRR, AD 2182, Section F, item 8, Luthuli to Quinton Whyte, 13 December 1960; also, UKZN, APC&SA, PC2/3/7/1, A. Luthuli to Peter Brown, 13 December 1960. Also found at LM, *Rand Daily Mail*, 'Luthuli Says: "End Ban on ANC and PAC" ', by Benjamin Pogrund, 9 December 1960.
32. Callinicos, *Oliver Tambo*, p. 283.
33. E. Reinertsen, 'Umkhonto we Sizwe 1961–1964: The Break with a Long Lasting Tradition of Non-Violent Opposition in South Africa' (Honours dissertation, University of Natal, 1985), p. 23.

Chapter 4: The Tempo Quickens

1. Karis and Carter (eds), *From Protest to Challenge*, Vol. 3, pp. 357–358.
2. A. Sampson, *Mandela: The Authorised Biography* (Johannesburg: Jonathan Ball, 1999), p. 142. See also Tom Lodge, *Mandela: A Critical Life* (Oxford: Oxford University Press, 2006), p. 84; see also p. 237 note 8. Lodge cited *Contact* (Cape Town), 6 April 1961.
3. Lodge, *Mandela*, p. 84; see also p. 237 note 10. Lodge cited Jordan Ngubane, *An African Explains Apartheid* (New York: Frederick Praeger, 1963), p. 172.
4. 'Treason Trial Verdict – "Law Upheld" ', publication unknown, 30 March 1961.
5. H. Joseph, *If This Be Treason* (London: André Deutsch, 1963), pp. 8–9.
6. This is not to say that Mandela was entirely sympathetic to these sentiments and was anti-white.
7. 'Why the South Africa United Front Failed: Disruptive Role of the Pan Africanist Congress', *New Age*, 29 March 1962.
8. *New Age*, 29 March 1962.
9. Luthuli indicated that he would like to include in the United Front: Ex-Chief Justices, Albert van der Sandt Centlivres, Henry Fagan, Sir David Pieter de Villiers Graaff, Dr Jan Steytler, Alan Paton of the Liberal Party, the Reverend Z.R. Mahabane of the Interdenominational African Ministers' Federation (IDAMF), Dr G.M. Naicker, president of the SAIC, P.R. Pather, president of the South African Indian Organisation (SAIO), Paramount Chief of the Abatembu, Sabata Dalindyebo (whom Luthuli had criticised in September 1959), Dr R.E. van der Ross of the Coloured Convention Movement, Archbishop Denis Hurley, Archbishop Joost de Blank, Mr Basson, Leon Levy, president of the South African Congress of Trade Unions (SACTU), L.C. Scheepers, president of the Trade Union Congress (TUC), Canon Alpheus Zulu, and J.N. Singh, banned vice president of the SAIC. *New Age*, 'Form United Front Now', May 1962.
10. N. Mandela, 'The Struggle for a National Convention', March 1961. Excerpt from an unidentified article, in S. Johns and R. Hunt Davis, Junior, (eds), *Mandela, Tambo and the African National Congress: The Struggle against Apartheid, 1948–1990, A Documentary Survey* (Oxford: Oxford University Press, 1991), pp. 96, 100.

11. 'Speech of a Nobel Prize-Winner: The Gell Memorial Address by A.J. Luthuli', *Forum*, November 1961, p. 7.

12. Govan Mbeki, Interview, in SADET, *The Road to Democracy*, Vol. 1, pp. 79-80.

13. 'The General Strike: Statement by Nelson Mandela on Behalf of the National Action Council Following the Stay-At-Home in May 1961', 3 June 1961. Found at: <http://www.anc.org.za/ancdocs/history/mandela/pr610603.html#1> accessed 30 April 2010.

14. Karis and Carter (eds), *From Protest to Challenge*, Vol. 3, p. 363.

15. BAPA, N. Mandela, 'Out of the Strike', *Golden City Post*, 3 June 1961. Cited in *Africa South-in-Exile*, October–December 1961.

16. M. Benson, *Nelson Mandela: The Man and the Movement* (London: W.W. Norton and Company, 1994), p. 86.

17. *New Age*, 8 June 1961. Cited in Karis and Carter (eds), *From Protest to Challenge*, Vol. 3, p. 364; see also p. 378 note 226.

18. Mandela, 'Out of the Strike', *Africa South-in-Exile*, October–December 1961. Found in Johns and Davis (eds), *Mandela, Tambo and the African National Congress*, p. 104.

19. Mandela, *Long Walk to Freedom*, pp. 319–320.

20. M. Benson, *Chief Albert Lutuli of South Africa* (London: Oxford University Press, 1963), p. 65. Benson is an informed source as she served as Luthuli's secretary for much of time between the announcement and reception of the Nobel Peace Prize. In fact, Benson's uncited quotations of Luthuli likely derived from her time as his personal secretary.

21. Reinertsen, 'Umkhonto we Sizwe', p. 13.

22. B. Bunting, *Moses Kotane: South African Revolutionary: A Political Biography* (London: Inkululeko, 1975), p. 268.

23. J. Slovo, *Slovo: An Unfinished Autobiography* (Johannesburg: Ravan, 1995), p. 147.

24. Benson, *Nelson Mandela*, p. 116. Yengwa's rendition of the meeting, through Benson, differs from Mandela's version presented in his autobiography in timing and content. First, chapter six conveys that Benson chronologically placed this meeting and conversation after Mandela's trip to North Africa (prior to his arrest in Howick) rather than immediately before he departed in January 1962. Second, Mandela's discussion with Luthuli following his tour of Africa did not focus on the issue of violence but rather the degree to which newly independent African countries identified and sympathised with the ANC's co-operation with non-blacks.

25. LM, Masabalala Yengwa Papers (MYP), 'Masabalala Bonnie Yengwa', Unpublished autobiographical manuscript, 23 January 1976, p. 106.

26. LM, Mangosuthu Buthelezi, 'The Awarding of the OAU Merit Award Posthumously to the Late Chief Albert Mvumbi Luthuli: President General of the Banned African National Congress: To be Presented on Behalf of the OAU by His Majesty King Moshoeshoe II', Maseru, 10 December 1974, p. 3. The event celebrated the tenth anniversary of the OAU's founding.

27. Buthelezi, 'The Awarding of the OAU Merit Award', p. 5.

28. Buthelezi, 'The Awarding of the OAU Merit Award', p. 9.

29. These sentiments are also expressed in Buthelezi's speeches: LM, 'Remarks Made on the Occasion of the Luthuli Memorial Foundational Meeting in Swaziland' (1976); '*Inkatha Yenkululeko Yesizwe Kgare Ya Tokoloho Ya Setjaba*: National Cultural Liberation Movement' (1982), address at Groutville, 1982; and in 'Prayer Rally for Peace and Progress in Negotiations' (1991).

30. This 'logical' assumption may be a fallacy, as Mandela also wrote the foreword to Slovo's autobiography.

31. S. Couper, 'Luthuli and the Armed Struggle: Nelson Mandela as the Historiographical Father', 14 March 2006. This paper can be found at: <http://www.history .ukzn.ac.za/?q=seminar_archive&op0=%3D&filter0=Couper> and subsequently at: <http://www.history.ukzn.ac.za/?q=node/636> accessed 25 January 2008.

32. Sisulu, *Walter and Albertina Sisulu*, p. 147.

33. Mandela, *Long Walk to Freedom*, p. 320. Also in Sampson, *Mandela*, p. 150; SADET, *The Road to Democracy*, Vol. 1, p. 88. SADET cited Mandela; Sisulu, *Walter and Albertina Sisulu*, p. 146; Meer, *A Fortunate Man*, p. 224.

34. Sisulu, *Walter and Albertina Sisulu*, p. 146.

35. Mandela, *Long Walk to Freedom*, p. 321.

36. When Lionel 'Rusty' Bernstein presented a report advocating armed force at a 1961 Communist Party conference, Turok recalled Mandela shared 'that it would be difficult to sell this to the ANC, particularly Luthuli'. UWC, RIMA. MCH 07, 8.4.5, tape No. 2, Interview, Ben Turok, 1973.

37. 'Naicker Remembers Chief Luthuli', *South African Beacon* Vol. 10, No. 2, Summer 2003, p. 20.

38. Mandela, *Long Walk to Freedom*, p. 322.

39. Mandela, *Long Walk to Freedom*, p. 322.

40. Mandela, *Long Walk to Freedom*, p. 322.

41. Meer conveyed that the NEC agreed to 'allow the formation of an organisation that would engage in violent forms of struggle'. The ANC NEC did not agree to the 'initiation' of violence or the 'launch' of an armed movement (Meer, *A Fortunate Man*, p. 224).

42. C. Ndlovu, Interview, found in SADET, *The Road to Democracy*, Vol. 1, p. 89; see also note 130.

43. Meer, *A Fortunate Man*, p. 224.

44. Mandela, *Long Walk to Freedom*, p. 323; Meer, *A Fortunate Man*, p. 224.

45. Mandela, *Long Walk to Freedom*, p. 323.

46. Mandela, *Long Walk to Freedom*, p. 324.

47. B. Feinberg and A. Odendaal (eds), *Nelson Mandela: The Struggle is my Life (His Speeches and Writings 1944-1990)*, revised edition (Cape Town: David Philip, 1994), p. 167.

48. Callinicos, *Oliver Tambo*, p. 280; see also p. 643 note 18. Callinicos cited H. Barrell, *MK: The ANC's Armed Struggle* (London: Penguin Forum Series, 1990), p. 24. Barrell quoted Joe Slovo in *Dawn*.

49. Mandela, *Long Walk to Freedom*, pp. 323-324.

50. UCT, MAD, Jack and Ray Simons Papers, BC1081/P28, no author cited, 'Chief Albert John Mvumbi Luthuli, Isitwalandwe, 1898–1967', *Sechaba*, Vol. 1, No. 8, August 1967, supplement insert.

51. UCT, MAD, BC1081/P28, no author cited, 'In Memory of Chief Albert Luthuli', *Spotlight on South Africa*, Vol. 5, No. 30, special issue, 5 August 1967, p. 3.

52. UCT, MAD, BC1081/P28.1, ANC South African Studies, *Lutuli Speaks: Statements and Addresses by Chief Albert Lutuli, President of the African National Congress of South Africa*, n.d., p. 6. (Also known as *Lutuli Speaks: Portrait of Chief Lutuli*.)

53. UCT, MAD, BC1081, 'The Road to Freedom is Via the Cross', *South African Studies* Vol. 3, n.d., p. 5.

54. ANC, Introduction to 'The Lutuli Page'. Found at: <http://www.anc.org.za/ancdocs/history/lutuli/> accessed 26 January 2008; Ethekwini Online, 'Chief Albert Luthuli' by Khaya ka Buthelezi. Found at: <http://www.ethekwini.gov.za/durban/discover-durban/ourdurban/history/famous_durbanites/politics/luthuli> accessed 14 March 2008.

55. This quote is attributed to Luthuli in the inside jacket covers of the 1961 Collins and April 1987 Fontana Paperbacks (thirteenth impression) editions of *Let My People Go*.

56. Luthuli, *Let My People Go*, p. 24

57. 'From Gandhi to Mandela', *Sechaba*, Vol. 3, No. 5, 5 May 1969, pp. 10–12. *Sechaba* cited Gandhi, 'Declaration on Question of the Use of Violence in Defence of Rights', *Guardian*, 16 December 1938.

58. A. Luthuli, 'Africa and Freedom', lecture delivered in Oslo, Norway, on 11 December 1961 upon receiving the 1960 Nobel Peace Prize, in Asmal, Chidester and James (eds), *South Africa's Nobel Laureates*, p. 22 (see Appendix 4).

59. 'Mr Luthuli's Honour', *Daily News*, 24 October 1961.

60. Jean Hill attested that the editor of *Ilanga*, Rolfes Robert Reginald Dhlomo (1901–1971), accompanied by Mahomed, shared the news with Luthuli. LM, Jean Hill, Interview with the author, 18 April 2005.

61. Jean Hill and her husband, Charles Hill, were members of the Musgrave Congregational Church in Durban. Jean, a white liberal Christian, had served on the Durban Joint Council of Europeans and Africans, a predecessor of the South African Institute of Race Relations. She was also a member of the multiracial International Club that sponsored the event at which she first met Luthuli. She also served the Women's Defence of the Constitution, the predecessor of the Black Sash. After unsuccessfully trying to set up a chapter of the Civil Rights League in Durban, Jean, Charles and others founded the Liberal Party. Much later, Jean was involved with the Defence and Aid Fund that provided legal defence and subsistence income to families of political prisoners. For this she earned the government's ire and a five-year banning order. See LM, Jean Hill, unpublished autobiographical manuscript.

62. 'Nobel Peace Prize for Luthuli: A Life for South Africa's Prestige', *Gazette*, 24 October 1961.

63. The Progressive Party broke away from the United Party in 1959. In many ways, it was similar to the Liberal Party especially as regards its qualified franchise policy.

64. 'The Man of the Hour, But His Old-World Courtesy Remains', *Daily News*, 26 October 1961.

65. E. Mphahlele, 'Albert Luthuli: The End of Non-Violence', *Africa Today* Vol. 14, August 1967, pp. 1–3.

66. R. Kally, *The Struggle: Sixty Years in Focus* (Durban: no publisher, 2004), p. 1.

67. M. Lloyd, 'Lutuli – The Impact of a Personality', *Sunday Tribune*, 29 October 1961.

68. M. Benson, 'You There, Luthuli . . .', *Observer*, 29 October 1961.

69. M. Lloyd, 'Lutuli – The Impact of a Personality', *Sunday Tribune*, 29 October 1961.

70. UKZN, APC&SA, PC2/3/4/2, Albert Luthuli to the Chairman of the National Executive of the Liberal Party, 23 March 1962. (Also found at LM.) Their shared belief in non-violence superseded any differences they may have had over a qualified franchise.

71. From 12 January 1960 to 30 April 1961, C.R. Swart (1894–1982) was the (last) governor general of the Union of South Africa. From 31 May 1961 he was the first state president of the Republic of South Africa for six years.

72. UKZN, APC&SA, P2/9/29/1, 'Report on Protest Meeting', p. 2.

73. 'Luthuli Wants to Go to Oslo for His Nobel Prize', *Daily News*, 24 October 1961.

74. In a draft article dated 31 August 1967, Mohammed Meghraoui claimed that the ANC mandated that 'he accept it on behalf of the ANC and not in his personal capacity'. University of Fort Hare (UFH), Howard Pim Africana Library (HPAL), ANC Archives, Box 23, Folder 4, draft article by Mohammed Meghraoui, 31 August 1967. This claim is spurious. On 23 October, the Nobel committee announced Luthuli would receive the award. The ANC could not have met, decided and communicated this mandate before Luthuli made his humble remarks the following day. Luthuli's remarks emanated, first, from his self-effacing nature, second, from his and the ANC's collective culture rather than from a specific mandate and, third, as a rationale to convince the ANC not to initiate violence.

75. 'Luthuli Proud – But With a New Burden', *Cape Argus*, 24 October 1961; 'Added Burden upon People of Liberation Movement', *Star*, 24 October 1961. Mary Benson told in her biography of Luthuli's response to the question, 'When had you first begun to believe in non-violence?'; Luthuli responded, 'I wouldn't say that there was ever a time when I consciously decided and said – now look, I am here deciding for non-violence. For one thing, when I came into Congress, the campaigns it was planning were in fact on non-violent lines and one was happy to fit in with that' (Benson, *Chief Albert Lutuli*, p. 64). *Sechaba*'s August 1967 tribute to Luthuli seems to be lifted from this quote by Luthuli. The similarities are striking. If so, *Sechaba* then, and ANC party nationalists today,

conveniently excise the last sentence where Luthuli states that to use violence would be 'suicide'.

76. Bunting related that no formal resolutions were taken on the use of violence at Lobatse. Rather, the 'turn to violence' was accepted and approved in private 'talks held outside the conference hall' (*Moses Kotane*, p. 273). Yengwa stated the 'subject of sabotage was not very controversial and the conference unanimously agreed to embark on the armed struggle' (unpublished draft autobiographical manuscript, p. 108). Bunting's appraisal is likely. The NEC in a statement emanating from the ANC's first conference as a banned organisation implied, but did not state explicitly, that it considered MK and the ANC to be linked. The statement described MK as 'the military wing of our struggle'. Karis and Carter's appraisal serves as an appropriate compromise ('The People Accept the Challenge of the Nationalists', statement 'issued by the National Executive of the ANC', 6 April 1963, Karis and Carter (eds), *From Protest to Challenge*, Vol. 3, p. 650).

77. 'Insult to Nobel Prize Committee – Luthuli', *Rand Daily Mail*, 27 October 1961.

78. 'Luthuli: Not Much Time Left to Save S. Africa', *Sunday Times*, 29 October 1961.

79. B. Pogrund, 'Non-Violence is Path to Freedom – Luthuli', *Rand Daily Mail*, 14 November 1961.

80. Pogrund, 'Non-Violence is Path to Freedom – Luthuli', *Rand Daily Mail*, 14 November 1961.

81. Reported in Sampson, *Mandela*, p. 159; see also p. 599 note 103.

82. 'Afrikaans Press Told Why Luthuli Cable Was Held', *Cape Times*, 20 November 1961.

83. Benson, *Chief Albert Lutuli*, p. 65. Luthuli's statement that those who resort to violence 'could not be blamed' is echoed in his Rivonia statement. Yet, as quoted by Benson here, the withholding of blame does not imply support or affirmation of the decision to resort to violence.

84. Only once before had a Nobel Peace Prize recipient been denied the opportunity to travel and accept the award. Carl von Ossietzky (1889–1938), who controversially won the award in 1936, was unable to claim it as he was in German custody. Ossietzky won the 1935 Prize which was, similar to Luthuli's, reserved to the following year.

85. In fact, the oversight not to include Sweden in the passport application's itinerary can be considered a grievous mistake by the Nobel committee and Luthuli. Only the Nobel Peace Prize is received in Oslo. All other Nobel prizes are awarded in Stockholm, Sweden. Customarily, the Nobel laureate for Peace would join all the other laureates for a conference in Stockholm. LM, Tor Sellström, Interview with the author, 17 June 2008.

86. M. Benson, "'You There, Luthuli . . .'", *Observer*, 29 October 1961.

87. 'Lutuli Goes to Oslo – But Not Tanganyika', reported in publication unknown, 8 November 1961.

88. 'More Than 10,000 Attend Rally to Honour Lutuli', *Daily News*, 10 November 1961.

89. 'Mr Luthuli in London Today: Delayed Flight from S. Africa', *Times*, 6 December 1961.

90. He had approved of Tambo's 1960 departure from South Africa to represent the ANC diplomatically. In 1962, he expressed the desire that Mandela should return home from his extended African tour.

91. 'Mr Luthuli in Oslo', *Times*, 8 December 1961; 'Audience with King of Norway: Very Tired Luthuli Faces Busy Three Days', *Daily News*, 8 December 1961; 'Luthuli Suffering from Strain', *Star*, 8 December 1961.

92. In fact, Tambo sought medical advice for Luthuli during their stay in Oslo.

93. 'Mr [Gunnar] Jahn delivered this speech on 10 December 1961, in the auditorium of the University of Oslo. At its conclusion he presented the Peace Prize for 1960 (reserved that year) to Mr Luthuli, who accepted [the Prize] in a brief speech. The English translation of Mr Jahn's speech is, with certain editorial changes and emendations made after collation with the Norwegian text, that which is carried in *Les Prix Nobel en 1960*, which also includes the original Norwegian text.' Asmal, Chidester and James (eds), *South Africa's Nobel Laureates*, pp. 20–21 and p. 274.

94. Mandela, *Long Walk to Freedom*, p. 338.

95. J. Allen, *Rabble-Rouser for Peace: The Authorised Biography of Desmond Tutu* (Johannesburg: Rider Books, 1997), p. 209. Allen reported to the author in a correspondence that the source of this information was Anne Ragnhild Breiby, a Norwegian researcher who did a Master's degree on the award of the Peace Prize to South Africans. In an interview with Allen, she was quite clear that, while in Oslo, Luthuli told at least one of his hosts about the decision to turn to violence. The one further detail of interest was that friends in Oslo at the time of the award found Luthuli very depressed – presumably because of the tensions he felt over the decision and his receipt of the prize. Note: The author does not agree with the assertion that the decision Luthuli felt bound by was to 'embark on sabotage'.

96. Informal discussions with the family suggest that Nokukhanya attempted to dissuade Luthuli from the perplexing decision to wear the regalia.

97. 'Lutuli featured in BBC TV Programme', *Daily News*, 12 December 1961.

98. BBC's current affairs programme, *Panorama*. Cited in 'Help from the World Welcomed', publication unknown, 12 December 1961.

99. LM, John Reuling to 'Family and Friends', 12 December 1961, p. 6.

100. 'Way of Violence Still Rejected', publication unknown, 12 December 1961. Quoted from Luthuli's Nobel Peace Prize speech found in Asmal, Chidester and James (eds), *South Africa's Nobel Laureates*, pp. 28–29. 'SA is "Museum-Piece of Our Time": Lutuli Surveys Africa Changes', publication unknown, 11 December 1961.

101. 'Lutuli Sings, Brings Crowd to Its Feet', *Daily News*, 12 December 1961.

102. Quoted in C. and M. Legum, *The Bitter Choice: Eight South Africans' Resistance to Tyranny* (New York: World Publishing Company, 1968), p. 62.

103. '100 Brave Cold to Greet Luthuli', *Rand Daily Mail*, 12 December 1961.

104. UWC, RIMA, Congress of Democrats (MCH 229), 'Congress Bulletin' issued by the National Consultative Committee of the SA Indian Congress, SA Coloured People's Congress, SA Congress of Democrats and the SA Congress of Trade Unions, November 1961, p. 6.

105. G. Houser and H. Shore, *I Will Go Singing: Walter Sisulu Speaks of his Life and Struggle for Freedom in South Africa in Conversation with George Houser and Herbert Shore* (Cape Town: Robben Island Museum, 2001).

106. P. Rule, M. Aitken and J. van Dyk, *Nokukhanya: Mother of Light* (Braamfontein: The Grail, 1993), p. 136.

107. Rule, Aitken and Van Dyk, *Nokukhanya*, p. 133.

108. Quoted in Feinberg and Odendaal (eds), *Nelson Mandela*, p. 123.

109. Due to an 'operational' anomaly, the first act of sabotage was committed in Durban early on 15 December 1961. It is recognised that violence takes many forms. A distinction is made between violent acts against people and violent acts against symbolic symbols of the apartheid regime, such as government infrastructure (sabotage). Yet, as was and is often the case, sabotage quickly leads to the loss of life despite the best intentions.

110. UWC, RIMA, MCH 150, *Dawn: Journal of Umkhonto we Sizwe – Souvenir Issue, Twenty-Fifth Anniversary of MK* (ANC, 1986), 'The Longest Three Minutes in My Life: An Episode by Comrade Joe Slovo', MK Chief of Staff, *Dawn*, 1986, p. 7.

111. Slovo, *Slovo*, p. 155.

112. 'December Sixteen '61 in Durban by Eric Mtshali', *Dawn*, 1986, p. 13.

113. 'Though We Had No AK47s Nor Revolvers by Ebrahim Ismail', *Dawn*, 1986, pp. 14-15.

114. 'How MK Grew by Bobby Pillay', *Dawn*, 1986, p. 20.

115. Bunting, *Moses Kotane*, p. 268.

116. Bunting, *Moses Kotane*, p. 269.

117. UWC, RIMA, MCH 07, 8.4.5, tape 2, Interview with Ben Turok, August–October 1973, 7-8.

118. Slovo, *Slovo*, p. 146.

119. 'The Sabotage Campaign by Joe Slovo', *Dawn*, 1986, p. 25.

120. 'MK is Born by Steve Tshwete', *Dawn*, 1986, p. 26.

121. 'The Sabotage Campaign by Joe Slovo', *Dawn*, 1986, p. 24.

122. 'The Least Dramatic Contribution by Albie Sachs' and 'Dynamite Thieves by Ronnie Kasrils', *Dawn*, 1986, pp. 16 and 17, respectively.

123. R.M.T. Ngqungwana, 'Vuyisile Mini', *Dawn*, 1986, p. 19.

124. S. Couper, '"An Embarrassment to the Congresses?": The Silencing of Chief Albert Luthuli and the Production of ANC History', *Journal of Southern African Studies*, Vol. 35, No. 2, June 2009, pp. 331-348.

125. Reinertsen, 'Umkhonto we Sizwe', p. 2.

126. B. Mtolo, *Umkhonto we Sizwe: The Road to the Left* (Durban: Drakensberg, 1966), p. 23.

127. Mtolo, *Umkhonto we Sizwe*, p. 191.

128. Mtolo, *Umkhonto we Sizwe*, pp. 23, 24, 25 and 26 respectively.

129. Mtolo, *Umkhonto we Sizwe*, p. 26.

130. Mandela, *Long Walk to Freedom*, pp. 342-343.
131. N. Mandela, in Feinberg and Odendaal (eds), *Nelson Mandela*, pp. 122-123.
132. Cited in Lodge, *Mandela*, p. 91.
133. Cited in Feinberg and Odendaal (eds), *Nelson Mandela*, p. 122.
134. UFH, HPAL, Meghraoui, draft article, unpublished, p. 3.
135. In fact, Luthuli tried to extend his stay so that he could travel to Sweden. The South African government refused the request, forcing Luthuli to return on the designated day.
136. UFH, HPAL, Meghraoui, draft article, unpublished, p. 4.
137. Benson, *Nelson Mandela*, p. 116.
138. 'Umkhonto we Sizwe Manifesto, 1961', in Feinberg and Odendaal (eds), *Nelson Mandela*, p. 122.
139. Mandela, *Long Walk to Freedom*, p. 320.

Chapter 5: Brave Just Men

1. Lodge, *Mandela*, p. 96 and 239; see also notes 53 and 54. Lodge cited 'Mandela Diary, entry for 3 January-13 July 1962, Exhibit R 17, Rivonia Trial Records, Brenthurst Library, Johannesburg, entry for 8 January 1962'.
2. UFH, HPAL, ANC, A2561, Box 70, Folder C 39, transcripts of the Rivonia Trial 1963-1964, Mandela's statement regarding the formation of MK on the opening of the defence case in the Pretoria Supreme Court, 20 April 1964, p. 9. Feinberg and Odendaal (eds), *Nelson Mandela*, p. 170.
3. UFH, HPAL, ANC Archives, A2561, Box 70, Folder C 3.9, transcripts of the Rivonia Trial 1963-1964, p. 10; Feinberg and Odendaal (eds), *Nelson Mandela*, pp. 170-171.
4. Lodge, *Mandela*, p. 96.
5. Lodge, *Mandela*, p. 100 and Mandela, *Long Walk to Freedom*, p. 363.
6. Mandela, *Long Walk to Freedom*, p. 351.
7. Mandela, *Long Walk to Freedom*, p. 355.
8. Mandela, *Long Walk to Freedom*, p. 362.
9. Mandela, *Long Walk to Freedom*, p. 363.
10. Luthuli, *Let My People Go*, p. 227. Luthuli also said in his book, 'We mean to continue to use such [non-violent and passive resistance] methods' and 'As long as our patience can be made to hold out, we shall not jeopardise the South Africa of tomorrow by precipitating violence today' (postscript, p. 218). A.R. Delius, 'A Different Perspective: Albert Luthuli's Autobiography', *Cape Times*, 22 February 1962.
11. Lodge, *Mandela*, p. 101 and 239 note 65. Lodge cited 'Nelson Mandela, PAFMECSA, Exhibit R13, *Rivonia Trial Records*, Brenthurst Library, Johannesburg, 1962'.
12. Exodus 3:7 (NIV): 'The Lord said, "I have indeed seen the misery of my people in Egypt. I have heard them crying out because of the slave drivers, and I am concerned about their suffering".'

13. Other evidence Luthuli visualised himself to be a participant in a typological re-enactment is a sermon he preached entitled 'Christian Life: A Constant Adventure' at Adams Mission one week prior to publicising 'The Road to Freedom is Via the Cross' in reaction to his being relieved of the chieftaincy (see Appendices 1 and 2).

14. The ten plagues of blood, frogs, gnats, flies, livestock, boils, hail, locusts, darkness and firstborn males are violent in the extreme (Exodus 7–11).

15. In fact, in his youth, Moses incurred the wrath of the state by killing an Egyptian who beat a Hebrew (Exodus 2:12). This killing resulted in Moses' self-imposed exile and prolonged refugee status (Exodus 2:15).

16. Exodus 4:10: 'Moses said to the Lord, "O Lord, I have never been eloquent, neither in the past nor since you have spoken to your servant. I am slow of speech and tongue".'

17. The actual refrain was: 'Let my people go, so that they may worship me', found in Exodus 8:1, 8:20, 9:1, 9:13. In Exodus 5:1, it reads: 'Let my people go, that they may hold a feast to me in the wilderness.'

18. Luthuli, Let My People Go, p. 235. This portion of Luthuli's statement is strikingly parallel with Martin Luther King Junior's speech 'I Have a Dream'. One can only wonder to what degree, if any, did Luthuli's statement inspire King? Did both consciously see themselves in a re-enactment of Moses' life? Did both have a premonition that 'the dream' would not be achieved in their lifetimes?

19. The book of Deuteronomy concludes: 'Since then, no prophet has risen in Israel like Moses, whom the Lord knew face to face, who did all those miraculous signs and wonders the Lord sent him to do in Egypt – to Pharaoh and to all his officials and to his whole land. For no one has ever shown the mighty power or performed the awesome deeds that Moses did in the sight of the Lord' (Deuteronomy 34:10–12).

20. Pillay (ed.), Voices of Liberation, Vol. 1, p. 126. Also found in Karis and Carter (eds), From Protest to Challenge, Vol. 3, pp. 456–463.

21. Luthuli, Let My People Go, p. 230. These sentiments can also be found in Martin Luther King Junior's speeches, for example, 'I Have a Dream'.

22. Durban Local History Museum, File number 545617, Accession number 99/3697 – 3699 – 4200 – 4204, Interview, Rowley Arenstein, n.d.

23. For example, in 1959 and 1960 he represented the women facing charges arising from the beerhall riots in Cato Manor, Durban.

24. A. Luthuli, 'What I Would Do If I Were Prime Minister', Ebony, February 1962, in UCT, MAD, Lutuli Speaks, p. 74.

25. A. Luthuli, 'If I Were Prime Minister', Atlantic Monthly, March 1962, pp. 61, 64.

26. Pillay (ed.), Voices of Liberation, Vol. 1, pp. 146–149.

27. BAPA, A. Luthuli, 'Our Way Is Right – We Must Keep On', Golden City Post, 25 March 1962.

28. UWC, RIMA, MCH, 229, Report of a meeting of the Congresses' Joint Executives held in March 1962, p. 7.

29. BAPA, Albert Luthuli, 'No Change In Heart Among The Whites', *Golden City Post*, 29 April 1962.
30. T. Sellström, *Sweden and National Liberation in Southern Africa: Volume 1, Formation of a Popular Opinion 1950-1970*, second edition (Uppsala: Nordiska Afrika-institutet, 2003), p. 193.
31. Cited in Karis and Carter (eds), *From Protest to Liberation*, Vol. 3, p. 664.
32. A. Luthuli, 'Our Struggle for Progress', *New Age*, 24 June 1962.
33. A. Luthuli, 'Statement on the "Sabotage Act", June 1962'. Found at: ANC, 'The Lutuli Page, <http://www.anc.org.za/ancdocs/history/lutuli/> accessed 25 June 2008.
34. 'Lutuli Now Silenced: Vorster Declares Ban', *Natal Mercury*, 4 July 1962.
35. One source incorrectly claims that F.W. de Klerk ordered the painting to be taken down. 'Defiance, Incarceration, Torture, House Arrest, Hope', brochure for Ronald Harrison's The Black Christ Foundation, n.d. It was actually his father who ordered the painting to be taken down.
36. Ultimately, Julius Baker, a South African exile, stored the painting in the basement of his London home until the late 1990s when he returned it to South Africa.
37. R. Harrison, *The Black Christ: A Journey to Freedom* (Cape Town: David Philip, 2006), pp. 66-67.
38. LM, Roland Harrison, Interview with the author, Cape Town, 14 January 2006.
39. 'The Legacy of Inkosi Albert Luthuli', commemorative brochure, 24 August 1963, p. 15.
40. The university approved Dr T. Honeyman, former director of the Glasgow art galleries, as Luthuli's representative.
41. Other candidates included a race car driver (Stirling Moss), race horse owner (the Earl Rosebery), British Sir and Member of Parliament (Edward Heath) and the Chairman of the Scottish National Party (Dr R. McIntyre). Moss subsequently withdrew, recommending Luthuli.
42. 'Students in Brawl after Election of Luthuli as Rector', *Star*, 23 October 1962; 'Luthuli Is Honoured – Then Scots "Rag" Police', *Rand Daily Mail*, 23 October 1962.
43. 'Rector of Glasgow on Phone', *Rand Daily Mail*, 26 October 1962.
44. 'Luthuli Letters Missing – Scots Student', *Rand Daily Mail*, 2 February 1963; 'Hertzog to be Asked about Luthuli's Missing Mail', *Sunday Times*, 3 February 1963; 'Luthuli's Missing Mail', *Daily News*, 6 February 1963.
45. 'Luthuli Has Asked for Passport', *Star*, 10 July 1963; 'Government's "No" to Lutuli Installation', *Daily News*, 24 January 1964.
46. 'Luthuli Has Asked for Passport', *Star*, 10 July 1963; 'University Is Upset Over Mr Lutuli', *Daily News*, 2 August 1963.
47. 'No Ceremony without Luthuli', *London Times*, 17 October 1963, 7a.
48. BAPA, A. Luthuli, 'Why I Believe in Non-Violence', *Golden City Post*, 28 May 1961.
49. Luthuli, 'Why I Believe in Non-Violence'.

50. Asmal, Chidester and James (eds), *South Africa's Nobel Laureates*, pp. 9-10. This frequently told narrative about chickens seems to derive from Mandela, *Long Walk to Freedom*, p. 322; see also Sampson, *Mandela*, p. 151.

51. 'Letter in the SA Press', by Charles Hooper, *Sechaba*, October 1967, p. 7. Colonel Claus von Stauffenberg (1907-1944) was the conspirator who attempted to assassinate Adolf Hitler (1889-1945) on 20 July 1944. The assassination attempt failed. Only one of two bombs was armed inside the suitcase Stauffenberg left in the conference room where Hitler examined a map. A large thick conference table and a member of Hitler's staff (who was killed) by chance shielded Hitler from the bomb blast. Hitler subsequently launched a brutal and bloody purge, killing thousands of those even remotely associated with the resistance and the conspirators, Bonhoeffer and Erwin Rommel 1891-1944) included. Rommel, though not involved in the plot, knew of it and thus Hitler gave him the option of suicide by poison or having his entire family killed before his execution. Stauffenberg was shot with other conspirators. Eight others were executed by being hung on meat hooks. Their agonising deaths were filmed and watched by Hitler.

52. Luthuli, 'Why I Believe in Non-Violence'.

53. 'Luthuli Proud - But with a New Burden', *Cape Argus*, 24 October 1961.

54. Pillay (ed.), *Voices of Liberation*, Vol. 1, p. 152.

55. Pillay (ed.), *Voices of Liberation*, Vol. 1, p. 150.

56. LM, Martin Luther King Junior to Albert Luthuli, 8 December 1959.

57. NobelPrizes.com, Martin Luther King Junior, 'Martin Luther King's Nobel Prize Acceptance Speech', 10 December 1964, Oslo, Norway. Found at: <http://www.nobelprizes.com/nobel/peace/MLK-nobel.html> accessed 18 August 2008.

58. UKZN, Gandhi-Luthuli Documentation Centre, Dr Martin Luther King Junior, or 'King' pages. Found at: http://scnc.ukzn.ac.za/doc/TEXTS/dc/dcking.htm, accessed 18 August 2008.

59. Martin Luther King Junior, *The Autobiography of Martin Luther King Junior*, Chapter three, 'Crozer Seminary'. Found at: <http://www.stanford.edu/group/King/publications/autobiography/chp_3.htm> accessed 18 August 2008. Also found in 'We Shall Overcome', author and publication unknown, pp. 205-206.

60. Amistad Research Centre (ARC), American Committee on Africa Collection (ACA), Box 100, Folder 20, Luthuli to various international leaders, September 1962.

61. ARC, ACA, Box 100, Folder 20, Luthuli to various international leaders, September 1962.

62. ANC, 'Appeal for Action against Apartheid', Luthuli and King, 10 December 1962.

63. ANC, 'Appeal for Action against Apartheid'.

64. ARC, ACA, Box unknown, Folder unknown, A. Luthuli, 'Tenth Anniversary of the American Committee on Africa', by Albert Luthuli, n.d.

65. King Encyclopedia, 'Houser, George Mills'. Found at: <http://www.stanford.edu/group/King/about_king/encyclopedia/houser_george.html> accessed 13 June 2008. King Encyclopedia, 'American Committee on Africa (ACOA)'.

66. ANC, from Albert Luthuli to the secretary general of the United Nations, U Thant, 9 March 1964. Found at: <http://www.anc.org.za/ancdocs/history/lutuli/let640309.html> accessed 25 June 2008.

67. Morocco's representative at the United Nations read out the statement to a meeting of the Security Council on the same day.

68. Karis and Carter (eds), *From Protest to Challenge*, Vol. 3, pp. 798-799; A. de Bragança and I. Wallerstein (eds), *The African Liberation Reader: The National Liberation Movements*, Vol. 2, (London: Zed, 1982), pp. 40-43; Pillay (ed.), *Voices of Liberation*, Vol. 1, pp. 151-152. The statement was taken from the text entitled *United Nations and Apartheid, 1948-1994*, pp. 282-283 and from a United Nations publication produced by the Unit on Apartheid, No. 22/69, 10 December 1969, pp. 34-35.

69. J. Zuma, 'Address by Deputy President Zuma at the Second Matthew Goniwe Annual Lecture on the Occasion of the Albert Luthuli Memorial Lecture Week', University of the Witwatersrand, Johannesburg, 2 August 2004, p. 2. Found at: <http://www.dfa.gov.za/docs/speeches/2004/zuma0803.htm> accessed 20 March 2008.

70. LM, MYP, unpublished typed manuscript, p. 108. See also Interview, Govan Mbeki; SADET, *The Road to Democracy* Vol. 1, p. 135 and p. 574.

71. Bunting, *Moses Kotane*, p. 273.

72. Gunnar Helander, Interview, Västerås, 12 February 1996, in Sellström (ed.), *Liberation in Southern Africa*, p. 286.

73. Sellström (ed.), *Liberation in Southern Africa*, p. 286. The second portion of Helander's quotation of Luthuli may derive from Benson or Kotane who attributed similar words to Luthuli.

74. The explanation may lie within the fact that one comment was made in May 1961 (when acts of violence were less prominent) and the other much later in 1964 (when other organisations had for some time conducted attacks that could be more closely associated, correctly or incorrectly, with 'terrorism'). Another explanation may simply be Luthuli's self-confessed disposition that 'affords a charitable interpretation' to people's characters until they prove irredeemably otherwise.

75. Lodge, *Mandela*, p. 110; see also p. 241 note 21. Lodge cited Joel Joffe, *The Rivonia Story* (Bellville: Mayibuye Books and the University of the Western Cape, 1995), p. 92.

76. Lodge, *Mandela*, p. 111; see also p. 241 note 22. Lodge cited Mtolo, *Umkhonto we Sizwe*, pp. 39-40.

77. 'Big Cash Award for Lutuli', publication unknown, 18 October 1964.

78. National Archives Repository (NAR), Pretoria, File 100/6/704, SA Embassy, Washington DC, Telegram, No. 140, to Secretary for Foreign Affairs, Pretoria, 'Secret: 1964 Society of Man Award', 15 October 1964, p. 2.

79. Edward A. Hawley is an ordained minister in the United Church of Christ, USA. Service in Great Britain immediately after the Second World War and participation in the Second World Conference of Christian Youth in Oslo,

NOTES TO PAGES 181-184

Norway, in 1947 created a deep interest in African affairs and worldwide race relations. As associate pastor for five years in Oberlin, Ohio, a town and college with a long history of pioneering in race relations and overseas missions, he then was for ten years the pastor of an interracial and bilingual church on the West Side of Chicago. His friendship with Edwardo Mondlane, the first president of FRELIMO, the Mozambique liberation movement, led him to apply for, and be chosen for, a position as pastor for refugees with the Christian Council of Tanganyika, specifically charged to work with the liberation movements from white-ruled southern Africa after, at President Nyerere's invitation, they had established offices in Dar es Salaam. He served in this position from April 1964 until the end of 1969, and in a somewhat similar position with the National Christian Council of Kenya through April 1971. He is now retired and lives in Denver, Colorado.

80. LM, Edward Hawley, Interview with the author, Grand Rapids, Michigan, 29 June 2009.

81. Luthuli, *Let My People Go*, 1962 edition, introduction, p. 12.

82. These reports likely emanated from Mary-Louise Hooper of the ACOA who told the United Nation's General Assembly Special Committee against Apartheid that Luthuli's health was deteriorating and the government prohibited him from being seen by a doctor. The South African government rightly denied this claim, indicating that 'any doctor, except one who is a "named Communist" or one who is himself subject to an order restricting his movements, could be summoned by Mr Lutuli'. ANC, 'Chief Lutuli and the United Nations: "Statement by Mrs Mary-Louise Hooper at the Forty-Fifth Meeting of the UN Special Committee against Apartheid", Annex III, 29 October 1964. ' "No Medical Care" Allegation Denied', publication unknown, 31 October 1964.

83. Correspondence from the South African minister A.M. Hamilton to the secretary, Stockholms Arbetarekommun, Stockholm, 3 June 1965. Cited by Sellström, *Sweden and National Liberation in Southern Africa*, Vol. 1, p. 239.

84. The ANC issued its first printed statement connecting MK to the ANC in April 1963 (SADET, *The Road to Democracy* Vol. 1, p. 135). In a statement arising from the Lobatse Conference, the ANC claimed the military wing and violence as a tactic (beyond sabotage) and emphasised the importance and primacy of political mass action. Nonetheless, the statement contradicts Luthuli's claim in the June 1964 Rivonia Trial statement that 'The ANC never abandoned its method of a militant, non-violent struggle . . .' The ANC and/or Luthuli cannot claim to prosecute a non-violent struggle and prosecute an armed struggle simultaneously. By pursuing the latter, the former claim is negated (see Appendix 5).

85. Reinertsen, 'Umkhonto we Sizwe', p. 13 and p. 12, respectively.

86. 'Kennedy, Come Back', by the Editor-In-Chief, *Rand Daily Mail*, 9 June 1966.

87. UKZN, KCAL, Book and Manuscript Collections, KCP 4144, 323.168 ROB, 'Robert Kennedy in South Africa', a souvenir booklet of Senator Kennedy's

1966 tour of South Africa compiled by the Rand Corporation, 1966; 'Day of Affirmation Speech', 6 June 1966, University of Cape Town, p. 7.
88. 'Kennedy, Come Back', *Rand Daily Mail*, 9 June 1966.

Chapter 6: Alone on the Tracks

1. D. Royle, 'Albert Luthuli: "Africa's Forgotten Man ..."', *Natal Witness*, 1 May 1964.
2. The note of congratulations is to the government and people of Zambia for their newly attained independence, written on 23 October 1964.
3. Rule, Aitken and Van Dyk, *Nokukhanya*, p. 137.
4. Howard Christofersen, Email to the author, Vol.1 August 2008.
5. Very little biographical information exists about Hugh Luthuli. He has suffered for many years from one or more conditions that render him unable to care for himself.
6. 'Chief Luthuli – In Hospital – May Be Going Blind', *Sunday Times*, 2 April 1967, p. 2.
7. Sellström, *Sweden and National Liberation in Southern Africa*, Vol. 1, p. 241.
8. UCT, MAD, Luthuli Papers, BCZA 78/46-47, CAMP MF 2914, Nokukhanya Luthuli, Inquest Report, Exhibit R, sworn testimony, 1 August 1967. There are discrepancies between Nokukhanya's recollection of events recorded in Rule's biography and her sworn statement soon after Luthuli's death. In Rule's book, Nokukhanya remembers, 'What was amazing about this whole incident was that there was a short cut through the cane fields which he had used on that previous Wednesday. But on the day of his death he decided to use the bridge. He had even remarked that the short cut was better than the long route. I don't know why he used the bridge.' Here, Nokukhanya made no mention of the new bridge under construction as she does in her 1967 sworn statement (p. 145). In her 1967 statement and in her interview with Rule, Nokukhanya remembers she advised Luthuli to take a route that was shorter. At the funeral, Nokukhanya sorrowfully disclosed in her address to the congregation, 'I had urged him to not use the bridge but to take a longer, safe route.'
9. Rule, Aitken and Van Dyk, *Nokukhanya*, p. 140.
10. BAPA, 'Luthuli's Last Hours – By His Son', *The Post*, 30 July 1967.
11. G.R. Naidoo, 'The Old Campaigner Starts a New Life', *Drum*, April 1964.
12. Ziphi Gumede knew Mbuyeseni only by his first name and Mpanza only by his surname. Apparently, the police took no statements from the two men. Presumably, the police assumed their testimonies would be identical to Gumede's, as she suggested in her testimony.
13. Naidoo, 'The Old Campaigner Starts a New Life', *Drum*, April 1964.
14. UCT, MAD, Luthuli Papers, BCZA 78/46-47, CAMP MF 2914, Stephanus Lategan, Inquest Report, Exhibit U, sworn statement, 24 July 1967.
15. UCT, MAD, Stephanus Lategan, Inquest Report.
16. UCT, MAD, Stephanus Lategan, Inquest Report.

17. UCT, MAD, Luthuli Papers, BCZA 78/46-47, CAMP MF 2914, Andries Pretorius, Inquest Report, Exhibit M, sworn statement, 25 July 1967.

18. Dr J.W.J. van Rensburg, Deputy Medical Officer of Health, Cape Town, wrote, 'Because of her intelligence and sharp mind, it was an exciting experience to work with her, though at times she had a tendency to take up "crusades" which sometimes had to be strongly contested, in the most amicable atmosphere. When she gave in, she did so with enduring and sometimes humorous grace. She was always scrupulously careful to ensure that the patients' rights were adequately protected and would fight furiously to see that they were.' Found at: <http://archive.samj.org.za/1993%20VOL%2083%20Jan-Dec/Articles/06%20JUNE/1.19%20IN%20MEMORIAM.pdf> accessed 19 April 2010.

19. UCT, MAD, Luthuli Papers, BCZA 78/46-47, CAMP MF 2914, Gwendoline Gregersen, Inquest Report, Exhibit A, sworn statement, 24 July 1967.

20. 'Luthuli's Last Hours - By His Son', The Post, 30 July 1967.

21. 'Luthuli's Last Hours - By His Son', The Post, 30 July 1967. Nokukhanya's memory of the event documented by Rule, Aitken and Van Dyk contradicts Christian's testimony recorded days after the accident in his article published by The Post. In her biography, Nokukhanya imagined that Luthuli had been 'alert right up to the time that he passed away . . . Because he was lucid right up to the end, [Christian] did not realise that he was dying' (Nokukhanya, p. 140). Nokukhanya also revealed that Luthuli did not wish to have a 'noise' over his death due to foul play. Nokukhanya added that Luthuli chose not to reveal who killed him. She visualised: 'When Christian, who was at home at the time, got the message and went to the hospital, he found him in great pain. "How are you father?" he asked. Albert said, "The pain is terrible." Christian never asked him how it happened. Albert could have talked and said, "Such and such a thing happened to me", but there was silence, and it's all the better' (p. 145). It seems that in writing about Luthuli's death and relating the family's suspicions, these authors also did not cross-check oral testimony with written documentary evidence, i.e., articles and testimony dating back to the time of death. Why they included these particular recollections of Nokukhanya in their book when they contradicted Christian's earlier recorded recollections and the sworn medical evidence of Luthuli's condition (i.e., semi-consciousness) that they had referenced is unknown.

22. UCT, MAD, Luthuli Papers, BCZA 78/46-47, CAMP MF 2914, M.J. Joubert, Inquest Report, Exhibit B, affidavit, 5 August 1967.

23. 'Ten Years of Democracy Celebrates Chief Luthuli's Ideas', BuaNews Online, 28 March 2004.

24. Mzoneli and Mthiyane's sentiments were reported in 'Ten Years of Democracy Celebrates Chief Luthuli's Ideas', BuaNews Online, 28 March 2004.

25. Carol Brown, 'The Many Mysteries of the Black Christ', Weekend Witness, 23 September 2006, p. 10.

26. UFH, HPAL, ANC Archives, Box 23, Folder 4, draft speech by the Zimbabwe African People's Union (ZAPU), July 1967.

27. UFH, HPAL, ANC Archives, Box 23, Folder 4, 'Mr Masha's Speech', Tanganyika African National Union (TANU), handwritten speech, July 1967.

28. UFH, HPAL, ANC Archives, Box 23, Folder 4, 'Statement by Jacob Kuhangua', the Secretary General of South West Africa People's Organisation (SWAPO), 24 July 1967.

29. UFH, HPAL, ANC Archives, Box 23, Folder 4, Uria T. Simango, vice president of the Mozambique Liberation Front, to the ANC (Dar es Salaam), 22 July 1967.

30. UFH, HPAL, draft article, unpublished.

31. Dr N.G. Maroudas, 'In Memoriam: Albert Luthuli', *Sechaba*, Vol. 2, No. 7, July 1968, p. 11. Maroudas also wrote insultingly: 'Sorry, dead chief, not even your Chief has won that victory yet: Your honoured Nobel Prize was not the prize of peace. To win that real prize it may be one has to use real weapons against real bullets.'

32. T. Makiwane, 'Somlandela uLuthuli', *Mayibuye*, Vol. 2, No. 29, 19 July 1968, p. 2.

33. C.J. Beyers (ed.), *Dictionary of South African Biography*, Vol. 4 (Durban: Butterworth and Company, 1981), p. 331. (The train actually struck Luthuli as he walked toward it and thus he faced it head-on.)

34. UCT, MAD, Luthuli Papers, (BCZA) 78/46-7, microfilm reel No. 1, inquest papers, N. Luthuli, Affidavit.

35. 'South African Memory: My Life with Chief Luthuli', *Trust*, March 1975. Nokukhanya Luthuli may have made these comments when recollecting the state of the body in the casket. She said in Rule, Aitken and Van Dyk's biographical book that the accident 'did not in any way distort his looks' (*Nokukhanya*, p. 146). In the casket, Luthuli's head appeared undamaged, though there appeared to be some bruising to the forehead. Nokukhanya's understanding that 'his body had no injuries' conflicts with statements she made during an interview included in the biography in which she stated, 'I think he was struck by a long object like the fork used for stoking the fire (*intshumentshu*) after the railway line was shifted to bring the engine close to him. This left a small hole in the back of his head' (p. 144). Note: The train and engine could not have been shifted to bring the train closer to a pedestrian walking along the bridge.

36. Confusion seems to exist as to whether the family recently requested a formal investigation of the accident. The February 2006 minutes of the Parliamentary Monitoring Group recorded a reporter's misunderstanding that the Luthuli family had requested an investigation. The Minister of Safety and Security, Charles Nqakula, replied denying that this was so.

37. Nokukhanya Luthuli suggested that the killing of Nkosinathi Yengwa, an ANC member in Maphumulo, by bush knives as he hid in a cane field was politically motivated (Rule, Aitken and Van Dyk, *Nokukhanya*, p. 142).

38. LM, Albertinah Luthuli, Interview with the author, 4 January 2006.

39. Rule, Aitken and Van Dyk, *Nokukhanya*, pp. 144–145.

40. Documentary film, *The Legacy of a Legend*, Amandla Communications, 2005.
41. *The Legacy of a Legend*, 2005.
42. UFH, HPAL, ANC Archives, A2561, Box 70, Folder C39, 'July 21'.
43. Rule, Aitken and Van Dyk, *Nokukhanya*, p. 142. Pretorius and Gregersen's testimony contradicts their assertion that it appeared as if Luthuli was dragged. They mistook Gregersen's middle names for her surname. They also stated that Gregersen 'suspects a fracture at the base of the skull and broken ribs' when Gregersen indicated that the fracture of the skull was 'visible', hence there was no 'suspicion'.

Postcript
1. Luthuli, *Let My People Go*, p. 29.
2. Mandela, *Long Walk to Freedom*, pp. 522–523.

Glossary

abasemakholweni	community of Christian converts
Abatembu	Tembu people
amakholwa	Christian converts
amakhosi	chiefs
amaSwazi	the Swazi nation
Angivumi	I don't agree with you
Baba	Father, used affectionately
Boer	Dutch descended settler
bliksem	cause grievous harm, used expletively
hamba kahle	go well, carefully
hawu	good grief!
impi	traditional Zulu warrior force
inkosi	chief
kholwa	Christian convert
laager	defensive formation using ox wagons
lalela	listen
predikant	pastor
somlandela	we will follow
umkandlu	council
usuthu	Zulu royalists
volksraad	governing council (of the Natalia Republic, 1839–1843)
voortrekker	migratory Dutch descended settler

Select Bibliography

Archives and repositories

African National Congress (ANC) online archives, website: http://www.anc.org.za.

African National Congress Headquarters, Luthuli House, Johannesburg, Archives Division.

Alan Paton Centre and Struggle Archives (APC&SA), University of KwaZulu-Natal (UKZN), Pietermaritzburg.

Aluka, from Africa Action Archive, website: http://www.aluka.org.

American Congregational Association Archives (ACAA), Boston, Massachusetts (USA).

American Board of Commissioners for Foreign Missions (ABCFM), Houghton Library, Harvard University, Cambridge, Massachusetts.

Amistad Research Centre (ARC), American Committee on Africa Collection (ACA), Tulane University, New Orleans, Louisiana (USA).

Bailey's African Photo Archives (BAPA), Johannesburg.

Charlotte Owen and Peter Corbett Papers (COPCP), Luthuli Museum (LM).

Congress of South African Trade Unions (COSATU), website: http://www.cosatu.org.za.

Durban Local History Museum, Durban.

Gandhi-Luthuli Documentation Centre, University of KwaZulu-Natal.

Howard Pim Africana Library (HPAL), ANC Archives, University of Fort Hare (UFH), Eastern Cape.

Inanda Seminary Archives, Inanda.

Killie Campbell Africana Library (KCAL), Campbell Collections, University of KwaZulu-Natal, Durban.

KwaZulu-Natal Archives Depository (KZNA), Pietermaritzburg Archives Repository (PAR).

Luthuli Museum (LM), Groutville, KwaDukuza.

McCord Hospital Archives, Durban.

National Archives Repository (NAR), Pretoria, (United States) SA Embassy.

Nobel Committee, Nobel Peace Prize, website: http://www.nobelprizes.com.

Rhodes University, Cory Library, Grahamstown.

Robben Island Mayibuye Archives (RIMA), University of the Western Cape (UWC), Cape Town.

Truth and Reconciliation Commission, website: http://www.justice.gov.za/trc/report/finalreport.

United Congregational Church of Southern Africa (UCCSA), Head Office Archives, Johannesburg.

University of Cape Town (UCT), Manuscripts and Archives Department (MAD), Legal Collections.

University of South Africa (UNISA), Library, Archives, Documentation Centre for African Studies (DCAS), Pretoria.

William Cullen Library, University of the Witwatersrand, Johannesburg.

Yale University, Divinity Library Special Papers, John and Eleanor Reuling Papers.

Audio-visual

Mayibuye Afrika: 'His Story', audio-visual documentary (Anglo American Corporation of South Africa, Shell and Durban Arts Association, 1993), UCCSA Head Office Archives.

The Legacy of a Legend: Chief Albert J.M. Luthuli, audio-visual documentary produced by Amandla Communications in co-operation with the National Film and Video Foundation, sponsored by the Department of Arts and Culture, aired on SABC, 2005.

'Servant of the People': A Commemorative Tribute to Chief Albert Luthuli, Rhubarg Productions, sponsored by the Office of the Premier, KwaZulu-Natal, audio-visual documentary, February 2007.

Books and articles

African National Congress, *African National Congress, South Africa: A Short History* (London: The Publicity and Information Bureau of the African National Congress, n.d.).

African National Congress, *ANC Speaks: Documents and Statements of the African National Congress* (African National Congress, n.d.).

African National Congress, *Forward to Freedom: Documents on the National Policies of the African National Congress of South Africa* (Morogoro: ANC, n.d.).

African National Congress, *Selected Writings on the Freedom Charter, 1955-1985: A Sechaba Commemorative Publication* (London: African National Congress, 1985).

African National Congress, 'Statement to the Truth and Reconciliation Commission' (Marshalltown: Department of Information and Publicity, August 1996).

African National Congress, *Afrika ke Nako, Ninety Years of Struggle: A History of the African National Congress 1912-2002* (Marshalltown: African National Congress, 2002).

African National Congress, Norway, *ANC 1912-1993* (Oslo: African National Congress, Norway, 1993).

Africa's Freedom (London: Unwin Books, 1964).

Ahlstrom, Sidney, *A Religious History of the American People* (New Haven: Yale University Press, 1972).

Allen, John, *Rabble Rouser for Peace: The Authorised Biography of Desmond Tutu* (Johannesburg: Rider Books, 1997).

American Friends Service Committee, *South Africa: Challenge and Hope*, revised edition, Lyle Tatum (ed.), (New York: Hill and Wang, 1987).

Anderson, Rufus. *Foreign Missions: Their Relations and Their Claims* (New York: Charles Scribner and Company, 1869).

Anon., *Chief A.J. Lutuli: African Patriot, World Statesman* (Durban: iAfrika Publications, n.d.).

Anon., 'Why the South Africa United Front Failed: Disruptive Role of the Pan Africanist Congress', *New Age*, 29 March 1962.

Anon., *Selected Writings on The Freedom Charter 1955-1985: A Sechaba Commemorative Publication* (London: African National Congress, 1985).

Asmal, Kader, David Chidester and Wilmot James (eds), *South Africa's Nobel Laureates: Peace, Literature and Science* (Johannesburg: Jonathan Ball, 2004).

Atkins, Gaius and Frederick Fagley, *History of American Congregationalism* (Boston: The Pilgrim, 1942).

Babenia, Natoo and Iain Edwards, *Memoirs of a Saboteur: Reflections on my Political Activity in India and South Africa* No. 58 of the Mayibuye History and Literature Series, (Bellville: Mayibuye Books, 1995).

Bailey, Jim (ed.), *The Beat of Drum: The Rise of Africa* (Johannesburg: Ravan, 2001).

Bailey, J.R.A. and Helen Lunn (eds), *Profiles of Africa* (Johannesburg: Drum, 1983).

Barrell, Howard, *MK: The ANC's Armed Struggle* (London: Penguin Forum Series, 1990).

Beinart, William, *Twentieth-Century South Africa*, revised edition (Oxford: Oxford University Press, 2001).

Benson, Mary, *Chief Albert Lutuli of South Africa* (London: Oxford University Press, 1963).

Benson, Mary, *The African Patriots: The Story of the African National Congress of South Africa* (London: Faber and Faber, 1963).

Benson, Mary, *The Struggle for a Birthright* (Middlesex: Penguin Books, 1966).

Benson, Mary, *Nelson Mandela: The Man and the Movement*, revised edition (London: W.W. Norton and Company, 1994).

Bernstein, Hilda, *The World That Was Ours: The Story of the Rivonia Trial* (London: SA Writers, 1989).

Beyers, C.J. (ed.), *Dictionary of South African Biography*, Vol. 4, (Durban: Butterworth and Company, 1981).

Biko, Steve, *I Write What I Like: Steve Biko, A Selection of His Writings*, Aelred Stubbs (ed.), (Johannesburg: Picador Africa, 2004).

Blom-Cooper, L.J., 'The South African Treason Trial: R. *v.* Adams and Others', *International and Comparative Law Quarterly*, Vol. 8, January 1959, pp. 59-72.

Boesak, Allan, *Black and Reformed: Apartheid, Liberation and the Calvinist Tradition* (Johannesburg: Skotaville, 1984).

Bonhoeffer, Dietrich, *The Cost of Discipleship*, revised edition (London: SCM, 1959).

Booth, Ian, 'Major Epochs in the History of Congregationalism', in *Papers Presented at the UCCSA Congregational Polity and Ecclesiology Consultation*, Carmel Christian Conference Centre, George, 21-23 August 2008, pp. 1-9.

Bredekamp, Henry and Robert Ross (eds), *Missions and Christianity in South African History* (Johannesburg: Wits University Press, 1995).

Briggs, D. Roy, A Covenant Church: Studies in the Polity of the United Congregational Church of Southern Africa in Terms of its Covenant (Gaborone: Pula, 1996).

Briggs, D. Roy and Joseph Wing, The Harvest and the Hope: The Story of Congregationalism in Southern Africa (Johannesburg: UCCSA, 1970).

Bunting, Brian, Moses Kotane: South African Revolutionary: A Political Biography (London: Inkululeko, 1975).

Buthelezi, Mangosuthu, 'A Tribute by Prince Mangosuthu Buthelezi' at the funeral of Dr Eliachim Thabani Zibusisoziyeza Mthiyane, 'ETZ', Noodsburg Congregational Church, UCCSA, 10 January 2007.

Butler, Alan, Kuruman Moffat Mission (Kuruman: Kuruman Moffat Mission Trust, 1987).

Callan, Edward, Albert John Luthuli and the South African Race Conflict (Kalamazoo: Western Michigan University, 1962).

Callinicos, Luli, Oliver Tambo: Beyond the Engeli Mountains (Cape Town: David Philip, 2004).

Carton, Benedict, John Laband and Jabulani Sithole (eds), Zulu Identities: Being Zulu, Past and Present (Pietermaritzburg: University of KwaZulu-Natal Press, 2008).

Chetty, Desarath and Deanne Collins (eds), The Deepest International Principles of Brotherhood and Humanity: The Albert Luthuli Memorial Lecture (Durban: Public Affairs and Corporate Communications, University of KwaZulu-Natal, 2005).

Christofersen, Arthur, Adventuring with God: The Story of the American Board Mission in South Africa (Durban: Lutheran Publishing House, 1967).

Cipolla, Benedicta, 'Reinhold Niebuhr is Unseen Force in 2008 Elections', Pew Forum on Religion and Public Life, 27 September 2007.

Clingman, Stephen, Bram Fischer: Afrikaner Revolutionary (Cape Town: David Philip, 1998).

Cohen, Ronald, 'Nigerian Nationhood is Endangered', Toward Freedom, Vol. 15, No. 10, November 1966.

Comaroff, Jean and John, Of Revelation and Revolution: Christianity, Colonialism and Consciousness in South Africa, Vol. 1 (Chicago: University of Chicago Press, 1991).

Cordier, Andrew and Wilder Foote, The Quest for Peace: The Dag Hammarskjöld Memorial Lectures (New York: Columbia University Press, 1965).

Couper, Scott, '"My People Let Go": A Historical Examination of Chief Albert Luthuli and His Position on the Use of Violence as a Means by which to Achieve South Africa's Liberation from Apartheid', International Congregational Journal, Mission, 5.1, Fall 2005, pp. 101–123.

Couper, Scott, 'Luthuli and the Armed Struggle: Nelson Mandela as the Historiographical Father', 14 March 2006. This paper can be found at: <http://www.history.ukzn.ac.za/?q=seminar_archive&op0=%3D&filter0=Couper> and subsequently at: <http://www.history.ukzn.ac.za/?q=node/636> accessed 25 January 2008.

Couper, Scott, 'Chief Albert Luthuli and the Bantustan Question', Journal of Natal and Zulu History, Vols. 24 and 25, 2006–2007, pp. 240–268.

Couper, Scott, 'Luthuli and Kairos', in The Nonconformist, Prince Dibeela (ed.), (Johannesburg: The Congregational, July 2007), pp. 32–43.

Couper, Scott, 'When Chief Albert Luthuli Launched "Into the Deep": A Theological Reflection on a Homiletic Resource of Political Significance', *Journal of Theology for Southern Africa*, Vol. 130, March 2008, pp. 76–89 and pp. 108–111.

Couper, Scott, '"An Embarrassment to the Congresses?": The Silencing of Chief Albert Luthuli and the Production of ANC History', *Journal of Southern African Studies*, Vol. 35, No. 2, June 2009, pp. 331–348.

Couper, Scott, 'Luthuli's Conceptualisation of Civilisation', *African Studies*, Vol. 70, No. 1, March/April 2011, page numbers unknown at time of publication.

Couzens, Tim, *The New African: A Study of the Life and Work of H.I.E. Dhlomo* (Johannesburg: Ravan, 1985).

Cubbin, A.E., 'Origins of Empangeni: Revd Aldin Grout's Mission Station Inkanyesi on the Mpangeni River, May 1841–25 July 1842', *Contree*, Vol. 31, 1992, pp. 25–30.

Davis, Merle (ed.), *The Economic and Social Environment of the Younger Churches: The Report of the Department of Social Economic Research of the International Missionary to the Tambaram Meeting 1938* (London: Edinburgh House, 1939).

De Bragança, Aquino and Immanuel Wallerstein (eds), *The African Liberation Reader: The National Liberation Movements*, Vol. 2 (London: Zed, 1982).

De Gruchy, John, *The Church Struggle in South Africa* (Cape Town: David Philip, 1979).

De Gruchy, John and Charles Villa-Vicencio, *Apartheid is a Heresy* (Cape Town: David Philip, 1983).

De Gruchy, Steve, 'Reinhold Niebuhr and South Africa', *Journal of Theology for Southern Africa*, No. 80, September 1992.

De Gruchy, Steve (ed.), *Changing Frontiers: The Mission Story of the UCCSA* (Gaborone: Pula, 1999).

De Gruchy, Steve and Desmond van der Water (eds), *Spirit Undaunted: The Life and Legacy of Joseph Wing* (Pietermaritzburg: Cluster Publications, 2005).

De Gruchy, Steve, G. Philpott and D. Ntseng, 'The United Congregational Church of Southern Africa: An Inventory of Land Holdings' (Pietermaritzburg: Church Land Programme, n.d.).

De Klerk, F.W., *The Last Trek – A New Beginning: The Autobiography*, second edition (London: Pan Books, 2000).

De Villiers, Peter, 'The Formation and Ethos of the United Congregational Church of Southern Africa 1967–1992' (M.A. dissertation, Department of Religious Studies, University of Cape Town, 1998).

Deane, Shirley, *Black South Africans: A Who's Who (Fifty-Seven Profiles of Natal's Leading Blacks* (Cape Town: Oxford University Press, 1978).

Denis, Philippe, 'From Church History to Religious History: Strengths and Weaknesses of South African Religious Historiography', *Journal of Theology for Southern Africa*, Vol. 99, November 1997, pp. 84–93.

Denis, Philippe (ed.), *The Making of Indigenous Clergy in Southern Africa* (Pietermaritzburg: Cluster Publications, 1995).

Dibeela, Prince (ed.), *The Nonconformist* (Johannesburg: The Congregational, July 2007).

Dinnerstein, Myra, 'The American Board Mission to the Zulu, 1835–1900' (Ph.D. dissertation, Modern History, Columbia University, 1971).

Drew, Allison (ed.), *South Africa's Radical Tradition: A Documentary History: 1943–1964*, Vol. 2 (Cape Town: University of Cape Town, 1997).

Dube, John, *Isita Esikulu Somuntu Omnyama, Nguye Uqobo Lwake* (Mariannhill, 1922).

Dubow, Saul, *The African National Congress* (Johannesburg: Jonathan Ball, 2000).

Dugard, Martin, *Into Africa: The Epic Adventures of Stanley and Livingstone* (New York: Broadway Books, 2003).

Duminy, A. and W.R. Guest, *Natal and Zululand* (Pietermaritzburg: University of Natal Press, 1989).

Elphick, Richard and Rodney Davenport (eds), *Christianity in South Africa: A Political, Social and Cultural History* (Cape Town: David Philip, 1997).

Enklaar, I.H., *Life and Work of Dr J.T. van der Kemp, 1747–1811: Missionary, Pioneer and Protagonist of Racial Equality in Southern Africa* (Cape Town: A.A. Balkema, 1988).

Etherington, Norman, *Preachers, Peasants and Politics in Southern Africa, 1835–1880: African Christian Communities in Natal, Pondoland and Zululand* (London: Royal Historical Society, 1978).

Feinberg, Barry and Andre Odendaal (eds), *Nelson Mandela: The Struggle is my Life (His Speeches and Writings 1944–1990)*, revised edition (Cape Town: David Philip, 1994).

Feit, Edward, *South Africa: The Dynamics of the African National Congress* (London: Oxford University Press, 1962).

First, Ruth (ed.), *No Easy Walk to Freedom: Articles, Speeches and Trial Addresses of Nelson Mandela* (London: Heinemann, 1965).

Friedmann, Marion (ed.), *I Will Still Be Moved: Reports from South Africa* (London: Arthur Baker, 1963).

Gamblee, Joanne, *Ahead of Their Time: Nineteenth-Century Miami County Women* (Wooster: The Wooster Book Company, 2001).

Gandhi, M.K., 'Between Cowardice and Violence', from *The Mind of Mahatma Gandhi*, pp. 1–3. Found at: <http://www.mkgandhi.org/nonviolence/phil8.htm> accessed 26 May 2008.

Gerhart, Gail, *Black Power in South Africa: The Evolution of an Ideology* (Berkeley: University of California Press, 1978).

Gish, Steven, *Desmond Tutu: A Biography* (Westport: Greenwood, 2004).

Gordimer, Nadine, 'Chief Luthuli', *Atlantic Monthly*, Vol. 203, No. 4, April 1959, pp. 34–39.

Gordimer, Nadine, *The Essential Gesture: Writings, Politics and Places*, Stephen Clingman (ed.), (Johannesburg: Taurus, 1988).

Gray, Mary, *Stories of the Early American Missionaries in South Africa* (Johannesburg: private print, n.d.).

Graybill, Lyn, *Religion and Resistance Politics in South Africa* (Westport: Praeger, 1995).

Grout, Lewis, *Zulu-land or Life Among the Zulu-Kafirs of Natal and Zulu-land South Africa* (Philadelphia: Presbyterian Publication Committee, 1864).

Guy, Jeff, *The Heretic: A Study of the Life of John William Colenso 1814–1883* (Pietermaritzburg: University of Natal Press, 1983).

Guy, Jeff, 'Class, Imperialism and Literary Criticism: William Ngidi, John Colenso and Matthew Arnold', *Journal of Southern African Studies*, Vol. 23, No. 2, June 1997.

Guy, Jeff, *The View across the River: Harriette Colenso and the Zulu Struggle against Imperialism* (Cape Town: David Philip, 2001).

Guy, Jeff, *The Maphumulo Uprising: War and Ritual in the Zulu Rebellion* (Pietermaritzburg: University of KwaZulu-Natal Press, 2005).

Hadland, Adrian and Jovial Rantao, *The Life and Times of Thabo Mbeki* (Rivonia: Zebra, 1999).

Harrison, Roland, *The Black Christ: A Journey to Freedom* (Cape Town: David Philip, 2006).

Hastings, A., 'Mission, Church and State in Southern Africa', *Mission Studies*, Vol. 2, No. 1, 1985, p. 22.

Heale, Jay, *They Made This Land* (Johannesburg: Ad. Donker, 1981).

Helander, Gunnar, *Zulu Möter Vit Man* (Stockholm: Sv. Kyrkans Diakonnistyrelses Bokförlag, 1949).

Heribert, Adam (ed.), *South Africa: Sociological Perspectives* (Oxford: Oxford University Press, 1971).

Heroes of Our Time (New York: E.P. Dutton and Company, 1962).

Hill, Jean, 'Autobiography of Jean Hill' (Unpublished, Luthuli Museum).

Hofmeyr, J.W. and Gerald Pillay (eds), *A History of Christianity in South Africa*, Vol. 1, (Pretoria: HAUM Tertiary, 1994).

Hooper, Charles, *Brief Authority* (New York: Simon and Schuster, 1960).

Houser, George and Herbert Shore, *I Will Go Singing: Walter Sisulu Speaks of his Life and Struggle for Freedom in South Africa in Conversation with George Houser and Herbert Shore* (Cape Town: Robben Island Museum, 2001).

Huddleston, Trevor, *Naught for Your Comfort* (Johannesburg: Hardingham and Donaldson, 1956).

International Missionary Council, *The World Mission of the Church: Findings and Recommendations of the International Missionary Council, Tambaram, Madras, India, 12–29 December 1938* (London: International Missionary Council, 1939).

Jenkins, Daniel, *Congregationalism: A Restatement* (London: Faber and Faber, n.d.).

Johns, Sheridan and R. Hunt Davis Junior (eds), *Mandela, Tambo and the African National Congress: The Struggle against Apartheid, 1948–1990, A Documentary Survey* (Oxford: Oxford University Press, 1991).

Johnson Daniel and Charles Hambrick-Stowe (eds), *Theology and Identity: Traditions, Movements and Polity in the United Church of Christ* (Cleveland: United Church, 1990).

Johnson, R.W., *South Africa: The First Man, The Last Nation* (Johannesburg: Jonathan Ball, 2004).

Jordan, A.C., *The Wrath of the Ancestors*, revised edition (Johannesburg: Ad. Donker, 2004).

Joseph, Helen, *If This Be Treason* (London: André Deutsch, 1963).

Kairos Document: Challenge to the Church, A Theological Comment on the Political Crisis in South Africa (Braamfontein: Skotaville, 1985).

Kairos Document: Challenge to the Church, second revised edition (Grand Rapids: William Eerdmans Company, 1996).

Kally, Ranjith, *The Struggle: 60 Years in Focus* (Durban: no publisher, 2004).

Karis, Thomas and Gwendolen Carter (eds), *From Protest to Challenge: A Documentary History of African Politics in South Africa 1882–1964*, Vol. 2, 'Hope and Challenge, 1935–1952' (Stanford: Hoover Institution, 1973).

Karis, Thomas and Gwendolen Carter (eds), *From Protest to Challenge: A Documentary History of African Politics in South Africa 1882–1964*, Vol. 3, 'Challenge and Violence, 1953–1964' (Stanford: Hoover Institution, 1977).

Karis, Thomas and Gwendolen Carter (eds), *From Protest to Challenge: A Documentary History of African Politics in South Africa 1882–1964*, Vol. 4, 'Political Profiles' (Stanford: Hoover Institution, 1977).

Karis, Thomas and Gwendolen Carter (eds), *From Protest to Challenge: A Documentary History of African Politics in South Africa 1882–1964*, Vol. 5, 'Nadir and Resurgence, 1964–1979' (Pretoria: UNISA Press, 1997).

Kasrils, Ronnie, *Armed and Dangerous: From Undercover to Freedom* (Johannesburg: Jonathan Ball, 2004).

Kathrada, Ahmed, *Memoirs* (Cape Town: Zebra, 2004).

Kelly, Geffrey and F. Burton Nelson (eds), *A Testament to Freedom: The Essential Writings of Dietrich Bonhoeffer*, revised edition (New York: Harper Collins, 1995).

Khumalo, Vukile, 'Head Rings or Top Hats? An Inquiry into the Shifting Meaning of Body Coverings in Nineteenth Century KwaZulu-Natal', *Chicago Art Journal*, Spring 2001, pp. 33–43.

Khumalo, Vukile, 'The Class of 1856 and the Politics of Cultural Productions in the Emergence of Ekukhanyeni, 1855–1910', in *The Eye of the Storm: Bishop John William Colenso and the Crisis of Biblical Inspiration*, J.A. Draper (ed.), (Pietermaritzburg: Cluster Publications, 2003).

Khumalo, Vukile, '"A Great Invitation": Publics, Assemblies and Opinion Formation in Natal, 1900–1910', University of KwaZulu-Natal, May 2010.

King, Martin Luther Jr., Letter to Albert Luthuli, 8 December 1959, in *The Papers of Martin Luther King Jnr*, Vol. 5, Clayborne Carson (ed.), (Los Angeles: University of California Press, 2005).

Kotzé, D.J. (ed.), *Letters of the American Missionaries, 1835–1838* (Cape Town: Van Riebeeck Society, 1950).

La Hausse de Lalouvière, Paul, *Restless Identities: Signatures of Nationalism, Zulu Ethnicity and History in the Lives of Petros Lamula (c. 1881–1948) and Lymon Maling (1889–c. 1936)* (Pietermaritzburg: University of Natal Press, 2000).

Laband, John, *Rope of Sand: The Rise and Fall of the Zulu Kingdom in the Nineteenth Century* (Johannesburg: Jonathan Ball, 1995).

Legum, Colin and Margaret Legum, *The Bitter Choice: Eight South Africans' Resistance to Tyranny* (New York: World Publishing Company, 1968).

Lelyveld, Joseph, *Move Your Shadow: South Africa, Black and White* (New York: Times Books, 1985).

Lerumo, A., *Fifty Fighting Years: The Communist Party of South Africa 1921–1971*, third revised edition (London: Inkululeko, 1987).

Lodge, Tom, *Black Politics in South Africa since 1945* (Johannesburg: Ravan, 1983).

Lodge, Tom, 'Paper Monuments: Political Biography in the New South Africa', *South African Historical Journal*, Vol. 28, May 1993, pp. 249–269.

Lodge, Tom, *Politics in South Africa: From Mandela to Mbeki* (Cape Town: David Philip, 2002).

Lodge, Tom, *Mandela: A Critical Life* (Oxford: Oxford University Press, 2006).

Loram, Charles, 'A Plea for Handwork in Our Native School (Continued)', *Native Teachers' Journal*, January 1921, pp. 44–47.

Luthuli, Albert, 'The Road to Freedom is Via the Cross', *South African Studies*, Vol. 3 (London: Publicity and Information Bureau of the African National Congress, n.d.).

Luthuli, Albert, 'Natal Native Teachers' Union', *Natal Teachers' Journal*, Vol. 12, No. 1, October 1932, pp. 50–51.

Luthuli, Albert, 'Natal Native Teachers' Union', *Natal Teachers' Journal*, Vol. 12, No. 2, January 1933.

Luthuli, Albert, 'The Vernacular as a Medium of Instruction', *Native Teachers' Journal*, Vol. 14, No. 2, October 1934, pp. 30–34.

Luthuli, Albert, 'Let Us Speak Together of Freedom', *Fighting Talk*, Vol. 10, No. 10, October 1954, pp. 4–5.

Luthuli, Albert, *Let My People Go: The Autobiography of a Great African Leader* (Johannesburg: Collins, 1962).

Luthuli, Albert, *Let My People Go: The Autobiography of the Great South African Leader* (Glasgow: Fontana Paperbacks, 1987).

Luthuli, Albert, *Let My People Go: The Autobiography of Albert Luthuli, Nobel Peace Prize Winner* (Cape Town: Tafelberg, 2006).

Lutuli, Albert, *Lutuli Speaks: Portrait of Chief Lutuli – Statements and Addresses by Chief Albert Lutuli President General of the African National Congress of South Africa* (German Democratic Republic [GDR]: Solidarity Committee of the GDR in co-operation with the United Nations Centre Against Apartheid, 1982).

Maharaj, Mac (ed.), *Reflections in Prison* (Cape Town: Zebra, 2001).

Mandela, Nelson, *I Am Prepared to Die* (London: International Defence and Aid Fund for Southern Africa, 1979).

Mandela, Nelson, *Long Walk to Freedom: The Autobiography of Nelson Mandela* (London: Abacus, 1995).

Marable, William, 'African Nationalist: The Life of John Langalibalele Dube' (Michigan: UMI Dissertation Services, 1976).

Marks, Shula, *Reluctant Rebellion: The 1906–8 Disturbances in Natal* (Oxford: Clarendon, 1970).

Marks, Shula, *The Ambiguities of Dependence in South Africa: Class, Nationalism and the State in Twentieth Century Natal* (Johannesburg: Ravan, 1986).

Mbeki, Govan, *South Africa: The Peasants' Revolt* (London: International Defence and Aid Fund, 1984).

McCord, James, *My Patients Were Zulus* (London: Frederick Muller, 1946).

McGrandle, Piers, *Trevor Huddleston: Turbulent Priest* (London: Continuum, 2004).

Meer, Fatima, *Higher Than Hope: 'Rolihlahla We Love You': Nelson Mandela's Biography on His Seventieth Birthday* (Johannesburg: Skotaville, 1988).

Meer, Ismail, *A Fortunate Man* (Cape Town: Zebra, 2002).

Meli, Francis, *South Africa Belongs to Us: A History of the ANC* (Harare: Zimbabwe Publishing House, 1985).

Meredith, Martin, *The State of Africa: A History of Fifty Years of Independence* (Johannesburg: Jonathan Ball, 2005).

Morris, Michael and John Linnegar (eds), *Every Step of the Way: The Journey to Freedom in South Africa* (Cape Town: HSRC Press, 2004).

Motlhabi, Mokgethi, *The Theory and Practices of Black Resistance to Apartheid: A Social-Ethical Analysis* (Johannesburg: Skotaville, 1984).

Mphahlele, Ezekiel, 'Albert Luthuli: The End of Non-Violence', *Africa Today*, Vol. 14, August 1967, pp. 1-3.

Mtolo, Bruno, *Umkhonto we Sizwe: The Road to the Left* (Durban: Drakensberg Press, 1966).

Mzala (Nxumalo, Jabulani), *Gatsha Buthelezi: Chief with a Double Agenda* (London: Zed, 1988).

Naidoo, Jay, *Tracking Down Historical Myths* (Johannesburg: Ad. Donker, 1989).

Naidoo, Phyllis, *Footprints in Grey Street* (Durban: Far Ocean Jetty, 2002).

Ngubane, Jordan, *An African Explains Apartheid* (New York: Frederick Praeger, 1963).

Nzo, Alfred, *Interviews in Depth: South Africa, African National Congress* (British Colombia: LSM, 1974).

Ó Siochrú, Micheál, *God's Executioner: Oliver Cromwell and the Conquest of Ireland* (London: Faber and Faber, 2008).

Oakes, Dougie, 'The Incredible Journey of South Africa's "Black Christ"', *Reader's Digest*, Christmas 2003, pp. 30-31.

Oakes, Dougie (ed.), *Illustrated History of South Africa: The Real Story*, second edition (South Africa: Reader's Digest Association, 1992).

Pampallis, John, *Foundations of the New South Africa* (Cape Town: Maskew Miller Longman, 1991).

Peel, Albert, *Inevitable Congregationalism* (London: Independent, 1937).

Pheko, Motsoko, *Apartheid: The Story of a Dispossessed People*, second edition (London: Marram Books, 1984).

Pillay, Gerald (ed.), *Voices of Liberation, Albert Luthuli*, Vol. 1, (Pretoria: Human Sciences Research Council, 1993).

Pogrund, Benjamin, *How Can Man Die Better: The Life of Robert Sobukwe* (Johannesburg: Jonathan Ball, 1997).

Reddy, E.S. (ed.), *Oliver Tambo and the Struggle against Apartheid* (New Delhi: Sterling, 1987).

Reddy, E.S. (ed.), *Luthuli: Speeches of Chief Albert Luthuli 1898–1967* (Durban: Madiba, 1991).

Reeves, Ambrose, *Shooting at Sharpeville: The Agony of South Africa* (London: Victor Gollancz, 1960).

Reinertsen, Elaine, 'Umkhonto we Sizwe 1961–1964: The Break with a Long Lasting Tradition of Non-Violent Opposition in South Africa' (Honours dissertation, University of Natal, 1985).

Rich, Paul, 'Albert Luthuli and the American Board Mission in South Africa', presented at the Conference on People, Power and Culture: The History of Christianity in South Africa, 1792–1992 at the University of the Western Cape (UWC) Great Hall and Genadendal Mission Museum, from 12–15 August 1992 by the UWC Institute for Historical Research. Found at the St Joseph's Theological Institute, Hilton, KwaZulu-Natal.

Roberts, Beatrice, *Albert Luthuli: They Fought for Freedom*, Ann van Bart (ed.) and John Pampallis (series ed.), (Cape Town: Maskew Miller Longman, 2006).

Robinson, Virgil, *The Solusi Story: Times of Peace, Times of Peril* (Washington, DC: Review and Herald, 1979).

Ross, Andrew, *John Philip (1775–1851): Missions, Race and Politics in South Africa* (Aberdeen: Aberdeen University Press, 1986).

Rule, Peter, Marilyn Aitken and Jenny van Dyk, *Nokukhanya: Mother of Light* (Braamfontein: The Grail, 1993).

Ryan, Colleen, *Beyers Naudé: Pilgrimage of Faith* (Cape Town: David Philip, 1990).

Saayman, Willem, *A Man with a Shadow: The Life and Times of Professor Z.K. Matthews: A Missiological Interpretation in Context* (Pretoria: UNISA Press, 1996).

Saayman, Willem, *Christian Mission in South Africa: Political and Ecumenical* (Pretoria: Unisa Press, 1991).

Sachs, Albie, *The Jail Diary of Albie Sachs* (London: Paladin Grafton, 1990).

Sampson, Anthony, *The Treason Cage: The Opposition on Trial in South Africa* (London: William Heinemann, 1958).

Sampson, Anthony, *Mandela: The Authorised Biography* (Johannesburg: Jonathan Ball, 1999).

Schadeberg, Jurgen (ed.), *Nelson Mandela and the Rise of the ANC* (Johannesburg: Jonathan Ball, 1990).

Schell, Jonathan, *The Unconquerable World: Power, Nonviolence and the Will of the People* (London: Penguin, 2003).

Selbie, W.B., *Congregationalism* (London: Methuen and Company, 1927).

Sellström, Tor, *Sweden and National Liberation in Southern Africa: Volume I, Formation of a Popular Opinion 1950–1970*, second edition (Uppsala: Nordiska Afrikainstitutet, 2003).

Sellström, Tor (ed.), *Liberation in Southern Africa – Regional and Swedish Voices: Interviews from Angola, Mozambique, Namibia, South Africa, Zimbabwe, the Frontline and Sweden*, second edition (Uppsala: Nordiska Afrikainstitutet, 2002).

Seme, Isaka, 'The Regeneration of Africa', *Journal of the Royal African Society*, Vol. 5, 1905–1906.

Sethi, Prakash (ed.), *The South African Quagmire: In Search of a Peaceful Path to Democratic Pluralism* (Cambridge: Ballinger, 1987).

Sillery, Anthony, *John Mackenzie of Bechuanaland 1835–1899: A Study in Humanitarian Imperialism* (Cape Town: A.A. Balkema, 1971).

Simpson, Thula, '"Total Onslaught" Reconsidered: The ANC in the 1980s' (Ph.D. dissertation, Birkbeck College, University of London, 2007).

Sisulu, Elinor, *Walter and Albertina Sisulu: In Our Lifetime* (Cape Town: David Philip, 2002).

Sithole, Jabulani and Sibongiseni Mkhize, 'Truth or Lies? Selective Memories, Imagings and Representations of Chief Albert John Luthuli in Recent Political Discourses', *History and Theory*, Vol. 39, December 2000, pp. 69–85.

Skota, T.D. Mweli, *The African Yearly Register: Being an Illustrated National Biographical Dictionary (Who's Who) of Black Folks in Africa* (Johannesburg: R.L. Esson and Company, n.d.).

Slovo, Joe, *Slovo: An Unfinished Autobiography* (Johannesburg: Ravan, 1995).

Smith, Adam, *An Inquiry into the Nature and Causes of the Wealth of Nations*, E. Cannan (ed.), (London: The Modern Library, 1937).

Smith, Edwin, *The Life and Times of Daniel Lindley 1801–1880* (England: Epworth, 1949).

Smith, Jack, *Buthelezi: A Biography* (Melville: Hans Strydom Publishers, 1988).

South African Democracy Education Trust (SADET), *The Road to Democracy in South Africa (1960–1970)*, Vol. 1 (Cape Town: Zebra, 2004).

Southey, Nicholas, 'History, Church History and Historical Theology in South Africa', *Journal of Theology for Southern Africa*, Vol. 68, September 1989, pp. 5–16.

Speckman, McGlory, 'An Analysis of Luke 19:41–44', delivered at Kairos '95: At the Threshold of Jubilee, September 1995.

Spottiswoode, Hildegarde (ed.), *South Africa: The Road Ahead* (Cape Town: Howard Timmins, 1960).

Stempowski, Pawel Loius, 'The Making, Experiencing and Memorialising of Space: The Adams College Experience' (Honours dissertation, Department of History, University of Natal, 1999).

Suttner, Raymond, 'The Road to Freedom is via the Cross: Just Means in Luthuli's Life' (unpublished article, n.d.).

Suttner, Raymond, 'Periodisation, Cultural Construction and Representation of ANC Masculinities through Dress, Gesture and Indian Nationalist Influence', *Historia*, Vol. 54, No. 1, May 2009, pp. 51–91.

Switzer, Les, *Power and Resistance in an African Society: The Ciskei Xhosa and the Making of South Africa* (Pietermaritzburg: University of Natal Press, 1993).

Tambo, Adelaide (ed.), *Preparing for Power: Oliver Tambo Speaks* (London: Heinemann, 1987).

Tatum, Lyle (ed.), *South Africa: Challenge and Hope*, revised edition (New York: Hill and Wang, 1987).

Temkin, Ben, *Buthelezi: A Biography* (Balgowan: J.B. Publishers, 2003).

Templin, Alton, *Ideology on a Frontier: The Theological Foundation of Afrikaner Nationalism 1652-1910* (Westport: Greenwood, 1984).

Thompson, Leonard, *A History of South Africa*, revised edition (New Haven: Yale University Press, 1995).

Thompson, Paul, *Bambatha at Mpanza: The Making of a Rebel* (South Africa: P.S. Thompson, 2004).

Trouillot, Michel, *Silencing the Past: Power and the Production of History* (Boston: Beacon, 1995).

Turok, Ben, *Nothing But the Truth: Behind the ANC's Struggle Politics* (Johannesburg: Jonathan Ball, 2003).

Vail, Leroy (ed.), *The Creation of Tribalism in Southern Africa* (Berkeley: University of California Press, 1989).

Villa-Vicencio, Charles, *Trapped in Apartheid: A Socio-Theological History of the English-Speaking Churches* (Cape Town: David Philip, 1988).

Villa-Vicencio, Charles, *Civil Disobedience and Beyond: Law, Resistance, and Religion in South Africa* (Cape Town: David Philip, 1990).

Villa-Vicencio, Charles (ed.), *Theology and Violence: The South African Debate*, revised edition (Grand Rapids: William Eerdmans, 1988).

Vowell, Sarah, *The Wordy Shipmates* (New York: Riverhead Books, 2008).

Wahlberg, Barbara, 'Jordan Khush Ngubane: Journalist or Politician' (Honours dissertation, University of Natal, Durban, 2002).

Wallace, Jonathan, 'Nonviolence', *Ethical Spectacle*, June 2001, pp. 1-8.

Walshe, Peter, *The Rise of African Nationalism in South Africa: The African National Congress 1912-1952* (Berkeley: University of California Press, 1971).

Wassermann, Johan, *A Man for All Seasons: Mohandas Gandhi* (Pretoria: Voortrekker Museum, Series No. 2, n.d.).

Webb, Pauline (ed.), *A Long Struggle: The Involvement of the World Council of Churches in South Africa* (Geneva: World Council of Churches, 1994).

Welsh, Frank, *South Africa: A Narrative History* (New York: Kodansha International, 1999).

Whitman, Alden, *The Obituary Book* (New York: Stein and Day, 1971).

Wildman, Wesley, *Fidelity with Plausibility: Modest Christologies in the Twentieth Century* (Albany: State University of New York Press, 1998).

William, Raymond, *Marxism and Literature* (London: Oxford University Press, 1977).

Williams, Oliver, *The Apartheid Crisis: How We Can Do Justice in a Land of Violence?* (San Francisco: Harper and Row, 1986).

Wilson, Monica, 'Missionaries: Conquerors or Servants of God?' *South African Outlook*, Vol. 110, March 1976.

Wilson, Monica (ed.), *Freedom for My People: The Autobiography of Z.K. Matthews: Southern Africa 1901 to 1968* (Cape Town: David Philip, 1983).

Wing, Joseph, *As One People: Commemorating the Tenth Anniversary of the United Congregational Church of Southern Africa* (Braamfontein: United Congregational Church of Southern Africa, 1977).

Wing, Joseph (ed.), *Jesus Is Lord in Church and World: Studies in the Nature of Congregationalism* (Johannesburg: United Congregational Church of Southern Africa, 1980).

Wintterle, John and Richard S. Cramer, *Portraits of Nobel Laureates in Peace* (New York and London: Abelard-Schuman, 1971).

Wood, Agnes, *Shine Where You Are: A History of Inanda Seminary (1869–1969)* (Pietermaritzburg: The Lovedale, 1972).

Woods, Donald, *Biko* (New York: Henry Holt and Company, 1978).

Index